Indigenous Knowledge and Ethics

Darrell A. Posey, who died in 2001, was internationally known for his advocacy of indigenous peoples: from his pioneering association with the Kayapó of Brazil to his global campaign to protect indigenous knowledge and practices using the concept of Traditional Resource Rights. He was an organizer of the First International Congress of Ethnobiology which resulted in the Declaration of Belém: the first instance of an international scientific organization recognizing an obligation to compensate native peoples for use of their knowledge and biological resources. In 1993, Posey received the United Nations Global 500 Award for Outstanding Achievement in Service to the Environment. *Indigenous Knowledge and Ethics: A Darrell Posey Reader* presents seventeen of his articles on indigenous knowledge, natural resource use, and intellectual property rights. Demonstrating his belief in the validity of indigenous knowledge systems, and his insistence that indigenous rights must be recognized and protected, it is an ideal introduction to his thought and work.

Studies in environmental anthropology
Edited by Roy Ellen
University of Kent at Canterbury, UK

This series is a vehicle for publishing up-to-date monographs on particular issues in particular places which are sensitive to both socio-cultural and ecological factors. Emphasis will be placed on the perception of the environment, indigenous knowledge, and the ethnography of environmental issues. While basically anthropological, the series will consider works from authors working in adjacent fields.

Volume 1: A Place Against Time
Land and environment in Papua New Guinea
Paul Sillitoe

Volume 2: People, Land and Water in the Arab Middle East
Environments and landscapes in the Bilâd as-Shâm
William Lancaster and Fidelity Lancaster

Volume 3: Protecting the Arctic
Indigenous peoples and cultural survival
Mark Nutall

Volume 4: Transforming the Indonesian Uplands
Marginality, power and production
Edited by Tania Murray Li

Volume 5: Indigenous Environmental Knowledge and its Transformations
Critical anthropological perspectives
Edited by Roy Ellen, Peter Parkes and Alan Bicker

Volume 6: Kayapó Ethnoecology and Culture
Darrell A. Posey, edited by Kristina Plenderleith

Volume 7: Managing Animals in New Guinea
Preying the game in the highlands
Paul Sillitoe

Volume 8: Nage Birds
Classification and symbolism among an eastern indonesian people
Gregory Forth

Volume 9: Development and Local Knowledge
Issues in natural resources management, conservation and agriculture
Edited by Alan Bicker, Paul Sillitoe and Johan Pottier

Volume 10: Indigenous Knowledge and Ethics
A Darrell Posey reader
Darrell A. Posey, edited by Kristina Plenderleith

Further series titles will be published by Berghahn Books.

Indigenous Knowledge and Ethics

A Darrell Posey Reader

Darrell A. Posey
Edited by Kristina Plenderleith

NEW YORK AND LONDON

First published 2004 in the USA and Canada
by Routledge
711 Third Avenue, New York, NY 10017

Simultaneously published in the UK
by Routledge
2 Park Square, Milton Park, Abingdon, Oxfordshire OX14 4RN

Routledge is an imprint of the Taylor & Francis Group

First issued in paperback 2011

© 2004 Taylor & Francis Books Ltd for selection and editorial material; individual extracts as elsewhere stated

Typeset in Times New Roman by
Newgen Imaging Systems (P) Ltd, Chennai, India

All rights reserved. No part of this book may be reprinted or reproduced or utilised in any form or by any electronic, mechanical, or other means, now known or hereafter invented, including photocopying and recording, or in any information storage or retrieval system, without permission in writing from the publishers.

Every effort has been made to ensure that the advice and information in this book is true and accurate at the time of going to press. However, neither the publisher nor the authors can accept any legal responsibility or liability for any errors or omissions that may be made. In the case of drug administration, any medical procedure or the use of technical equipment mentioned within this book, you are strongly advised to consult the manufacturer's guidelines.

Library of Congress Cataloging in Publication Data
A catalog record for this book has been requested

British Library Cataloguing in Publication Data
A catalogue record for this book is available
from the British Library

ISBN 978-0-415-32363-5 (hbk)
ISBN 978-0-415-51121-6 (pbk)

Contents

List of illustrations	viii
Preface	x
Foreword	xii
Acknowledgements	xiv
1 Introduction to ethnobiology: its implications and applications	1

PART I
Ethnoentomology   7

2 Topics and issues in ethnoentomology with some suggestions for the development of hypothesis-generation and testing in ethnobiology   9

3 Ethnoentomological survey of Brazilian Indians   23

4 Entomological considerations in south-eastern aboriginal demography   34

5 An ethnoentomological perspective of the south-eastern Indian belief system   43

PART II
Wider applications of indigenous knowledge   51

6 The application of ethnobiology in the conservation of dwindling natural resources: lost knowledge or options for the survival of the planet   53

7 Ethnobiology and ethnodevelopment: importance of
traditional knowledge and traditional peoples 63

8 Ethnoecology as applied anthropology in
Amazonian development 70

9 The perception of ecological zones and natural resources
in the Brazilian Amazon: an ethnoecology of Lake Coari 88

10 Diachronic ecotones and anthropogenic landscapes
in Amazonia: contesting the consciousness of conservation 121

11 Indigenous knowledge, biodiversity, and international
rights: learning about forests from the
Kayapó Indians of the Brazilian Amazon 133

PART III
Intellectual property rights and ethical concerns 141

12 Intellectual property rights: what is the position
of ethnobiology? 143

13 Indigenous knowledge and green consumerism:
co-operation or conflict? 148

14 Traditional Resource Rights (TRR): *de facto*
self-determination for indigenous peoples 155

15 Finders keepers won't do any more: Darrell Posey says
the time has come for a rethink on bioprospecting 169

16 Indigenous peoples and Traditional Resource Rights:
a basis for equitable relationships? 172

17 The 'balance sheet' and the 'sacred balance': valuing
the knowledge of indigenous and traditional peoples 195

Appendices 206
1 *Ethnobiology* 206
2 *The Declaration of Belém* 208
3 *The Convention on Biological Diversity (extracts)* 210
4 *United Nations Draft Declaration on the Rights of Indigenous Peoples* 210
5 *The Covenant on Intellectual, Cultural, and Scientific Resources* 218
6 *Traditional Resource Rights* 222

7 *Summary of Principle Intellectual Property Rights Instruments 223*
8 *Scientific and Professional Societies that have developed Guidelines on Intellectual Property Rights 225*
9 *Research Principles for Community-controlled Research with the Tapirisat Inuit of Canada (Selected Principles) 226*
10 *Kari-Oca Declaration and Indigenous Peoples Earth Charter 226*
11 *Principles for 'Equitable Partnerships' established by the International Society for Ethnobiology 235*

Notes	237
Bibliography	240
Index	270

Illustrations

Figures

9.1	Location of Coari within Amazonia	92
9.2	Location of major resource units, Lake Coari area	93
9.3	Generalized schematic of aquatic and terrestrial/arboreal vertical levels in the Lake Coari region	97

Tables

3.1	Insect species involved in this study and their local names	24
8.1	Representative gathered plants of the tropical forest and their uses	74
8.2	Principal species of Apidae utilized by the Kayapó Indians	76
8.3	Game animals most frequently hunted by the Yekuana of southern Venezuela	79
8.4	Feed conversion ratios	80
8.5	Commonly cultivated food plants of Amazonia	82
8.6	Representative plants commonly found in reforestation sequence of 'abandoned' Kayapó fields and animals associated with each	85
9.1	Glossary of resource units as defined by a caboclo of the Lake Coari region	94
9.2	Some general characteristics of the resource units encountered in the Lake Coari region	99
9.3	Varieties of aquatic animals important to caboclo subsistence	106
9.4	Mammals important to caboclo subsistence	109
9.5	Birds important to caboclo subsistence	111
9.6	Lizards, snakes, and turtles important to caboclo subsistence	114
9.7	Knowledge of floral and faunal associations utilized in hunting and fishing	115
9.8	Fishing equipment used for various types of fish and turtles in the Lake Coari region	118
9.9	Resources used in arts, crafts, and medicinals	119

16.1	Findings and Recommendations from the Workshop held at Green College, Oxford, 28 June 1995	174
16.2	The past and present contribution of biodiversity-rich countries to humanity	179
17.1	Inadequacies of intellectual property rights	201
17.2	Some principal rights affirmed by the UN Draft Declaration on the Rights of Indigenous Peoples	202

Preface

This book is the second of the two companion volumes of selected papers and articles by Darrell Posey to be published in the Studies in Environmental Anthropology series. The first book, *Kayapó Ethnoecology and Culture*, focussed on Darrell's work and relationship with the Kayapó Indians in Brazil.

Darrell's interest in indigenous knowledge systems began well before he went to Brazil. At Louisiana State University he progressed from a science-based first degree studying entomology to an MA in geography and anthropology. The subject of his Master's thesis was the Freejacks of Louisiana, descendants of ex-pirates and assorted renegades of many racial origins who lived in geographical and social isolation in south-eastern Louisiana where they had developed their unique culture. Study of these isolated people, and his friendship with fellow-Kentuckian William Haag, Professor of Anthropology at LSA, inspired Darrell to develop his pioneering work in ethnoentomology during the late 1970s, first in the United States, and then in Brazil where his PhD thesis focussed on the ethnoentomology of the Gorotire Kayapó of Central Brazil. Out of his practical experiences with the Kayapó grew his belief in the validity of all indigenous knowledge systems, and his insistence that indigenous rights must be recognized, promoted, and protected – a creed that was realized at Rio in 1992 and subsequently developed in his lecturing, teaching, and regular attendance at international meetings.

This book aims to reflect Darrell's career before and after his time with the Kayapó: his early interest in ethnoentomology (Part I); the wider field of ethnobiology (Part II); and the growth of his fight for indigenous rights (Part III). Chapter 17, 'The balance sheet and the sacred balance: valuing the knowledge of indigenous peoples' is based on the Introduction to his final major work, editing the all-encompassing *Cultural and Spiritual Values of Biodiversity*, published by the United Nations Environment Programme in 1999. This massive book embracing all facets of indigenous and traditional cultures is a testament to the diversity of these cultures and peoples on Earth at the end of the twentieth century. Documenting, protecting, and acknowledging this disappearing diversity was Darrell's life's work.

The Appendices in this book provide the statements and texts included in the original publications, but study of Darrell's later work can be much enhanced by referring to two books he published during his collaboration with Graham Dutfield and the Working Group on Traditional Resource Rights whilst based in Oxford. These two books, *Beyond intellectual property: toward traditional resource rights for indigenous peoples and local communities* (1996), and *Traditional resource rights: international instruments for protection and compensation for indigenous peoples and local communities* (1996), bring together the texts of many international documents and statements central to the study of the international human and indigenous rights movements at the end of the twentieth century that are referred to here but not reproduced.

Kristina Plenderleith

Foreword

It is with great pleasure that I introduce this volume of papers by Darrell Posey. I knew him from early in his career, met him all over the world, but especially in Brazil, attended several stimulating meetings organized by him, and admired the enthusiasm and energy with which he always approached his work. His friendly and outgoing nature enabled Darrell to make many friends and to get on so well with the peoples he studied, but at the same time he made a major contribution to ethnoscience. After his detailed studies of the Kayapó people of Brazil, which have been brought together in another volume, *Kayapó Ethnoecology and Culture*, Darrell became increasingly concerned about the more general aspects of his subject and therefore played an important role in the development of the sciences of ethnobiology and ethnoecology. This was a logical follow up of the broad interdisciplinary approach he had used to study the Kayapó.

The time at which Darrell was working in Amazonia coincided with a vast increase in deforestation and the loss of traditional cultures and languages in the region. It is therefore not surprising that he became deeply concerned with the conservation of both biological species and of cultures. Following on from his interest and concern for biological diversity was his application of indigenous knowledge to both conservation and to a more rational and sustainable use of resources. Unlike many ethnobiologists Darrell spent long and extended periods with his Kayapó friends. With his language fluency and in-depth knowledge Darrell developed a deep understanding of the Kayapó myths and ceremonies that are so important to interpret if indigenous knowledge is to be applied more widely. I am particularly glad to see some of his papers on ethnoentomology included here. This is a comparatively little studied area in which Darrell made significant contributions to both basic knowledge and to the practical application of the information that he gathered. Darrell showed that insects play a much larger role in indigenous culture, behaviour and beliefs than had previously been suspected. His work on ethnoentomology is one of his major contributions to science.

As the threat to indigenous peoples increased it was a logical development that Darrell became deeply concerned about the intellectual property rights of these people. He became an outspoken defender of rights of all tribal peoples and frequently called for a code of ethics to protect them. This is hardly surprising from someone who earlier had risked his whole career by taking two Kayapó to Washington to oppose the building of a hydroelectric dam that would infringe on their territory. Darrell showed both courage and concern in his defence of traditional rights. The papers about intellectual property rights brought together here are still a challenge for action and I hope that their republication will help to stimulate many more people to become involved. Despite such legal documents as the Convention on Biological Diversity that Darrell pushed so strongly, there is still much exploitation of indigenous people. As the last paper in this volume clearly states, despite more international recognition of indigenous peoples, their role in the conservation of biodiversity has been underestimated. We ignore their wisdom and their rights at our peril. This book has brought together an important collection of papers by one of the great Amazonists of today and I am sure it will be of great use to anyone who wants to follow in his footsteps.

Professor Sir Ghillean Prance FRS, VMH
McBryde Professor, National Tropical Botanical Garden

Acknowledgements

On behalf of Darrell Posey the editor and publishers would like to thank the following people and organizations who supported Darrell in achieving the work represented here:

The publishers of the papers reproduced in this book, and in particular, the co-authors of Chapter 8, J. Frechione, J. Eddins, L. F. da Silva, D. Myers, D. Case, and P. MacBeath, and Chapter 9, J. Frechione and L. F. da Silva.

Funding and support was received from the Carnegie Museum of Natural History, Pittsburgh, Pennsylvania; the Center for Latin American Studies, University of Pittsburgh, Pittsburgh, Pennsylvania; the Ford Foundation of Brazil; and the World Wildlife Fund, Washington, DC.

Friends and colleagues who supported and worked with Darrell Posey during the time covered by this book, included: Wagner Alhadef, Murray Blum, Márcio Campos, Susan Canney, Antonia Carvalho, D. Case, Charles R. Clement, Clarice Novaes da Mota, L. F. da Silva, José Flâvio Pessôa de Barros, Guilherme M. de la Penha, William Denevan, Rachel Duncan, Graham Dutfield, J. Eddins, Elaine Elisabetsky, John Frechione, Caspar Henderson, Charles Hogue, Carol Jones, Rosana and Hélio Kerr, Warwick E. Kerr, Sarah Laird, Daniel Linger, George Monbiot, Emilio Moran, D. Myers, Nazaré Paes Loureiro, Reinaldo Lourival, P. MacBeath, Sandra Machado, Celso Pinto Martins, Graça Overal, William L. Overal, Nelson Papavero, Kristina Plenderleith, Mark Plotkin, Berta Ribeiro, Laura Rival, Marisa Rotenberg, Mary Ann Schmid, William Smole, Crispin Tickell, Oliver Tickell, Martha Valle, H. Weidner, and many, many more friends and colleagues throughout the world.

Every effort has been made to obtain permission to reproduce copyright material. If any proper acknowledgement has not been made, we would invite copyright holders to inform us of the oversight.

Chapter 1

Introduction to ethnobiology

Its implications and applications*

From 19 to 22 July 1988, the First International Congress of Ethnobiology was held in Belém, Pará, Brazil.[1] Scientists and native peoples from twenty-five countries met to discuss the importance of traditional knowledge and its application to the development of socially equitable and ecologically sustainable options for the planet. (See Appendix 1 for a definition of 'ethnobiology'.)

There were many examples of indigenous knowledge systems in diverse ecological regions, with wide-ranging suggestions for applications of native concepts. Yet, one common theme appeared and reappeared throughout the Congress: the richness and relevance of traditional knowledge and the global threat to native peoples and their cultures.

For many years there have been warnings of the impending destruction of native cultures and the implications of those losses for all of humanity. As Goodland and Irwin (Goodland and Irwin 1975: 65) pointed out for the Amazonian region: 'Scientists are competing with extinction in their race to inventory what the world contains. Amerindians are the only societies with the necessary knowledge, expertise, and tradition to prosper in the Amazon jungle. Amerindians not only profoundly appreciate what exists, but also understand ecological interrelations of the various components of the Amazonian ecosystem better than do modern ecologists. Indians perceive specific relationships which biologists are only now discovering to be accurate.'

Traditional knowledge of medicinal plants, natural insecticides and repellents, fertility regulating drugs, edible plants, animal behaviour, climatic and ecological seasonality, soils, forest and savanna management, skin and body treatments, to cite just a few examples, attest to the diversity of the categories of knowledge that can contribute to new strategies for ecologically and socially sound sustained development.

Yet, native peoples and their knowledge systems are threatened with imminent destruction. Ribeiro (1970) estimates that eighty-five Brazilian Indian groups

---

* *Ethnobiology: Implications and Applications*. Proceedings of the First International Congress of Ethnobiology (Belém 1988). D. Posey (ed.) Museu Paraense Emílio Goeldi/CNPq. Belém, Brazil, (1990), 1, 1–7.

became extinct in the first half of this century. In the Amazonian region, a conservative estimate would be that, on an average, one Amerind group has disappeared for each year of this century. Unfortunately we have no calculations showing the worldwide extent of cultural extinction.

In many cases, indigenous societies are disappearing at an even faster rate than the ecosystems of the regions they have traditionally inhabited. Culture change is so rapid for many groups that 'young people no longer learn the methods by which their ancestors maintained fragile regions' (Clay 1988: 4). This is a global tragedy, for 'with the disappearance of each indigenous group the world loses an accumulated wealth of millennia of *human* experience and adaptation' (Posey 1983b).

Clay (1988) warns, however, that one should not be too hasty in the pronouncement that native peoples are all becoming extinct. Demographically, native groups with guarantees of land rights, as well as political and economic independence, have some of the fastest growing population rates in the world. The diverse and enthusiastic presentations from around the world at the First International Congress of Ethnobiology also attest to the continuing richness and resistance of indigenous peoples and their cultures.

Native leaders at the Congress affirmed that, given basic conditions for survival, indigenous societies will prosper, and with that prosperity, the entire planet will benefit.

The basic conditions for survival

The first and foremost condition for survival of native peoples is *land*. For this reason, right to land is viewed as a basic human right of all native peoples. Other essential conditions include: equal opportunities under the law, access to vocational and educational institutions, adequate social security and health assistance, right to decide which group(s) and individual(s) are to be considered 'indigenous', and respect of native language, laws, and customs.

The First International Congress of Ethnobiology produced a position statement of the International Society for Ethnobiology founded during the Congress. The 'Declaration of Belém' (Appendix 2) attempts to translate native rights into terms of responsibility for scientists and the world economic and political leaders. Article 7, for example, calls for scientists who work with native peoples to return the products of their research efforts in useful forms to the peoples they study, and in the native language.

Perhaps the most progressive Article deals with the intellectual property rights (IPR) of native peoples. The Declaration of Belém is the first international document to specifically call for the just compensation of native peoples for their knowledge and the legal defence of indigenous Intellectual Property Rights. Article 4 reflects the concerns of the International Society for Ethnobiology for the economic dependence that native peoples must confront, even if their lands and legal rights have been secured.

Congress participants expressed concern for young indigenous leaders, who too frequently see their only option for economic security is to follow the ecologically destructive ways of the 'Industrialized World'. How can traditional knowledge be defended and valued within a native society when, in fact, such knowledge offers little economic benefit to indigenous groups caught in the economic maze of consumerism and basic survival?

Kayapó chief, Paiakan, told participants in the Congress how warriors from his people travelled to the Brazilian capital during the Constitution Convention in order to defend native peoples against proposals that, if included in the new constitution, would have stripped many groups of their protective status as Indians. Had the physical presence of the Kayapó lobby not been evident during the Constitutional Convention, he explained, Indians would not have achieved the new laws that guarantee to them rights to independent legal representation and protection from decisions about their lands and resources being made behind closed doors by government officials.

The Kayapó were in a fortunate position: they are relatively wealthy Indians, whose money comes from mining and lumber extraction.

Ironically, with all of the much-heralded biological and ecological richness of Amazonia, the only products that command stable and reasonable prices are cattle, minerals, and timber, all of which require the destruction of tropical ecosystems in order to be attained!

It was with gold and timber money that the hundred-strong Kayapó warrior delegations went on costly one-thousand kilometre trips to Brasilia. 'If we did not have that money', explained Chief Paiakan, 'Brazilian Indians would have had to sit helplessly on their reserves while the politicians did exactly what they wanted. The government certainly was not interested in funding our journeys to the capital. Indians these days must have financial resources too. Our people want radios and batteries for their tape recorders. We need the White Man's clothes when we go to the city, and we must go to the city to defend ourselves against those who would dispossess us of our lands and turn us all into fourth-class citizens with no food, medicine, or money.'

The Kayapó experience was echoed in the International Congress of Ethnobiology by representatives of the Maori from New Zealand, the Cuna from Panama, and various representatives from Africa and Asia. Native peoples must have economic sources, and, if such income is to preserve the land, the people and their cultures, then traditional knowledge itself must be compensated in real terms. Otherwise, native peoples themselves must revert to ecological destruction, associated with atrophy of their own knowledge systems, in order to acquire the economic power they need to survive.

Indigenous knowledge and its worth

Industry and business discovered many years ago that indigenous knowledge means money. In the earliest forms of colonialism, extractive products (called 'drogas do sertão' in Brazil) were the basis for colonial wealth. More recently, pharmaceutical industries have become the major exploiters of traditional medicinal knowledge for major products and profits.

The annual world market value for medicines derived from medicinal plants discovered from indigenous peoples is US$43 billion. Estimated sales for 1989 from three major natural products in the US alone was: digitalis, US$85 million; reserpine, US$42 million; pilocarpine, US$28 million (Data from Dr Elaine Elisabetsky, Fundação Brasileira de Plantas Medicinais – FBPM).

Although no comparable figures are available for natural insecticides, insect repellents, and plant genetic materials acquired from native peoples, the annual potential for such products is easily that of medicinal plants. Research into these natural products is only beginning, with projections of their market values exceeding all other food and medicinal products combined. The international seed industry alone accounts for over US$15 billion per year, much of which derived original genetic materials from crop varieties 'selected, nurtured, improved and developed by innovative Third World farmers for hundreds, even thousands of years' (*South*, September 1989: 95).

Likewise, natural fragrances, dyes, body and hair products are coming to account for major world markets. Figures from the Body Shop, considered to be one of the new stars of success in international enterprise, show an annual sales of $90 million with a growth rate last year of 60 per cent (*Time*, 23 April 1990: 39). The 300 Body Shop products are derived from plants, are not tested on animals, and mostly come from 'Third World' countries. These products are marketed as coming from ecologically sustainable projects managed by the native peoples themselves. The success of Anita Roddick, founder of the 14-year-old British company, has earned her the title of Britain's 'Retailer of the Year'. Such renown will not go unnoticed by the hundreds of would-be clones that will appear to take up Anita's marketing strategy.

Growing interest and catapulting markets in 'natural' food, medicinal, agricultural, and body products signals increased research activities into traditional knowledge systems. Now, more than ever, the IPR of native peoples must be protected and just compensation for knowledge guaranteed. We cannot simply rely upon the 'good will' of companies and institutions to 'do right by' indigenous peoples. If something is not done now, mining of the riches of indigenous knowledge will become the latest, and ultimate, neo-colonial form of exploitation of native peoples.

Confronting the problem of securing intellectual property rights for native peoples will be the major ethical, intellectual and practical problem that ethnobiologists will have to face in the 1990s and is the major barrier to the advance of the discipline.

Eco-ethno ethics?

Perhaps what is needed is a reordering of priorities and values: a new code of *eco-ethno ethics*. The code would not depend upon any international laws or conventions, would not be legislated in congresses or parliaments, nor depend upon enforcement of 'copyrights' or 'patents'.

It would depend upon scientists who explained to the natives they study as to what they are doing and why it is important for the people themselves; on researchers who voluntarily sign contracts with native groups guaranteeing a percentage of any profits from medicines, films, new plant varieties, books, or whatever; on businesses that would guarantee excellent prices for natural materials, help local peoples add value to those materials and profit from their activities, help them market the products, and return a percentage of the profits to the community; and on film and television crews that pay generous prices for filming native peoples and return some of the profits.

Utopia? Yes, intentionally so. Miracles are necessary now to reverse the devastation of native peoples and surviving natural ecosystems. Professional societies, like the Society for Ethnobiology and the International Society for Ethnobiology, simply by discussing these issues in public meetings and ethics committees, can bring to light the ethical need of researchers to change their relationships with their 'subjects'.

A few successful projects working with native communities to develop their own natural products, markets, and distribution contacts, would go a long way. Or, alternatively, a few more successful projects utilizing native medicinal or edible plants, or cosmetic preparations that really take care to study the social and ecological impact of management decisions and work with the communities to determine 'just compensation', would be more effective than hundreds of national and international laws.

The Declaration of Belém was nothing short of an urgent call for this new ethic. It stands as a challenge to ethnobiologists to lead the way in a new form of responsible science that works *with* native peoples for a better future, and not just treats them as *subjects* for the advancement of White Man's science.

Implications and applications

The current devastation of native peoples and the ecological systems that they have conserved, managed, and intimately known for millennia, require that new and drastic steps be taken to reorient world priorities. All channels and organizations, whether governmental, non-governmental, professional or business, must work together to reverse the current momentum in loss of cultural, ecological, and biological diversity of this planet.

Ethnobiology seems uniquely placed to lead the way to this new understanding, since it bridges disciplines and cultures through a practical focus on the implications and applications of traditional knowledge for all of humanity.

To achieve this leadership role, ethnobiologists must find ways to: (i) give economic value to the *living* forest and natural habitats through the valorization of 'natural products'; (ii) demonstrate scientifically that native peoples have invaluable tools to aid the rational use and management of living natural areas; and (iii) develop legal and practical mechanisms for the 'just compensation' of native peoples for their knowledge through the guarantees of intellectual property rights for traditional knowledge.

These tasks will be the themes of the Second International Congress of Ethnobiology in Kunming, China, from 21 to 25 October, 1990 (see Chapter 7). This Congress will be the next step towards the development of a position of ethnobiologists towards IPR and the 'just compensation' of native peoples for their knowledge.

I hope that the Society for Ethnobiology and the International Society for Ethnobiology will take the intellectual lead, as well as the appropriate actions, towards the development of a new ethic that serves as a model for other disciplines. The following actions are suggested:

(i) Support an international call, through its members in all countries that participate in United Nations activities, for UN action on the question of IPR.
(ii) Seek national legislation to secure indigenous IPR rights in all countries where native populations exist.
(iii) Encourage funding agencies and development banks to support research into traditional knowledge, its practical applications, and ways that native peoples can be 'justly compensated' for their knowledge.
(iv) Establish a special Working Committee to investigate the issues of IPR in relation to native rights and report to the Society with guidelines for international and national legislation.
(v) Include on the agenda of an Ethics Committee the issues of IPR in relation to activities of researchers with indigenous populations.

The Declaration of Belém was a clear call to a new order. It was appropriate that such a call would come in Belém, the unofficial capital of the Amazon and one of the regions most threatened by unbridled 'development'. It is equally appropriate, if not prophetic, that the Second International Congress of Ethnobiology be held in China, where threats of a different order affect the future of native peoples, science, nature, and planetary harmony.

Ethnobiology finds itself on centre stage: now more than ever dialogue must take place between disciplines and peoples. It will take our best minds from all fields and cultures to find socially and ecologically viable options for the survival of the planet. One might ask if ethnobiology is capable of such miraculous tasks. The only response can be: if we do not try, who will. Surely exchange of knowledge between disciplines and cultures on an equal basis is at least the right road to finding acceptable solutions.

The Proceedings of the First International Congress of Ethnobiology assembles the published results of attempts of scientists from many different backgrounds and cultures to establish a new scientific synthesis. It is a first step towards the establishment of ethnobiology as a positive new force that unites peoples and cultures in an attempt to preserve the ethnic, biological, and ecological diversity that remains on this planet.

Part I

Ethnoentomology

Chapter 2

Topics and issues in ethnoentomology with some suggestions for the development of hypothesis-generation and testing in ethnobiology*

Introduction

Definitions, even for ethnoentomology, are often difficult to formulate, and, once formulated, are usually unsatisfactory. Insight and understanding is sometimes increased through a comparison with a related term or concept, hence the juxtaposition of 'cultural entomology' and 'ethnoentomology' in the discussion that follows.

Cultural entomology treats the influence of insects upon the 'essence of humanity as expressed in the arts and humanities' (Hogue 1980). Cultural anthropologists usually restrict their studies to 'advanced', industrialized, and literate societies, maintaining that entomological concerns of 'primitive' or 'noncivilized' societies are in the domain of ethnoentomology. They are principally interested in written forms of cultural expression and limit their studies to physically recorded sources of literate societies. It is well to note that this, like many divisions, is an artificial one, and it implies an ethnocentric 'we/they' bias built upon assumptions of fundamental differences between 'primitive' and 'civilized' classification and thought. Thus far, anthropological research has not substantiated such assumptions.

Although the prefix 'ethno' generally indicates knowledge of 'folk' societies and the word cell 'ento' refers to insects (thus ethnoentomology is concerned with the knowledge and use of insects in different human societies), defining the term is not as easy as might be expected. A fundamental problem is that of delimiting entomology itself. Even though the concept 'insect' is clearly defined by Western science, entomologists also frequently study 'related arthropods'. Since these two concepts gradually developed in Western science, it cannot be assumed that they are universal and, in folk societies, must be elicited using *emic* procedures that 'discover' conceptual paradigms rather than methods that impose preconceived concepts upon the society under study.

There are a number of areas within ethnoentomology which can be successfully researched through analyses based upon observations and data collection using the categories of Western science, that is, using the *etic* approach, without

---

* *Journal of Ethnobiology* (Special Volume: New Directions in Ethnobiology) (1986), 6:1, 99–120.

diminishing their ethnoscientific contribution. Examples include studies of insects as food, the role of arthropods in disease transmission, hallucinogenic insects, the use of insects for ornamentation, problems in contamination of food with insects and so on. Few studies have passed from the *etic* to the cognitive *emic* level. Yet the native (folk) view of insects – their naming, classification, and use – is surely the ultimate goal of ethnoentomology.

This chapter gives a general survey of both *emic* and *etic* topics in ethnoentomology, utilizing the general Western concept 'insects and related arthropods' as a unifying category for comparative study. Cultural entomology is treated as a subdivision of ethnoentomology that deals with recorded sources in literate societies. Cultural entomological interests will, therefore, be incorporated throughout the chapter, although no attempt is made to review the vast literature.

The purpose of this review is to outline areas of interest for future ethnoentomological investigation, with an attempt made to establish ethnoentomology, and ethnobiology in general, as a hypothesis-generating and testing mechanism. That is, to show how folk knowledge and beliefs can serve to generate new ideas and hypotheses which can then be investigated and tested by our own science. This approach provides an intellectual bridge between Western and folk sciences as well as the basis for a non-culturally biased world science. The chapter argues that folk specialists must be treated as scientists, with their respective systems regarded as invaluable codifications of human observations of natural phenomena.

A brief history of ethnoentomology

Development of entomology as a folk science has been traced for Egypt (Efflaton 1929), the Middle East (Harpaz 1973), Greece and Rome (Scarborough 1979a), and other parts of the world (Essig 1931; Montgomery 1959). Modern entomology acquired a distinctively humanistic flavour (and perhaps its 'ethno' tendencies) from entomologist-philosophers such as William Morton Wheeler, Maurice Maeterlinck, and Jean Henri Fabré, who 'not only described insect phenomena with imagination and brilliance, but wrote and spoke of their meaning on a human intellectual plane' (Hogue 1980). Contemporary ethnoentomology began in the nineteenth century with the works of Bates (1862a), Daoust (1858), Glock (1891), Hagan (1863), Katter (1883), Liebrecht (1886), Marshall (1894), Wagner (1895), and Wallace (1852). Writings by Arndt (1923), Barrett (1925), Caudell (1916), Dammerman (1929), Ealand (1915), Gudger (1925), Knortz (1910), Laufer (1927), and Nordenskjöld (1929) brought the subject into the twentieth century. Essig's (1934) survey of the importance of insects to the Indians of California established the traditional categories of ethnoentomological interest.

Zinsser's (1935) *Rats, Lice and History* remains a classic because of its perspective of insects as forces in human social and biological history. *Insects as Human Food* (Bodenheimer 1951) likewise brought insects to world attention in a more positive light as a potential and important source of protein. Wyman and Bailey (1952) were the first to use the term ethnoentomology in print in their seminal work on the Navajo Indians.

The writings of Schimitschek (e.g. 1968, 1977) certainly establish him as a major force in cultural and ethnoentomology. Other general works include those by Clausen (1954), Cloudsly-Thompson (1976), Hitchcock (1962), Hogue (1980), Kevan (1974, 1979, 1980), Posey (Chapters 2, 4 and 5 this volume, 1978, 1979a, 1980a), and Ritchie (1979).

Conklin's (1973) general bibliography of folk classification offers an important section of entries on ethnozoology (including ethnoentomology) and provides a bibliographic framework to link ethnoentomology with its theoretical roots in ethnoscience.

Insects and human history

Zinsser's (1935) work popularized the knowledge of the association of insects with the spread of epidemic diseases that demolished empires and changed the course of human history. Subsequent works (Cloudsly-Thompson 1976; Hare 1954; McNeill 1976; Ritchie 1979; Singerest 1951; Smith 1973) trace the plagues and pestilence caused by insect-borne diseases such as bubonic plague, typhus, yellow fever, and trypanosomiasis. Bushvine (1976) details the effects of ectoparasites on human hygiene and medical history.

Crosby (1972) analyses the complexities of transatlantic exchanges of insect-transmitted diseases and emphasizes the destructive impact on such aboriginal populations of the New World. Often such devastation extended well into regions with no direct contact with Europeans. This was due to extensive aboriginal trade routes that brought goods infested with insect vectors deep into the hinterlands (Posey, Chapter 4 this volume). The complete impact of insect-related diseases is still little known for the Americas (Dobyns 1966).

Certainly the role of insects in human evolutionary history is indisputable. Students interested in this broad area should begin their studies by consulting the bibliographies of the above works.

Insects and human food

The most extensive literature in any subject of ethnoentomology concerns the relationship between insects and human food. The study of entomophagy, the direct use of insects as human food, has a long and varied history. *Why Not Eat Insects?* (Holt 1885) stimulated a series of studies concerning the nutritional potential and importance of insects to the human diet. Subsequent general surveys (e.g. Bergier 1941; Bodenheimer 1951; Conconi *et al.* 1981; Curran 1939; Dufour 1981; Gorham 1976a,b; Harlan 1976; Hoffman 1947; Meyer-Rochow 1973, 1975, 1976, 1985; Ruddell 1973; Taylor 1975) have investigated the variations in cultural practice of entomophagy. Other studies have documented the biological efficiency of insect reproduction and the consequent production of protein (de Foliart 1975; Dufour 1981; Meyer-Rochow 1975, 1976). Recent works discuss the practical problems of insect foods for Western societies, including socio-economic factors, manpower, preparation, handling, and marketing (Conconi 1982; Dufour 1981; Gorham 1979; Kok 1983; Ramirez *et al.* 1973).

Insects are also consumed indirectly through the ingestion of contaminated foods. This is because of the impossibility of complete removal of insect parts from food products (Caron 1978). Contamination necessitates the establishment of a complex set of rules and standards utilized by government food- and drug-regulating agencies (Taylor 1975). Detailed works outline the hazards of insect ingestion which include allergic reactions, poisoning, tumorigenic stimulation and related health problems (Choovivathanavanich *et al.* 1970; Dufour 1981; Gorham 1975; Pimentel *et al.* 1977; Taylor 1975).

The major factors affecting insect consumption are not health hazards, however, but cultural biases. Bodenheimer's (1951) book on insects as human food stimulated a series of works regarding cultural traditions and taboos of insect eating (e.g. Aeschlimann 1982; Catley 1963; Meyer-Rochow 1973; Ruddell 1973; Taylor 1975; Tihon 1946). Although Western societies have a particularly strong bias against insects as food, with honeybees being the only Arthropod systematically exploited for human food (Dufour 1981), many other societies have a long and extensive inventory of useful and edible species (e.g. Aldrich 1921; Catley 1963; Daoust 1858; Silow 1976, 1983; Tindale 1953; Wallace 1852). Techniques for the evaluation of insect nutritional qualities have been developed (Conconi 1977; Conconi *et al.* 1981, 1984; de Foliart 1975; Teotia and Miller 1974) and allow for the generation of numerous lists of species and their dietary potentials (e.g. Dufour 1981; Redford and Dorea 1984; Taylor 1975). Such techniques are not without problems and refinements in protein and nutrient evaluation are still needed (Redford 1986).

Other indirect effects of insects include the enormous cost of agricultural chemicals used to control them. A dramatic worldwide increase in mechanized monocultural planting has led to sharp rises in epidemic outbreaks of insect pests and the resultant rise in crop loss (Altieri 1983b; Cooper and Tinsley 1978). This trend, combined with soaring energy costs, has created serious global problems and threatened the stability of food prices in both developed and under-developed countries (Altieri 1985). Other farming trends, such as 'no-till' planting, have led to increased vulnerability to some crop pests and greater dependency on herbicides; these herbicides, in turn, often increase the susceptibility of some crops to other insects and microbial pests (Oka and Pimentel 1974). This situation stimulates even greater dependency upon insecticides. All of these have contributed to re-establish the viability of traditional agriculture and the necessity of studying folk agriculture in detail.

Apart from the high costs of chemical agents, health hazards are alarming and ominous. Fatal and non-fatal poisoning from pesticides is common, and the long-term effects of ingestion through contaminated food and water are of wide concern (Gorham 1975, 1979; Pimentel *et al.* 1977; Taylor 1975).

Another problem is that for cosmetic and psychological reasons many types of insects are considered repulsive (Hosen 1980). That certain species are relished as edible delicacies in one society and viewed with dread or horror in another is a question of cultural 'tastes'. Yet as Dufour (1981) points out, attitudes towards insects can change. As world food supplies dwindle and long-term space travel becomes a way of life, consumption of insects may have to become acceptable (Pimentel 1971). Insects are potentially one of the ideal sources of food and components in waste recycling in outer space because of their light weight, high quality of animal protein, and rapid reproductive rates (Miller 1981). Even so, any major changes in world diet will require a 'desensitizing' to produce more positive attitudes towards insects in general and innovative marketing to introduce insect-based products (Dufour 1981).

Insects and medicine

It is in China that we find the most ancient and complete record of the use of insects in medicinal preparations. Read (1935) gives a detailed inventory of useful medicinal species. Chinese veterinary medicine had evolved to a point that curative diets and remedies were used to treat ailing crickets and silkworms (Laufer 1927; Read 1935).

Scarborough (1979b, 1981) gives evidence of the importance of certain insects in ancient Greek and Roman medicine. Numerous other surveys record diverse examples of insects in various cultures (Greenlee 1944; Kevan 1979; Meyer-Rochow 1985; Posey 1978; Swanton 1928). For example, in Brazil termites are used to treat bronchitis, catarrh and influenza, constipation, dog bite, goitre, incontinence, measles, protruding umbilicus, rheumatism, whooping cough, sores, boils, ulcers and so on. The treatments range from teas made from crushed insects or their nests, to inhalation of smoke from burning termite cartons (Mill 1982).

In Brazil cockroaches and wasps have multiple medicinal uses (Lenko and Papavaro 1979), and the Kayapó use bees and bee products widely in their medicine (Posey 1983d,e,f; Posey and Camargo 1985) (see Chapter 3). Mixtures of wasps are thought to be aphrodisiacs. Ant and wasp infusions are widely used to cure goitre, paralyses, and rheumatism (Ealand 1915).

Other diverse uses include Tindale's (1953) observation of grubs being used in Australia by the aborigines as a 'substitute teat' to wean their children. The aborigines also commonly treat stomach ache and colds with a liquid prepared from crushed green-tree ants and larvae (McKeown 1944); crushed cockroaches are used to treat cuts (Ruddell 1973). Cloudsly-Thompson (1976) provides a long list of medicinal uses of insects in the ancient and modern world.

Beekeeping and insect rearing

From ancient cave paintings of honey raids, to beekeeping in Babylon, and the use of beeswax to embalm the dead in Assyria, Ransome (1937) traces the importance of 'the Sacred Bee' in ancient times. Crane (1984) describes the 'archaeology' of beekeeping recorded in historical texts and art. Crane (1979) also provides a comprehensive survey of production, collection and use of beeswax in many parts of the world. The literature is so extensive on the keeping of *Apis* in ancient and contemporary times that it cannot be reviewed herein.

Keeping of stingless bees (Meliponinae) is a much less known area of ethnoentomology. Yet the keeping of meliponine species was a highly developed science amongst native peoples of Africa and the Americas (Parent *et al.* 1978; Schwarz 1945, 1948).

Schwarz (1948) provides one of the most complete studies on the domestication of meliponines by the Maya of Central America. These Indians were expert in the genetic manipulation of different bees to increase honey and wax productivity, and perfected many methods for the division of colonies and the rearing of numerous species. Highly ornamented man-made hives were employed in special shelters constructed for the sacred bees and bee gods. The Maya had several methods to attract and 'tame' wild swarms, which included attraction with plantations of flowering plants preferred by the bees. Such practices continued into modern times and are still observed in México, Panama, and other parts of Central America (Bennett 1964, 1965; Hendricks 1941; Luhrmann 1981; Weaver and Weaver 1981).

Stingless beekeeping was also highly developed in pre-Colombian South America. Nordenskjöld (1929) provides an interesting survey of South American folk apiculture observed during the first half of this century.

For stingless bees in Brazil, Lenko and Papavaro (1979) recorded 171 folk names, the majority of which were of indigenous origin. Many scientific names are actually taken directly from their Tupi Indian language origin (Nogueira-Neto 1970).

Although some species of Meliponinae were undoubtedly fully domesticated in South America, many species were only semi-domesticated. Chagnon (1968) and Metraux (1948b) describe bee management by the Yanomamo and Guarani Indians, but they fall short of describing the bees as fully domesticated.

Contemporary Kayapó Indians of Brazil name and classify at least fifty-six folk species of stingless bee (Posey 1983e,f); nine species are semi-domesticated. Hives of these species are raided, and a portion of the brood comb (with some honey and pollen) is returned to the nest before resealing, so that the bees re-establish the colony and the Indians continue to exploit the hive in subsequent years. In addition to the nine semi-domesticated species, the Kayapó mark the nests of several others and carefully observe the progress of the colonies. When the Indians think that the quantity of honey and/or wax is sufficient, the nest is raided. Nests of some species, when found in the forest, are actually brought to the village to be observed on a daily basis (Posey and Camargo 1985). Other social insects reported to be 'managed' include the sauva (*Atta* spp.) (Lenko and Papavaro 1979), various wasp species (Baldus 1937; Chagnon 1973; Metraux 1984a), and honey-producing wasps (*Brachygaster*) (Lenko and Papavaro 1979).

Beetle grubs (Phalaenidae and Buprestidae) are raised by several South American tribes (Chagnon 1968; Steward and Metraux 1948). Palm trees are deliberately cut to provide fodder for egg-laying adults. The Indians know exactly when to return to the decaying pith to extract the numerous, large grubs. Coimbra

(1984) offers detailed information on the rearing of four species of *Bruchidae* and *Curculionidae* larvae by the Sun Indians of Rondonia (Brazil).

A sizeable bibliography exists regarding insect-rearing for laboratory experiments as well as livestock food (Calvert *et al.* 1969; Chambers 1977; MacHargue 1917; Vanderzant 1974). One interesting study deals with the commercial management of *Hermetia illucens* larvae, which are used as fish bait in Brazil (Santos and Coimbra 1984).

Insects have been reared for a number of purposes. Laufer (1927) describes in detail how elaborate carved gourds and miniature houses were prepared for singing and fighting crickets in China. Special shelters were prepared for them during the summer, with clay beds built for each individual. Elaborate diets were recognized for different species in different lunar cycles. Special diets and medicines were available for ailing crickets. Intricate porcelain dishes were created for feeding the prized individuals. Even delicately carved 'ticklers' were created to urge reluctant cricket warriors to battle. Kevan (1979) notes that American Indians likewise raised crickets 'simply to enjoy their songs'. Similar reports are found in Bates (1862a), Caudell (1916), and Floericke (1922). Posey and Camargo (1985, also in Posey 2002, ch.11) report on the keeping of stingless bees purely because of the Kayapó Indians' fascination with social insects. Of course, cultivation of silk worms (*Bombyx mori*) is another ancient Chinese tradition in insect rearing. The details of this folk science are described by Read (1935) and Cloudsly-Thompson (1976).

Scale insects (*Coccus cacti*) that feed on prickly pear (*Opuntia* spp.) are still raised in México, Honduras, the Canary Islands, Algeria, Spain, and Peru because of their use in the production of the carmine-red pigment cochineal (Cloudsly-Thompson 1976; Ealand 1915). Similarly, 'lac insects' (*Laccifer lacca*) are reared in Thailand, Burma, and India for their production of shellac, polishes, and sealing wax (Cloudsly-Thompson 1976).

Pests and pest control

Was it a tarnished plant bug that caused the potato rot which led to the great Irish potato famine? Quite possibly, according to Wheeler (1981). If so, it probably was not the first ecological and social disaster wrought by insect pests. Although the role of insects in agricultural history remains little known, we do know that today world-wide deforestation and the dominance of crop monocultures have provoked a sharp rise in insect pests (Cooper and Tinsley 1978; Thresh 1982). Likewise there have been dramatic increases in insect-borne diseases caused by blood parasites and arboviruses. These situations, along with the high costs of pesticides and energy for their application, have stimulated a refreshing new emphasis upon studies of pest management in traditional agriculture (Altieri 1985).

Western agriculturalists have generally assumed traditional agricultural systems to be of low productivity and have used 'bigger yield' as their justification for expensive technologies and chemical dependency (Alverson 1984). Yet in many cases, native agriculture has been shown to be both productive and efficient in its use of local skills available energy, and materials (Egger 1981; Kerr and Posey 1984; Parker *et al.* 1983; Posey 1983a,b; Wilken 1977). One of the major reasons for this effectiveness is efficient pest management.

Traditional cropping systems have 'built-in suppression mechanisms' (Altieri 1983a,b). These include: (a) arrangement of crops, (b) composition and abundance of non-crop vegetation in and around fields, (c) genetic diversity of domesticates and semidomesticates, (d) matching of soil varieties with crop varieties, (e) 'natural corridors' between fields, and (f) variation of field sites and long-term management of old fields (Altieri 1985; Denevan 1971; Denevan *et al.* 1984; Parker *et al.* 1983; Posey 1984b).

Brown and Marten (1984) point out that crop losses in native fields may be as high as 40 per cent, and such losses are still within the range of losses in modern agriculture using pesticides. One major difference exists: elimination of pesticides from modern systems can produce losses approaching 100 per cent (Schwarz and Klassen 1981), whereas pest damage in traditional agricultural systems almost never exceeds reasonable bounds (Altieri 1985).

The relationship between agricultural polycultures and lower pest incidence is currently under investigation (Altieri and Letourneau 1982; Perrin 1980; Risch *et al.* 1983). Maintenance of a broad genetic base certainly diminishes attacks from host-specific pests (Brush 1982; Gliessman *et al.* 1981; Pimentel and Goodman 1978). A variety of management techniques have been described for different societies. Use of resistant native cultivars, crop rotation, variation in planting times, and use of shade to shelter useful insects, are only a few keys to successful traditional agriculture. In Nigeria, for example, okra is planted to divert flea beetles (*Podagria* spp.) from cotton (Perrin 1980). Variations in relative corn and bean planting dates are also used to reduce leafhopper and armyworm damage (Altieri and Letourneau 1982). Many studies detail other management techniques (Altieri 1983a,b, 1985; Bunting 1972; Glass and Thurston 1978; Golob *et al.* 1982; van Huis *et al.* 1982; Khan *et al.* 1978; Litsinger *et al.* 1978a,b; Matteson *et al.* 1984; Wilken 1977).

The effects of spatial arrangement, for example, row spacing, are still little known but appear to have significant impact on pest management. Matteson *et al.* (1984) document a significant difference in crop loss between cowpeas (*Maruca testulalis*) planted in intra-rows rather than inter-rows with maize. Kerr and Posey (1984) report that interdispersal of *aria* (*Calathea aloua*) with tuber crops reduces nematodes and *Collembola*-borne virus attacks in Kayapó fields.

Management of 'weeds' is also an important factor in the overall practices of traditional agriculturalists. 'Relevant weeds', according to Altieri (1983a,b, 1985), support rich natural enemy fauna that provide alternative prey/hosts, pollen or nectar, or favourable microhabitats unavailable in weed-free fields. Most of what Western agriculturalists would consider 'weeds' in a Kayapó field are, in fact, useful semi-domesticates for the Indians (Posey 1986b). Altieri and Letourneau (1982) provide examples of cropping systems in which the presence of weeds has enhanced biological control of insect pests.

Western science has only begun to seriously study traditional agricultural science. Yet existing evidence already points to the richness of ideas and data available to interested researchers (Brokensha *et al.* 1980; Parker *et al.* 1983; Posey *et al.* Chapter 8 this volume). Some laboratories have begun the serious study of toxicological potentials of native pesticides. Results have been promising (Ganjian *et al.* 1983; Kubo and Matsumoto 1984; Kubo *et al.* 1984). Other entomologists, agriculturalists, and ethnoentomologists should devote more attention to the investigation of integrated pest management by native peoples.

Mythology, ritual, and 'natural models'

Reports of insects in mythology and ritual are widespread. Bushnell (1910) and Mooney (1972) discovered many insects as key figures in the belief systems of Indians of south-eastern North America. For the Louisiana Chocktaw, for example, grasshoppers and men were created at the same time and were once brothers; ants were likewise considered as having human ancestors (Bushnell 1910). Ant clans existed in many tribes (Gilbert 1943; Grinnel 1899) and ant people were thought to have been the first to have inhabited the underworld (Bushnell 1910). Water beetles (*Hydrophilidae*) were responsible for the formation of the earth because they had brought up the mud from beneath the waters to form the first dry land (Mooney 1972).

The Cherokee attributed the origin of 'Sacred Fire' to the heroic efforts of the water spider, which brought fire on its back while crossing the ocean (Mooney 1972). Diseases and crop pests were cast upon people, according to legend, by Grubworm, who organized his fellow insects to punish humans for their abuse of nature (Posey Chapter 5 this volume; Swanton 1928).

Insects also play an important role in Australian aboriginal lore (Meyer-Rochow 1985). Spencer and Gillen (1899) reported thirty insect totems; Berndt and Berndt (1964) provide further evidence of insect-named clan and totemic groupings. One of the major cosmogenic myths of the aborigines refers to the famous witchetty grub that served as humankind's first food. Numerous examples of insects in mythology can be found in various compendia (e.g. Armstrong 1970; Clausen 1954; Cowan 1865; Dentan 1968; Ealand 1915; Griaule 1961; Kevan 1974, 1979, 1980; Posey 1978, 1980a, 1981; Reim 1962, Rutschky 1981; Schimitschek 1968, 1977; Wyman 1973).

Insects are also important components in many ceremonies. The Cherokee shamans employed many insect names in their sacred chants (Kilpatrick and Kilpatrick 1970) and had an elaborate 'extraction' ritual to remove disease-causing insects from their patients' bodies (Greenlee 1944; Lawson 1937; Morphi 1932). Fortune-telling rituals used insects as indicators of the future (Mooney 1972). The ordeal undergone by young Maué boys in Brazil before they may marry (Biard 1862) is described in Chapter 3.

Accounts such as those previously related are generally recorded out of cultural context and, consequently, are of limited significance to the folk entomologist.

Recent studies (e.g. Brown and Chase 1981; Gregor 1983; Luhrmann 1981; Malkin 1956; Posey 1984e; Waddy 1982; Wilbert 1981) have attempted to provide a broader cultural framework for the interpretation of insects in myth and ceremony. Natural 'models' based upon insect examples and recognized by native peoples themselves have been shown to be useful for the organization of folk scientific data and are significant alternatives to the imposed models of traditional anthropological structuralism and Western science (Posey 1981).

Oral literature and ecological knowledge

Oral literature is a major vehicle for ecological information. Santos and Posey (1986) witnessed an old man in the Ilha de Lencois (Brazil) describing his pursuit of a mythological animal. The 'plot' of the story could take only three minutes to relate, but the master story teller kept his audience of local youth spellbound for nearly 45 minutes. Analysis of the folk tale reveals that the minute detail used to embellish and add credence to the story is also instruction in local ecology and survival.

Myths are concentrated symbolic codes that transmit cultural information, including social rules and standards of behaviour. Ecological information, such as knowledge of animal behaviour and 'coevolutionary complexes', can also be communicated in myth form (Posey 1983a). Baldus (1937, 1970) recorded Taulipang myths describing the commensal relationships between birds and wasps. Kayapó lore describes commensalism between stingless bees and acrids (Posey and Camargo 1985).

Mill (1982) points out that widespread stories of 'weeping termites' in Brazil reflect folk knowledge of the biological fact that ground nesting termites (*Nasutitermes, Velocitermes,* and *Cortaritermes*) exude droplets of exocrine secretions for chemical defence when disturbed. A Kamaiura myth describes termite nests that glow in the night (Villas-Boas and Villas-Boas 1972). These glowing nests are not superstitious nonsense, but rather recognition of a natural phenomenon caused by periodic invasions of termite mounds by phosphorescent *Lampyridae* larvae (Redford 1982).

Oral literature has not been sufficiently studied as a transmitter of biological information. This is because of the highly symbolic language of myth and folklore, which is frequently considered as nonsense by those who do not understand the linguistic and cultural codes. Researchers who take the time to learn the language of the societies they study and prepare themselves with training in folkloristics can indeed make a significant contribution to myth interpretation and ethnoentomology.

Miscellaneous topics

Several miscellaneous topics deserve mention. Brief examples will be given to illustrate each topic.

Use of insects as ornaments and decorations

Berlin and Prance (1978), Covarrubias (1971), Kennedy (1943), Lothrop (1964), and Outram (1973) review the importance of insects in art and ornamentation in the New World. Meyer-Rochow (1975) reports the use of green tenebrionid beetles, as well as scarabaeids and buprestids, among the Wahgi Valley people of New Guinea. The Kayapó inherit the right to use iridescent elytra of *Euchroma goliatha* and make elaborate ceremonial hats from meliponine batumen (Posey 1983f). Butterfly wings are commonly used in the Americas for adornment and decoration (Posey 1986b). Klots and Klots (1959) report the use of luminous beetles (*Pyrophorus* spp.) to decorate the hair of Indian girls.

Insects as objects of entertainment

The keeping of stingless bees by the Kayapó Indians out of interest has been mentioned earlier (Posey and Camargo 1985; Posey 2002). Dragonfly catching is a favourite and developed sport in the Banda Islands (Simmons 1976). Butterfly wings are important play objects for Trobriand Island youth (Meyer-Rochow 1985). In Papua New Guinea, large weevils (*Rhynchophorus ferruginius*) are used as musical instruments by letting the human mouth serve as a variable resonance chamber for the wing vibrations of the beetle (Meyer-Rochow 1973). Staged fights between lucanid beetles are reported in Thailand (Meyer-Rochow 1975). Lenko and Papavaro (1979) give several examples of the keeping of *Pyrophorus* spp. beetles for entertainment, as well as for their light. Dances inspired by insect movements are reported in several North American Indian groups (Bushnell 1910; Gilbert 1943; Schoolcraft 1851; Swanton 1928, 1946).

Insects as indicators

Due to the sensitivity of the head louse to minute changes in body temperatures, some native groups diagnose illness of patients by the presence or absence of lice. Slight fevers can cause an exodus of body lice that indicates oncoming illness (Malinowski 1929; Raths and Biewald 1974). Absence of certain insects can be taken as a sign of environmental pollution (Englehardt 1959), while the presence of other species (such as greenflies that are attracted to decaying matter) can indicate unhealthy conditions (Meyer-Rochow 1985). Water striders, for example, are indicators of polluted water to the Trobrianders (Meyer-Rochow 1985). Meyer-Rochow (1985) reports how Australian aborigines use the contents of spider webs to indicate the proximity of honey bees. The presence of 'mutucas' (*Tabanus*) near river banks indicates the presence of game to indigenous hunters of Brazil (Lenko and Papavaro 1979).

Insects as UFOs

Many tribes in Papua New Guinea report the presence of 'flying light spots' in areas where luminescent creatures are not reported by entomologists (Callahan and Mankin 1978). These sightings may be explained by flying insects that enter into electric fields caused by thunderheads; the result is that ordinary insects appear to 'emit sparks' (Meyer-Rochow 1985).

Insects and utilitarian concepts

Insects are frequently used as fish bait in preliterate cultures (Kevan 1979). *Nasutitermes* mounds are used for construction material by Brazilian Indians, who prize the natural insulating qualities of the nests extensive galleries (Posey 1979b). Nests of *Azteca* ants are buried with newly planted crops to stimulate plant growth (Kerr and Posey 1984). Beeswax and batumen are extensively used for artefact production and paint bases by indigenous tribes of South America (Crane 1979, 1984; Posey 1978, 1980a; Schwarz 1945, 1948). In Papua New Guinea and Northern Australia, ants and maggots are used to clean skeletons and bones. Cantharid beetles are the source of poisons for arrow points for some South American Indians (Meyer-Rochow 1985).

Hallucinogens

Insects have been found as sources of hallucinogens used by some indigenous groups (Meyer-Rochow 1985). It is unclear if the hallucinogenic properties are due to the insects themselves or the plant sources upon which they feed (Blackburn 1976).

Insects and archaeology

Insects are frequently found in archaeological sites. The presence of seasonal species has been shown to be useful to the archaeologist in determining seasonality of site use and the historic ecological setting (Gilbert and Bass 1967; Hevly 1982; Hevly and Johnson 1974).

Urban ethnoentomology

A current topic in entomology is the ecology of insects in urban environments (Frankie and Ehler 1978). Studies in this area focus upon the adaptations of insects to the special climatic and edaphic conditions created by intense human manipulation of the natural environment. 'Synanthropy' describes the nature of this coexistence with humankind over an extended time (Povolny 1971); a formula for determining the degree of synanthropy has even been developed (Nuorteva 1963). This specialized area of human–insect relationships might also be called 'urban ethnoentomology'.

Hypothesis-generation: the ethnobiological bridge

The interdisciplinary Kayapó project has developed methodological procedures to scientifically test hypotheses generated through its ethnobiological investigations of indigenous ecological knowledge (Posey 1986b). Native concepts and beliefs are used by Western scientists as *emic* guides for their research designs (Posey 1983c, 1984b). Data collection utilizes indigenous categories for floral and faunal inventories, while ethnoecological concepts (often couched in myth and natural symbols) establish the basis for interdisciplinary dialogue and research. In this manner, indigenous knowledge of biological communities and ecological relationships can be studied; when non-Western notions arise, these are formulated as hypotheses and tested by respective specialists.

Posey (1983g), for example, reports the discovery of nine new species of stingless bees (Meliponinae) through the comparison of Kayapó and Western taxonomic systems. Posey and Camargo (1985) record the utility of Indian knowledge about bee behaviour in the development of studies in areas little known to ethnoentomologists, such as: differences in odour characteristics, swarming behaviour, flight patterns, and habitat choices between or within meliponine species. They also propose scientific investigations based on indigenous knowledge of bee species distribution in relation to ecological zones and habitat sharing by certain species clusters. Indian ideas of acrid commensalism and use of odour trails by species for which such activity is unreported have also spurred further studies by entomologists of stingless bee behaviour.

Overal and Posey (1986) have effected a large inventory of arthropod agricultural pests based on Indian information and confirmed by field collections. They also report the development of research into the highly effective control of agricultural pests in indigenous gardens through intercropping, use of trap crops and natural predators. The Indians attribute much of this natural control to predatory ants, wasps, and termites, all of which are glorified in Kayapó myth and song. Roles of these insects in crop pest control are being investigated following indigenous guidelines.

Kerr and Posey (1984) report how the Kayapó utilize *Azteca* spp. ants to repel leaf-cutting sauva (*Atta* spp.). Likewise, Kerr (1986) reports the indigenous use of several natural pesticides and calls for their testing by Western science. At least in the case of *Azteca* spp., Overal and Posey (1986) report very positive results from scientific tests to determine their effectiveness in the protection of Amazonian citrus.

Anderson and Posey (1985) and Posey (1984b) report the intentional planting of certain plant species by Indians to attract bees. Such knowledge can be helpful in the investigation of tropical pollination and aid in the improvement of apiculture.

Many bee species are thought by the Kayapó to have important medicinal properties (Posey 1983f). Although almost practically unknown by pharmacologists they need to be investigated for their effectiveness and potential for a natural pharmacopeia (Elisabetsky and Posey 1986).

These are but a few examples from a single ethnobiological project of how indigenous knowledge can stimulate new ideas for Western science. No researcher is expected to accept *prima facie* all native beliefs. Much indigenous knowledge, as we have already seen, is highly symbolic and difficult for even the most experienced anthropologist to interpret, however, nothing can be dismissed by the ethnobiologist no matter how ridiculous it may initially sound. The most seemingly ludicrous ideas today may offer the greatest insights tomorrow when their symbols are finally decoded.

Refusal by Western scientists to study native beliefs is, after all, not a very scientific attitude. It is much more scientific to test the validity of native observations through the testing of hypotheses generated by ethnobiological study.

Concluding remarks

Knowledge, classification, and use of insects in human societies is diverse but relatively unstudied in a systematic manner. Lack of anthropological and linguistic training by entomologists – and entomological training by anthropologists and linguists – hampers ethnoentomological research. A true science of ethnoentomology will not develop until researchers have sufficient expertise in all three fields to investigate the native *emic* view of 'natural worlds'.

This situation does not prevent the elaboration of studies in cultural entomology that attempt to investigate insect importance in literate societies. Nor does it inhibit important research into the potential uses of insects as foods and medicines. Indeed, insects have played a significant role in human history and may be even more important in the future. Whether as protein sources in space flight or as key elements in integrated biological pest control, insects will continue to be studied and manipulated for human welfare.

From the theoretical side, folk biological studies can discover 'natural models' used by other peoples to define their own world in their own terms. Instead of imposing paradigms of anthropological structuralism and Western science upon non-Western peoples, we must learn to elicit and organize our data within the cognitive bounds of the societies we study.

Folk systems of knowledge have in most cases developed for many millennia and are frequently more ancient than Western science. They reflect the diversity of ways in which the natural world can be ordered and provide detailed information of ethology, ecological communities, useful species, and biological diversity. Folk knowledge can also serve to generate new ideas and hypotheses that can be investigated and tested with the rigorous controls of occidental science.

Studies of folk knowledge as outlined in this chapter offer a powerful 'intellectual bridge' between different peoples. Understanding the sciences of other cultures enriches Western science and provides the philosophical bases for the understanding and appreciation of other peoples *on* and in their own terms.

Chapter 3
Ethnoentomological survey of Brazilian Indians*

Introduction

Amerindian populations had undergone thousands of years of adaptation to the New World prior to the arrival of Europeans. Dominant European culture, aided by epidemics of diseases brought by colonists, missionaries, and conquistadores, left indigenous peoples decimated; today Indians remain only in the most remote, inhospitable parts of the Americas (Crosby 1972).

In addition to remaining Indian groups, many 'caboclos' (peasants) are inheritors of remnant indigenous information and culture (Posey *et al.* Chapter 8 this volume; Parker *et al.* 1983). Thus, to varying degrees, traditional knowledge about ecology and biological diversity of the Americas can still be decoded from indigenous and folk societies.

One of the most important ecological considerations for people living in tropical America has always been insects. Arthropods in general threaten public health, crop productivity, and are effective competitors for human food and living space. Thus it is predictable that insects would play an important role in cultural knowledge, material culture and belief systems of Amerinds. This chapter is a brief survey of the importance of insects to native peoples of Brazil and the Amazon Basin. Table 3.1 gives a record of all species mentioned in this study.

Reports and discussions

Food and useful products

The pre-Columbian agricultural system of Latin America was slash and burn with regular shifting of field plots. Starchy root crops were the principal food source in most of the lowlands tropical areas (Carneiro 1960). Protein intake through hunting and fishing appeared to have been very low in many areas (Gross 1975), although this may reflect incomplete data collection. Scientists tend to focus on eating at 'mealtimes', which often do not exist in indigenous groups, who gather

---

* *Entomologia Generalis* (1987), 12:2/3, 190–202. Stuttgart, Germany.

Table 3.1 Insect species involved in this study and their local names.

Ordines	Familiae	Genus and species	Local name
Coleoptera	Buprestidae	*Euchroma gigantea* (Linnaeus 1758)	mae do dol
Coleoptera	Scarabaeidae	*Megasoma acteon*	—
Coleoptera	Scarabaeidae	*Strateagus* sp.	—
Diptera	Tabanidae	*Tabanus* spp.	motuca
Homoptera	Fulgoridae	*Fulgora lanternaria*	jaquiranaboia
Hymenoptera	Formicidae	*Atta cephalotes* (Linnaeus 1758)	sauva, iça, tanajura
Hymenoptera	Formicidae	*Atta sexdens*	sauva, iça, tanajura
Hymenoptera	Formicidae	*Atta* spp.	sauva, iça, tanajura
Hymenoptera	Formicidae	*Azteca* spp.	—
Hymenoptera	Formicidae	*Paraponera clavata* (Fabricius 1775)	tocandeira
Hymenoptera	Meliponidae	*Frieseomelitta* sp.	—
Hymenoptera	Meliponidae	*Melipona rufiventris flavolineata* (Friese 1900)	—
Hymenoptera	Meliponidae	*Partimona cupira*. (Smith 1863)	—
Hymenoptera	Meliponidae	*Scaptotrigona nigrohirta* (Moure 1945)	—
Hymenoptera	Meliponidae	*Tetragonisca angustula fiebrigi* (Schwarz 1939)	—
Hymenoptera	Meliponidae	*Trigona amazonensis* (Ducke 1916)	—
Hymenoptera	Meliponidae	*Trigona branneri* (Ckll 1912)	—
Hymenoptera	Meliponidae	*Trigona cilipes pellucida* (Ckll 1912)	—
Hymenoptera	Meliponidae	*Trigona fulviventris* (Guerin 1829)	—
Hymenoptera	Meliponidae	*Trigona recursa* (Smith 1863)	—
Hymenoptera	Sphecidae	*Stictia signata* (Linnaeus 1758)	—
Hymenoptera	Vespidae	*Brachygaster lecheguana* (Latreille 1824)	enxu, sissuira
Hymenoptera	Vespidae	*Polybia liliacea* (Fabricius 1804)	—
Siphonaptera	Tungidae	*Tunga penetrans* (Linnaeus 1758)	bicho de pe
Lepidoptera	Pieridae	*Phoebis*	were-ngránga

food constantly and eat it on the spot. As Lyon (1974) noted, unless researchers follow on routine gathering ventures, constantly recording and weighing the gathered foods, the importance of many gathered products may be grossly underestimated. This is probably the case with most insect sources of protein. Denevan (1971) realized the significance of larvae, ants, beetles, and other insects, as important protein sources for the Campa. Insects offer a rich supply of protein and fats and are readily available throughout tropical America (Taylor 1975). Additional works detailing the importance of insects as food include those by Bodenheimer (1951) and Ruddell (1973).

Ants (Formicidae) are one of the most popular insect foods gathered in tropical regions. Tribes of the Uapés-Caquetá region of the Amazon eat large quantities of 'cuqui' ants (Goldman 1963); the Roamaina and Iquito Indians prefer flying ants (Metraux 1948b); the Tucuna fancy the abdomen of red ants (Nimuendajú 1952). These are all probably the same ant, the 'saúva' (*Atta* spp.), which is definitely identified as such for the Mave and Arapium Indians. They roast, pound, then add the saúva to their manioc flour. Steward (1948b) describes the practice of adding whole ants to manioc cakes. Eggs of some ant species (e.g. *Atta cephalotes*) are also considered delicacies.

Lenko and Papavaro (1979: 276–86) provide a rich inventory of saúva used as food throughout Brazil. Indians are attributed with teaching the 'sertanejos' how to eat ants, particularly the juicy abdomen of the saúva; Gabriel Soares de Souza, in describing scenes from Brazil in 1587, noted:

> ...the Indians, both men and women, anxiously await in groups for the ants to leave their earthern caverns; the Indians run with excitement and pleasure to take the ants, filling their pots or gourds, then returning to their homes to roast them in earthen basins. Roasted as such, the ants can be preserved for many days.
> (translated from Lenko and Papavaro 1979: 276)

The value to the ant as food which Indians give is expressed by Padre Ancieta, who noted:

> ...the Indians raise in this land an ant they call *icas*...that they roast over fires with great zeal to provide a delicious dinner.
> (quoted in Lenko and Papavaro 1979: 276–7)

Heads of some soldier and worker ants are also eaten (Carvalho 1951: 15). The Uananas utilize the saúva for food during female initiation (Lenko and Papavaro 1979: 278); the Tucano require that the father of the newborn child eat three times per day the saúva (Giacone 1949: 15).

Other social insects are also intentionally reared by Indians and their life cycles are known in great detail. Both Chagnon (1968) and Metraux (1948a) suggest various unnamed wasp species that can be considered semi-domesticates.

Honey-producing wasps (*Brachygastra*) are common sources of food: not only is their honey eaten, but also their larvae and pupae (Lenko and Papavaro 1979: 173). The Tapirapé eat wasp larvae (unidentified species) roasted in their combs, then extracted with small sticks and eaten alone or mixed with manioc flour (Baldus 1970). Baldus (1937) also reports the use of wasp larvae as fish bait.

Undoubtedly the most common and highly prized insect food is honey. Stingless bees (Meliponinae) are generally well known by indigenous peoples. Lenko and Papavaro (1979: 321–44) record 171 folk names for stingless bees, most of which have indigenous origins. Many of the scientific species names of Meliponinae are taken from Tupi folk taxonomy (Nogueira-Neto 1970). Both Chagnon (1968) and Metraux (1948b) refer to the semi-domestication of stingless bees. After robbing the hive the Guarani intentionally leave a portion of the brood comb with larvae and some honey so that bees will return (Metraux 1948b).

Beekeeping is also reported for the Kayapó of Pará (Posey 1983a,e,f) who recognize and name fifty-six folk species of bees. Honey, wax, and other products associated with Meliponinae are some of the most important economic elements in Kayapó society. One of the principal reasons men give for going to hunt is to procure honey.

Termites and termite nests also provide dietary input, although not as frequently as might be expected considering their abundance (Mill 1982). The Macú Indians eat termites during shortages of other foods (Giacone 1949); the Maué make a paste of termites and ants which is roasted in banana leaves (Pereira 1954). Jacob (1974) reports that the Uaica eat pulverized termite mounds, just as do the Kayapó (Posey 1979a). In the latter case, at least, this is not done only in times of hunger, but is a general practice that results from a craving for such termite and ant 'dirt'.

Eating of grasshoppers and crickets is reported as a widespread practice by Kevan (1979) in the Americas. Hitchcock (1962), Levi-Strauss (1948), Posey (1978) and Ruddell (1973) are a few amongst many that report the hunting and eating of Orthopterans by indigenous peoples.

According to Chagnon (1968) the Yanomamo also eat spiders and caterpillars (probably Phalaenidae and Morphidae), which are wrapped in leaves and thrown into the coals to roast. These are said to become crunchy and have a texture and form like 'cheese pone'. Beetle grubs (Scarabaeidae and Buprestidae) are one of the most important insect food sources. The Kayapó prize various types of grubs which they eat raw, fry in their own fat, or mash and make into a gruel with boiled plantain. Steward and Metraux (1948) observed the Peban tribes preparing a favourite sauce of red peppers, maize flour, and large fat grubs. The Yanomamo prepare large grubs for cooking by biting the insects behind their heads: a quick pull removes the head and intestines. If the grub is damaged in the process, the parts are eaten raw instead of being saved for roasting in leaves. The soft, white bodies that remain are said to taste like bacon. Liquid fat left over from the cooking is also licked off the leaves (Chagnon 1968).

Chagnon (1968) suggests that the Yanomamo come very close to 'animal domestication' in their techniques of exploiting grubs. They deliberately cut down palm trees (various genera of Palmae) to provide fodder for developing grubs. The pith attracts adult beetles to lay their eggs in the decaying palm heap. The Indians have learned when to return to the fodder to extract the numerous large grubs. A fair-sized palm tree will yield 3–4 pounds of these grubs, some of which are 'as big as mice'. Thus one tree may provide a rich protein source readily available and always near a Yanomamo settlement.

Pests and pest control

Although grasshoppers and locusts are occasional pests of indigenous crops, they do not pose the threat that they do in more arid climates of the Americas. For the Kayapó, crickets (Grylloidea) signal abundant crops and are excellent fish baits; mole crickets (Gryllotalpidae) are a sign of rains.

The most serious pest is the saúva ant (*Atta* spp.). Lenko and Papavaro (1979: 273–4) document how this great pest prevented early settlers from planting anything. It appears the Indians fared better in coexisting with the saúva, for they devised various ways of controlling the ant. A variety of poisonous plants were used including: copaiba, jasmi-de-cacharro (*Melia azedarach*), and various timbos (*Lonchocarpus* sp.). Mamona (*Ricinus officinalis*) is another plant known to resist or even repel saúva (Teixeira 1937: 357).

The Kayapó employ another ant called 'mrum kudja' (the 'smelly ant' *Azteca* sp.), which they say has a smell that is repugnant to the saúva. The nests of the *Azteca* are systematically divided and the parts redistributed in order to facilitate the spread of mrum kudja colonies. They attempt to ring their fields with nests of this small ant in order to prevent the entrance of saúva into their fields. The Kayapó have also developed six varieties of papaya that are resistant to saúva. These papaya (katè-bàri) are also planted to ring their fields to produce a barrier against saúva. I have seen 10–20 saúva-resistant papaya planted in large saúva-nests in order to expel the colony of ants effectively (Kerr and Posey 1984).

The Kayapó use a toxic vine called 'kangàra kané' (*Tanaecium nocturnum*), whose bark is scraped to produce fragrant shavings. These shavings are put into openings of bees' hives and saúva nests in order to kill the insects, and are very effective (Kerr and Posey 1984).

Lice are a common problem in most societies. Removal of lice is a daily activity in Indian and caboclo villages, with special rules usually developed to determine who can pick lice off whom. Much can be learned by anthropologists who study the social patterns and implications of this important ethnoentomological pursuit. Lenko and Papavaro (1979: 120–2) list a variety of traditional ways lice can be removed, including use of ashes of certain plants, and the employment of various oils (e.g. oils of *Simaruba versicolor*, *Carapa guyanensis*, and *Nerium oleander*). The Kayapó claim to have various treatments to rid lice, but the most effective is the use of tobacco smoke. Women are the usual removers of lice from the heads of their husbands and relatives. They blow smoke into the hair of their client, ruffle the hair, and wait for the lice to move about to avoid the smoke. The lice are then plucked and bitten or crushed. Removal of lice is a time-consuming activity, but one of great social pleasure and importance for indigenous societies.

Pubic lice are usually prevented by shaving off pubic hair, which is seen by most indigenous groups as extremely ugly and antisocial. Small gnats and bees that tend to be attracted to eyes are also avoided by plucking or shaving eyebrows and lashes.

Genipapo (*Genipa americana*) and urucú (*Bixa orellana*) have also been found effective as insect repellents. Tobacco may also be chewed and the mixture with saliva passed over the skin to repel noxious insects (Posey 1978, 1980a).

Smoke is the universal repellent of insects. Holmberg (1950) reported that the Siriono have a fire smouldering at all times between each hammock to repel mosquitoes. Wagley and Galvão (1948) observed the same practice among the Tenetehara.

General adaptation

Coping with insects is an unrelenting task for Amerind groups. Whether it is the daily routine of delousing the family, the formation of natural insect repellents, or the production of fly fans, Amerinds have refined techniques for adapting to insects.

Careful settlement site selection and house type variation are two ways of modifying cultural forms to diminish contact with pests. Steward (1948b) observed that the Witotan tribes of the upper Amazon were quite careful to select village sites that were dry and 'some distance from the river for protection from enemies and mosquitoes'. Denevan (1971) observed that in spite of poorer soils, the Campa preferred sloped sites because of their greater exposure to sunlight and wind and the corresponding decrease in insect pests.

Mosquitoes, black flies, and sand flies will fly only a few feet above their breeding sites (Borror and de Long 1976); thus elevated houses often reduce numbers of these pests. Tabanids are sensitive to minute wind currents as are midges and black flies. Prevailing winds are also an important consideration for coastal groups who seek to locate upwind from mosquito-filled swamps. The Yanomamo select a rise or hump for their villages to minimize insect attacks. Their houses are rounded with only a smoke hole at the top. Smoke from smouldering fires repels most insects and hinders species that live in thatch. Palm fronds and banana leaves are arranged at the entrances to the houses to keep in the smoke and to form an effective barrier to most flying insects (Chagnon 1968).

Various house types have developed to adapt to local insect problems. The Jura take refuge from mosquitoes in small oven-like structures made of earth (Metraux 1948b). the small thatch hut is as ubiquitous as insects in the tropical lowlands. They are generally tightly thatched and closed except for small doorways. Metraux attributes this construction as a protection against mosquitoes, though the thatch itself is subject to severe infestations of other insects. Barrett (1925) reports that cockroaches in the thatch of buildings are one of the greatest problems of the lowland tropics. For many tribes like the Jivaro the infestation is so bad that every 3–5 years sites are abandoned and built anew somewhere else. The Yanomamo completely burn their entire villages every 2 years because of tremendous populations of cockroaches, spiders, and scorpions in the thatched roofs (Chagnon 1968). Amerinds were using and producing mosquito netting long before the arrival of Europeans; mats of tightly woven cane and reeds were widespread in Latin America (Steward and Metraux 1948).

Sleeping platforms are also common throughout the Americas. The Cayapa utilize sleeping platforms both inside and outside their huts. These are 5–7 feet above the ground and provide remarkable protection against pests like horse flies, black flies, and sand flies that rarely attack above this level (Borror and de Long 1976). Occasionally 'flea beds' are also seen in Latin America. These are built at a distance off the ground 'beyond which a flea cannot jump' (Dunn 1973).

Termites are another insect to which humans must adapt. Termites that threaten wooden house structures frequently have their nests and trails burned on a regular basis. The Kayapó raise woodpeckers in their houses to eat the termites that infest their residences. Other animals are also raised by the Kayapó to help control house pests, including various genera of spiders that eat mosquitoes, and a small iguana that lives off cockroaches. Xingú Indians are also reported to use lizards to help control crickets (Carvalho 1951), which are kept on cords and allowed to feed where there are too many crickets (Kevan 1979: 61). In some parts of Amazonia army ants are intentionally diverted by Indians into their villages: the Indians leave their houses while the army passes through eating every living creature left behind, including cockroaches, scorpions, mice and others. When the ants leave and the Indians return, spring house-cleaning is complete and thoroughly effective.

Medicinal uses, illnesses, and cures

Insects are used extensively by indigenous peoples in their medicinal knowledge. Termites, for example, are used to treat many afflictions (Mill 1982: 215 and see Chapter 2, this volume).

Principal insect groups listed in Brazil by Lenko and Papavaro (1979: 189–93) for the variety of their medicinal uses are: cockroaches (to treat alcoholism, asthma and bronchitis, colitis, constipation, tooth ache, etc.); and wasps (for stomach ache, wounds, spider bites, constipation, burns etc.).

Bees are important in Kayapó medicine. Different honeys are thought to have different medicinal properties and are used for a variety of diseases. Pollen (collected by bees), larvae and pupae likewise have medicinal qualities. Smokes from different waxes are the most important and powerful curative substances: patients are either 'bathed' in smoke or inhale it. Houses are also 'cleansed' by smokes from burnt beeswax, batumen and resin (Posey 1983a,e,f).

One of the most feared, though harmless, insects is the 'jaquiranabóia' (Fulgoridae), a Tupi word meaning 'snake insect'. There are two species of *Fulgora* in Latin America that are given a variety of indigenous names. The Xerente call it the 'anquecedarti' (winged snake). The insect is believed almost without exception to be deadly, with a bite for which there is no cure. Both Spix and Martius (1823–31) and Bates (1864) reported native fear of the insect and tales of deaths caused by it. It is still a mystery why such an inoxious insect could provoke fear of death and disease.

Wasp infusions are widely used to cure such things as goitre, paralyses, and rheumatism (Ealand 1915). Mixtures of wasps are thought to be aphrodisiacs. Parts of the horns of the rhinoceros beetle, *Megasoma acaeon* (Dynastidae), are also thought to give great strength and sexual stamina (Lenko and Papavaro 1979: 205, 336). One of the most amazing medical associations with any insect is that of stinging ants and wasps and cures for crippling arthritis (cf. *Journal of Ethnobiology* 3 (1): 970, 1983). Stings from these Hymenoptera are apparently effective in curing arthritis. Cures for certain types of blindness are also attributed to wasp stings (Araújo 1961: 174). The Uapixana and Tirió Indians also use ant stings for curing various maladies (Lenko and Papavaro 1979: 239–40).

A famous use of insects in Brazil is that of the enormous mandibles of *Atta* to suture. The ants are allowed to bite the sides of the wound; when they close their jaws, their heads are broken off and the closed mandibles hold the wound together (Gudger 1925).

Fleas that burrow into the skin are of widespread concern in Brazil. These 'bicho-do-pé' (*Tunga penetrans*) were described as dangerous pests by early travellers in Brazil (e.g. Staden and de Léry) and can cause large holes in the skin where the fleas have laid their eggs. If not removed, the developing insect will cause pain and leave a hole that is easily infected. These 'buracos' (holes) are treated by the Indians with juice of the cajú and other fruits. Urucu (*Bixa orellana*) is also used to treat such wounds. Lenko and Papavaro (1979: 501–5) report that 'bicho-do-pé' attacks were said to have been prevented by some Indians by keeping their dogs on special platforms or hammocks. The Kayapó simply keep all grass cleared from near their houses and in the village plaza so that only bare earth remains in areas of human activity. The Kayapó watch carefully the crevices of their feet to detect the penetration of *Tunga*. At the first itching, they open the egg pouch with the thorn of a special vine they plant near their houses and gardens.

Mythology and folklore

Indigenous oral literature is rich in references to and beliefs about insects. Myths encode important ecological information, as well as social rules and codes of behaviour. Thus what superficially may seem to be nonsense or superstition may be structurally codified to transmit a variety of fundamental ideas at different semantic levels. Posey (1983a), for example, shows how oral tradition can encode information about ecological 'coevolutionary complexes'. Another example is the belief in 'weeping' termites common in Mato Grosso, which is really recognition of the biological reality that ground-nesting termites (*Nasutitermes, Velocitermes,* and *Cortaritermes*) exude droplets of exocrine secretions for chemical defence when disturbed (Mill 1982: 214–15). Likewise the Kamaiurá myth of termites with nests that light up at night (Villas-Boas and Villas-Boas 1972) is not mythological nonsense, but a way of encoding in oral tradition the biological fact that on certain occasions larvae of Lampyridae do inhabit and light up the nests of termites. This phenomenon is well known by the Kayapó, who take great delight in the rainy season event.

Social insects figure in the origin myths of numerous other tribes, including the Kadiueu (Ribeiro 1950: 177) and the Uitoto do Rio Chorero, as well as the Tucuna (Pereira 1967: 480, 457). Their myths also encode the Indians' ethological knowledge of the insects. The Kalapalo myth places the wasp (genus *Stictia*) in symbolic relationship with a series of plants that are actually part of a co-evolved ecological community (Carvalho 1951) and describes the predatory nature of *Stictia* on 'motucas' (Tabanidae) (Lenko and Papavaro 1979: 175).

Baldus (1937: 244) recorded a Taulipang myth describing the commensal relationships recognized between birds and wasps. The Kayapó recognize many special commensal and symbiotic relationships observed in nature, including those Meliponinae and acrids, as well as between different species of stingless bees that share habitats (Posey and Camargo 1985).

Most indigenous and 'caboclo' groups seem to hold life of all creatures in respect and their myths function to preserve nature (Posey 1984b; Smith 1983). The Kaingang, for example, associate ants with spirits of their ancestors and therefore do not kill ants (Baldus 1937). Cabral (1963) and Fernandes (1941) report similar beliefs. Bates (1862a) found the same associations with ant colonies and beliefs in resuscitated life. The Kayapó afford great power to the 'krã-kam-djware' (rhinoceros beetle, Dynastidae) they believe to be the chief and protector of all insects, except 'nhy' (the social insects) that are the 'õ-krit' (wards) of the 'hàk' (eagles).

We can therefore conclude that insects for the Amazonian Indians are not necessarily seen as objects that must be eliminated from their world. Rather they are viewed as integral and important components of nature and are given personalities through the use of myth and folklore. Oral literature also functions to transmit encoded biological and ethological information important to survival. Although some examples have been given as to how myth functions to preserve and promulgate beliefs about social relations and knowledge about nature, these functional aspects are still little studied or appreciated by scientists.

Ritual and ceremony

There are numerous works describing the importance of insects in indigenous art and ornamentation (e.g. Covarrubias 1971; Lothrop 1964). The elytra of iridescent beetles like *Euchroma gigantea*, for example, are highly prized. For the Kayapó, elytra of these beetles form a part of specialized 'nêkrêtx' (inheritance) and only certain persons can use them under prescribed ritual contexts.

Ceremonially one of the most dramatic uses of insects is in the Kayapó 'fight' with social wasps (Banner 1961; Diniz 1962; Vidal 1977: 126). The Kayapó may receive dozens of stings during the ceremony and may participate in 'fights' a dozen or more times in their lives. The Indians are constantly searching for the nest of the most powerful and aggressive wasps, 'amuh-djà-kèn' (*Polybia liliacae*). When a nest is found that is sufficiently large (usually 1.5 metre long by 0.5 metre in diameter), scaffolding is erected, at night when the wasps are inactive, to prepare for a re-enactment of the ancient event. The warriors dance and sing at the foot of the scaffolding, then ascend the platform to strike the massive hive with their bare hands. Over and over again they strike the hive to receive the stings of the wasps until they are semi-conscious from the venomous pain.

The wasp nest is a symbolic statement of unity and serves as a model of the universe. The hive is divided into parallel 'plates' that seem to float just like the layers of the universe. The Kayapó say that today they live on one of the middle plates. But in ancient days, they believe they lived on another plate above the sky.

Equally impressive as the Kayapó wasp 'fight' is the ceremony of marriage by the Maués using the tocandeiro (*Paraponera clavata*). Spix and Martius (1823–31) described the Maué marriage ritual for boys of up to 14 years of age. The powerful stinging ants are placed in a special glove of palm fibre and dozens are allowed to sting the youths, who are to show no sign of pain because their lack of fear is a sign of strength and manhood. After the ceremony the stings are treated with manioc juice and, when life returns to normal, the boy is free to marry. Biard (1862) described a similar ceremony for the Maué.

Insects are important in many other ceremonies and rituals, but these few examples suffice to illustrate this aspect of ethnoentomology.

Miscellaneous uses

The variety of uses of insects is enormous (see Chapter 2 for more examples). I will mention only a few of the more exotic variations in order to illustrate the complex role of insects in indigenous society.

For the Kayapó, termite mounds furnish soil to enrich plantations, as well as to form part of a mixture with ant nests to create planting zones in the savanna (Posey 1984c). Ant nests of *Azteca* are buried with some newly planted crops to increase growth of the plant; the results are said by the Kayapó to be phenomenal (Kerr and Posey 1984).

Kevan (1979: 61) notes the keeping of crickets and katydids by Indians simply to enjoy their 'songs'. This is confirmed by Bates (1862a), Caudell (1916) and Floericke (1922). Posey and Camargo (1985) report the keeping of stingless bees (Meliponinae) by the Kayapó Indians simply because they are fascinated by insect behaviour.

Insects are important as fish baits, as noted by Kevan (1979: 62) and Posey (1979), and even for hunting. According to Magalhães (quoted in Lenko and Papavaro 1979: 440) the 'mutuca' (*Tabanus*) was used by Indians of São Paulo and Minas Gerais to aid in hunting: where swarms of the insects were observed, especially near the water's edge, the hunter knew game was not far away.

Insects, especially ants and wasps, are also frequently used by the Kayapó to mix with urucu to paint hunting dogs (Posey 1979). Kayapó 'dog medicine' using insects is so elaborate that it merits special study to determine if crushed social insects can actually affect the olfactory functions of canines (Elisabetsky and Posey 1986).

Final comments

A final note is necessary to mention the importance of insects as an aesthetic part of Brazilian life. Nothing is more thrilling or beautiful than the flight of *Morpho* butterflies, filling the dark trails of tropical forests with scintillating blue flashes from their iridescent wings. Likewise there is no more beautiful natural spectacle than that of the literally millions of shimmering yellow, orange, and white 'sulphur' butterflies that fill the tropical skies and river beaches during the summer months. To the Kayapó Indians, at least, nothing typifies more their land than these scenes. I have sat for many pleasant hours with the Kayapó watching the kilometres-long strings of 'were-ngrãngrã' (Pieridae, *Phoebis*) and their ribbons of colour as they hover, drink and flutter on the sandy beaches and river banks. I have spent just as many hours watching the Indians watching the butterflies. They are keen observers of nature and fascinated by all that composes their natural world. This chapter is but a tribute to indigenous knowledge of nature and their respect for life in its many forms.

Ethnoentomology is not only the study of indigenous 'folk' science, but also the relationship between humans and nature. It is sad, but necessary, to end on a negative note: both Indians and nature are in peril in the Amazon. Indigenous knowledge of nature, and nature herself, are disappearing at alarming rates. As scientists we must work not only to record Indian knowledge, but also to protect the very lands and people who encompass countless millenia of accumulated information and experience in coexisting with nature.

Chapter 4
Entomological considerations in south-eastern aboriginal demography*

Insects are one of the most important ecological factors affecting any human population (Southwood 1977: 30). Insects are the 'dominant group of animals on the earth today'. Surpassing all other terrestrial fauna in numbers, insects live nearly everywhere. Scientists have already described several hundred thousand kinds of insects – 'three times as many as there are in the rest of the animal kingdom' (Borror and de Long 1976: 1). As Southwood (1977: 36) pointed out, 'about one in six of mankind is suffering from an insect-borne disease and...one in five is malnourished, while insects consume enough food to satisfy those needs...'. Why, then, have anthropologists and cultural ecologists almost totally ignored the impact of insects upon human societies?

Edward Hall (1969: 45) mentioned that anthropologists and the rest of our modern Western society live in a world of sensory deprivation and blandness. We strive to isolate and to insulate ourselves from the natural world to avoid any and all unpleasant stimuli. Thus, an ethnocentric bias due to western technology has skewed our data concerning the impact of insects upon less technological peoples. We do not conceive of insects as being anything other than incidental pests, for we have subdued the really harmful ones. We find it difficult, therefore, to imagine any reason for other peoples to be aware of or concerned with such creatures.

Patricia Lyon (1974: 70) pointed out a basic weakness in the overwhelming majority of anthropological studies conducted today. She criticized anthropologists for their lack of understanding of agricultural systems, not to mention their paucity of knowledge about ecology and biology. Perhaps the new emphasis on cultural ecology will change this currently accurate indictment, but little evidence has been produced to date that fills the gap in our knowledge about the role of insects in human ecosystems.

The purpose of this chapter is therefore twofold. First, to establish that insects were extremely important ecologically and culturally to Indian groups in the south-eastern United States. Second, to show that these Amerind groups

---

* *Ethnohistory* (1976), 23:2, 147–60.

recognized their importance and developed a sophisticated knowledge of insect behaviour. In short, they were magnificent applied insect ethologists.

One of the easiest ways to document which insects were important to the Indian is their use as a food. Ethnohistorical accounts are full of references to eating insects. Insects contain high proportions of fats, minerals and protein. They remain, therefore, one of the earth's greatest potential food sources (Bodenheimer 1951: 25–38). Locusts, cicadas, and beetles are frequently listed by earlier chroniclers as being a part of the south-eastern Indian diet (Swanton 1946: 252–3, 290–1). Spiders, fleas, and lice were regularly observed as food sources (Lawson 1714, in 1860 edition 277–8). Even today, certain eastern Cherokee groups greatly relish a gruel made of locusts. Cicadas are also roasted and eaten like popcorn. The pupae of wasps is one of the greatest of treats, especially when roasted or browned in grease (Witthoft, personal communication). Ethnohistorical sources reveal that the consumption of pupating *Hymenoptera* was the most widespread example of insect eating. As John Lawson (1714, in 1860 edition 290–1) described 'hunting' such food, the combs of ants, wasps, and bees were raided, 'when they [the pupae] are white in the combs, before they can fly'. These were 'esteemed [as] a dainty,' Lawson continued.

The Indians may have turned to insects to supplement their diets during the late summer and early autumn when the store of maize was exhausted and the supply of insects was still plentiful (Gilbert 1943: 294). Or, they may have depended on insects as a regular and important component whenever available, seizing upon the right seasons to capitalize on the high quantities of certain species due to normal pupation cycles. As skilful naturalists, the Indians would have known when the optimum times would have been to collect their favourite insects. Woodsmen of today have inherited a keen sense of accumulated knowledge, for example, about when is the best time to raid the local bee tree.

The question of bees and honey in the aboriginal South-east is itself one of the most fascinating to consider. The only species of honeybee in the United States today is the European-imported bee (*Apis mellifera*). There are no native honeybees. Yet the earliest narratives of De Soto (Bourne 1904: 74) and Laudonnière (1586: 9) clearly refer to both bees and honey. Later, Bartram (1909: 38–9), Mooney (1972: 82), and Lawson (1714, in 1860 edition 182) documented an extensive trade network of honey and beeswax. Where did these bees come from? Were they *Meliponidae* brought from Mesoamerica, where we know of their semi-domestication (Calkins 1974: 4)? What happened to this native species that it would survive in Latin America and not in the United States? Suffice it to say that bee larvae, honey, and beeswax were all significant to the south-eastern Indian (Robertson 1933: 74, 110).

To what extent insects fit into the total diet is difficult to document. Coprolitic analysis from the amazingly well-preserved Bajou Jasemine site in Louisiana may soon offer some information on at least one aboriginal south-eastern population (Hang and Neuman, personal communication). To utilize insects and insect products to any extent presupposes a folk knowledge about insects and their behaviour, and that is an important point.

36 Ethnoentomology

A sophisticated folk knowledge of insect behaviour is revealed through an analysis of the oral traditions that in some way involve insects. A search of the remnants of the belief systems preserved for us indicates how insects are encoded into some rather significant myths. For example, Bushnell (1910: 526) recorded the creation myth of the Louisiana Choctaws, which explained how grasshoppers and men were created at the same time deep in a great cavern in the earth (see Chapter 5 in this volume). Grasshoppers were one of the major crop pests for Amerind groups. This myth established why grasshoppers had good reason to seek destructive revenge upon important horticultural commodities. Furthermore, one can infer that grasshoppers and ants were both rather important in Choctaw belief to have been included in this major cosmogonic myth.

A similar tradition persists among the Cherokee, whose myths and sacred formulae Mooney (1972: 250–2, 308) recorded. The central story of Kanati and Selu in 'The Origin of Corn and Game' explains why bedbugs, fleas, lice, and gnats were released to punish man. In 'The Origin of Diseases and Medicine', another extremely important myth, it is the Grub worm that leads the council of animals that seek reprisals against humans for wrongs suffered at their hands (see Chapter 5 in this volume).

There is no real significance to the content of these myths other than simply their symbolism. These myths also point to knowledge about insect behaviour which I call 'folk ethology'. In the Cherokee creation myth, for example, the 'Little Water Beetle' is responsible for having formed the earth plane (Mooney 1972: 239).

How the Earth was made

When all was water, the animals were above in *Gallant*, beyond the arch; but it was very much crowded, and they were wanting more room. They wondered what was below the water, and at last *Dayunisi*, 'Bearer's Grandchild', the little Water-beetle, offered to go and see if it could learn. It darted in every direction over the surface of the water, but could find no firm place to rest. Then it dived to the bottom and came up with some soft mud, which began to grow and spread on every side until it became the island which we call the earth. It was afterward fastened to the sky with four cords, but no one remembers who did this.

Another example involves the water spider (*Pisauridae*) and man's acquisition of fire (Mooney 1972: 240–1). Lightning was sent from the sky and struck a sycamore tree on an island. Fire was given to the earth in this manner, but the creatures of the earth could not get the fire because none of them could swim or fly well enough to go to the island – none, that is, except the water spider.

The tusti *bowl*

In the beginning there was no fire, and the world was cold, until the Thunders, who lived up in *Galunlati* sent their lightning and put fire into the bottom of a hollow sycamore tree which grew on an island. The animals knew it was there, because they could see the smoke coming out at the top, but they could not get to it on account of the water, so they held a council to decide what to do. This was a long time ago.

Every animal that could swim or fly attempted to go after the fire, but all failed. In desperation the water beetle volunteered. This is not the water spider that looks like a mosquito, but the other one, with black downy hair and red stripes on her body. She can run on top of the water or dive to the bottom, so there could be no trouble to get over to the island, but the question was, How could she bring back the fire?

'I'll manage that,' said the Water Spider; so she spun a web from her body and wove it into a *tusti* bowl, which she fastened on her back. Then she crossed over to the island and through the grass to where the fire was still burning. She put one little coal of fire into her bowl, and came back with it, and ever since we have had fire, and the Water Spider still keeps her *tusti* bowl.

The 'tusti' bowl referred to in the myth is the egg sac normally carried by the water spider under the cephalothorax of the female. This is a distinctive trait used by entomologists today in field identification of *Pisauridae* (Borror and de Long 1976: 645–6) which can, indeed, travel on, in and under the water as the Indians well knew.

The contribution of fire by the water spider was not forgotten by the Indians. It became the symbol of fire itself and was often represented on shell gorgets and other artefacts (MacCurdy 1913: 402–3). Another distinctive morphological feature of *Pisauridae* is the marking on top of the thorax. This resembles a cross encompassed by a circle. The 'cross-and-circle motif' is very common in southeastern aboriginal iconography and represents the all-important 'sacred fire' (Swanton 1946: 210; Waring 1965: 35).

To prove by citing documents that such a folk ethology existed is not enough. One major purpose of this chapter is to show how such knowledge was put to very practical use. Every aspect was harnessed to alleviate the myriad problems that beset the Indian because of insects.

Village sites were selected to avoid as many insect pests as possible. Ridges were preferred because of their dryness and commanding positions, but this openness and slight elevation reduced the number of mosquito species that would be bothersome and also regulated which species would be encountered. Mosquitoes are quite sensitive to microenvironmental changes due to height, and will fly only certain species-determined distances above their breeding grounds (Borror and de Long, 1976: 494; Johnson 1969: 364, 374–6). Mosquitoes are also light-sensitive. Lower strata species, for example, tend to prefer the dawn and dusk (Borror and de Long 1976: 471–4). Those species with an affinity for maximum darkness are much higher fliers (Horsfall 1955; Matheson 1944: 41–5). Thus, by choosing a site on higher ground, a choice of night-flying mosquitoes would be made. This would coincide with periods of least activity in an Indian camp. Cane matting, which was used as a type of mosquito netting (Chmurny 1973: 235; Lawson 1937: 14; Price

1973: 2, 69), and constantly burning smudges inside and outside the houses were effective in repelling the bothersome night-time species (Ehrmann 1940: 177; Milanich 1972).

Gnats, sandflies, or midges are also sensitive to minute variations in the environment. Their activity is severely altered by wind currents (Borror and de Long 1976: 475; Frost 1959: 214–15). The slightest breeze can silence their maddening attacks (Johnson 1969: 380). By careful site selection, Indians could maximize wind currents and minimize the problems caused by gnats. This is borne out by studies of sites along the Georgia coast (De Pratter 1975, 1976). In swampy coastal areas, significant improvement in conditions could be achieved simply by moving to the top of a natural ridge, a mound, or a man-made midden (Broyles 1971: 12–14; Milanich 1971: 192, 1972: 59). Shell middens are common along southern coastal areas, and Alvar Nuñez Cabeca de Vaca (Hodge 1907: 54) observed Indians retiring to their midden tops for a night's rest, relatively free from the insect swarms. Bushnell (1909) also observed 'domiciling mounds' four to five feet high among the Louisiana Choctaw (Nash 1968).

Deer flies and horse flies are another terror when their numbers swell during various natural cycles. These animals are also quite light-sensitive. They will not enter dark areas and refuse to pass through tight spaces or wind turbulence. The Indian had two solutions to fit this ethological pattern. Tribesmen built windowless huts with small doorways to insure relative darkness within their houses, and they hung palmetto leaves (or something else appropriate) from the top of the small doorway (Bushnell 1909: 7; Lawson 1714, in 1860 edition 180; Price 1973: 42–7; Swanton 1946: 392–3). The swaying of the leaves or branches created a type of screen and created air currents around the doorway. This combination was effective in repelling the *tabanids* and is still in common use by Amerind groups in Latin America (Chagnon 1968: 26; Metraux 1948b: 443).

Sleeping platforms were standard in most south-eastern Indian groups. These were generally four to twelve feet high (Ehrmann 1940: 177; Swanton 1946: 387–8, 422, 427). In addition to the reasons already explained, the minimum height was selected to be above the distance fleas could spring. As James Adair (1775: 421) recorded: 'The inside of their houses is furnished with genteel couches to sit, and lie upon, raised on four forks of timbers of a 'proper height' to give the swarming fleas some trouble in their attack, as they are not able to reach them with one spring.'

When European explorers made their ways through the South-east, they frequently came across either burned or abandoned villages (Robertson 1933: 66–7; Smith 1907: 384–5). They immediately assumed, as have archaeologists ever since, that such vacant villages were the remnants of tribal warfare. What else could it be? Indian huts were almost always thatched. With time, all thatch becomes riddled with insect infestation. Even in temperate climates this occurs over a period of four to five years. In subtropical areas a total infestation may take only two to three years (Chagnon 1968: 26). Cockroaches, fleas, scorpions, spiders, lice, and a myriad of other creatures find thatch environmentally quite suitable (Barrett 1925: 18). It is probable that tribes found it easier to abandon

Entomological considerations in aboriginal demography 39

a site or burn it and start anew a few months or a season later, than to dismantle all the huts and rebuild immediately on the same site. It is a fairly common pattern in Mississippian archaeological sites in the South-east to show sequential burnings of villages with intermediate periods of habitation (Price 1973: 18, 65, 67, 98). The reason? Ceremonial, of course! It may have simply been an extreme but effective way of ridding one's village of noisome insects. This is a standard pattern today among Amerind groups in tropical areas. Villages are periodically burned to rid them of infestations and then rebuilt on the same site or a former site that has been allowed to stand for a while since it was likewise burned (Barrett 1925: 18; Chagnon 1968: 26, 1973: 20; Harner 1972).

James Price (1973: 99–100) reported this substantiating evidence from the Snodgrass site of South-east Missouri: 'Since the village was probably quickly destroyed [by fire], inhabitants would have had very little time to save goods and foodstuffs once it started. Yet the structures had almost all easily portable goods removed prior to the fire.' In other words, the physical evidence implied 'that the inhabitants had prior knowledge of the fire and may actually have set it intentionally since they had removed small vessels that would have been broken in the collapsing structures.'

Finally, a few words should be said about horticultural systems. Evidence of shifting horticulture is found in several areas of the South-east. In Georgia, slash-burn plots were shifted every two to three seasons (Larson 1970: 13, 296, 293; Murphy 1968: 108; Zubillaga 1946: 294–6). In the past this has been explained by depletion of soil fertility. Research in shifting agricultural systems has shown, however, that in temperate climates a plot is capable of 70 per cent productive capacity for up to 30 years (Carneiro 1973; Miller and Huddleson 1921: 32). We can, therefore, no longer rely on the simplicity of soil depletion to explain shifting cultivated plots. The alternation of fields was more probably due to an influx of insect pests. Over successive seasons, insect populations tend to build up rapidly in cropped areas – especially in warmer climates where there is no sustained freeze to kill overwintering insect forms (Andrews 1952; Andrewartha and Birch 1973: 234–7; Price 1975: 375, 378, 405). By shifting field sites, however, insects are denied their food sources and must migrate elsewhere in search of a host (Nicholson 1970: 3–59). The population of insects is naturally limited and checked by this means (Price 1975: 38–49, 346–9; Thompson 1970: 60–93).

The very distribution pattern of field plots is also important in insect control (Price 1975: 38–49, 346–9). If fields are spaced far enough apart, there can be no overlap of insect populations that centre around the crop. If fields were too close, populations could build up rapidly and cause an amplifying effect (Price 1975: 4–8, 30–48) in terms of crop damage. Fields spread far apart, as was the case in shifting horticultural systems in the South-east, would prevent such population build-ups (Clark et al. 1967: 22–5).

Other means were also employed to minimize insect infestation. Like most American folk culture that has been recorded in books, old gardening manuals are filled with choice practical garden advice, most of which was acquired from

Indians (Hedrick 1950: 2–23). Planting sunflowers at the edge of a garden or field is one effective way of luring many potential pests away from the real crop (Earle 1901: 178; White 1858: 92–3).

Even the maize–bean–squash complex developed out of years of trial and error experimentation – called 'science' in western culture. This trilogy proved to do well in the South-east as a field combination (Murphy 1968: 127–32; Zurel 1976: 7). This success stemmed from efficient use of land and reduced attacks from insects (Meggers 1971: 27). This trio of plants is less susceptible to insect invasions than if each plant were planted separately. We are only now beginning to understand why this is the case. Recent advances in entomological research in visual perception in insects (Wehner 1972) may explain the extraordinary success of the 'American Trilogy'. The tree plants growing close to each other may create a type of visual pollution or confusion that inhibits the traditional insect pests from identifying their hosts. In other words, one plant tends to camouflage the other. This undoubtedly represents one of nature's greatest symbiotic creations. One cannot go so far as to suggest that Indians knew about this, but they were abundantly aware of the success of this plant triad.

The Indian also associated insects with disease, and consequently with witchcraft (Kilpatrick and Kilpatrick 1970: 86–90; Swanton 1946: 794). The ethnohistorical material indicates that they had a notion of insect vectors. This is not the same concept developed to fit the germ theory of disease, but Indians felt that certain illnesses were carried by specific insects (Adair 1775; Greenlee 1944: 319). Lice, for example, were associated with boils (Gilbert 1943: 386), a very curious notion when considered with the next point.

There were certain severe health problems that the Indian could not have understood – in particular those brought to the New World by Europeans (Crosby 1972: 35–8). Here two major insect-borne diseases, typhus and plague, will be discussed.

Williams (1909: 340–9) assembled the first historical descriptions of plague in New England. Packard (1931) documented the advance of plague among the Indians of the English colonies. Ashburn (1947) discussed typhus and plague. Yet, neither disease has been adequately considered as a factor in the devastation of the Amerind population. This is particularly due to ethnographic parallels observed in modern times that explain the rapid decrease of Amerind populations as due totally to lack of immunity to smallpox, measles, and similar diseases. To explain decline in Amerind groups in terms of these diseases alone is to posit a one-sided analysis of the whole situation. It is to ignore the tremendously high mortality rate among crews and passengers aboard European ships, and to overlook records that show decrease in colonial settlements of up to 60 per cent in non-malarial areas (Dobyns 1963: 504–6).

Examining the situation more thoroughly, we find that plague was rampant in Europe during the entire period of early exploration and settlement of the New World (Campbell 1966: 1–5). In London, for example, the so-called 'Great Surge' began in 1497, but did not climax until 1665 (Bell 1951: 1–15). It is probable that a significant number of crewmen or passengers on any given ship were plague carriers. For the disease to spread across the vastness of the ocean, there had to be both rodent and insect vectors.

Ship rats were far more numerous than ship crews and passengers combined. Rats were ubiquitous and impossible to flush from a ship, regardless of effort. Dunn (1973: 305) pointed out that 'the colonists came...on crowded, filthy ships. They seldom bathed and wore dirty, vermin-infested garments...Excrement and garbage lay everywhere...to be picked up by the rats.' Captain John Smith (1907: 185) recorded that 'ship rats are a major problem. Thousands of rats [have] increased first from the ships, [so] that we know not how to keep that little we had.' Smith (1907: 332) later cited rats as a continuing and major problem, with explicit reference to rats spilling over from the ships and invading the granaries.

There seems to be little doubt the plague was transported to the New World with the earliest of European explorers (Dobyns 1963: 500, 503). Once the rodent carriers were transported to this virgin territory, the plague would have rapidly spread as wild native rodent populations became reservoirs of the dreaded disease.[1] The transmission of the plague organism from the rodent to man occurs via the flea (*Xenopsylla cheopis*). Few, if any, animals except the louse were more common in Indian and colonial camps. Lawson (1937: 30) wrote that 'the Indian cabin [was] often fuller of such vermin than any dog kennel.'

A vast network of trade and exchange existed throughout the South-east. Furs, blankets and shawls were given as signs of tribute and esteem. Early explorers were forced to exchange these commodities to establish good relations with Indian groups (Swanton 1946: 189, 237). Cabeza de Vaca (Hodge 1907: 103, 165, 173–4, 189, 206, 220, 237) observed extensive blanket and fur trading through his travels. These trade items were flea-ridden (Lawson 1714, in 1860 edition 180; Smith 1907: 366), and this trade network made transmission of the plague easy (Dobyns 1976: 3).

Thus, the World Health Organization's recording of the first case of plague in the United States as having occurred in 1903 is extremely misleading. That date may mark the first medically proven case of plague, but the disease is surely as old in the country as any in the European heritage.

A similar case can be built for typhus. Typhus results from an insect-borne organism, *Rickettsia prowazekii*. The louse (*Pediculus immanus*) is the insect vector. As already mentioned, lice were one of the major Amerind pests. The number of references to flea and louse infestations is extraordinary in early literature – especially considering the Europeans of that period were not themselves cleanliness fanatics. It is likely, therefore, that typhus, too, was a far more important disease among Amerind populations of the South-east than currently realized.

In conclusion, the importance that insects had for Amerind groups of the south-eastern United States bears emphasis. Insects and insect products were used and traded exclusively by Indians and most groups consumed insects as food. Insects were associated with disease in lore and myth and occurred in sufficient numbers to dictate modifications in life styles and seasonal activity.

The Amerind possessed a sophisticated knowledge of insect behaviour – of 'folk ethology' – that is reflected in mythology, but was manifest in many practical ways. Site selection, horticultural systems, house types, and numerous aspects of daily life were affected by adaptations to insects. Finally, depletion of Amerind populations may be closely correlated with the transport from the Old World of typhus and plague, both of which depend upon insect vectors for their transmission. There are certainly many other ways in which insects affected Amerind populations as one of the most significant components of the ecosystems of the South-east. The few examples cited in this chapter will underscore the absolute necessity of ethnoentomological considerations in any future evaluation of aboriginal demography in the south-eastern United States, or in studies of any native group, wherever it might be found.

Chapter 5

An ethnoentomological perspective of the south-eastern Indian belief system*

Introduction

The Indians of the South-east had undergone thousands of years of adaptation to the environment of the area prior to the arrival of the Europeans. Those Europeans who first encountered the Amerinds hardly took time to record or notice many of the details of Indian life, for they were too struck by the more profound cultural differences between themselves and the 'savages' to record routine activities.

Since the South-east lacked the cities of silver and gold of the so-called 'high cultures' in Middle and South America, Europeans quickly came of the opinion that Indians were certainly inferior, if not sub-human. It is no wonder then that the early historical accounts attribute little wisdom or intelligence to the Indian. The paucity of information concerning the native inhabitants of the South-east is also in large part due to what Murphy (1968: 1) calls an 'historical accident'. The rapid depletion, or total extinction, of Amerind populations immediately after European contact left many groups without even as much as the incomplete and ethnocentric accounts written by early settlers and missionaries that were afforded some 'savages'.

Later settlers began to understand, or at least appreciate, some of the Indian customs. This is evidenced by the adoption of many Indian ideas about nature, folk cures and notions of illness, recipes and ways of cooking, Southern folk culture, with so many borrowings and influences from Indian traditions, persists even today, though now in the possession of a dangerously small number of bearers. It has only been in the past decade or so – perhaps the result of a general awakening to the near extinction of this folk knowledge – that scientists have begun to discover that many of these folk traditions indicate a very accurate knowledge about plants and animals and are, indeed, founded upon what we today have rediscovered and called 'scientific principles'.

In the relatively sterile, air conditioned, insulated and padded world of modern man, it is easy to overlook the profound impact of such environmental factors as insects. Due to what Edward Hall calls modern man's sensory depravity and

---

* *Human Mosaic* (1977) Spring, 11:1, 1–9.

blandness (Hall 1969: 45), it is especially difficult for us to weigh the importance of such ubiquitous creatures as insects upon peoples of simple technology. Yet their impact was great, and, since insects were an environmental force that had to be reckoned with daily, it is not surprising that insects would of necessity play a key role in the belief systems of the Indians. This chapter attempts to consider the Indian myths and traditions that involve insects. Such a reanalysis of available data from an ethnoentomological perspective can offer valuable insights into the place of insects in the belief systems of the Indians of the South-east and, furthermore, show that these groups had a sophisticated, complex, and accurate knowledge of insects and insect behaviour.

Preliminaries

The geographic area dealt with in this chapter is that of the 'South-eastern tribes' (Hudson 1975: 4; Swanton 1946: 10). This classification is based on political considerations, as well as linguistic and cultural similarities. The South-east in aboriginal times was certainly not a homogenous area. Yet most of the inter-regional differences were quantitative rather than qualitative (Murphy 1968: 50); thus the similarities within the area outweighed the differences and a regional pattern is clearly indicated (Hudson 1975: 2–9; Murphy 1968: 50–1; Swanton 1946: 1–10).

The term 'insect' will be utilized in this chapter in a modified linear sense. Technically, 'insects' are those invertebrates in the Order *Insecta*. Most entomologists, however, tend to incorporate other related Orders such as *Arachnidea* (spiders, ticks, scorpions, daddy long legs, mites), *Chilopoday* (centipedes) and *Diplopoda* (millipedes) into their studies (see Borror and de Long 1976: 6–36, 46–55; Ross 1965: 25–49). This is appropriate, for these are orders of the phylum *Arthropoda* and closely related anatomically, physiologically and behaviourally. The term 'insect' as used in this chapter does not, therefore, conform strictly to the standard taxonomy, but does also reflect practical scientific usage.

It is also important to point out that the scientific term 'insect' does not necessarily coincide with the folk classification of insects in standard usage today by peoples of the South-east. Many people would probably recognize a category of 'creepy-crawly' which would subsume half of the known animal species of the world. Thus the category 'insect' is a contrived one, a convenient agreement within science, and should be treated as such.

There is insufficient documentary evidence to determine the native taxa used by the south-eastern Indians. It is probable that their systems were elaborate, complex and carefully correlated with the key characteristics deemed important to distinguish certain insects. With certainty one can say that the average Indian knew considerably more about his environment, including insects, than the average person living in the South-east today. The only extensive insect folk taxonomy developed for any North American Indian group has been compiled by Wyman and Bailey (1964; see also Wyman and Bailey 1952: 97–103) for the modern Navajo. Other insect taxa for a few current Indian tribes have been treated in a limited way under the broader heading of 'ethnozoology' (see Conklin 1973 for a complete bibliography up through 1971).

Though documentation is scarce concerning the South-east Indians' belief systems, several very important Spanish, French and English documents have been preserved. These were written by early explorers and missionaries who were themselves dealing intimately with all the environmental rigours of the Southeast. Many manuscripts may still remain undiscovered in European archives. There remain others that are untranslated and analysed. Therefore, there are still prospects for further ethnoentomological investigation.

Insects in the belief system

Ants, grasshoppers, spiders and water beetles have important roles in the creation myths of the south-eastern Indians. According to the Louisiana Choctaw legends, recorded by Bushnell in 1910, grasshoppers and men were created at the same time and in the same sacred place called Nane Chaha. The legend is as follows:

> Soon after the earth, 'yahne' was made, men and grasshoppers came to the surface through a long passageway that led from a large cavern, in the interior of the earth, to the summit of a high hill, Nane Chaha. There deep down in the earth, in the great cavern, man and the grasshoppers had been created by Aba, the Great Spirit, having been formed of the yellow clay.
>
> For a time the men and the grasshopper continued to reach the surface together, and as they emerged from the long passageway they would scatter in all directions, some going north, others south, east or west.
>
> But at last the mother of the grasshoppers who had remained in the cavern was killed by the men, and as a consequence there were no more grasshoppers to reach the surface, and ever after those that lived on the earth were known to the Choctaw as 'eske ilay' or 'mother dead'. However, men continued to reach the surface of the earth through the long passageway that led to the summit (of Nane Chaha) and, as they moved about from place to place, they trampled upon many grasshoppers in the high grass, killing many and hurting others.
>
> The grasshoppers became alarmed as they feared all would be killed if men became more numerous and continued to come from the cavern in the earth. They spoke to Aba, who heard them and soon after caused the passageway to be closed and no more men were allowed to reach the surface. But as there were many men remaining in the cavern he changed them to ants and ever since that time the small ants have come forth from holes in the ground.
>
> (Bushnell 1910: 526–7)

Grasshoppers (*Tetrigidae* and *Tettigonidae* are the major Orthopteran pests in the South-east) were one of the major insect problems for the Indian. This myth not only explains why grasshoppers would seek such destructive revenge on man, but also justifies the ravenous attacks by the insects upon the important agricultural commodities of the Indian. It is still believed by modern Indian groups that grasshoppers are sent by witches to destroy crops.

Ants are also important in this creation myth. Since ants come from below the earth, they are seen as being invaders of the upper world. By virtue of being from two parts of the world – upper and lower – ants were considered anomalous to the Indian. Ants were denizens of the lower world and, therefore, associated with witchcraft.

The Cherokee, however, admired the 'warlike proclivities' of ants, and the 'ant clan' was an important one in many tribes (Gilbert 1943: 185). Ant mythology seems to permeate Indian belief systems throughout the Americas. 'Ant people' were among the first to inhabit the dark underworld. The Emergence myths recorded by Bushnell (1909) record that the first people of the earth were all insect people, and the different colours of ant species account for the different coloured races of man.

Another insect associated with cosmogonic myths is the water beetle (*Hydrophilidae* and/or *Gyrinidae*). These insects were particularly anomalous to the Indian, for they are equally at home under the water as well as on the surface. Often they are also attracted to lights or fire at night (Borror and de Long 1976: 277–82). The Choctaw conceived of the earth as a great island floating in a sea of water. Cords hanging from a sky vault of solid rock held the earth in suspension (see Chapter 4).

The notion that the water beetle could dive to the bottom of a body of water and bring up soft mud is an excellent example of the sophisticated knowledge the Indians must have had about the habits of insects. Water beetles do indeed create little soft mud cells on the shore of pools and streams wherein pupation occurs (Borror and de Long, 1976: 280). The morphology of the water beetle may also be significant. The shape of the water beetle is a near perfect oval, with a lateral division being formed by the elytra. Thus a perfectly straight line is formed three-quarters through the centre of the oval. A case could be made to suggest that the Indian may have held the water beetle in special esteem by virtue of its shape. The barrel-oval, a sacred symbol to the south-eastern Indian, may have been seen in a natural manifestation in the water beetle.

This may not be such a far-fetched notion, for the water spider (*Pisauridae*, commonly called the fishing spider) is seen throughout the South-east represented on shell gorgets (MacCurdy 1913: 402–3). The 'cross and circle' motif is very common and represents 'sacred fire' (Swanton 1942: 210; Waring 1965: 35). The water spider has a design on its thorax reminiscent of the cross and circle. The water spider also has an anomalous nature because of its ability to walk on land as well as on water. This explains why these creatures are important in Indian mythology. The water spider is attributed with bringing fire to the tribes (see Chapter 4).

It is in association with disease, and therefore witchcraft, that insects are most important in the belief systems of the south-eastern Indians. In the famous

Cherokee myth of Kanati and Selu, 'The Origin of Corn and Cane', bedbugs, fleas, lice and gnats were released by Kanati from jars in a cave to punish his evil boys. 'They screamed with pain and fright and tried to beat off the insects but the thousands of vermin crawled over them and bit and stung them until they both dropped down nearly dead' (Mooney 1972: 244). The insects mentioned here must have been considered some of the most pestilent species, and were believed to have been released into the world because of man's evil actions. This seemed justifiable and reasonable to the Indian for another reason also: the insects were seeking revenge for the cruelties and injustices they had suffered from man. In the myth about the 'Origin of Diseases and Medicine' (Mooney 1972: 250–2), this is explained most clearly. In a special council, with Grub-worm (the grub of *Allorhina nitida* says Mooney (1972: 308)) as chief, the birds, small animals, and insects sought reprisals for the wrongs they suffered at the hands of man:

> They began then to devise and name so many new diseases, one after another, that had not their intention at last failed them, no one of the human race would have been able to survive. The Grub-worm grew constantly more pleased as the name of each disease was called off, until at last they reached the end of the list, when someone proposed to make menstruation sometimes fatal to woman. On this he rose up in his place and cried, 'Wadan! (Thanks!) I'm glad some more of them will die, for they are getting so thick that they tread on me.' The thought fairly made him shake with joy, so that he fell over backward and could not get on his feet again, but had to wriggle off on his back, and the Grub-worm has done so ever since.

The anger of the grub-worm might have been due to the utilization of the insect as a food by the Indian. Throughout the Americas Indians rely upon grubs of various insect species as a source of protein and fats (see Lawson 1937: 290–1; Swanton 1946: 81, 252, 277, 295). The grub of *Allorhina nitida* is an especially large and fat one, and is commonly seen curled up on its side. The spiral form of the curled grub might have been of special symbolic importance to the Indians, for the 'spiral' is seen in much iconography in the South-east (see Waring and Holder 1965: 9–29).

Nearly every human ailment not directly traceable to witchcraft is thought to be caused by insects. 'The reason is plain,' explains Mooney (1972: 308). 'There are such myriads of them (insects) everywhere in the earth and in the air that mankind is constantly destroying them wholesale, without mercy and almost without knowledge, and this is their method of taking revenge.'

Ants, for example, were thought to contribute their 'collective stings' to the witches, and grains of sand from red ant hills were useful to shamans for causing illness. A Cherokee shaman often used insects or insect parts in effecting cures. This would generally be in the form of a chant or formula (Kilpatrick and Kilpatrick 1970: 86, 96), or perhaps a performance of an elaborate 'extraction' ritual to remove the culprit insect from the patient's body (Greenlee 1944; Lawson

1937: 30; Morphi 1932: 35–6). Insects were so closely associated with disease that even to dream of a louse, for example, meant impending sickness or boils (Gilbert 1943: 386).

Because of their close association with witchcraft, insects were thought to have special powers to foretell the future. A certain song of a katydid (*Tettigonidae*) meant death to the hearer (Mooney 1972: 401). Crickets (*Gryllidae*) could tell a pregnant woman if she would give birth to a girl or a boy depending upon which song was sung (Mooney 1972: 401). The song of the jar-fly (*Cicada auletes*) which begins in mid-summer, is taken to signal the ripening of beans and the coming of the green corn (Mooney 1972: 309). The appearance of greenflies (probably *Calyptrata*) was an omen of a good harvest (du Pratz 1774: 136–47), and an abundance of ticks (*Acarina*) was a sign of an abundant crop of beans (de Spinosa 1927: 68; Swanton 1942).

The power of some insects was so great that coming into contact with them or any of their parts could have profound effects. The Cherokee admired the mole cricket (*Gryllotalpa*) because of its flawless singing. Infants that were slow in learning to speak had their tongues scratched with the claw of the cricket 'in order that they may soon learn to speak distinctly and be eloquent, wise and shrewd of speech as they grow older'. The same could be accomplished with older persons, but with greater difficulty. In such a case 'it is necessary to scratch the inside of the throat for four successive mornings, the insect being pushed down with the fingers and then withdrawn' (Mooney 1972: 309). Butterfly setae (scales) were used in some cases to rub on the legs of men and boys about to go to war or to run: this was said to make them fly with the speed of the butterfly.

Dances named after insects were also widespread throughout the South-east, and some remain in modern Indian groups. The 'ant dance', 'tick dance', and the 'mosquito dance' are the most widespread (Bushnell 1909: 22; Gilbert 1943: 260; and Swanton 1928: 523). These dances all appear to be quite similar. Schoolcraft noted that 'in general the dances are performed with the most violent contortion of the limbs, and an excessive excretion of the muscular power' (Schoolcraft 1856: 277).

It has already been noted that several clans chose to adopt the name of an insect. The Ant Clan was a widespread clan in the South-east, possibly in admiration of the ant's constant activity and warring nature (Bushnell 1909: 22). Other clans in the South-east included the Dragonfly Clan (sometimes called the Daddy Long Legs Clan) and the Weevil Clan (Bushnell 1909: 16; see Swanton 1946: 658, table 4).

Conclusion

Insects are a key part in the belief systems of the south-eastern Indians. Not only do these creatures play considerable roles in the cosmogonic myths, but they are also prominent in many other stories and legends. Insects are most important in the Indian's concepts about disease and curing. Many diseases not directly attributable to witchcraft are thought to be caused by insects. Because of the association of some insects with the 'underworld', however, insects are also considered to be used by witches to cause man injury and harm. An analysis of myths that refer to insects indicates that the south-eastern Indian possessed a rather detailed and sophisticated knowledge about insects and insect behaviour. It is for this reason that some groups chose to name their clans after insects and to create dances in their honour. It is unfortunate that more detailed descriptions of the Indian do not exist, for most certainly these would reveal that insects play a much greater role in the belief systems than is suggested in the literature.

Part II

Wider applications of indigenous knowledge

Chapter 6

The application of ethnobiology in the conservation of dwindling natural resources

Lost knowledge or options for the survival of the planet*

Introduction

Conservation has always been a cultural question, although environmentalists have acted for decades as though the preservation of nature had nothing to do with the human species. Humans were seen as innately destructive and set in some cosmic world in absolute opposition to nature. Indeed, the Judaeo-Christian tradition establishes such a dichotomy, but – fortunately for the species – not all societies see the human role as the one that dominates 'lesser things'.

Most experienced environmentalists and conservationists have discovered that unless people have a direct stake and interest in conservation, then the best designed projects in the world stand little chance for long-term success.

Recently scientists have begun to demonstrate how native peoples can teach us new models for sustained natural resource use and management. Their ancient traditions, developed through millennia of experience, observation, and experiment, do have relevance in providing options for the future of the planet.

The basic argument is that native peoples know how to utilize and conserve the forest, which is currently being destroyed, in part, for lack of knowledge about how to utilize the vast diversity of medicines, foods, natural fertilizers and pesticides and so on.

Fundamental to the preservation of the forest and those peoples living in it, is to show that standing, living forests are more valuable than cut, burned ones. The sad truth is that, as hard as it may seem to believe, currently the forest is only economically valuable for cattle, lumber, and gold – all of which are attained only through the destruction of tropical forests and savannas. Indigenous peoples can teach us how to give greater value to the tropical forest.

Disgusting 'primitives' and cuddly creatures

I began my research with the Kayapó Indians of the Xingu Basin of Brazil's Para State in 1977 in order to complete a PhD dissertation on ethnoentomology.[1] Soon

---

* Proceedings of the First International Congress of Ethnobiology (Belém, Pará). D. Posey (ed.) Museu Paraense Emílio Goeldi/CNPq. Brazil (1990), 1, 47–61.

after I arrived, I began to understand why it is easier to mount campaigns to save exotic species than it is to muster efforts to salvage endangered peoples.

My first lesson came when I went to the Xingu River Indian post of Kokrajmoro. There was very little meat in the village for some time, and the Indians were anxious to kill some game animals. A hunting trip was mounted and I was invited to participate. After most of the day in the forest, we were fortunate enough to kill a sizeable tapir. A large hunk of meat was brought back to the cabin where I was staying. It was processed by rubbing the meat with salt and storing it in a bowl of brackish water in the dark storage room.

The cabin residents left to go down river, promising to return within two days. I was asked to keep an eye on things, which I gladly did. After five days, however, I found myself still alone in the cabin. I decided to go into the back room to look at our meat. To my horror, I discovered the meat covered with fly maggots. I was originally trained as an entomologist and do not actually have anything against fly maggots, but that does not mean they are good for meat. 'Who would eat spoiled meat?' I reasoned, then threw out the noxious mess.

Several Indians from a neighbouring cabin happened by, saw the meat being thrown away, looked at me strangely, asked for the meat – which I gladly gave them – and meandered off looking quite pleased. I was not quite sure why.

The next day, my hosts arrived from their prolonged journey. They were hungry for tapir meat and immediately ask about the prepared tapir.

I said: 'Well, it was full of maggots and I threw it out.'

'What!!!', the head of the household exclaimed angrily. He then threatened to throw me out of the cabin.

Some maggots, it seems, as they grow exude enzymes which help break down the more gristly parts of the meat. They look awful, but do a great service. One has only to remove the maggots with a good washing to find a very nice tender piece of meat that is much more edible than before the processing. The meat is then hung up to dry in the sun and it becomes traditional 'charque'. But who would want to live with people who eat such horrible things?

Sometimes such prejudices are so deep-seated that we are not even aware of them. I remember one of the most powerful experiences I ever had living with the Kayapó. A young child lay dying in the cabin where I was visiting in Gorotire village. Up until that time, I had been shielded from seeing death for all of my 30 years. I did not know how to deal with death. I heard the piercing wails, watched people beating themselves in the chest and screaming in anguish, and observed the burial preparations. I felt that, as an anthropologist, I should put myself physically as far away as I possibly could from the bereaved relatives. I chose a relatively unoccupied, dark corner on the opposite side of the mourning spot. What I did not know was that I had put myself not in a position away from the action, but instead had managed to place myself exactly in the focus of the human drama.

The quiet old woman next to me in the corner was the grandmother. She was preparing to ritually mutilate herself in anguish. She took out from under a pan, upon which my arm was resting, a rusty-bladed machete and started pounding herself in the head. I grabbed the machete to take it out of her hand so she would not in fact kill herself. It was a reflex, tempered by my own cultural instincts, that took me out of the scene as an observer and into the life of my 'subjects'. To the Kayapó I had acted as a concerned relative and was later adopted into her family.

The violent screams and self-mutilation that I had witnessed that day with the Kayapó struck deep into my cultural prejudices. How could I ever understand such people?

There was one custom associated with the mourning and burial, however, that sent even deeper daggers of revulsion into my cultural subconscious: I call it 'snot-slinging'. During the wailing, great streams of mucus would run down the mourners' faces. They would resolve the problem by taking their fingers and slinging the excess off to the side with great skilful, forceful flicks. One sizeable blob landed on my leg. Of all of the events of that day, that blob left the most indelible mark.

These three examples are given to stress how cultural differences are much more difficult, personal and emotional for us to deal with than just the 'unpleasant habits' of otherwise loveable, cuddly critters. We become confused about the importance of preserving these cultures that do not have the same concepts of cleanliness, or who mutilate themselves in ways that we don't, or who have six wives instead of one. It offends deep prejudices in our own cultural system, and we don't like it.

We have to deal with those very fundamental questions of who are these people, and are they, in fact, really more 'primitive' than we are. This is a profoundly difficult problem, particularly because we frequently use these differences to justify our imposition of what we consider to be order and progress and civilization on native peoples.

Interpreting 'reality'

One of the most intriguing aspects of the study of traditional knowledge is the degree to which native peoples are 'conscious' of their management activities, and, indeed, if they have any 'real' concepts of ecological conservation at all. These questions pierce at the heart of the most fundamental problems that have driven the evolution of anthropological theory and practice since the inception of cross-cultural investigation: how to separate scientific interpretation from the 'reality' of those societies under study.

The structural and functional theorists that dominated anthropology for many decades of this century established the 'right' of researchers to 'flesh out' structures and activities not 'seen' by the native and even to interpret behaviour in ways not agreed upon, or in some cases acceptable to, the local society.

Thus marriage could be interpreted as an economic union between two kin groups rather than the love match espoused by the newlyweds. And schools were shown to function to keep young adults off the job market, rather than quench their thirst for knowledge as argued by jobless teachers. All societies have their own myths, and anthropologists work to 'demyth' human culture, exposing the structural elements that function to preserve societies.

Emic and etic distinctions

In an attempt to separate cultural interpretations by the investigator from explanations by the native, anthropologists and ethnobiologists adopted the linguistic distinction of 'emic' and 'etic'. 'Emic' interpretations reflect cognitive and linguistic categories of the natives, whereas 'etic' interpretations are those that have been developed by the researcher for purposes of analysis.

It would be nice if such distinctions clearly existed. After 12 years of studies of the Kayapó Indians and their environmental management activities in Southern Pará State, Brazil, however, I have learned and relearned that dialogue between researcher and informant obscures these categories. This is only natural, since individuals from two different cultures inevitably think and speak with different cognitive 'realities'. For mutual interpretation to occur, sharing of 'realities' must also occur.

Sharing realities

I have written extensively about Kayapó planting along trailsides, in old fields, in 'forest islands', at old village sites and others (e.g. Posey 1985a and 2002). The concept of 'planting' obviously implies a certain degree of consciousness on the part of indigenous peoples. But some Kayapó do not agree with my use of the word 'planting' to describe their activities.

Recently one of the young chiefs, who can read Portuguese, commented on an article I had published in a Brazilian journal about Kayapó planting. 'We don't really do that,' he told me.

I responded in a manner considered most unbefitting of an ethnobiologist. 'I'm terribly sorry,' I said, 'but you're wrong. You do do that!'

I continued to defend my position: 'I have seen many non-domesticated plants being taken out of the ground by your people and then planted in their backyard and along the trailsides. I've seen Beptopoop take orchids and epiphytes from the forest and tie them on trees near his medicinal garden. And I've watched many times Uté and Kwyrà-kà take tubers and seedlings from way over there and then plant them along the trails near the village.'

'Yes,' said the Chief, 'but these are natural plants. They grow in the forest anyway. They are not *planted*; they are natural.' He then continued in his critique: 'We do plant piquiá (*Caryocar villosum*) trees, as you said we do. These are not the kind of plants that we plant.'

'But,' I argued, 'I've seen the people throw piquiá seeds into the (termite) holes and I've also seen them step on those seeds (to push them into the soil).' My defence continued: 'I've had people tell me: "If you step on the seeds, then they'll grow. If you don't, then they don't come up".'

'Yes,' he somewhat relented, 'but that is not planting – that is something else completely different.'

For me, these were all obvious examples of conscious planting. But not for my Kayapó friend. He insisted that only plants that could not grow *without the help of humans* are *planted*; all other species are 'natural'.

We then proceeded to spend most of the evening discussing why it was that I thought that they did something that he contended they did not do. We finally came to the source of the problem: our differing concepts of 'domesticated' and 'natural'.

My Kayapó friend was using concepts that were more restrictive than mine. To him, 'domesticated' plants are those species that would not exist if Indians did not plant them. Knowledge about the care and propagation of 'domesticated' plants are handed down through generations. All other plants that can survive alone in the forest or savanna are 'natural', and, consequently, not 'planted' – even though their seeds, tubers, or cuttings might be intentionally spread great distances from site to site and reflect millennia of genetic selection by the Kayapó.

Thus most of the fruit trees and medicinal species that I have described as planted by the Kayapó, to my Kayapó friend belong to the category of 'natural' and, therefore, *non-plantable*.

I would defend my 'right' as an anthropologist, however, to contend for purposes of analysis that these species are indeed intentionally managed and – well, planted.

What I had learned most from the dialogue with my Kayapó friend was that my concept of 'planting' was much broader than his, and that to understand the 'emic' view of the matter, I had to return to a cognitive analysis of Kayapó words and expressions related to seed scattering, tuber replanting, epiphyte spreading, and a potential field of many additional unknown, unnamed, or still unimagined (to me) categories.

Consciousness of reality

Sometimes the 'consciousness' of knowledge is just a matter of putting an abstract label on a well-known, but unconscious, non-verbalized phenomenon. Edward T. Hall (Hall 1969) points out how culturally different perceptions of space change social interactions. Living in a Latin culture, for example, one quickly learns that intimate spaces are closer between people than in northern European cultures. Latins are seen as 'pushy' or 'forward' by 'gringos', while the 'gringos' are considered 'cold' and 'formal' by Latins. Different perception of space is to a large extent to blame for these generalized differences in behaviour.

Behaviour in elevators teaches the conscious observer much about the organization of unconscious, interpersonal space. One needs only a book like Hall's to become consciously sensitized to the well known, but generally overlooked, behaviour of persons in elevators. As the number of users changes in the restricted space, 'common sense' rearrangements of individuals occur to re-establish the proper interpersonal space.

So it is with the conscious of native people and their management practices. The native can become conscious of certain 'common sense' acts of 'management' when alerted to the phenomenon by the researcher, as in the case of observing an Indian throwing seeds on the ground and stepping on them.

'Yes, we do that,' he may say, 'but that's not planting or management.' At least the phenomenon is agreed upon by researcher and researched, even if the 'emic' and 'etic' terminologies are different. But the informant too learns of the categories being used by the researcher and may even modify his own way of looking at his own culture.

The distinction between 'interpretation' and 'reality' becomes even more complicated when dealing with higher levels of abstraction, such as the notion of spirits and mythological beings or forces. Native peoples generally make a point of saying that the forest for them is not just an inventory of natural resources, but represents the spiritual and cosmic forces that make life what it is. What, then, is the role of metaphysical concepts in management practices?

The Kayapó, for example, believe that old, abandoned village sites are full of spirits. Fear of spirits puts these old sites off-limits for many Indians. Only those who deal with spirits (shamans) and special hunting parties go to these sites. Thus, these abandoned camps and villages effectively become protected reserves, with a high diversity of secondary growth that also attracts many animals. The spirits effectively serve as ecological protective agents.

Consider what the Kayapó call the 'pitu' plant (actually a grouping of plants from several botanical families). Pitu is one of the few plants that is thought to have a spirit – a very powerful spirit that once killed thousands and thousands of Indians. The spirit of this plant is so dangerous that if people go near it, or touch it, they will die. It is said, however, that pitu can be planted by shamans in specialized, secret medicinal gardens. Fear of coming into contact with pitu is sufficient to keep out unwanted guests in these gardens and to guarantee the secrecy of the garden and its contents.

An etic interpretation of pitu maintains that the fear of its spirit functions to protect medicinal gardens and restrict use to specialists of medicinal plants. It would be impossible, however, to find an Indian who would say: 'Well, yes, the pitu spirit functions in our society as an ecological management agent to protect our medicinal plantations.'

So, we return to the initial problem of interpreting 'reality' of native peoples. It is the problem of emic versus etic analyses that has scared biologists and ecologists away from anthropology, which they consider unscientific. Botanists and zoologists do not, after all, have to confirm their scientific analyses with their biological subjects. Having only an etic level of analysis makes scientific investigation much easier. It is important, however, not to confuse scientific objectivity with the obscuring of reality. There is much to learn from the interpretation of indigenous myths, legends, and folk taxonomies whether or not the methods meet the rigours of some scientists.

A raging debate is now occurring within anthropology itself as to whether cultural interpretation can ever become scientific. To the ethnobiologist, the debate is rather inane. Ethnobiologists attempt to use all of the scientific tools that can be borrowed from botany, zoology, geography, pedology, genetics, ecology and so on. But that does not mean abandoning the quest for an 'emic' view as well. If searching for native 'realities' noses a bit too far into metaphysics or 'fuzzy-science' for some hardliners, then we must conclude that not everyone can or should be an ethnobiologist. We cannot forget, however, that attitudes regarding 'what is true science' seriously divide the social and natural sciences.

Methodological barriers

One of the greatest barriers to interdisciplinary scientific investigation is the differential time frames for research used by social and natural scientists. Biologists consider a few months to be a reasonable field period, whereas anthropologists think in terms of years in order to dominate a language well enough to delve into native perceptions of natural resources, concepts of management, mythological forces, and other levels of conscience or unconscious knowledge. For this fundamental difference alone, it is justifiable to develop a hybrid field of ethnobiology that trains students to weigh as equally important the cognitive analysis of semantic fields as the gathering of basic biological and ecological data.

Another fundamental barrier to research into traditional knowledge is the methodological problem of assessing the degree to which knowledge is shared within a society. Even in the smallest of societies, individuals do not know the same things. Scientists who have worked with native peoples have painfully learned this – or ignored it in their data analyses.

The Kayapó and other Jê peoples, for example, have highly specialized knowledge. Twenty-six per cent of the population of the Kayapó village of Gorotire (population approximately 700) are medicinal curing specialists. Each specialist knows certain types of animal spirits that provoke diseases and can only be treated with a specific array of medicinal plants, magical songs, and curing rituals.

Roughly 15 per cent of Gorotire inhabitants can identify and name at least thirty-five species of stingless bees (Meliponidae). The remaining 85 per cent have difficulty recognizing more than eight. But some specialists can tick off sixty-five species, including details of their morphological characteristics, nesting habits, flight patterns, seasonal production of honey, and varied uses of their wax, batumen, pollen, and honey.

To complicate matters, specialists frequently do not agree on details of knowledge. Two specialists in 'fish diseases' ('tep kane'), for example, may vehemently disagree about which method for preparing 'fish medicine plants' is most effective – or even which plants can be used for which type of the disease.

The hypothesis-testing bridge

These methodological problems can be handled by trying to construct statistically significant survey and analytical methods to describe 'typical' Kayapó knowledge, but such endeavours are nightmares for field researchers and result in questionable benefits. If it is the detailed knowledge of biological and ecological knowledge that is of interest, then careful documentation, checking and cross-checking to find anomalies and contradictions between informants is adequate to advance ethnobiological research. More importantly, it is adequate to advance hypotheses (Posey Chapter 2 in this volume).

Most ethnobiological studies have tended to search in native knowledge only for what is already known from science. So we look for categories of plant use, animal behaviour, ecological relationships, soil types, and landscapes that already exist in our own knowledge system.

Utilizing indigenous concepts, however, short cuts, or even breakthroughs, in scientific investigation can occur through the quite appropriately scientific method of hypothesis-generation and testing. No ethnobiologist has ever insisted that traditional knowledge be taken at face value, but rather that such statements be used to guide researchers to look for unknown categories of knowledge or unknown relationships, that is, to proposed hypotheses to test indigenous concepts.

In this manner, new species and subspecies of bees have been 'discovered' from bee specialists, interesting active compounds have been isolated in laboratories as a result of ethnopharmacological research with medicinal curers, diets of animals have been analysed with the help of skilled hunters, pioneering behavioural studies of little-known species have been carried out with the help of native specialists, and soil–plant–animal complexes have been learned from veteran agriculturalists.

The decisions of scientists as to how to propose their hypotheses based upon indigenous knowledge reveals the arbitrary nature of this basic step in the scientific pursuit, since the researcher must frequently discard from his formulations the 'unlikely' or 'unbelievable' elements of informants' statements. But what is unlikely and unbelievable more often reflects the researcher's ability to grasp native 'reality' than any real scientific criteria. Nonetheless, the proposal and testing of hypotheses provides the methodological and theoretical bridge necessary to link scientific research with traditional knowledge.

Discarding archaic dichotomies

Despite the many problems that complicate the study and use of traditional knowledge, some important advances have been made. Pioneering emic studies of indigenous knowledge and management practices are appearing (Alcorn 1984, 1989; Boster 1984; Carneiro 1978; Chernela 1989; Conklin 1957; Johnson 1989; Ribeiro and Kenhiri 1989; Salick 1989; and others) to reveal the sophistication of folk knowledge. More and more evidence is now available to show that what were once considered 'natural' landscapes are really 'human artefacts' (Alcorn 1981; Anderson and Posey 1985; Balée 1989a; Balée and Gély 1989; Clement 1989; Denevan and Padoch 1988; Frickel 1959; and others). And very slowly, the deeply embedded concept of 'abandoned fields' is being replaced with data on field successions and their long-term roles in natural resource management (Balée 1989b; Denevan and Padoch 1988; Irvine 1989; Posey 1985a; and others).

Yet most of these advances continue to be ignored in general scientific literature. Readers continued to be plagued with archaic dichotomies. Plants must be either domesticated or wild, native peoples must be either hunter–gatherers or agriculturalists, and agriculture is considered mutually exclusive of agroforestry.

Some years ago I coined the term 'nomadic agriculture' to describe the widespread manipulation of *semi-domesticated* plants by the Kayapó Indians (Posey 1983a). The term was intended to emphasize that most plants used by the Kayapó are *not* domesticates, nor are they 'wild', if wild means uninfluenced by human manipulation. Over 76 per cent of the species used by the Kayapó that are not domesticates are nonetheless systematically selected for desirable traits and propagated in a variety of habitats. During times of warfare, the Kayapó could abandon their agricultural plots and survive on the semi-domesticated species that had for millennia been scattered in known spots throughout the forest and savanna. Old field sites became hunting preserves and orchards, since as younger fields they had been planted by the Indians to mature for such purposes. In other words, agricultural plots were designed to develop into productive agroforestry plots dominated by semi-domesticated species, thereby allowing the Kayapó to shift between being agriculturalists and hunters–gatherers. Such patterns appear to have been widespread in the lowland tropics and make archaic the traditional dichotomies, which, unfortunately, still persist.

Future research and the discovery of history

Far too many biologists and ecologists still assume ecological systems to be 'natural', instead of investigating the historical and prehistorical activities of humans in the region. This ignores a sizeable literature documenting the widespread effects of humans on environmental communities that is reflected, amongst other ways, in the genetic diversity of a region. Future biologists will have to become aware of anthropological, archaeological, ethnobiological and historical research in order to produce credible results.

Many of the assumed historical processes that produced today's landscapes, are, in fact, current processes as well. The formation of 'terra preta do indio' can still be observed in Amazonian Indian villages. Kayapó ethnopedological studies (Hecht and Posey 1989; Posey 2002) have shown that even some agricultural soils should be considered human artefacts due to the extensiveness of manipulation by indigenous agriculturalists.

Likewise the processes of genetic selection of thousands of species is currently underway throughout the Amazon (Clement 1989; Kerr 1987; Kerr and Clement 1980; Patiño 1963). Domestication, therefore, is not just an historical question, but a dynamic one that can be studied today in many Indian villages. Yet we continue to read mostly theory about domestication as though it were only some archaic process to be encountered in libraries.

Application of traditional knowledge

Major international policy shifts by governments, lending institutions, research institutions, private foundations, and industry should occur to support research into traditional knowledge use and its potential applications in solving modern world problems. Applied research centres need to be established so that experimental plots, analytical laboratories, and field research stations can investigate ways for sustained resource management based on indigenous models.

New categories of plant and animal use (as cosmetics, alternative building materials, and other natural products) should be investigated along with international markets for these products. Pragmatically, if economic value cannot be given to the myriad of natural products – and the people who know how to propagate, prepare, and use them – then there is little chance to save the planet's remaining environments and native peoples.

Once the diversity of native products and their market potentials are known, it will be possible to design reforestation and forestation projects that are productive in all stages of their development. A real challenge rests with the implementation of forestation programmes and forest reconstruction projects that include native peoples as *intellectual* participants in all stages of project planning and implementation.

Intellectual property rights (IPR)

Headway has been made in convincing the world that native peoples have much to teach us about the ecological and biological diversity of the planet. Until there are international agreements to protect the IPR of indigenous peoples and to compensate them for their knowledge, however, then ethically it will be difficult to proceed much further in the application of traditional knowledge. Development of these policies and procedures should be given highest priority.

Lingering thoughts

There are lingering Rousseauean notions that 'true' native peoples are totally adapted to their environment and languish in perfect harmony with nature. If natives begin to wear clothes and wristwatches, drive cars, use video cameras, and drink Coke, then they have been polluted and acculturated and have nothing more to tell us.

This notion is both incorrect and dangerous. Even in the most acculturated, devastated societies valuable knowledge resists. 'Caboclos' (Amazonian peasants), for example, have an enormous amount to teach us. In fact, caboclos have been applying indigenous models to changing and modernizing situations for centuries. Romantic idealism must not be allowed to blind researchers from the remnants of traditional knowledge that may in fact be close to home.

Finally, those who study traditional knowledge and attempt to find its modern applications are not proposing that the world revert back to a tribal existence. We are merely calling out to any and all that will listen to help stop the senseless destruction of the planet's natural resource and the native peoples who best know them. There are options for the survival of man in the biosphere, and many of those options lie encoded within the 'realities' of native peoples.

Chapter 7

Ethnobiology and ethnodevelopment
Importance of traditional knowledge and traditional peoples*

Introduction

It is curious that 1992 marks not only the planet's first Earth Summit (known in Brazil as Rio '92 or EOC '92), but also commemorates the 500th anniversary of the 'discoveries' of the Americas. Ironically, the preparatory meetings for the United Nations Conference on Environment and Development (UNCED) have dealt extensively with the necessity to 'discover' how to conserve biodiversity, how to develop new forms of natural resource exploitation, and how to effect sustainable ecological management. It seems that after 500 years, the 'developed' world still has not learned that much of what it seeks already exists and already existed within the thousands of traditional societies that already conserve, manage, and utilize the biodiversity of Planet Earth.

This paper outlines the importance of traditional knowledge in the 'discovery' of Amazonia's riches – economic, cultural, and ecological. The basic argument is that traditional peoples (Indians, caboclos, rebeirinhos, serengeiros, quilombos, etc.) have vast experience in the utilization and conservation of biological and ecological diversity, which is currently being destroyed, in part for lack of appreciation of the economic potential of native species for medicines, foods, natural fertilizers, pesticides and so on. Preservation of biological and ecological diversity depends upon the recognition that healthy, living ecosystems are more valuable than barren degraded ones. Unfortunately, today most economic activities in Amazonia depend upon cattle, lumber, and gold – all of which provoke destruction of tropical forests and savannas. Traditional peoples can teach us how to give greater value to the living resources of Amazonia, but only if their diversity of cultures survives, and we can learn to give them equal status in the future of the region.

---

* This paper was presented to the Second International Congress of Ethnobiology, Kunming, Yunnan, China, 22–26 October 1990, and published in *The Challenges of Ethnobiology in the Twenty-first Century*. Proceedings of the Second International Congress of Ethnobiology (Pei Shengji, Su Yong-ge, Long Chun-lin, Ken Marr, and Darrell A. Posey, eds). Yunnan Science and Technology Press (1996).

Ethnobiological research

Ethnobiology combines the interdisciplinary and multidisciplinary forces of Western science to document, study, and give value to the knowledge systems of traditional peoples. Ethnobiologists present these peoples not as exotic creatures with strange cultural habits, but rather as societies that live in close association with their environments. Many of them have done so for centuries or even millennia. Frequently, traditional peoples have been seen as merely exploiters of their environments – not as conservers, manipulators, and managers of natural resources. Researchers are finding, however, that many presumed 'natural' ecological systems in Amazonia are, in fact, products of human manipulation (e.g. Alcorn 1981, 1989; Anderson and Posey 1985; Balée 1989a,b; Balée and Gély 1989; Clement 1989; Denevan and Padoch 1988; Frickel 1959; Irvine 1989; Posey and Overal 1990; and others).

Traditional knowledge is an integrated system of beliefs and practices distinctive to different cultural groups. In addition to general information, there is specialized knowledge about soils, plants, animals, crops, medicines, and rituals. Such knowledge often deals with higher levels of abstraction, such as the notion of spirits and mythological beings or forces. Traditional peoples generally make a point of saying that 'nature' for them is not just an inventory of natural resources, but represents the spiritual and cosmic forces that make life what it is.

In an attempt to separate cultural interpretations by the investigator from explanations by the native, anthropologists and ethnobiologists adopted the linguistic distinction of 'emic' and 'etic'. Emic interpretations reflect cognitive and linguistic categories of the traditional peoples, whereas etic interpretations are those that have been developed by the researcher for purposes of analysis. Emic analysis frightens biologists and ecologists, who do not have to confirm their scientific analyses with their biological subjects. Many scientists feel that ethnobiological research (ethnobotany, ethnozoology, ethnoecology, ethnopharmacology, etc.) is not 'hard' science and therefore is invalid. There is much to learn, however, from the interpretation of indigenous myths, legends, and folk taxonomies, whether or not the methods meet the rigours of some scientists. Ethnobiologists attempt to use all of the scientific tools that can be borrowed from botany, zoology, geography, pedology, genetics, ecology, and others without deserting the search for other systems of perception, use, management, and knowledge of natural resources.

One of the greatest barriers to interdisciplinary scientific investigation is the differential time frames for research used by social and natural scientists. Biologists consider a few months to be a reasonable field period, whereas anthropologists, ethnobiologists, and linguists think in terms of years in order to understand language and culture well enough to delve into native perceptions of natural resources, concepts of management, mythological force, and other levels of overt and covert knowledge. For this fundamental difference alone, it is necessary to develop a hybrid field ethnobiology that trains students to weigh as equally important the cognitive analyses of semantic fields as the gathering of basic biological and ecological data.

Another fundamental barrier to research into traditional knowledge is the methodological problem of assessing the degree to which knowledge is shared within a society. Even in the smallest of societies, individuals do not know the same things. Scientists who have worked with traditional peoples have painfully learned this (or ignored it in their data analyses).

Most ethnobiological studies have tended to search in traditional knowledge only for what is already known from science. By utilizing indigenous concepts, however, short cuts – or even breakthroughs – in scientific investigation can occur. No ethnobiologist has ever insisted that traditional knowledge be taken at face value, but rather to guide researchers to look for unknown categories of knowledge or unknown relationships. The decisions of scientists as to how to propose their hypotheses based upon indigenous knowledge reveal the arbitrary nature of this basic step in the scientific pursuit, since the researcher must frequently discard from his formulations the 'unlikely' or 'unbelievable' elements of informants' statements. But what is 'unlikely' and 'unbelievable' more often reflects the researcher's inability to grasp native 'reality' than any real scientific criteria. Nonetheless, the proposal and testing of hypotheses provides the methodological and theoretical bridge necessary to link scientific research with traditional knowledge (Posey 1983a and 2002: 58)

Categories of knowledge

A 'complete view' of indigenous knowledge, is therefore difficult (or even impossible) to convey because of its underlying cultural complexity. It is possible, however, to identify categories of indigenous knowledge that indicate new research directions, even shortcuts, for Western science.

Ethnoecology

Traditional peoples identify specific plants and animals as occurring with particular ecological zones. They have a well-developed knowledge of animal behaviour, and also know which plants are associated with particular animals. Plant types in turn are associated with soil types. Each ecological zone represents a system of interactions among plants, animals, soils, and, of course, the people themselves.

Ethnopedology

Surveys of indigenous and native soil taxonomies show sophisticated horizontal and vertical distinctions, as well as qualities of texture, colour, drainage qualities, friability, and stratification. Soil classification is frequently used to predict floral and faunal components associated with specific taxonomic categories. Where agriculture is practised, native soil classifications determine differential management activities, including organization of fields, as well as selection and distribution of cultivars.

Ethnozoology

Hunting societies are generally very knowledgeable about animal anatomy, giving special attention to stomach contents of game animals. They are also astute observers of many aspects of animal behaviour, including feeding, nesting, and sexual habits. Ethnozoological studies can also reveal sophisticated relationships between animals, their habitats, and other ecological associations.

Ethnomedicine and ethnopharmacology

Almost every indigenous and caboclo household has its complement of common medicinal plants, many of which are domesticates or semi-domesticates. Folk categories can be more elaborate and detailed than their Western counterparts. Ethnopharmacologists and physicians frequently forget that disease categories, like all phenomena, are culturally classified and not universal. Thus, not only can new medicines be discovered, but new symptom patterns can be detected that can facilitate disease diagnosis.

Ethnobotany

Traditional ethnobotanical knowledge can serve to provide new uses for existing plants, uses for previously unknown plants, and new sources of useful known compounds. Existing plant genetic selection activities can also offer insights into the ancient domestication processes. Traditional peoples frequently use upwards of 75 per cent of all available species, in sharp contrast to the less than 2 per cent currently being economically exploited in Amazonia. Thus, traditional knowledge is one of the greatest riches that Amazonia has, since it is the key to a myriad of new foods, drugs, colourings, oils, essences, and others.

Ethnoagriculture and agroforestry

Agriculture and forestry have historically been separated as different academic disciplines. Yet, traditional peoples frequently integrate these systems through the use of 'old fallows' that serve as concentrations of useful 'semi-domesticated' plants and animals. Thus, agricultural plots actually become a phase of forest management and domesticated plants become secondary to the overall utility of the system. This system offers a much more vast array of useful plant species, while preserving the integrity of the forest. Transfer of this technology to 'modern' agriculture and agroforestry could offer many promising options for Amazonia.

Knowledge as business

Industry and business discovered many years ago that traditional knowledge means money. It was one of the earliest forms of colonial wealth. More recently, pharmaceutical industries have become the major exploiters of traditional medicinal knowledge for major products and profits, with an annual world market value of US$43 billion (source: Fundacao Brasileira de Plantas Medicinais, FBPM).

Although no comparable figures are published for natural insecticides, insect repellents, and plant genetic materials acquired from traditional peoples, the annual potential for such products is only beginning, with projects of their combined market values exceeding all other food and medicinal products. The international seed industry alone accounts for over US$15 billion per year, much of which is derived from original genetic materials from crop varieties selected, improved and developed by innovative traditional farmers for hundreds, even thousands of years.

Growing interest and catapulting markets in 'natural' food, medicinal, agricultural, and body products signals increased research activities into traditional knowledge systems. Now, more than ever, the intellectual property rights (IPR) of traditional peoples must be protected and just compensation for knowledge guaranteed. Otherwise, mining of the riches of traditional knowledge will become the latest, and ultimate, neo-colonial forms of exploitation of traditional peoples. It is in the interest of the Amazonian region, as well as Brazil, to give priority to the protection of IPR for its citizens, since traditional knowledge is increasingly becoming the basis for a considerable international market.

Ecologists are also concerned with the ecological impact of production of 'natural products' because of the tendency towards monoculture cash crops. Many worry that international demands may spell the end of biodiversity, rather than encourage conservation of natural resources as initially desired (Soulé and Kohm 1989).

Suggestions for the future

The following suggestions are offered to guide future research into traditional natural resource management techniques and their applications:

1. Genetic manipulation of flora and fauna by traditional peoples remains relatively little known. Research into selection procedures, decisions behind selection choices for different species and varieties, inter- and intra-tribal variations in selection of variables, and evolutionary consequences of differential selective behaviour should be systematically studied.
2. More extensive studies should be made to describe how traditional peoples modify landscapes and environments.
    (i) Fire management is immensely important in almost all traditional systems, yet few details of fire use are available, such as when to burn; what can or cannot be burned and when; temperature of burn; frequency of burning; protection from burning; products of burning (use of charcoal, ashes, stumps, charred root systems) and so on. Likewise,

little is known of the effects of fire on biological communities, such as which species are destroyed; which are stimulated; the effects of burning on blooming and fruiting timing and production; modification of morphological structures due to burning and others.

(ii) Most research to date has focussed on indigenous manipulation of forests and agricultural plots. Yet evidence exists showing that other habitats may also be significantly modified. Scrub forests and savannas, for example, are certainly moulded by the use of fire. Creation of apêtê (forest islands) in campo-cerrado (scrub-grassland) by the Kayapó shows that ecological communities can even be human-made with a high diversity of useful plants from very distant areas. Hillsides, trails, and even rocky outcroppings are also modified to maximize resource availability (Posey 1985a and 2002). To get a more complete picture of indigenous adaptation and management, future research should emphasize investigations into traditional management of these studied habitats.

(iii) Rivers, streams, and seashores also can be modified by indigenous activities. Although extensive documentation of the dependence of traditional peoples on fresh and salt water species exists, only scattered evidence (Chernela 1989) is available on how traditional peoples manage these ecosystems.

3 Baseline studies are necessary to establish wildlife population composition, numbers, and carrying capacities. Many researchers have observed that old fields are favoured hunting areas. I have proposed that where old-fallow management is practised, wildlife populations may indeed be higher in number and species diversity (Posey 2002). This hypothesis goes against traditional thinking that traditional peoples are innately destructive to wildlife populations. To prove or disprove the thesis, baseline data from uninhabited areas must be available for comparison with managed inhabited areas.

4 Ethnolinguistic studies can provide valuable data on the historical relationships between peoples and the botanical interchanges that occurred between them (see Balée 1989a), or the cognitive geographical maps that link resources with the physical world. Myths, legends, ceremonies, rituals, and songs are filled with ecological and biological information, but very few studies have systematically analysed their content.

5 More long-term sequence studies of fallows and other managed habitats are needed to understand the ecological transitions that accompany growth. These studies, coupled with knowledge of the traditional uses of resources in the growth sequences, can give a much clearer picture of options for forestation and reforestation schemes.

6 Multidisciplinary research teams should be encouraged, despite the conceptual and time difficulties that separate disciplines. Focussing upon the study of traditional knowledge can indeed be used to reunite the fragmented disciplines of science.

7 Special ethnobiological academic and training programmes should be established to develop the interdisciplinary field, combining the methods and techniques of ecology, biology, anthropology, and linguistics.
8 Ethnobiological research centres should also be established to co-ordinate multidisciplinary research and experimental programmes for the application of traditional knowledge. These centres should include laboratories for the analysis of medicinal compounds, the nutritional value of edible plants, the chemical characteristics of natural fertilizers, and experimental plots and field research stations to investigate ways for sustained resource management based on indigenous and traditional models.
9 Major international policy shifts by governments, lending institutions, research institutions, private foundations, and industry should occur to support research into traditional knowledge use and its potential applications in solving modern world problems.
10 New categories of plant and animal use (as cosmetics, alternative building materials, and other natural products) should be investigated along with international markets for these products. Once the diversity of native products and their market potentials are known, it will be possible to design reforestation, and environmental restoration projects that are productive in all stages of their development.
11 Immediate funding and planning priority must be given to environmental restoration of degraded areas utilizing native species of economic potential. The key to success of such a reorientation will be the recognition of traditional uses of native species.
12 A real challenge rests with the implementation of alternative projects that include traditional peoples as full intellectual participants in all stages of project planning and implementation.
13 Brazil should establish as high priority the guarantee of IPR for traditional knowledge. This will require a complete re-orientation of existing laws, which have historically been used only to protect industrial property. Existing pressures on Brazil from industrialized countries through the 'Uruguay Round' GATT (General Agreement on Trade and Tariffs) are forcing the opening of 'free markets' and protection of intellectual property – but only to the benefit of technologically rich countries. If the same 'rights' to intellectual and biogenetic property were to be demanded for local, traditional farmers, then Brazil would have a decided advantage in future negotiations.
14 Development of alternative market infrastructures that are sensitive to local communities and their needs. If market mechanisms cannot be developed that respect both the ecological balance and the cultural and social integrity of traditional peoples, then there is little hope that our consumer-based society can survive.

Chapter 8

Ethnoecology as applied anthropology in Amazonian development*

Introduction

> To find alternative paths for the development of hinterland regions that led to greater human riches for more people, we need to begin with a less arrogant view of the superiority of our world of shiny hardware, a greater appreciation of the wisdom – and the potential power – of the villagers we would teach and guide.
>
> (Keesing 1980: 6)

Amazonia is considered to be one of the last terrestrial frontiers of the planet. Tremendous ecological and social devastation has followed in the wake of recent attempts to 'develop' this region (Davis 1977; Denevan 1973, 1981; Foweraker 1981; Sioli 1980; Smith 1982). The early history of economic exploitation in Amazonia was characterized by enterprises based upon the promotion of simple technology, decentralized extractive activities that relied upon the knowledge and labour of indigenous peoples who were most often subjected to a system of 'quasi-slavery' (Barbira-Scazzocchio 1980: xv; Reis 1974: 34). Little natural environmental degradation occurred, although the indigenous population appears to have been devastated (Denevan 1970; Dobyns 1966; Morey 1978; Myers 1978). Gradually, however, changes in world market demand, the structure of capital investment and returns, and general social, economic, and political development resulted in two problems that, by the 1970s, were commonly shared by the South American countries whose national territories encompass portions of Amazonia. First, these nations had all become net food importers (World Bank 1980); and second, they all had developed severe balance of payment deficits (Hecht 1982b: 62, table 1). In order to rectify these problems, these nations turned to their Amazonian hinterlands with a variety of developmental goals.

---

* Posey, D. A., Frechione, J., Eddins, J., and da Silva, L. F., with Myers, D., Case, D., and MacBeath, P. (1984). *Human Organization* 43:2, 95–107.

These goals were:

(i) to increase basic food production;
(ii) to expand exports;
(iii) to alleviate population and political pressures in non-Amazon regions of the countries;
(iv) to improve access to non-agricultural resources such as timber, minerals, hydropower and so on;
(v) to promote economic integration;
(vi) to secure national boundaries (Hecht 1982b: 63).

To achieve these goals, the Amazonian countries instigated large-scale development projects such as road-building, colonization programmes, monocrop agriculture, cattle ranching, and mining in their Amazon territories.

From a purely economic viewpoint, the performance of these development projects in Amazonia has been poor. Highly proclaimed commercial forest schemes, like the Jari Project, have proven unprofitable (Hecht 1982b: 78). Cattle ranching, the major vector for development funds and enterprise in the Brazilian Amazon during the last decade (Goodland 1980: 18), has similarly failed to generate long-term, fiscally sound development (Hecht 1982a: 27–8). For example, in the Brazilian Amazon approximately 95 per cent of all cleared land is used for cattle ranching; yet, in the Paragominas region of Para alone, 85 per cent of the recently established cattle ranches are now unproductive due to pasture degradation (Hecht 1982b: 96).

From a social standpoint, the results of development projects in the Amazon are equally poor. Indigenous populations in Amazonia have suffered significantly from efforts to develop and 'conquer' the region. Entire groups have been eliminated (Davis 1977; IAFB 1974). At least eighty-seven Amerindian societies have become extinct in the Brazilian Amazon alone over the past 75 years (Ribeiro 1970: 238). Caboclos and colonos[1] have fared little better even though one of the major justifications for varied development projects in Amazonia has been the provision of new lands for settlement and small-holder farming which would contribute to relieve population pressure, poverty, and unemployment (Bunker 1981; Schmink 1981). However, colonization projects from the Tocantins to the Trans-Amazon Highway have abysmal social success records (Moran 1981; Smith 1982).

Development projects are also accelerating rates of deforestation, soil destruction, and desertification in Amazonia (Cultural Survival 1982; Fearnside 1979). Amazonia constitutes the largest tract of tropical rain forest in the world, over 55 million hectares. Despite controversy over the current amount of deforestation in Amazonia (see Fearnside 1982; Hecht 1982b: 65–6), authorities agree that land clearing is occurring at an alarming rate that threatens the viability of the entire region. Deforestation destroys the ecosystem nutrient cycle, and inevitably and rapidly leads to leaching, soil compaction, soil erosion, and flooding (Goodland

and Irwin 1975: 23–6; Sioli 1980). This is followed by water pollution, changes in water turbidity, and changes in pH that reduce or destroy aquatic life (Lovejoy and Schubart 1980: 23–4; Schubart 1977). It is estimated that continued deforestation in the Amazonian rain forests, one of the most species-diverse regions in the world (Goodland and Irwin 1975: 78–111; Sioli 1980: 264–5), will push to extinction up to 90 per cent of the natural inventory of organisms before even basic taxonomic descriptions, much less scientific evaluations of their value, can be made (Gottlieb 1981: 23).

Largely because of poor economic performance, and partially due to the adverse environmental and social effects of large-scale developments, Brazil (the country with sovereignty over the largest section of Amazonia) has reduced the rapid pace of some forms of Amazonian development (Goodland 1980: 22). Formulation of a new policy of development in the Brazilian Amazon was supposed to begin in 1979 (Goodland 1980: 9). However, Brazilian Amazonian development still appears to be directed towards large-scale projects (currently concentrating upon mining and hydroelectric dam construction) that retain many of the unsound ecological and social aspects associated with the development projects of the last two decades (Wright 1983).

Failure of the bulk of Amazonian development projects underscores the necessity for radically different strategies if development is to be humane, productive, and ecologically sound. This chapter argues that indigenous systems of resource perception, utilization, and management can contribute significantly to these alternative strategies and are the logical products of applied ethnoecological research.

It must be noted, however, that a critical aspect of alternative strategy development as proposed herein is the formulation and implementation of equitable indigenous rights policies throughout Amazonia. Respect for the cultural integrity of Amazonian indigenous and peasant populations has been growing. In reality, many Amazonian nations already have laws guaranteeing indigenous populations rights to their lands and to the retention of their particular cultural practices (e.g. for Brazil see Ramos 1980: 228; and for Venezuela see Frechione 1981: 139–42). Generally these laws have been ignored or have been difficult to enforce due to the remoteness of Amazonia within the infrastructure of the region's nations. The continuing integration of Amazonia into national and international systems has made it more difficult for these laws to be ignored, or for negligence to escape attention.

In addition, indigenous and folk societies are now organizing themselves into political and economic interest groups with the power to represent their interests within the regional, national and international systems (Barbira-Scazzocchio 1980: xv). The Shuar Federation in Ecuador (Salazar 1981) and the Union Makiritare de Alto Ventuari in Venezuela (UMAV) (Frechione 1981) are examples of such successful movements. Groups are becoming politicized and are knowledgeable of the potential value of their ethnoecological expertise and the natural resources of their territories. In some areas, they are attempting to limit exploitation in their territories without their participation, or the assurance of equitable recompense (UMAV 1978, personal communication).

In this chapter we do not suggest a policy of isolation for Amazonian populations or a complete 'hands off' policy for the development of the area in general, but rather a co-operative strategy for the formulation of development planning based upon a combination of indigenous ethnoecological knowledge and western scientific knowledge that is fostered by the Amazonian nations and by the international community.

Indigenous roots

Ethnoecology may be defined as indigenous perceptions of 'natural' divisions in the biological world and plant–animal–human relationships within each division. These cognitively defined ecological categories do not exist in isolation; thus ethnoecology must also deal with the perceptions of interrelatedness between natural divisions (Posey 1981). The diversity of indigenous strategies aimed at the integrated utilization of natural resources is witness to the complexity and richness of Amazonian ecosystems. The strategies themselves are interrelated, forming an overall cultural system inextricably wrapped in myth, ceremony, kinship, and politics (Posey 1981). For purposes of clarity in this chapter, however, we divide the text into six sub-headings with suggestions for the incorporation of indigenous ideas into new development strategies. These six areas of consideration are: (i) gathered products, (ii) game, (iii) aquaculture, (iv) agriculture, (v) resource units, and (vi) cosmology.

Gathered products

Gathering refers to procurement of wild plants, animals and animal products, and various inert elements for food, materials or medicines. The array of wild plants collected by Amazonian Indians is known to be extensive, but taxonomic, pharmacological, and nutritional data remain scanty. A limited number of wild food sources have been described in detail (e.g. Cavalcante 1972, 1974). Gathered plants are used for cordage, thatch, oils, waxes, fuels, ointments, tools, ornaments, perfumes, timber, pigments, dyes, gums, resins, and fibres to name a few (e.g. Prance *et al.* 1977; Steward 1948a; Verdoorn 1945). Many plants also have medicinal value (cf. Kreig 1964; Poblete 1969), but ethnopharmacology is a regrettably under-emphasized field of research. Table 8.1 lists some representative plants gathered by Amazonian Indians and the uses of these plants (see also Fidalgo and Prance 1976; Prance *et al.* 1977).

Insects are another major gathered product (Ruddell 1973). Entomophagy, insect eating, is widely reported (cf. Beckerman 1979: 538–9; Posey 1980b; Smole 1976: 163–7) but not systematically studied in the Amazon. However, substantial evidence now documents the importance of bees (*Apidae*) and bee products (resin, wax, honey, pollen) to indigenous groups (see Posey 1981, 1983b). Table 8.2 lists a number of species of bees that are exploited by the Kayapó Indians of Brazil.

Table 8.1 Representative gathered plants of the tropical forest and their uses (based upon Lowie 1948: 7–10).

Common name	Scientific name	Use
Drugs and poisons		
Assacu, possumwood, sandbox tree	*Hura crepitans*	Fish drug
Ayahuasca, cayapi, hage, huni	*Banisteriopsis* spp.	Hallucinogenic drug
Cunambi	*Clibadium surinamense*	Fish drug
Curare, curari	*Strychnos toxifera*	Hunting poison
Curupa	*Mimosa aracioides*	Cathartic drug
Floripondia, campa, datura	*Datura arborea*	Hallucinogenic drug
Guayusa	*Ilex* sp.	Anaesthetic agent
Parica, yupa, niopo	*Mimosa acacioides*	Hallucinogenic drug
Timbo	*Paullinia pinnata*	Fish drug
Yoco	*Paullinia yoco*	Hallucinogenic drug
Foods and manufactures		
Almecega	*Tetragastris balsamifera*	Resin used for fuel
Ambaiba	*Cecropia* sp.	Various products
Anaja, palm	*Maximiliana regia*	Fibre used in basketry
Andirobá, Brazilian mahogany	*Carapa guianensis*	Oil used for fuel
Angelim	*Andira* sp.	Wood for canoes
Aratazeiro	*Anonaceae* sp.	Wood for bows
Arrow reed	*Gynerium saccharoides*	Arrow shafts
Assaí palm, palm	*Euterpe oleracea*	Fruit eaten
Palm	*Attalea humboldtiana*	Fruit eaten
Palm	*Attalea spectabilis*	Fruit eaten
Pine tree	*Araucaria brasiliensis*	Nut eaten
Babassú palm	*Orbignya speciosa*	Oil and fruit eaten
Bacaba palm	*Oenocarpus bacaba*	Oil for cooking
Bactrix marajá, palm	?	Fruit eaten
Castanha, Brazil nut, Paránut	*Bertholetia excelsa*	Nut eaten
Buriti, murití, achua, palm	*Mauritia flexuosa*	Numerous products
Bussú palm	*Manicaria saccifera*	Leaves for thatch
Cabacinho	*Theobroma* sp.	Pith eaten
Cajú, cajueiro, cashew	*Anacardium occidentale*	Fruit eaten
Camayuva cane	*Guadua* sp.	Arrow shafts
Carayuru	*Bignonia chico*	Pigment from leaves
?	*Carludovica trigona*	Material for baskets
Cedar	*Cedrela angustifolia*	Wood for canoes
Cumarú	*Coumarouna odorata*	Condiment from bean
Cupuassú	*Theobroma grandiflorum*	Pith eaten, oil from seeds
Curauá	?	Fibre for cordage
Curuá piranga	*Attalea monosparma*	Leaves for thatch
Embira	*Couratari* sp.	Fibre for cordage
Greenheart	*Nectandra rodioei*	Seeds eaten
Guaraná	*Paullinia sorbilis*	Medicine and condiment
West Indian locust, Brazilian copal, anami gum	*Hymenaea courbaril*	Resin used as glaze

Table 8.1 continued

Table 8.1 Continued.

Common name	Scientific name	Use
Iacareva	Calophyllum sp.	Wood for canoes
Itauba	Ocotea megaphylla	Wood for canoes
Itauba	Silvia itauba	Wood for canoes
Itauba	Silvia duckei	Wood for canoes
Jabotá	Cassia blancheti	Bark for canoes
Jatahy	?	Bark for canoes
Jauary	Astrocaryum jauary	Various products
Jerimú, jerimum	?	Fruit eaten
Manga, mango	Mangifera indica	Fruit eaten
Masaranduba	Mimusops excelsa	Fruit eaten
?	Moronobea coccinea	Gum used for glue
Nibi	Carludovica sp.	Vine used in basketry
?	Oenocarpus sp.	Fruit eaten
Palo de balsa	Ochroma sp.	Wood for rafts
Pau d'arco	Tecoma sp.	Wood for bows
Paxiuba, pashiuba palm	Iriartea ventricosa	Materials for houses
Leopardwood	Brosimum aubletii	Wood for bows
Pequí, pequiá	Caryocar villosum	Seeds for oil and food
?	Pratium heptaphyllum	Resin used for fuel
Siriva palm	Cocos sp.	Wood for clubs
Tucumä	Acrocomia officinalis	Cordage, edible fruit
Tucumä	Bactris setosa	Cordage, edible fruit
Tucumä	Astrocaryum tucuma	Cordage, edible fruit
Urucurí palm	Attalea excelsa	Resin used as glaze

The initial developmental value of indigenous and folk knowledge concerning gathered products is likely to be based on the identification of products having pharmacological and industrial applications within the western system. Indigenous knowledge of wild plants has already made significant contributions to modern pharmacology (e.g. Kreig 1964). Generally, the indigenous peoples have not benefited from this application of their knowledge. An equitable system of remuneration is required if this type of development is to be successful both economically and ethically.

Gathering could also be part of an integrated development plan, with the collection and marketing of already important wild forest products, such as Brazil nuts and rubber, taking place during the appropriate season. When given the opportunity, Amazonian Indians have proven themselves quite capable of successfully directing such enterprises. For example, the Gaviões of central Brazil now profitably collect and market Brazil nuts in their area. This is due in large part to their having taken control over the production, transport, and marketing of their products (Ramos 1980). In this case, it is important to note that in some areas of Amazonia a dense stand of Brazil nut trees '...generates more revenue than an equivalent area of pasture' (Bunker 1981: 56) devoted to cattle herding.

Table 8.2 Principal species of Apidae utilized by the Kayapó Indians.

Kayapó name	Scientific name	Wax use[a] Util	Wax use[a] Cer	Wax use[a] Med	Honey Seasonal	Honey Amount	Larva eaten	Pupa eaten	Pollen eaten	Resin used	Aggressive	Distinctive traits
ngài-peré-ỳ	Apis mellifera	+	+		All year	Very much			+		****	Honey taken during New Moon
ngài-ñy-tỹk-ti	Melipona seminigra	+	+	+	Dry season	Average					**	Bee parts used for hunting magic
ngài-kumrenx	Melipona rufiventris	+	+	+	All year	Average						Wax used for mẽ-kutôm
ngài-re	Melipona compressipes	+	+	+	All year	Much						Has markings like the 'ants'
ngài-kàk-ñy	Partamona sp.											Wax used in magic to make enemy weak
mykrwàt udjy	Frieseo-melitta sp. Trigona amalthea	+	+	+	All year Dry season	Average Average	+	+	+			Bee parts mixed with urucú for hunting magic
kukraire	Trigona dallatorreana				All year	Much			+		*	Break off limb with nest and run to expel bees
mehnòra-kamrek	Trigona cilipes			+	All year	Little				+		Has shiny eyes like jaguar
mehnòrã-tỹk	Scaura longula			+	All year	Little				+		Used for hunting magic
kagnàra-krã-kamrek	Oxytrigona tataira	+	+	+	All year	Average	+	+	+		***	Cut entire tree to take honey
kangàra-krã-tyk	Oxytrigona sp.	+	+	+	All year	Average	+	+	+		**	Bees causes blisters on skin

Kayapó name	Species				Season	Amount			Aggressiveness	Notes
kangàrà-udja-ti	Oxytrigona sp.	+	+	+	All year	Average	+	+	***	Bees used in hunting magic
kangàrà-ti	Oxytrigona sp.	+	+	+	All year	Average	+	+	***	Wax used for mẽ-kutôm
mỳre	T. pallens	+	+	+	All year	Average		+	*	Sometimes fell tree
ngôi-tênk	Trigona sp.	+	+		All year	Average		+		Live in termite nests
djô	Trigona fuscipennis	+	+	+	All year	Little				Live in termite hills
imrê-ti-re	Trigona [?] chanchamayoensis				All year	Little	+	+		Live in ant nests
kukoire-kà õ-i	Partamona sp.				All year	Average			*	Nests in termite nests
	Tetragona sp.	+	+		Dry season	Little				Very acidic honey; fell entire tree
tôn-mỳ	Tetragona sp.	+	+		Dry season	Average		+		Fell tree to take honey
rĩ	Tetragona sp.	+	+		All year	Much		+		Bee thought to be 'stupid' and weak
mehr-xi-we'i	Tetragona goettei	+	+		All year	Average				Found only in the Xingu
mẽnire-udgà	T. quadrangula	+	+		All year	Average		+		Opening of nest like a vagina
mehnõdjành	Frieseomelitta varia		+		Dry season	Little				Smoke from wax used for curing
mehñy-kamrek	Trigona spinnipes	+	+		Dry season	Little	+	+	*	Wax burned; smoke causes dizziness
mehñy-tyk	Trigona branneri	+	+		Dry season	Little	+	+	*	
djô	Trigona fulviventris	+	+		Dry season	Little		+	*	Bee deposits drops of resin on skin

Notes
Nests of aggressive bees are raided using smoke and fire to expel bees first (*** very aggressive; ** moderately aggressive; * slightly aggressive).
a Wax use: utilitarian; ceremonial; medicinal.

Indigenous ethnoentomological knowledge is being utilized in southern Venezuela where a group of Sanema (Yanomamo) Indians have established bee hives with plans to market the honey (UMAV 1982, personal communication).

Some potentially valuable wild plants may also be suitable for more controlled production. For instance *Calathea lutea*, a tall herb that grows wild in swamps in the Amazon Basin, produces a wax similar to carnauba. This plant is easy to cultivate and harvest, and could provide jobs and income while exploiting otherwise unusable swampy areas in the region (NAS 1975: 137–40).

These brief examples indicate that indigenous knowledge of gathered products has potential for inclusion in development planning for Amazonia.

Game

Indigenous inhabitants of Amazonia hunt many forms of mammals and birds (see Table 8.3 for an example of game species hunted by the Yekuana of southern Venezuela). The Jivaro have knowledge of the significant details of animal behaviour, including cries and calls, preferred foods, types of excrement, scents, teeth marks on fruit, and so forth (McDonald 1977; Ross 1978). According to Hames (1979: 7–8, 20), some Yekuana and Yanomamo alternate hunting activities among a number of hunting zones to benefit from the increased fauna produced by an 'edge effect' linked to numerous overlapping biotopes of the hunting zones. Reichel-Dolmatoff (1978: 286) states that Desana shamans continually inventory resources and game to channel group exploitative activity. These represent attempts at resource management.

Game animals are efficient in use of available food, with high protein-to-fat ratios and resistance to diseases (de Voss 1977; Sternberg 1973; Surujbally 1977). Some game animals could potentially be cropped in a form of 'semi-domestication' in abandoned garden sites (see section on 'Natural and human-made resource units' below), or in an integrated management system combining the animals with plantations of fruit-bearing trees favoured by the animals, and to which they are attracted (Smith 1977). This 'game farm' strategy has been suggested as a viable system for sustained Amazonian development (Goodland and Bookman 1977; Goodland *et al.* 1978; Smith 1977; Vasey 1979).

The immediate application of game farming would be to improve the subsistence methods of small farmers (Goodland 1980: 17) and their diet. It is also important to note that some small animals, such as the agouti (*Dasyprocta* sp.) and capybara (*Hydrochoerus hydrochaeris*), and birds, like the curassow, might be susceptible to 'semi-domestication' in enclosed areas (fenced, abandoned garden sites or areas adjacent to household gardens) for significant surplus production and sale.

Aquaculture

One of the most promising strategies of aboriginal resource utilization with potential for large-scale development is aquaculture, or systems of water resource

Table 8.3 Game animals most frequently hunted by the Yekuana of southern Venezuela (from Frechione 1981: 50).

Scientific name	Common name
Birds	
Anhinga anhinga	Anhinga, snake bird
Ara macao	Scarlet macaw
Cairina moschata	Muscovy duck
Colinus cristatus sonnini	Quail
Columba cayenninsis	Forest dove
Columba subvinacea purpureotineta	White-tipped dove
Cripturellus soni soni	Ponchita
Cripturellus undulatus	Forest chicken
Leptolila varreauxi	Ruddy pigeon
Mitu tomentosa	Crestless currasow
Neochen jubata	Duck
Odontophorus gujanesis	Wood quail
Ortalis motmot motmot	Guacharaca
Pauxi pauxi	Black curassow
Penelope grani	Guan
Penelope marail	Forest turkey
Ramphastos sulfuratus	Toucan
Tinamus major serratus	Great tinamou
Monkeys	
Alouatta seniculus	Red howler monkey
Ateles belzebuth	Spider monkey
Cebus apella fatuellus	White monkey
Callicebus torquatous lugens	Window monkey
Pithecia chiropes	Saki
Terrestrial mammals	
Cuniculus paca	Paca, lapa
Dasyprocta aguti lunaris	Agouti
Dasyprocta fuliginosa	Picure
Dasypus novemcinctus	Nine-banded armadillo
Hydrochoerus hydrochaeris	Capybara
Mazama nemoriaga	Brocket deer
Tapirus terrestris	Tapir
Tayassu pecari	White-lipped peccary
Tayassu tajacu	Collared peccary

management (Goodland 1980: 14). Indigenous populations in Amazonia make use of numerous species of fish, reptiles, and water mammals, as well as some forms of riverine and lacustrine vegetation. Amazonia contains the most diverse freshwater fish fauna in the world (Smith 1981: 18).[2] Fish provide substantial portions of protein for most indigenous groups (Ross 1978; Sternberg 1973). Fish also have high quantities of essential amino acids (Bell and Canterbury 1976) and are superior to meat animals in terms of feed/protein conversion ratios as illustrated in Table 8.4.

Table 8.4 Feed conversion ratios (from Ackefors and Rosen 1979).

Meat animals	Dry weight feed: live weight	Dry weight feed: shredded weight (flesh)
Cow	7.5 : 1	12.6 : 1
Pig	3.25 : 1	4.2 : 1
Chicken	2.25 : 1	3.0 : 1
Rainbow trout	1.5 : 1	1.8 : 1

During the past two decades, commercial fishing in Amazonia has become a profitable industry. However, little is actually known of the life cycles of even the most important commercial fish species (Smith 1981: 121) and commercial exploitation appears to be drastically reducing the populations of these fishes (Goulding 1980: 154).

Turtles are also efficient in meat/protein production (Smith 1974: 85). Turtle meat is a delicacy in many parts of the world, and would be a highly exportable and valuable commodity. Since aboriginal times, Indians have corralled turtle-breeding groups for year-round cropping of their meat and eggs (Smith 1974: 85; Sternberg 1973: 258).

Caimans (various species) may prove important in large-scale aquaculture because they too can be bred in captivity (Montague 1981). They can provide both meat for local consumption and skins for export. They also play an important role in nutrient cycling in Amazonian waters (Fittkau 1973).

The manatee (*Trichechus inongrus*) can also be managed to produce meat while at the same time contributing to the larger aquacultural system by keeping waterways clear of vegetation and releasing large amounts of nutrients into the water to stimulate primary fish production (Myers 1979: 178; Spurgeon 1974: 239).

Lacustrine and riverine vegetation do not appear to have been directly exploited to any great degree by indigenous groups in Amazonia. However some groups in the Xingu River area did make a kind of salt by burning the leaves of the water hyacinth (*Eichornia crassipes*). Nonetheless, this vegetation shows considerable potential for inclusion in a highly productive aquaculture. Water hyacinth (*Eichnornia crassipes*) purifies water (1/3 hectare can purify one tonne of sewage per day (Myers 1979: 78). These floating meadows provide food for numerous invertebrates that in turn are consumed by fish (Smith 1981: 13).

Detailed studies of Amazonian aquatic ecosystems and their relationship to terrestrial environments are only now being undertaken (Goulding 1980; Smith 1981). These studies suggest that the clearing of várzea forests, a process related to some types of development projects, appears to have a direct adverse effect upon aquatic fauna (Goulding 1980: 252–3; Smith 1981: 125–7). These data support the ethnoecological knowledge of indigenous groups who are well aware of the interrelationship between the forest and aquatic fauna (e.g. Chernela 1982).

As noted above, some aquatic faunal and floral species appear to present possibilities for surplus production within an integrated system of management. The potential for implementing aquatic management systems is an area requiring considerably more study. As Goulding (1980: 254) points out, '...a better understanding of the natural fisheries and their proper management will be the best method for assuring a continual supply of fish to the Amazon region for years to come'. Those persons possessing the best understanding of the natural fisheries in Amazonia are the indigenous populations who have successfully exploited these resources for millennia.

Agriculture

The domesticated plant inventories of the indigenous populations of Amazonia are extensive, yet their potential for consumption and industrial uses is poorly evaluated and largely ignored by development planners. An exemplary list of some major cultivars is provided in Table 8.5. Some of the aboriginal domesticates are well known and form an impressive list of New World inventions (Ucko and Dimbleby 1969). Many other cultivars remain unknown, or if known are seldom utilized in Western agriculture (Kerr *et al.* 1978).

Numerous Amazonian domesticates demonstrate a great economic potential and lend themselves to large-scale exploitation (NAS 1975; Williams 1960). Indigenous uses of these plants include more than just foodstuffs; plants are frequently used as medicinals, insect repellents, dyes, and as raw materials for production. Indigenous varieties of cultivars attest to the great diversity of genetic stock in existence, and afford the opportunity for scientific experimentation in crop adaptations to various tropical soils and environmental factors.

The Western approach to agricultural development has been to eliminate complexity and impose a limited and controlled range of specific cash crop monocultures. In the process, the local natural environment has been destroyed, perhaps irretrievably in light of predictions about the effects of the current rate of deforestation (Denevan 1981; Myers 1981). The genetic diversity and economic utility of local wild and domesticated plants is being lost (Gottlieb 1981). The attempt to impose mid-latitude agricultural practices in Amazonia has resulted in soil erosion, soil compaction, leaching, and the outbreak of epizootic pests and diseases, with concomitant rapidly decreasing agricultural yields (Lovejoy and Shubart 1980; Sioli 1980).

Justification for the imposition of mid-latitude agricultural methods traditionally has been that the shifting cultivation systems of the indigenous populations are primitive and inefficient. However, scientists now recognize that the range of indigenous agricultural systems is more complicated and, generally, better adapted to tropical conditions than was previously assumed (Conklin 1969; Dickinson 1972; Frechione 1981; Geertz 1963; Lovejoy and Shubart 1980).

Indigenous agriculture depends heavily upon native plants that demonstrate an adaptation to localized climatic conditions (Alvim 1972, 1981; Lathrap 1970: 37–8).

Table 8.5 Commonly cultivated food plants of Amazonia (based principally upon Lowie 1948: 3–5 and Denevan 1974: 101).

Common name	Family	Scientific name
Tubers		
Arracacha	Umbilliferae	*Arracacia xanthorrhiza* Bancr.
Achira	Cannaceae	*Canna edulis* Ker.
Dali-dali	Marantaceae	*Calathea allouia* (Aubl.) Lindl.
Kupa	Vitaceae	*Cissus* sp.
Taro*	Araceae	*Colocasia esculenta* (L.) Schott.
Yam*	Dioscoreaceae	*Discorea alata* L.
Yam	Dioscoreaceae	*Discorea trifida* L.
Sweet potato	Convolvulaceae	*Ipomoea batas* (L.) Lam.
Arrowroot	Marantaceae	*Maranta arundinacea* L.
Yam bean	Leguminosae	*Pachyrrhizus tuberosus* (L.) Spreng.
Potato	Solanaceae	*Solanum tuberosum* L.
Tania	Araceae	*Xanthosoma sagittifolium* (L.) Schott.
Fruits and seeds		
Bacaiuva palm	Palmae	*Acrocomia* sp.
Cashew	Anacardiaceae	*Anacardium occidentale* L.
Pineapple	Bromeliaceae	*Ananas comosus* (L.) Merr.
Peanut	Leguminosae	*Arachis hypogaea* L.
Pigeon pea*	Leguminosae	*Cajanus cajan* (L.) Millsp.
Jack bean	Leguminosae	*Canavalia ensiformis* (L.) DC.
Chilli pepper	Solanaceae	*Capsicum* spp.
Papaya	Caricaceae	*Carica papaya* L.
Piquí	Caryocaraceae	*Caryocar* spp.
Star apple	Sapotaceae	*Chrysophyllum cainito* L.
Watermelon*	Cucurbitaceae	*Citrullus lanatus* (Thunb.) Mansf.
Lemon*	Rutaceae	*Citrus limon* (L.) Burm. f.
Orange*	Rutaceae	*Citrus* sp.
Squash	Cucurbitaceae	*Cucubita* spp.
Hyacinth bean*	Leguminosae	*Dolichos lablab* L.
Surinam cherry	Myrtaceae	*Eugenia unifora* L.
Peach palm	Palmae	*Bactris gasipaes* (Kunth.
Mangabeira	Apocynaceae	*Hancornia speciosa* Gomes
?	Leguminosae	*Inga* spp.
Bottle gourd	Cucurbitaceae	*Lagenaria* sp.
?	Sapotaceae	*Lucuma* sp.
Mango*	Anacardiaceae	*Mangifera indica* L.
Plantain, banana*	Musaceae	*Musa* x *paradisiaca* L.
Granadilla	Passifloraceae	*Passiflora ligularius* Juss.
Avocado	Lauraceae	*Persea americana* Mill.
Lima bean	Leguminosae	*Phaseolus lunatus* L.
Kidney bean	Leguminosae	*Phaseolus vulgaris* L.
Guava	Myrtaceae	*Psidium guajava* L.
Sicana	Cucurbitaceae	*Sicana odorifera* (Vell.) Naud.
Frutas de lobo	Solanaceae	*Solanum lycocarpum*
Pepino	Solanaceae	*Solanum muricatum* Ait.
Cocona	Solanaceae	*Solanum quitoense* Lam.
Topiro	Solanaceae	*Solanum topiro*
Cacao	Sterculiaceae	*Theobroma cacao* L.
Corn, maize	Gramineae	*Zea mays* L.
Other		
Sugar cane	Gramineae	*Saccharum officinarum* L.

Note
* Post-Columbian introduction.

They have also been found to be more efficient in their utilization of micro-nutrients and less dependent upon nutrients considered essential for good soil-fertility in the mid-latitudes (Hecht 1981, personal communication). Indigenous farmers act upon their knowledge of the localized adaptation of certain domesticates by developing what might be termed intra-garden microzonal planting patterns which match specific cultivar varieties with soils, drainage, patterns and other climatic features (Frechione 1981: 55; Hames 1980: 20–1; Johnson 1974; Leeds 1961: 19; Smole 1976: 132–5).

Indigenous agricultural systems generally result in positive soil conservation effects. For example, aboriginal field utilization practices minimize the time that soils are exposed to the destructive impact of direct sunlight and tropical rains. Vegetative cover is maintained at various heights to deflect the impact of tropical rainfall and provide sufficient shade, thus helping to prevent rapid erosion and leaching.

Indigenous horticulturists usually rely on small, dispersed garden sites. Garden dispersal contributes to the maintenance of the ecosystem and the success of native horticulture. The spatial dispersal minimizes the epizootic growth of insect pests and plant diseases (Pimental *et al.* 1978; Posey 1979b; Stocks 1980), thus eliminating the need for expensive and environmentally dangerous pesticides. Garden dispersal also stimulates the growth of wildlife populations (Hames 1979; Linares 1976; Ross 1978). Perhaps most important, indigenous agricultural systems always include 'natural corridors' between garden sites. These natural corridors form valuable ecological refuges for plant and animal species (Gomez-Pompa *et al.* 1972; Lovejoy and Schubart 1980). Therefore, species are not only protected from extinction but are reserved close at hand for re-establishment in the 'abandoned fields'.

Shifting cultivation gardens are highly productive in terms of yields per unit of labour expended (Carneiro 1973; Harris 1972: 247) and yield per unit of land actually under cultivation (Carneiro 1973). Manioc and plantain, for example, are especially productive relative to the yield of calories per hectare. The Barafiri Yanoama are capable of producing 23.16 tonnes of plantain per hectare yielding 15.6 million calories per hectare from the edible portion of the fruit (Smole 1976: 150). The Yekuana of southern Venezuela have produced as much as 30 tonnes of manioc per hectare, yielding 23.8 million calories from the raw tubers, and approximately 6 million calories per hectare from processed manioc products (Frechione 1981: 101).

The idea that indigenous shifting cultivators of Amazonia are incapable of producing significant crop surpluses is no longer generally accepted (Carneiro 1973; see also Allen and Tizon 1973; Kloos 1971: 38–9; Smole 1976: 192–3). Recent research also indicates that properly managed monozoned and basically monocultural gardens planted in native cultigens are no more deleterious to the forest ecosystem than are polycultural gardens (Frechione 1981: 102–5; Harris 1971).

Tropical forest cultivators can produce surpluses through shifting cultivation with a minimal amount of labour expended, but they generally lack the necessary economic and political stimuli to do so (Allen and Tizon 1973; Carneiro 1973). As early as 1930, Nimuendajú (1974: 115–16) noted that the Ramkokamekra were capable of producing surplus manioc flour, but were deterred from doing so consistently because they lacked the means of transporting this surplus to the marketplace.

Thus, although shifting cultivation is usually discounted as a focus of possible development in Amazonia (Goodland 1980: 14–15), it is suggested here that it does have developmental potential. Marketable surpluses of native cultigens can be produced immediately under long-fallow systems in areas where population pressure is low. However, it is usually these areas that lack the transportation facilities and stable markets necessary to encourage such development.

Shifting cultivation can also serve as the basis for the development of ecologically sound and profitable models for agricultural development (e.g. Dickinson 1972; Janzen 1973; and Sioli 1980: 266–9), and as an initial stage in an integrated agroforestry system (Denevan et al. 1982).

Natural and human-made resource units

A further manifestation of sophisticated and ecologically sound adaptations to tropical forest ecosystems by the indigenous populations of Amazonia is their recognition and utilization of 'resource units', both natural and human-manipulated. The procurement of resources from these units tends to overlap the measurable or statistically quantifiable neat boundaries of hunting, gathering, and horticulture, thereby making it difficult for Western science to recognize or measure the effects of the use of such areas (Posey 1981, 1982c).

Resource units are intimately known and periodically visited to harvest produce (Posey 1982c). Some are the result of naturally occurring concentrations of trees, plants, and animals. Others are artificially induced. For example, the Kayapó Indians systematically gather a variety of forest plants and replant them near camps and major trails to produce 'forest fields' (Posey 1982c). There are at least fifty-four species of plants used in these forest fields, including several types of wild manioc, three varieties of wild yams, a type of bush bean, and three or more wild varieties of kupa. This transplanting of wild plants into human-made, higher density forest fields intimates a transitional process of plant semi-domestication (Posey 1983b), and a type of ecological strategy largely overlooked by Western science.

Abandoned garden sites could be considered yet another type of resource unit. Although the principle agricultural production from shifting cultivation gardens culminates in two to three years, the sites are not totally abandoned after this period (cf. Basso 1973: 34–5; Bergman 1974: 147–8; Hames 1980: 9; Smole 1976: 152–6). In addition, indigenous populations gather a range of plants that appear in abandoned sites as part of the natural reforestation process (Denevan et al. 1982; Posey 1982c; Yde 1965: 28, 54). A representative inventory of these plants for the Kayapó are listed in Table 8.6.

Abandoned garden sites also produce a variety of foods that attract wild animals such as wild pig, coati, paca, agouti, deer, and others (Gross 1975: 536;

Table 8.6 Representative plants commonly found in reforestation sequence of 'abandoned' Kayapó fields and animals associated with each (based upon Posey 1982a).

Plant	Kayapó name	Associated animal*	Use of plant Man	Animal
Humiria balsamifera	bã-rerek	A,B,C,D,E	Eat fruit	Eat fruit
Psidium guineense	kamokãtytx	F	Eat fruit	Eat fruit + leaves
Zingiberaceae	madn-tu	F	Use root for tea; smoke leaves	Eat leaves
Peschiera sp.	pita-teka	—	Use for paint	—
Catasetum sp.	pitu		Medicinal	—
Bignoniaceae	ngra-kanê	C,F	Medicinal	Eat leaves
Cissampelos sp.	tep-kanê	C,D	Fish bait	Eat fruit
Piperaceae	mãkrê-kanê	A,B,C,D	Fish bait	Eat fruit
Amasonia sp.	pidjô-rã	—	Prophylaxis	—
Oenocarpus distichus	kamêrê (bacaba)	A,B,C,D	Eat fruit	Eat fruit
Macrostaychia sp	kukrytmyka	H	Use wood	?
Monotagma sp.	kũryre	F	Grind leaves; eat roots	Eat leaves; eat roots
Myrcia sp.	kônôkô	A,C,D,F	Eat fruit	Eat fruit + leaves
Cecropia leucocoma	atwyra'ô'	H,F	—	Eat fruit + leaves
Polypodiaceae	tôn-kanê	—	Medicinal	—
Clarisia ilicifolia	pidjô-nirê	F	Medicinal	Eat leaves
Centrosema carajaense	akrô	—	Fish poison	—
Cassia hoffmanseggii	pidjô-kakrit	C,D,F	Medicinal	Eat fruit + leaves

Note
* A = white-lipped peccary; B = white paca; C = agouti; D = tortoise; E = red paca; F = red agouti; G = deer; H = tapir.

Ross 1978: 10), as illustrated in Table 8.6. Many birds, particularly sparrows, macaws, and parrots, are attracted to these areas and are hunted by the Amerinds (Ross 1978: 10). The Kayapó are aware of the attractiveness of these abandoned garden sites to wildlife populations, and in dispersing their fields great distances from their villages maximize the area they can efficiently manage. This large-scale management strategy produces forest reserves where game is attracted in artificially high densities, thereby improving yields from hunting efforts.

Resource units should be identified, initially preserved and studied, and then evaluated on the basis of their potential economic value *vis-à-vis* alternative development schemes that might eliminate these units. Study of indigenous knowledge of these units also provides invaluable information on ecosystem relationships.

Cosmology

Further information concerning the complex ecosystems of Amazonia and the various ways in which they can be exploited may be found expressed, directly and indirectly, in the cosmologies, myths, and rituals of the indigenous groups of the region. These concepts influence, and to varying degrees are influenced by, perceptions about the ecosystems with which the indigenous populations interact, and provide important information on ecological interrelationships critical to the functioning of micro-ecosystems.

McDonald (1977) and Ross (1978) have suggested the possible operation of myth-based food taboos in preventing the over-exploitation of various fauna. Reichel-Dolmatoff (1976, 1978) has discussed the Desana shaman's attempts to manage the group's use of natural resources by using sanctions and cosmological constructs which promote the maintenance of balance in a closed system of economic, social, and spiritual forces. Posey (1983b) has sketched the function of Kayapó ceremonial cycles in dispersing knowledge concerning the systematic utilization of renewable resources. Furthermore, myth has been shown to encode intricate ecological relationships between the human and natural worlds (Berlin and Berlin 1979; Chernela 1982; Posey 1983b).

Conclusions

Development projects for Amazonia have been based upon the imposition of mid-latitude technology and methodology which promotes large-scale forest clearing for ranching and the production of monocultures of a limited number of cash crops. On the whole, these projects have resulted in ecological, economic, and social failures. This chapter has suggested the need for systematic study of indigenous systems of knowledge and utilization of the Amazonian ecosystems. It appears that such study can contribute to the formulation of ecologically sound, efficiently productive, profitable, labour-intensive, and integrated management systems of agriculture, aquaculture, and the cropping of wild and semi-domesticated plants, mammals, fish, reptiles, birds, and insects. Besides being commercially productive, such systems would blend with the natural Amazonian ecosystems, thereby preserving the diverse natural genetic stock with its unknown potential for commodities with nutritional, medicinal, and industrial use.

Indigenous knowledge of Amazonian ecosystems is sophisticated and extensive. Amerindians perceive a myriad of ecological zones, the elements composing these zones, and the interrelationships with and between such zones. They discern associations between soils, plants, animals, topography, drainage, and so forth, and rely upon a complex understanding of animal and insect behaviour. They manipulate various semi-domesticated and wild floral and faunal species and depend upon long-term use of abandoned garden sites and resource concentrations.

In order to change the nature of development in Amazonia towards one promoting ecologically and socially sound long-term sustained yield systems based upon indigenous knowledge, it is necessary for the international community to sponsor and support appropriate research in a timely manner. National and local governments within Amazonia must allow scientists access to Amerind groups and indigenous areas. Experimental stations need to be established to test the productivity and commercial viability of various integrated management systems. Nutritional, medicinal, and industrial values of commodities derived from native Amazonian plants also need testing.

Special emphasis should be given to the study of:

1   Folk ecological zones and their complexity, for example, the floral, faunal, edaphic, and climatic associations within zones as perceived by indigenous populations.
2   Forms of shifting cultivation, for example, the special adaptations of native plants, the function of vegetative cover, and the importance of spatial distribution of crops within gardens for pest and weed control and optimal production.
3   Natural corridors and their role in the preservation of biological diversity and facilitation of reforestation.
4   Manipulation of semi-domesticated plants and animals in 'abandoned fields' and 'resource units'.
5   Sustained yield aquaculture focussed upon the integrated and controlled cropping of riverine and lacustrine flora and fauna.
6   Large-scale management of animals and forests to develop 'forest-game reserves'.

Finally, indigenous societies of Amazonia are in rapid decline. There are a few aboriginal cultures still relatively intact, but little time remains to salvage the valuable information resulting from millennia of accumulated ecological knowledge. Anthropology offers the mechanisms for investigating ethnoecological knowledge, the application of which offers new strategies for ecologically and socially sound sustained yield development strategies for Amazonia.

Chapter 9

The perception of ecological zones and natural resources in the Brazilian Amazon
An ethnoecology of Lake Coari*

Introduction

A great obstacle to Amazonian development has been generalization about its ecology and a tendency to see the vast region as one homogeneous 'counterfeit paradise' or 'green hell' in which developmental activities either threaten the fragile balance of the rainforest ecosystem (e.g. Goodland and Irwin 1975; Meggers 1971), or can have no appreciable effect on the area due to its sheer size and homogeneity (e.g. see Pandolfo 1978; Rebelo 1973; Schmithusen 1978). In fact, Amazonia is composed of highly variable 'ecological zones' of enormous biological complexity (Denevan 1984; Moran 1981; Sioli 1975; and many others). Moreover, it has been demonstrated that indigenous knowledge of this ecological diversity can be both complex and sophisticated (Carneiro 1978; Chernela 1982; Denevan *et al.* 1984; Moran 1981; Parker *et al.* 1983; Posey 1983b; Reichel-Dolmatoff 1976; Smole 1976; Vickers 1979), offering new models for sustained and ecologically sound development (see Chapter 8). Systematic investigation of folk ecological knowledge systems (or 'ethnoecology') can, therefore, not only provide useful scientific data about the heterogeneity of Amazonian ecosystems, but can also elucidate interrelatedness of biological communities that are relevant to new strategies of natural resource utilization (Posey 1985b).

This chapter presents an outline of one individual's perceptions of the ecology of his natal region – the Lake Coari area in the Brazilian Amazon. It does not propose that this knowledge be considered 'correct' in any Western scientific sense, but rather serve as the basis for a cognitive ethnoecological model to guide future field research. The information provided herein is an example of the way in which one caboclo inhabitant of the region views his surroundings and the implications of this view for the exploitation of the region. The chapter does not suggest that all Amazonian caboclos, nor even all Coari caboclos, share the level

---

* Reprinted by permission from "The Perception of Ecological Zones and Natural Resources in the Brazilian Amazon: An Ethnoecology of Lake Coari," by John Frechione, Darrell A. Posey, and Luiz Francelino da Silva, from *Resource Management in Amazonia: Indigenous and Folk Strategies*, D. A. Posey and W. Balée, Editors, Volume 7 in Advances in Economic Botany, pp. 260–82, © 1989 The New York Botanical Garden.

of knowledge of this particular individual. However, since the information reflects this individual's enculturation as a member of a local population, it is a preliminary ethnoecology of the area as well as a personal in-depth interpretation of an Amazonian river environment.

Ethnoecology, biotopes, and ecological zonation

Ethnoecology can be defined as indigenous perceptions of 'natural' divisions in the biological world and soil–plant–animal–human relationships within each division. These cognitively defined ecological categories do not exist in isolation; thus, ethnoecology must also deal with the perceptions of interrelations between 'natural divisions' (Posey 1983b). These perceptions form a framework for personal interactions with the natural environment. As Frake (1962: 55) indicates, the purpose of ethnoecological investigation is to '...describe the environment as the people themselves construe it according to the categories of their ethnoscience'. Often, there is a high correlation between folk perceptions of biological reality and Western scientific classification systems (Hunn 1975). For example, resource units (*lugares de fartura*) as discussed herein, are relatively analogous to 'biotopes' as presented in the scientific literature. Biotope has been defined as '...a microenvironment with relatively uniform landform, climate, soil, and biota. It is with such units of nature that individual humans interact, not with a polymorphous "tropical forest"' (Denevan 1984: 311–12).

Biotopes do not exist in isolation, but rather in 'environmental gradients' reflecting biological diversity in relation to geographic distribution (Porter 1965). It is this geographic aspect that allows scientists to talk of 'horizontal zonation' to refer to closely related biotopes that characteristically co-occur in a geographical area. The same principles of relatedness allow caboclos to talk of 'resource units' that frequently co-occur in specific 'ecological zones'. That is, specific 'ecozones' are recognized by a characteristic resource unit or combination of units. Ecological zones, therefore, exhibit biotic variation but nonetheless show an overall ecological uniformity and, most importantly, predictability of natural resource locations.

Landforms and hydrology

As a starting point in dealing with the heterogeneity of the Amazonian biome, scholars have proposed an array of general typologies (see, e.g. Parker 1981; Pires 1974; Prance 1979; Sioli 1975). In a recent work, Denevan (1984: 312) suggests the following six major subdivisions: (i) humid forest, (ii) seasonal forest, (iii) montane forest, (iv) dry savanna, (v) wet savanna, and (vi) floodplain.

This chapter deals predominately with the floodplain and adjacent habitats. The floodplain, of which there may be nearly 30 million hectares in Amazonia (Goodland 1980), is one of the most ecologically heterogeneous habitats (Denevan 1984). According to Denevan (1984: 314–15), the floodplain varies greatly in width and biotope composition and is defined based on the following major landforms: (i) the river channel, (ii) islands within the river channel, (iii) natural levées (*restingas*), (iv) side channels (*paranás*), (v) backswamps (*igapos*), which may consist of permanent or seasonally inundated grasslands or forests, (vi) oxbow lakes, (vii) mouth bays or floodplain lakes, (viii) point bars (parallel ridges between loops of meanders), and (ix) sand and mud beaches (*praias*).

For graphic illustrations of Amazonian floodplain landforms and associated vegetation, see the cross-sections provided by Sioli (1975: 210) and Smith (1981: 6).

Another classificatory scheme employed when discussing the Amazonian region is based upon the water colour of rivers. In this system, Amazonian rivers are classified by the optical properties of their waters: white-water, clear-water, and black-water (McIntyre 1972). White-water rivers (like the Amazon) have low transparencies due to high carrying content of silt and phytoplankton. Clear-water rivers (like the Tocantins, Xingu, and Tapajós) have low-nutrient levels which result in high transparency. Black-water rivers (like the Negro) drain interfluvial surfaces (*terra firme*) and contain dissolved colloidal acid compounds that are toxic to many organisms.

Landforms and water types influence floral and faunal distribution. Other significant determinants of biological complexity include the macroclimatic factors of rainfall and length of dry season for the floodplain. Both of these '... are secondary in importance to the rise and fall of rivers, which are controlled by climatic events external to the floodplains themselves' (Denevan 1984: 317).

Amazonian forests are influenced by inundations of water for which Prance (1979: 26) has developed a seven-fold typology: (i) seasonal *várzea* – forest flooded by regular annual cycles of white-water rivers, (ii) seasonal *igapó* – forest flooded by regular annual cycles of black-water rivers and clear-water rivers, (iii) mangrove – forests flooded twice daily by saltwater tides, (iv) tidal *várzea* – forest flooded twice daily by freshwater backed up from tides, (v) floodplain forest – on low-lying ground, flooded by irregular rainfall, generally in upper reaches of rivers, (vi) permanent white-water swamp forest, and (vii) permanent *igapó* – black-water forest.

Forests on *restinga* are inundated irregularly and briefly but, nonetheless, bear distinctive floral and faunal characteristics due to periodic disturbance flooding. These forests are generally not as high density, diverse, nor as old as the true upland (*terra firme*) forests. The dynamics of the river system thus foster a variety of ecological zones and biological heterogeneity as recently critiqued by Denevan (1984).

Water-level variations are pervasive in caboclo thinking and subsistence strategies. Flood waters are mixed blessings. They may leave rich alluvial sediments and destroy crop pests and unwanted vegetation, thus making land clearing unnecessary and minimizing crop losses due to pests (Denevan 1984). On the other hand, floods may cause changes in landforms, destroying land in one place and creating it in another (Sternberg 1975). Early or unusually high floods can completely destroy crops and properties. Therefore, a successful caboclo must not only intimately know ecological zones, biotopes, and associated natural resources, but must also be an expert on river geography and hydrology.

The caboclo and the river

When Leandro Tocantins (1968) wrote *O Rio Comanda A Vida (The River Commands Life)*, he was reflecting on the centrality of the Amazon River and its tributaries to the life of native caboclos. The river provides food and means of communication and transportation.

The floodplain and adjacent *terra firme* soils supported most of the aboriginal and modern Amazonian populations and their agriculture (Denevan 1966a; Ross 1978). Aboriginal populations were both extensive and diverse on the floodplain or *várzea* (Denevan 1976; Lathrap 1970; Meggers 1971; Roosevelt 1980), but were devastated by European epidemics and encroachment soon after, if not prior to, presumed contact. For example, extensive aboriginal trade networks carried European epidemics deep into the hinterlands well before the actual arrival of Europeans, resulting in a considerable underestimation of aboriginal populations.

Caboclo cultures are a mixture of Amerindian and colonial elements and are the intellectual inheritors of indigenous folk knowledge. As Moran (1981: 99) notes, 'The culture of the Amazonian caboclo developed during the colonial period and represents an adaptive system to prevalent Amazonian ecological and micro-economic conditions. The resources of the forest are utilized in ways which closely replicate aboriginal patterns.' Caboclo subsistence is built upon resource diversity, and diverse resource use requires complex knowledge of ecological heterogeneity.

Methods

The information presented in this chapter is based upon discussions and interviews conducted with Luiz Francelino da Silva between 1981 and 1983 in Pittsburgh, Pennsylvania, USA. Dr Francelino da Silva was born in 1947 in the Lake Coari region of the Brazilian Amazon (see Figure 9.1) and participated fully in the caboclo lifestyle of his family until his early teens. Subsequently, he pursued his education in Belém and Manaus before coming to the United States in 1972. After receiving a master's degree from California State University at San Diego in 1973, he returned to Manaus to work as an educational planner and, later, to teach at the University of Amazonas, Manaus. While pursuing his studies and working in Brazil, he maintained close contact with his family in Coari – returning there on vacations and holidays. In 1980, he entered the International Development Education Program at the University of Pittsburgh and received his PhD in 1984. It was during this period that he met the other two authors, both of whom had undertaken ethnoecological field research among Amerindian populations in Amazonia. Informal discussions among the three revealed that Francelino da Silva was a veritable font of unstructured information on the folk ecology of

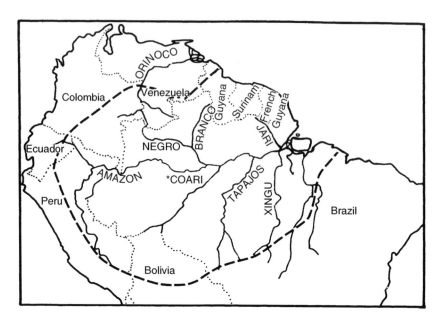

Figure 9.1 Location of Coari within Amazonia.

the Lake Coari area. Borrowing concepts revealed through their own studies (such as resource units), Posey and Frechione began to interview Francelino da Silva on the general characteristics of the Coari area. This led to the map of the Coari region, and the glossary of resource units (see Figure 9.2 and Table 9.1). The effort then mushroomed into a further delineation of the composition of resource units and their interrelationships.

The term caboclo is used differently in different parts of Brazil, but consistently refers to 'backwoods' people of mixed racial and cultural heritage. It is very important to realize that there is confusion in the use of the label caboclo even in Amazonia. Many recent (one to three generation) immigrants are considered caboclos, but know little about the ecology of the region. The 'true' caboclo has roots in indigenous cultures and is the inheritor of an adaptive system developed over millenia. As employed here, the term refers to these 'true' caboclos who live on small homesteads or in small villages in the interior of the Amazon Basin.

Dr Francelino da Silva is an ex-caboclo whose ethnoecological perceptions have been affected by his exposure to the Western educational system and concepts derived therefrom. Nonetheless, the considerable amount of detailed information that he presented allowed us to establish categories of information that could serve as a starting point for field research to test and verify his cognitive ethnoecological model. Thus the descriptions, figures, and tables that follow reflect his cognitive model and are intended to be the comparative basis for research with resident caboclos of the Coari region.

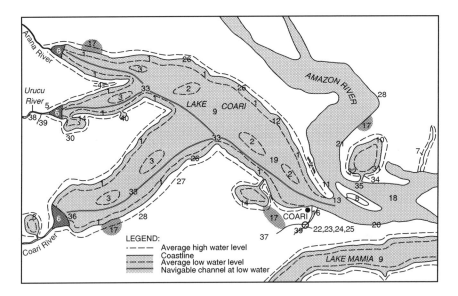

Figure 9.2 Location of major resource units, Lake Coari area.

In order to make the data useful and comparable, tentative scientific identifications for many of the animals listed in the tables (based upon Francelino da Silva's names for the animals) were provided by Drs Michael Goulding (fishes), David Oren (birds), William Overal (invertebrates), and Anthony B. Anderson (plants), all of whom are associated with the Museu Paraense Emílio Goeldi, Belém, Pará, Brazil.

Background: Coari on the Amazon

The major components of the Coari River system are the three relatively small black-water rivers that join to form the 80 kilometre long by 20 kilometre wide Lake Coari. Lake Coari in turn flows into the Amazon, a white-water river, at the town of Coari (see Figure 9.2). For the caboclos, different resources are associated with each river type. The mixture of white-water and black-water is said to produce especially rich areas characterized by many resource units.

The dynamics of the river system hinge upon the high and low water levels of the Amazon River and Lake Coari. Flooding is usually predictable, with the maximum flood level occurring in June (the rainy season extends from January until April). The lowest water level occurs in October (the dry season extends from June to November). December and May are transition months. The average difference between extremes is approximately 10 metres. Once every 7–10 years there are unusually high flood waters. Although these damaging flood waters occur rarely and erratically, floral and faunal distributions, as well as human activity, are limited by their occurrence.

Table 9.1 Glossary of resource units as defined by a caboclo of the Lake Coari region (see Figure 9.2 for locations).

Unit number	Unit name	Definition
1	Praia branca	Dry season, white sandy beaches of Lake Coari where birds and turtles lay their eggs
2	Praia suja	Dry season, wet or muddy beaches where a great number of birds feed
3	Praia verde	Dry season beaches, covered in short vegetation, where birds feed on weeds and insects
4	Restinga	Natural river levees, usually covered in forest, and not inundated during the dry season
5	Charco	Swamp area found within the várzea ecological zone
6	Chavascal	Transition area between rivers draining into Lake Coari and the lake itself, characterized by low vegetation which is mostly inundated during the rainy season and which during the dry season forms a labyrinth of dead-end and river-like branches, *ressacas, poços* and *pocinhos* surrounded by large areas of muddy land
7	Igapó	Forest area which is flooded during the height of the rainy season
8	Laguinho	Small lake connected to the river by a narrow stream during the rainy season and only accessible by land during the dry season
9	Lago grande	Large lake, such as Lake Coari or Lake Mamiá
10	Lago	Lake connected to the river by a passage navigable by canoe or boat
11	Costa	Margin (bank) of the Amazon River
12	Enseada	Gulf-like section of a large lake, usually characterized by calm waters
13	Encontro das águas	Point where the Lake Coari water system flows into the Amazon River
14	Poço grande	Deep section in a sharp turn of a smaller river, characteristic of the sinuosity of these rivers
15	Ressaca	Lake-like formation connected to a small river
16	Igarapé	A black-water stream flowing from deep in the forest to a river
17	Castanhal	The *terra firme* forest where the *castanheiras* (*Bertholletia excelsa*) are located
18	Águas fundas brancas	Deep white waters of the Amazon, where the *piraíbas* (*Brachyplatystoma* spp.) are caught
19	Águas fundas pretas	Deep-water areas of Lake Coari, associated with scarcity of resources except when in close proximity to the banks of the lake
20	Barreiras	High vertical banks of the Amazon River, characterized by swift currents and an abundance of clay varieties

Table 9.1 continued

Table 9.1 Continued.

Unit number	Unit name	Definition
21	Embaubal	Section of the *várzea* where *embatiba* trees (*Cecropia* spp.) are predominant
22	Buritizal	A concentration of *buriti* palms (*Mauritia flexuosa*)
23	Jauarizal	A concentration of *jauri* trees (*Astrocaryum jauari*), usually at critical zones during periods of medium water level
24	Açaizal	A concentration of *açaí* trees (*Euterpe oleracea*) in the *terra firme*
25	Bacahal	A concentration of *bacaba* trees (*Oenocarpus distichus*) along *igarapés*
26	Aratizal	A concentration of *arati* bushes at the critical zone during periods of medium water level
27	Capoeira alta	An abandoned garden site more than 10 years old
28	Capoeira baixa	An abandoned garden site approximately 5 years old
29	Baixio	Shallow section of the Amazon River opposite the channel side, characterized by the predominance of *oeirana* trees (*Salix martiana*)
30	Tabocal	A concentration of green-and-yellow bamboo (*Guadua* spp.) in the high *várzea*
31	Canaranal	A floating meadow dominated by *canarana* (*Panicum spectabile*), commonly used as cattle fodder
32	Mariruzal	A floating meadow dominated by *muriru* (numerous species, see Smith 1981: 14), providing food for fish and turtles
33	Canal seco	Navigable channel in the lake during low water
34	Boca de cima (lago)	Point where a lake narrows into a stream before entering a river
35	Boca de baixo (rio)	Point where the water from a lake flows into a river
36	Matupazal	A floating meadow dominated by *matupá*
37	Roçado novo	A recently planted slash-and-burn garden site
38	Roçado velho	A slash-and-burn garden site which is still being systematically utilized
39	Igarapezinho	A clear-water rivulet which provides drinking water; also called a *fonte*
40	Pocinho	A small lake which does not dry up during periods of low water, usually located near *ressacas* and *chavascals*, and where fish are easy to catch by hand

To the caboclos of Lake Coari, all life is coloured by the high water/low water changes. Nothing escapes the important influences of annual river cycles and unusually high flood waters. Houses and towns rest on *terra firme* or in the *várzea* on stilts well above the highest water mark; trails and roads avoid the flood zone; plantations and orchards are placed safely out of reach. Nonetheless, because the lower soils are relatively fertile due to alluvial deposits, caboclos may choose to plant a significant part of their crops on the lower lands to achieve increased productivity. Rarely are all crops planted on the lower alluvial deposits, despite the incentive of higher yields. Successful caboclo farmers are those who can accurately predict when devastating floods will come. The behaviour of water birds (*marrecos*, *mergulhões*, *patos*) is most frequently utilized by caboclos to predict water level. When these birds arrive at the beaches (*praias*) before the water has receded from the adjacent forest, caboclos say there will be an early dry season followed by unusually heavy rains and early floods during the following season.

According to Francelino da Silva, the caboclos believe that deforestation in the region has led to more erratic flooding near Coari, and has made farming on the lower lands less predictable with much greater risks to crops. Thus, in the Coari region, much rich cultivable land has recently been taken out of cultivation because of the increased frequency of devastating floods.

Figure 9.2 shows the Lake Coari area with both high-water and low-water levels. Numbers on the map indicate resource units (called *lugares de fartura* by the caboclos) recognized and named by Francelino da Silva. His folk taxonomy contains forty units, whose precise locations are subject to variability due to shifts in long-term river cycles. Table 9.1 is a glossary of these units.

Vertical levels

For the caboclo it is not enough to talk about the horizontal distribution of resources. It is also necessary to talk about 'vertical levels', since verticality is a criterion for taxonomic contrast within resource units and ecozones. Figure 9.3 illustrates these vertical levels for the Coari region.

Five terrestrial and/or arboreal levels (T-1 to T-5) are generally distinguished:

T-1: area below ground level, where most burrowing animals and large roots/tubers are found.
T-2: ground level to approximately 20 centimetre below, where organic matter is concentrated and the plant/animal communities associated with the superficial root zone are located.
T-3: understorey (1–10 metre above ground), which predominates in *capoeira* or 'open forest'. This is the area of smaller trees and shrubs and is attractive to many birds and mammals; when this zone exists, hunting is good.
T-4: middle canopy (7–15 metre above ground), which occurs in most mature forests and is the principal zone for arboreal mammals and large birds (e.g. macaw, parrots, etc.).
T-5: high canopy (15+ metre above ground), which characterizes the *terra firme* high forest. This is known to have arboreal mammals and birds, but hunting them is difficult because of the height. Forests with 1–5 zones are more useful for their forest products, including *castanha* (nuts) and honey.

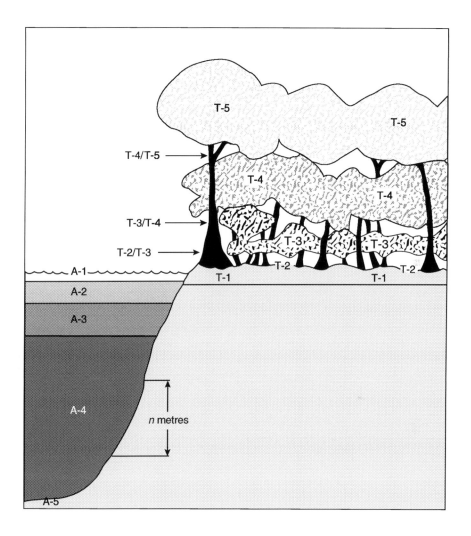

Figure 9.3 Generalized schematic of aquatic and terrestrial/arboreal vertical levels in the Lake Coari region.

Three 'intermediate zones' can also exist in the forest between the five terrestrial/arboreal levels. These are indicated in Figure 9.3 and are seen as movement corridors for birds and other animals. Because of the relative openness of the intermediate zones (T-2/T-3; T-3/T-4; T-4/T-5), visibility of game is improved for hunting.

Five vertical aquatic levels (A-l to A-5) are also generally distinguished:

A-1: surface level (0–1 metre below surface), where water-surface insects and top-feeding fish as well as water snakes are found.
A-2: upper level (1–4 metres below surface), where the greatest number of fish and eels can be caught.
A-3: middle level (4–10 metres) is less productive, but hosts some fish species.
A-4: lower level (various depths from A-3 to bottom) is the least productive zone.
A-5: river/lake bottom, which is rich in bottom-feeding fish and sting-ray species.

Intermediate aquatic zones are not discerned, although great variability is recognized due to changes in water level and seasonality. The vertical water levels presented here, like the terrestrial/arboreal levels, are generalized categories. Not all levels occur in all situations, and the actual complexity of categories is too detailed to be dealt with in this chapter. Caboclo perception of water resources is complicated and has been the focus of major studies by Goulding (1980), Parker (1981), and Smith (1981).

Resource use

Caboclo classification of ecological divisions is based on the recognition of soil–plant–animal relationships of practical importance. Thus resource units are characterized by natural resources upon which the caboclo depends and upon such criteria as water level, water colour, and vertical level.

Table 9.2 presents a listing of the resource units identified in Figure 9.2 and indicates some of the general characteristics of each. *Water level* is divided into a typology of low, medium, and high. These designations indicate the water level or levels when the unit is best exploited. *Water colour* refers to general characteristics of Amazonian rivers. In addition to the white-water, clear-water, and black-water categories discussed previously, mixed water occurs when black-water flows into white-water or vice versa. The designations listed in the column *Vertical level* are based upon the breakdown of vertical spatial dimensions presented in Figure 9.3. The level or levels indicated for each unit are those where the associated faunal components are most frequently exploited. The final column, *Faunal components*, indicates at a very general level the most common types of fauna found in each unit.

Table 9.2 Some general characteristics of the resource units encountered in the Lake Coari region.

No.	Resource unit	Water level(s) when resource unit occurs	Water colour	Vertical level(s) where faunal components occur	Faunal components
1	Praia branca	Low	Black	T-2	B, I, Rt
2	Praia suja	Low	Mixed	T-2	B, I
3	Praia verde	Low	Black	T-2	A, B, I
4	Restinga	Low	Mixed	T-1, 2, 3, 4	A, B, I, Rt
5	Charco	Low/Medium	Mixed	T-2; A-1	A, B, F, I, Rt
6	Chavascal	Low/Medium	Mixed	T-1, 2, 3; A-1	A, B, F, I, Rt
7	Igapó	High	Black/White/Mixed	T-1, 2, 3; A-1, 2	A, B, F, I, Rt
8	Laguinho	Low	Black/White/Mixed	A-1, 2	B, F, I, Rt
9	Lago grande	Medium/High	Black	A-1, 2, 3, 4	B, F, Rt
10	Lago	Low/Medium	Black/White/Mixed	A-1, 2, 3	B, F, I, Rt
11	Costa	Low/Medium/High	White	A-1, 2, 3, 4, 5	A, B, F, I
12	Enseada	Low/Medium/High	Black/White	T-1, 2, 3, 4, 5; A-1, 2, 3, 4, 5	A, B, F, I
13	Encontro das águas	Low/Medium/High	Black/White	A-1, 2, 3, 4, 5	A, B
14	Poço grande	Low/Medium	Mixed	A-1, 2, 3, 4	A, B, F, I, Rt
15	Ressaca	Low/Medium	Mixed	T-2, 3	A, B, F, I, Rt
16	Igarapé	Low/Medium	Black	T-1, 2; A-1	A, B, F, I, Rt
17	Castanhal	Low/Medium/High		T-1, 2, 3, 4, 5	A, B, I
18	Águas fundas brancas	Low/Medium/High	White	A-1, 2, 3, 4, 5	F
19	Águas fundas pretas	Low/Medium/High	Black	A-1, 2, 3, 4, 5	F
20	Barreiras	Low/Medium/High	White	T-1, 2, 3, 4, 5; A-1, 2, 3, 4, 5	B, F, I
21	Embaubal	Low/Medium/High	White	T-1, 2, 3; A-1, 2	A, B, F, I, Rt
22	Buritizal	Low/Medium/High	Black	T-1, 2, 3, 4, 5	A, B, I, Rt
23	Jauarizal	Low/Medium/High	Black/White	T-1, 2, 3; A-1, 2	A, B, F, I, Rt

Table 9.2 continued

Table 9.2 Continued.

No.	Resource unit	Water level(s) when resource unit occurs	Water colour	Vertical level(s) where faunal components occur	Faunal components
24	Açaizal			T-1, 2, 3, 4, 5	A, B, I, Rt
25	Bacabal			T-1, 2, 3, 4, 5	A, B, I, Rt
26	Aratizal	Low/Medium	Black	T-1, 2; A-1, 2	A, B, F, I
27	Capoeira alta			T-1, 2, 3, 4	A, B, I
28	Capoeira baixa			T-1, 2, 3	A, B, I
29	Baixio	Low/Medium	White	T-1, 2, 3; A-1, 2	A, B, F, I
30	Tabocal			T-1, 2, 3, 4	A, B, I
31	Canaranal	Low/Medium/High	Black/White	T-1, 2; A-1	A, B, F, I
32	Muriruzal	Low/Medium/High	Black/White	A-1	B, F, I
33	Canal seco	Low	Mixed	A-1, 5	A, B, F, Rt
34	Boca de cima (lago)	Low/Medium	Black	T-1, 2, 3, 4; A-1, 5	A, B, F, I
35	Boca de baixo (rio)	Low/Medium	White	T-1, 2, 3; A-1, 5	A, B
36	Matupazal	Low/Medium	Black/White	T-2; A-1	A, B, F
37	Roçado novo			T-1, 2	A, B, I, Rt
38	Roçado velho			T-1, 2, 3, 4	A, B, I
39	Igarapezinho	Low/Medium/High	Black	T-1; A-1	A, B, F, I
40	Pocinho	Low	White	A-1, 5	F

Note
Letters represent the following: A = animals (these are generally mammals); B = birds; F = fish; I = insects; Rt = reptiles/turtles.

Tables 9.3, 9.4, 9.5, and 9.6 respectively list major fish (sixty-two varieties), mammals (thirty-eight varieties), birds (ninety-two varieties), and reptiles (thirty-one varieties) important to caboclo subsistence. These tables also list each animal by the resource unit(s) in which it is most commonly sought. In addition, Table 9.7 provides a list of flora by resource unit(s) and the fauna associated with each as well as the vertical level(s) in which the attracted fauna is sought.

Table 9.2 indicates that of the forty resource units, thirteen occur and are exploitable throughout the sequence of changing water levels (i.e. year round); eleven occur during both low and medium water; seven occur only when the water level is low; one only during high water; and one during both medium and high water. The occurrence and exploitation of the other seven resource units have no direct relation to water level. The importance of water level for various units is that the natural cycles in the Lake Coari region are based primarily on these levels. During low water, certain resource units are more productive than others. During high water, some units disappear entirely from the caboclo's ecological world. Water/land variations also determine blooming of trees and other plants and thus movements of fish and wildlife that are attracted to special plant varieties or products. During high water, the flooded forest (*várzea* and *igapó*) is a haven for fish that feed off blooming and fruiting trees. During low water, other species of trees provide food for birds and animals, while fish must find food in the streams (*igarapés*) and shrunken rivers. For example, in the *lagos* (ten), seven varieties of fish, eight varieties of birds, and two varieties of reptiles are best exploited when the water level is low; while four other varieties of fish can be exploited throughout the cycle (low, medium, or high); and three other varieties of fish, two varieties of mammals, and one bird are best exploited when water level is low or medium, but not high. With such information for forty different resource units – and assuming the information is correct – individuals can facilitate their subsistence endeavours throughout the year by exploiting relatively predictable seasonal resources.

For example, the tables reveal that, for Francelino da Silva, the *igapó* is most commonly exploited for fish (eleven varieties) and birds (six varieties). Only one mammal [the *preguiça-real* (sloth)] is coded for this resource unit, although Table 9.7 shows that some monkeys and rodents are periodically attracted to the *igapó* by the existence of the *ingá-de-fogo* plant in that unit. Only one snake (*jibóia*) is coded for the *igapó*.

Furthermore, the data in Table 9.3 indicate that five of the fish varieties exploited in the *igapó* are available throughout the flooding sequence (low to medium to high to medium to low water level); five other varieties occur during high water only; and one occurs during both medium and high water. The *preguiça-real* is also best exploited during the period of high water; while water level is not particularly important to the hunting of birds (except for two varieties) in the *igapó*. Moreover, in the case of fish, since particular fish species have preferred food sources and vertical water levels, the caboclo must employ a variety of fishing strategies. Table 9.8 lists types of fishing gear and bait used for fishing at various levels.

Inter-unit ecological relationships: the chavascal and castanhal

Categorization of resource units and respective components is complemented by knowledge of ecological relationships between units. Units 6 (*chavascal*) and 17 (*castanhal*) have been selected to represent this knowledge of ecological relatedness.

There is a close and critical interplay between these two units. In the dry season, animals come to the *chavascal* (six) from the *castanhal* (seventeen) in search of water that can be found in small pools and streams left by receding flood waters. Small birds and mammals are also attracted to dry-season vegetation that flourishes in the damp beaches (*praias*) that rim the *chavascal*. Likewise, wading birds are abundant because of the presence of small fish in the shallow waters. Birds, such as *massarico* and *gaivota*, and turtles (*tartaruga, tracajá,* and *iaçá*) lay their eggs in the white sand beaches (*praias brancas*). Their eggs attract the *jacuraru* and other lizards, as well as man. Birds like the *cujubim* feed off seeds and nuts that they then transport to other regions through their droppings. Small mammals like the paca are also agents of seed dissemination because they store a portion of their food in earthen caches which are often abandoned. Jaguar (*onça*) and hawks (*gavião*) come into the *chavascal* to feed off the many small mammals and birds.

During the rainy season, the *chavascal* is flooded and its resources become available to large fish. Caboclos exploit these fish using deep-water circular throwing nets, bows and arrows, and poles with line and hook. They also collect *arati* fruit from their canoes. The primary focus of activity during the wet season is, however, the *castanhal*. Here, *castanhais* (Brazil nuts) are collected for subsistence and for market. In addition, the mammals and birds that have been forced to the *castanhal* by the high waters in the *chavascal* are hunted. Game is sought depending upon vertical level(s) occupied. Birds like the *juriti, inambu,* and *bacurau*, as well as anteaters (*tamanduá*), are found in level 1–3 (see Figure 9.3) because their preferred foods (insects such as *formiga* and *saúva*) are most abundant at that same level. Certain birds (*graúna, pipira,* and *mururé*) are found in levels 1–3 and 1–4 because of the prevalence of *taracua* (another type of insect) in these levels. Other birds (*japó, japiim, arara, periquito,* and *papagaio*) nest during the wet season at level 1–4 in the *castanhal*.

In addition to the seasonal variations of the *chavascal* and *castanhal*, there are daily movements, particularly of birds, into and out of these units. *Massarico, marreco,* and *mergulhão* move between the two units at regular intervals during the day. In the early morning, *mergulhão* and *garça* fish in the *lagos* and *laguinhos* near the *chavascal*, then move to the open areas to sun and dry themselves in the midday before returning to their *castanhal* roosts in the evening.

No Amazonas tudo da: a caboclo's view

To early travellers and explorers, life in the Amazon seemed naturally abundant. Plant and animal life was lush in this green paradise. The native caboclos wanted for little on their simple, but self-sufficient, homesteads (*sitios*). Yet, the caboclos appeared to be lazy and indolent, living only for thick sweet *cafezinhos* and prolonged naps in their hammocks. Obviously, the visitors concluded, caboclos have to do little for self-preservation because 'no Amazonas tudo da' (in the Amazon, everything grows well). Nature itself automatically supports this human existence.

By extrapolation, large agricultural and colonization projects should easily work in Amazonia. But such projects have failed: crops and plantations fell prey to pests and soil depletion; 'new caboclo' colonists perished in vain attempts to survive in the Amazonian 'paradise'. Perhaps the native caboclos knew some secrets for survival after all; perhaps some adaptive ecological knowledge did lie hidden beneath the apparent slovenliness.

It might take a year living with caboclos before the outsider could begin to piece together the logic of native existence. For example, to the caboclo, a year does not consist of twelve months, nor four seasons. It has a dry, high-water season, a dry, medium-water season, and a dry, low-water season followed by a 'stop' season, 'tempo de parada'; then a rainy, low-water season, a rainy, medium-water season, and a rainy, high-water season followed by another 'stop' time. Thus the year actually has eight units of natural time. The dry/rainy, low water/high water, 'enchente/vazante', divisions are of critical importance to the agricultural and subsistence cycles.

In the *terra firme*, the forest is cleared for planting one week after the rainy, high-water season ends. The humidity of the forest drops and the drying (*secagem*) begins until the felled trees are ready to burn. A well-timed burn (*queimada*) will reduce most of the trees and brush to nutrient-rich ash. Remaining trunks and limbs will be dumped into a *coivara* (a large hole in the ground with a chimney opening at one end) and burned to produce charcoal. Sales from the charcoal are sufficient to purchase a few items not produced on site: tobacco, salt, kerosene, and clothing.

When the river stops receding (the dry, low-water season), it is time for planting (*plantação*). Ideally, this occurs ten days to two weeks before the first rains of the 'false' rainy season (*enxurradas* and *repiquetes*) in October and is determined by watching cumulus cloud formations. These critical rains bring moisture to the parched soils and carry the dissolved nutrients from the ash to the new roots of garden crops. The developing plants prosper after the rains temporarily stop (the 'false' rainy season). Root systems are developed sufficiently to secure plants in the soil during the deluges of the following 'true' rainy season (*tempo de chuva*).

If corn or rice is to be planted, it is necessary to leave two or three large dead trees standing in the middle of the garden (*roçado*). The dead trees attract the *caboré*, a hawk whose presence keeps away birds like the *papa-arroz* that devour grain. The *bem-ti-vi* is a small bird that does not fear the hawk and also takes up residence in the standing trees, eating large quantities of ants and other insects.

After the initial annual crops have been harvested, tuberous and perennial cultigens take over. After 3–5 years, reforestation through succession begins, although fields continue to produce bananas, *urucú, mamão* and a variety of other fruits and vegetables. Even after these crops disappear, the caboclo keeps a sharp eye on his old gardens (*capoeira*) because they produce many medicinal plants, edible fruits and nuts, and attract a variety of game animals.

The garden is only one part of the caboclo's life. Other resources come from gathered items in surrounding resource units. But the homestead itself is a concentration of resources. Seeds of wild and domesticated plants are tossed by the caboclo and his family along paths and in old fields. Birds and animals attracted to the old fields also bring seeds from diverse plants to disseminate them through their droppings. The *pipira* bird, for example, is noted as an agent in the distribution of *mamão* (papaya), which is one of its preferred foods. Other birds attracted to the old fields of the homestead disseminate seeds of the nutritious *canapum* fruit.

Anyone who has lived in remote parts of Amazonia knows there is little waste; most things have some use (see Table 9.9 for some examples). The caboclo wife, for instance, is an agent in stimulating fish populations. She religiously throws scraps of food and game entrails into the river or stream. These serve as food for *piracatinga, sardinha, tucunaré,* and *piramutaba*. All family members have a place in maintaining the caboclo homestead, because cash income is low and survival is a task for the whole family. Children forage in the forest, collecting fruits and nuts while eating along the way. They then toss seeds and leftovers over their shoulders, thereby contributing to the perpetuation of ecological diversity. Adults carefully observe their manioc, maize, and papaya, selecting tubers and seeds from those plants that yield better, and replanting the healthier varieties next season. It is incorrect to think that caboclo ecological knowledge is a static entity. Quite the contrary. It may have ancient, indigenous roots, but caboclos are constantly experimenting with new plant varieties and different hunting/gathering strategies. Their knowledge is an accumulation of countless generations of refining ecological adaptation. All the more reason to take seriously the folk experts on Amazonian diversity and natural resources.

But it is not easy for the scientist to get at this folk knowledge; asking the proper questions is difficult. For example, if the outsider asks, 'What is the distance between this place and the next?' the answer may be, 'Nemperto, nem longe' (Not near, not far). If the researcher asks, 'How do you get such successful crops on your sitio?' the answer is likely to be, 'E assim que nós faz, seu doutor' (That's how we do it, Mr Doctor). One might easily conclude, as have countless outsiders in the past, that caboclos are stupid.

But if the proper question is asked, then the information flows: 'How many curves, beaches, and straits to the next village?' Answer: 'Four curves, three beaches, and two straits.' Question: 'Why do you leave those three dead trees in your *roçada*?' Answer: 'To keep the *papa-arroz* from attacking the grain.'

Knowing how to ask the right questions is no secret kept hidden in some mysterious anthropological methodology. The right questions only come when scientists spend enough time with caboclos to accept with humility that there are other experts in Amazonia.

Conclusion

The study of ethnoecology is valuable in understanding the ecological heterogeneity of the Amazon Basin. Francelino da Silva's perceptions of the Lake Coari region reveal a diversity of natural resources systematically exploited in integrated subsistence strategies. This diversity is reflected in his recognition of at least forty resource units. Each resource unit is characterized by a particular combination of faunal and floral components which allows for predictability of natural resource location both spatially and temporally. Vertical levels, both terrestrial and aquatic, allow the caboclo to classify floral/faunal components of the environment by what are perceived as natural strata above and below ground and water. Knowledge of interrelatedness between units and levels apparently allows the caboclo to fine-tune his hunting, gathering, and agricultural activities to maximize gain with minimal time and effort

For anthropologists, ethnoecology can provide an additional dimension for understanding human behaviour; for ecologists, it can serve as a point of embarkation for study in specific areas and, possibly, as a guide to certain ecological relationships; for development planners, it can indicate important resources and ways of choosing and adapting development schemes to local socio-natural systems.

Table 9.3 Varieties of aquatic animals important to caboclo subsistence.

Common name (Portuguese)	Scientific name	Resource unit(s) where fish are found	Water level(s) when fish is best exploited	Vertical level(s) where fish is commonly found
Acará	Geophagus sp.	10	Low/Medium	A-5
Acari	Pterygoplichthys sp.	8	Low	A-5
Acari-cachimbo	Lecostomus emmaginatus	10	Low	A-5
Acaru	Leporinus sp.	7	High	A-3
Acaru rajado	Leporinus fasciatus	7	High	A-3
Aruanã	Osteoglossum bicirrhosum	10	Low	A-1
Arraia	Potamotrygon or Disceus	6, 29	Low	A-2, A-5
Bacu	Pterodoras granulosus	10	Low/Medium	A-1
Baiacu	Colomasus asellus	11	Low/Medium	A-5
Bico de pato	Sorubim lima	10	Low	A-2
Bicudo	?	—	?	A-3
Boto tucuxi	Sotalia fluviatilis	9	Low/Medium/High	A-3
Boto vermelho	Inia geoffrensis	9	Low/Medium/High	A-3
Branquinha	Curimata latior	11	?	A-2
Candiru	Cetopsis sp.	13	?	A-1
Candiruí	Cetopsis and Hemicetopsis	29	?	A-3
Caparari	Pseudoplatystoma tigrinum	7, 10	Low/Medium	A-5
Cará-bandeira	Pterophyllum scalare	7, 10	Low/Medium/High	A-1
Cará-branco	Chaetobranchopsis sp.	7, 10	Low/Medium/High	A-1
Cará-preto	?	7, 10	Low/Medium/High	A-3
Cará-roxo	Cichasoma severum	23	Low/Medium/High	A-3, A-5
Caranguejo	Various genera	20	Medium	?
Carauaçu	Astronotus ocellatus	6	Low/Medium	A-2, A-5
Charuto	2 or 3 genera possible	9	Low/High	A-2
Cubiu	Anodus elongatus	9	Low	A-2
Cuiú-cuiú	Oxydoras niger	10	Low/Medium	A-2
Curimatá	Prochilodus nigricans	7	High	A-3

Dourada	Brachyplatystoma flavicans	29	Low/Medium	A-5
Jaraqui de escama fina	Semaprochilodus laeniurus	19	High	A-2
Jaraqui de escama grossa	Semaprochilodus insignis	19	High	A-2
Jatuarana	Brycon sp.	26	Low	A-2
Mapará	Hypophthalmus spp.	10	Low	A-3
Matrincha	Brycon hilari	7	High	A-2
Matupiri	Tetragonopterus chalceus	15	Low	A-2
Muçum	Symbranchus marmoratus	40	Low	A-3
Orana	Anodus cf. orinocensis	10	?	A-2
Pacamum, jaú	Paulicea luetkeni	18	Low/High	A-5
Pacu branco	Mylossoma cf. aureus	10	?	A-2
Pacu jumento	Myleus schomburgkii	10	?	A-3
Pacu vermelho	Mylossoma cf. albiscopus	7	?	A-2
Peixe-agulha	Boulengerella lucius	7	Medium/High	A-1
Peixe-boi	Trichechus inunguis	6	Low	A-3
Peixe-cachorro	Rhaphiodon vulpinus	15	Medium	A-2
Pescada	Plagioscion squamosissimus	20	Low/High	A-3
Piau	Leporinus piau	9	Low	A-2
Piracatinga	Callophysus macropterus	14	?	A-5
Piraíba	Rrachyplatystoma filamentosum	18	?	A-5
Piramutaba	Brachyplatystoma vaillanti	18	High	A-5
Piranambu	Pinirampus pirinampu	14	?	A-5
Piranha-branca	Serrasalmus rhombeus	7	?	A-2
Piranha-caju	Serrasalmus nattereri	6	Low	A-2
Piranha-preta	Serrasalmus rhombeus	9	High	A-5

Table 9.3 continued

Table 9.3 Continued.

Common name (Portuguese)	Scientific name	Resource unit(s) where fish are found	Water level(s) when fish is best exploited	Vertical level(s) where fish is commonly found
Pirapitinga	Colossoma bidens	10	Low	A-3
Pirarara	Phractocephalus hemiliopterus	29	Low/Medium	A-5
Pirarucu	Arapaima gigas	6, 10	Low	A-3
Sardinha	Triportheus rotundatus	9, 10	Low/Medium/High	A-1, A-3
Surubim	Pseudoplatystoma fasciata	29	Low/Medium	A-5
Tambaqui	Colossoma macropomum	7	High	A-3
Tamboatá	Callichthys callichthys	8	?	A-3
Traíra	Hoplias malabaricus	40	Low	A-5
Tucunaré	Cichla ocellaris	10	Low	A-2

Table 9.4 Mammals important to caboclo subsistence.

Common name (Portuguese)	Scientific name	Resource unit(s) where animal is found	Water level(s) when animal is best exploited	Vertical level(s) where animal is commonly found
Anta	Tapirus terrestris	4	Low	T-2
Ariranha	Pteronura brasiliensis	10	Low/Medium	A-1, T-2
Catetu	Tayassu tacaju tacaju	17	Low	T-2
Capivara	Hydrochoerus hydrochaeris	10	Low/High	T-2
Coati	Nasua nasua	17		T-2
Cotia	Dasyprocta sp.	17		T-2
Guariba	Alouatta seniculus	4, 10		T-5
Guariba	Alouatta belzebul	4, 10		T-5
Irara	Eira barbara	4		T-2
Jupará	Potosflavus	17		T-2
Lontra	Lutra brasiliensis	10	Low/Medium	A-1, T-2
Macaco barrigudo	Lagothrix lagothricha spp. (3 subspecies in Brazil)	17		T-4
Macaco caiarara	Cebus albifrons	17		T-4
Macaco coatá	Ateles paniscus	17		T-4
Macaco-da-noite	Aotus trivirgatus (various species)	17		T-4
Macaco prego	Cebus apella spp.	4		T-4
Macaco soim	Saguinus sp. (various species and subspecies)	4		T-3
Maracajá	Felis tigrina	28	High	T-2
Maracajá-açu	Felis pardalis	4	High	T-2
Mucura xixica	Caluromys philander	4		T-3
Onça-d'água	Chiromectes minimus	4		A-1
Onça pintada	Panthera onca	22		T-2

Table 9.4 continued

Table 9.4 Continued.

Common name (Portuguese)	Scientific name	Resource unit(s) where animal is found	Water level(s) when animal is best exploited	Vertical level(s) where animal is commonly found
Onça-vermelha (parda ou sussuarana)	Felis concolor	17		T-2
Paca	Cuniculus paca	17		T-2
Porco espinho	Coendou prehensilis	21		T-2
Preá	Cavia sp.	7		T-1
Preguiça	Bradipus tridactylus	27		T-3
Preguiça-real	Choloepus didactylus	17		T-3
Quandu	Coendou sp.	17		T-2
Quatipuru	Scurus aestuans	17		T-2
Queixada	Tayassu albirostris			T-2
Tamanduá-bandeira	Myrmecophaga tridactyla	17		T-2
Tamanduá-açu	Tamandua tetradactylus	17		T-2
Tamanduaí	Cyclopes didactylus	17		T-2
Tatu-bola	Tolypeutes tricinctus	17		T-1
Tatu-canastra	Priodontes giganteus	17		T-1
Veado capoeira	Mazama americana	17		T-2
Veado galheiro	Cervus polodosus			T-2
Veado roxo	Mazama gouazoubira			T-2

Table 9.5 Birds important to caboclo subsistence.

Common name (Portuguese)	Scientific name (Anseriformes, Passeriformes, etc.)	Resource unit(s) where bird is found	Water level(s) when bird is best exploited	Vertical level(s) where bird is commonly found
Alencórnio	Anhima cornuta	32	Medium	A-1
Andorinha	Progne chalybea	Varies	—	T-3, T-4
Andorinha	Hirundo rustica	Varies	—	T-3, T-4
Andorinha	Atticora fasciata	Varies	—	T-3, T-4
Anum	Crotophaga ani	28	—	T-3
Aracua	Ortalis motmot	17	—	T-2
Arara amarela	Ara ararauna	7	—	T-3
Arara azul	Anodorhynchus hyacinthinus	7	—	T-3
Arara vermelha	Ara macao	7	—	T-3
Ariramba	Ceryle torquata	Varies	—	T-3
Bacurau de praia	Caprimulgus rupestris	26	Low	T-3
Bacurau do mato	Nyctidromus albicollis	4	—	T-2
Beija-flor	Campylopterus largipennis	Varies	—	T-3, T-4
Bem-te-vi	Megarynchus pitangua	6, 16, 17	—	T-3
Bem-te-vi	Tyrannus melancholicus	6, 16, 17	—	T-3
Bem-te-vi	Pitangus lictor	6, 16, 17	—	T-3
Bem-te-vi	Myiozetetes cayenensis	6, 16	—	T-3
Caboré	Glaucidium brasilianum	27	—	T-5
Caga-sibite	Coereba flaveola	17	—	T-3
Canário	Sicalis columbiana	Varies	—	T-3
Cararã	Anhinga anhinga	8	Low/Medium	A-1
Caraxuê	Turdusfumigatus	17	—	T-2, T-3
Cauré	Falco rufigularis	Varies	—	T-5
Cigana	Opisthocomus hoazin	5	—	T-3
Colhereiro	Ajaia ajaja	2	Low	T-2
Coroca	Crotophaga major	7	High	T-3
Coro-coro	Mesembrinibis cayennensis	7	—	T-2
Coruja	Otus sp.	17	—	T-4
Corujão	Pulsatrix perspicillata	17	—	T-5

Table 9.5 continued

Table 9.5 Continued.

Common name (Portuguese)	Scientific name (Anseriformes, Passeriformes, etc.)	Resource unit(s) where bird is found	Water level(s) when bird is best exploited	Vertical level(s) where bird is commonly found
Corta-água	Rynchops nigra	1	Low	A-1, T-2
Cujubim	Pipile cujubi	24	—	T-5
Curica	Pionus menstruus	17	—	T-3
Curió	Oryzoborus angolensis	28	—	T-2
Curió-preto	Oryzoborus maximiliani	28	—	T-2
Gaivota	Phaetusa simplex	Varies	Low/Medium/High	Varies
Galega	Columba plumbea	27	—	T-3
Garça	Casmerodius albus	6, 10	Low/Medium	T-2
Gavião real	Harpia harpyja	Varies	—	T-2, T-3
Graúna	Scaphidura oryzivora	17	—	T-3
Inambu	Tinamus major	17	—	T-2
Jaburu	Jabiru mycteria	10	Low	A-1, T-2
Jacamim	Psophia leucoptera	4, 17	—	T-2
Jaçana	Jacana jacana	31	Low	A-1
Jacu	Penelope jacquacu	10	Low	T-3
Japiim	Cacicus cela	Varies	—	T-4
Japó	Psarocolius decumanus	17	—	T-4
Juriti	Leptotila verreauxi	17	—	T-2
Macucaua	Tinamus tao	17	—	T-2
Maguari	Ardea cocoi	2, 6, 10	Low	A-1, T-2
Maracaná	Ara severa	17	—	T-3
Marrecão	Dendrocygna autumnalis	2, 6	Low	T-2
Marreco	Amazonetta brasiliensis	2, 6	Low	T-2
Massarico	Hoploxypterus cayanus	2, 3, 6	Low	T-2
Mergulhão	Phalacrocorax olivaceus	2	Low	A-1
Mutum	Crax globulosa	4	—	T-2
Papagaio	Amazona festiva	7	High	T-4
Pato	Neochen jubata	6, 10	Low	A-1, T-4
Pato	Cairina moschata	6, 10	Low	A-1, T-4

Pavão	Eurypyga helias	8	—	T-2
Periquito	Brotogeris sanctithomae	17	—	T-3
Periquito	Forpus passerinus	17	—	T-3
Pica-pau	Dryocopus lineatus	Varies	—	T-4
Pipira	Ramphocelus carbo	17	—	T-3
Rolinha	Columbina talpacoti	37	—	T-2
Sabiá	Turdus sp.	17	—	T-3
Sabiá-una	Turdus albicollis	17	—	T-3
Sanhaçu azul	Thraupis episcopus	17	—	T-3
Sanhaçu pardo	Thraupis palmarum	17	—	T-3
Seringueiro	Lipaugus vociferans	4	—	T-4
Socó boi	Tigrisoma lineatum	6, 9, 10	Low	T-2
Socó branco	Egretta thula	6, 9, 10	Low	T-2
Socoi	Butorides striatus	6, 9, 10	Low	T-2
Surucuá amarelo	Trogon rufus	17	—	T-2
Surucuá	Trogon melanurus	17	—	T-2
Tesoureiro	Tyrannus savana	27	—	T-4
Ticoá	Piaya cayana	27	—	T-3
Tucano açu	Ramphastos tucanus	25	—	T-4
Tucano araçari	Pteroglossus araçari	25	—	T-3
Tucano papo-amarelo	Ramphastos vitellinus	25	—	T-4
Tulião-galinha	Charadrius collaris	2, 3, 6	—	T-2
Tulião-galinha	Tringa flavipes	2, 3, 6	—	T-2
Tulião-galinha	Tringa solitaria	2, 3, 6	—	T-2
Tulião-galinha	Arenaria interpres	2, 3, 6	—	T-2
Tulião-galinha	Calidris pusillus	2, 3, 6	—	T-2
Tulião-galinha	Callinago paraguayae	2, 3, 6	—	T-2
Uirapuru	Cyphorhinus arada	4	—	T-3
Uru-mutum	Nothocrax urumutum	17	—	T-2
Urubu	Coragyps atratus	Varies	—	T-5
Urubu-rei	Sarcoramphus papa	17	—	T-5
Urubu-tinga	Cathartes aura	25	—	T-4

Table 9.6 Lizards, snakes, and turtles important to caboclo subsistence.

Common name (Portuguese)	Scientific name	Resource unit(s) where animal is found	Water level(s) when animal is best exploited	Vertical level(s) where animal is commonly found
Cabeçudo	Peltocephalus tracaseus	6	Low	A-1
Calango	Tropidurus torquatus	38	—	T-2
Calango marrom	?	38	—	T-2
Camaleão	Iguana iguana	21	—	T-3
Capitari	Podocmenis expansa	6	Low	A-5
Cobra cascavel	Crotalus durissus marajoensis	38	—	T-2
Cobra cipó	Oxybelis aeneus	17	—	T-2
Cobra jararaca	Bothrops atrox	17	—	T-2
Cobra papagaio	Bothrops bilineatus bilineatus	17	—	T-3
Cobra papa-ovo	Spilotes pullatus pullatus	1	Low	T-2
Cutimbóia	Tseustes sulphurens sulphurens	6	Low	A-1, T-2
Iaca	Podocmenis sp.	6	Low	A-5
Jabuti	Chelonoidis denticulata	6	Low	T-2
Jacaré-açu	Melanosuchus niger	6	Low	A-1
Jacaré-tinga	Caiman crocodilus	6, 10	Low	A-1
Jacuraru	Tupinambis nigropunctatus	1, 6	Low	T-2
Jibóia	Boa constrictor constrictor	7	High	A-1
Matá-matá	Chelus fimbriatus	10	Low	A-5
Mussuã	Kinosternon scorpioides	6	—	A-5
Mussurana	Rhachidelus brazili	4	—	T-2
Perema	Callopsis punctularia	6	Low	T-2
Rã	Leptodactylus pentadactylus	Varies	—	T-2, T-3
Sapo	Bufo marinus	Varies	—	T-2
Sucuriju	Eunectes murinus	6, 14	—	A-1, A-2
Suissi	?	6	Low	A-5
Surucucu	Lachesis muta muta	17	—	T-2
Tartaruga	Podocnemis expansa	6	Low	A-5
Teju	Tupinambis teguxin	38	—	T-2
Tracajá	Podocnemis unijilis	6	Low	A-5
Tuíra	?	6	Low	A-5
Zé prego	?	6	Low	A-5

Table 9.7 Knowledge of floral and faunal associations utilized in hunting and fishing.

Plant (Portuguese)	Scientific name	Resource unit(s) where association occurs	Water level(s) when association is exploited	Vertical level(s) where association occurs	Associated fauna
Abiu	Lucama caimito	17		T-3	Birds
Abiurana	Neologatia cuprea	7	High	A-1	Fish
Abiurana	Lucama lasiocarpa	7	High	A-1	Fish
Apuri-grande	Duroia saccifera	4	High	T-4	Birds, rodents
Apuruizinho	Alibertia edulis	4	High	T-2	Birds, rodents
Araçá	Myrcia fallax	12	Medium	A-1, T-2	Birds, fish
Araçá	Psidium araca	12	Medium	A-1, T-2	Birds, fish
Araçá-boi	Eugenia stipitata	12	Medium	A-1, T-2	Birds, fish
Arati	?	12	Medium	A-1, T-2	Birds, fish
Araticum-cagão	Annona montana	17		T-4	Birds, insects
Araticum-do-mato	Annona densicoma	17		T-4	Birds, insects
Açai	Euterpe oleracea	24		T-2, T-4	Birds
Bacaba	Oenocarpus distichus	25		T-4	Birds
Bacaba-açu	Oenocarpus bacaba	25		T-2, T-4	Birds
Bacabai	Oenocarpus multicaulis	25		T-4	Birds
Bacabinha	Oenocarpus minor	25		T-4	Birds
Bacuri	Platonia insignis	11	Medium	T-2, T-4	Birds
Bacurizinho	Rheedia benthamiana	27		—	—
Biribá	Rollinia mucosa	22		T-2, T-4	Birds, insects
Buriti	Mauritia vinifera	22	Low	A-1, T-4	Birds, fish
Buritirana	Mauritia martiana	27	Low	A-1, T-4	Birds, rodents
Cacau	Theobroma speciosa	4		T-2, T-4	Birds, rodents
Cacaui	Theobroma sylvestris	17		T-2, T-4	Birds, rodents
Caiaué	Elaeis melanococca	17		T-2, T-3	Rodents, reptiles, insects
Cajá	Spondias dulcis	38		T-2, T-4	Birds, rodents

Table 9.7 continued

Table 9.7 Continued.

Plant (Portuguese)	Scientific name	Resource unit(s) where association occurs	Water level(s) when association is exploited	Vertical level(s) where association occurs	Associated fauna
Canapum	Physalis angulata	31		T-2	Birds
Canarana	Panicum spectabile	17	Low/Medium	A-1	Fish, birds, rodents
Capitiú	?	27		T-2	Birds
Castanha	Bertholletia excelsa	27	High	T-1, T-2, T-5	Birds, rodents
Cumaru	Dipteryx odorata	27		T-2, T-4	Rodents
Cupuaçu	Theobroma grandiflorum	27		T-2, T-4	Birds, rodents
Cupuí	Theobroma subincanum	17		T-2, T-4	Birds, rodents
Fruta-pão	Artocarpus sp.	23		T-2, T-4	Rodents
Goiaba	Psidium pomiferum	17		T-2, T-3	Birds, insects
Graviola	Annona muricata	17		T-4	Birds, insects
Inajá	Maximiliana regia	17	Low	T-3	Birds
Ingá-açu	Inga cinnamomea	17		T-3	Monkeys, rodents
Ingá-cipó	Inga edulis	17		T-3	Monkeys
Ingá-de-fogo	Inga velutinosa	23		T-2	Monkeys, rodents
Ingá-de-macaco	Inga fagifolia	17		T-2, T-3	Monkeys, rodents
Ingá-xixica	Inga alba	17		T-3	Monkeys
In gaí	Inga heterophylla	17		T-3	Monkeys, rodents
Jatobá	Hymenaea courbaril	17		T-2, T-5	Rodents, birds
Jauari	Astrocarium jauari	23	Low/Medium	A-1, T-2,	Fish, birds
Jenipapo	Genipa brasiliensis	17		T-4	Birds, insects
Jenipaporana	Guatteria augusti	7	High	A-1, T-4	Birds, fish
Maracujá-do-mato	Passiflora nitida	17		T-3	Birds
Marajá	Bactris maraja	23	Low	T-2, T-3	Birds, rodents
Mari	Poraqueiba sericea	17		T-4	Rodents

Mari-mari	*Cassia leiandra*	7	High	A-1	Fish
Marirana	*Couepia subcordata*	17		T-3	Birds, rodents
Miriti	*Mauritia flexuosa*	22	Low	A-1, T-2, T-4	Birds, rodents
Oeirana	*Salix martiana*	29		A-1, A-2; T-2, T-3	—
Parujá	*Pleragina sp.*	17		T-2, T-4	Birds
Patauá	*Oenocarpus bataua*	25		T-2, T-4	Birds
Piquiá	*Caryocar brasiliensis*	17		T-2, T-5	Rodents
Pitomba	*Melicocca bijuga*	17		T-4	Birds, rodents
Pitombinha	*Talisia esculenta*	17		T-4	Birds, rodents
Pupunha	*Guilielma speciosa*	27		T-2, T-4	Birds, rodents
Sapotilha	*Acras sapota*	17		T-4	Rodents
Sapucaia	*Lecythis spp.*	17		T-2, T-5	Monkeys, rodents
Sorva	*Couma macrocarpa*	4	Medium	A-1, T-3	Birds, fish
Sorvinha	*Collophora utilis*	4, 7	Medium/High	A-1, T-3	Birds, fish
Taperebá	*Spondias lutea*	17		T-2, T-4	Birds, rodents
Taperebá-açu	*Poupartia amazonica*	17		T-2, T-4	Birds, rodents
Tucum	*Astrocaryum vulgare*	17		T-2, T-4	Rodents
Tucumã	*Astrocaryum tucuma*	17		T-2, T-4	Birds, rodents
Uixi	*Endopleura uchi*	17		T-2, T-4	Birds, rodents
Uixirana	?	4	High	A-1, T-4	Birds, fish

Table 9.8 Fishing equipment used for various types of fish and turtles in the Lake Coari region.

Fishing equipment		Area utilized	Vertical level(s) where fish occur	Fish caught	Bait used
Portuguese	English				
Arco e flecha (peixe)	Bow and arrow	Lake, small river	A-1	Several types	None
Arco e flecha (tartaruga)	Bow and arrow	Lake, river	A-1	Turtles	None
Arpão	Fish harpoon	Lake, river	A-1	*Pirarucu, peixe-boi*	None
Arrastão	Net	Large river	A-1, A-2	Numerous types	None
Cam un	Buoy with hook and line	Lake	A-5	Turtles	Cooked palm heart
Canico	Pole and line	Lake, river	A-1, A-2	Several types	Insects, fish, worms, fruits
Espinhel	Line and hooks strung across water	Igapó	A-1	*Tambaqui*	Rubber fruit seed
Jatecá	Turtle harpoon	Lake, river	A-2, A-5	Turtles	None
Linha comprida	Hook and line	Lake, river	A-2, A-5	Several types	Fish, meat
Linha curta	Hook and line	Lake	A-1, A-2	Several types	Insects, fish, worms, fruits
Paneiro	Basket trap	River	A-1	*Camarao*	None
Pinauaca	Pole, line and spinner	Lake	A-1	*Tucunaré*	Red feather
Poita	Large buoy with hook and line	River	A-4	*Piraiba*	Fish
Rapiché	Net with handle	River, lake	A-1	Several types	None
Tarrafa de boca	Net on line (deep water)	River	A-3	Several types	None
Tarrafa de saco	Net on line (shallow water)	River, lake	A-1, A-2	Several types	None
Timbó	Poison	Lake	All levels	Several types	None
Zagaia	3-pronged spear	River, lake	A-1	Several types	None

Table 9.9 Resources used in arts, crafts, and medicinals.

Source (Portuguese)	Scientific name	Part used	Uses
Agrião	Spilanthes oleryacea	Leaf	Medicine for fever
Alfavaca	Ocinum minimum	Leaf	Medicine for headache
Arruda	Ruta graveolens	Leaf	Medicine for intestinal disorder
Arumã	Desmoncus sp.	Bark	Baskets, manioc squeezer, sieves, fire fan, sleeping mat, canoe, shelter
Barro		Clay	Stoves
Buriti	Mauritia vinifera	Leaf stem	Arrow shaft
Cabacinha	Luffa operculata		Medicine for fever
Capim-santo	Cymbopogon sp.	Leaf	Medicine for stomach ache
Caxinguba	?	Latex	Medicine for worms
Cera de abelha		Bee's wax	Adhesive for fixing points and feathers to arrows, small buoy for fishing
Cipó uambé	Philodendron uambe	Vine	Baskets, rope, brooms
Copaíba	Copaifera guyanensis	Topical oil	Medicine for bruises, inflammation
Crajiru	Arrabidaea chica	Leaf	Medicine for inflammation and venereal disease
Cuieira		Shell of fruit	Water containers, bowls, ladles
Itaúba	Acrodiclidium itauba	Trunk	Canoe, paddle, flooring
Jambu	?	Leaf and flower	Medicine for intestinal problems
Mamão	Carica papaya	Seeds	Medicine for worms
Massaranduba	Mimusops balata	Stem, trunk	Axe handles, boat keels, house support poles
Massaranduba	Mimusops balata	Sawdust	Medicine for liver problems
Mastruz	Chenopodium ambrosioides	Leaf	Medicine for worms, cuts, inflammation
Mucura-caá	Petiveria alliacea	Leaf	Medicine for fever
Munguba	Bombax munguba	Bark	Rope
Mutum	Crax nigra	Feather	Feather for arrows
Palha branca	?	Leaf	Roof
Paracuúba	?	Centre of trunk	Arrow, box, harpoon pole
Pau-de-preciosa	Mespilodaphne preciosa	Bark	Tea

Table 9.9 continued

Table 9.9 Continued.

Source (Portuguese)	Scientific name	Part used	Uses
Paxiúba	*Iriartea exorrhiza*	Stem	Floors, walls, bows, harpoon and spear poles
Pião-roxo	*Jatropha gossypifolia*	Leaf	Medicine for stomach problems
Piassava	*Leopoldinia sp.*	Vine	Broom
Piranheira	*Piranhea trifoliata*	Trunk, stem	Charcoal
Pirarucu	*Arapaima gigas*	Scales	Sandpaper
Pirarucu	*Arapaima gigas*	Tongue	Grater
Preciosa	*Aniba canelilla*	Bark, stem	Medicine for intestinal problems
Quebra-pedra	*Phyllanthus stipulatus*	Leaf	Medicine for kidney stones
Seringueira	*Hevea brasiliensis*	Sap	Boots, purses, cartridge bags, soccer balls
Sorvinha	*Collophora utilis*	Gum	Wax, canoe sealant
Sorvinha	*Collophora utilis*	Fruit	General medicinal
Tacana	*Gynerium saccharoides*	Stem	Arrows
Tucum	*Astrocaryum vulgare*	Fibre	Hammocks, rope
Ubim	*Genoma sp.*	Leaf	Roofing
Ucuúba	*Virola surinamensis*	Bark juice	Medicine for sore throat

Chapter 10

Diachronic ecotones and anthropogenic landscapes in Amazonia

Contesting the consciousness of conservation*

Overspecialization of Western science has helped to obscure human–environmental aspects of co-evolutionary relationships between Amerinds and Amazonian ecosystems. Social anthropologists have traditionally been inadequately trained in field aspects of natural sciences, while biologists seldom consider the cultural components – historical and present – of ecological systems. Biologists and ecologists find it difficult to accept as empirical the knowledge of scientifically untrained folk experts, whose practical experiences have generated well-adapted ecological management systems. On the other hand, romanticists have undermined scientific investigations with simplistic allegations that natives live in harmony with nature (Alvard 1993; Johnson 1989; Redford 1990; Stearman 1994). Thus the day-to-day realities of success and failure in indigenous experiments with strategies of natural resource management have generally been overlooked and understudied.

Much investigation of folk knowledge stops at inventories of native plants and animal names and their uses. Attempts to correlate basic inventories with folk taxonomic systems and related utilitarian patterns of behaviour inevitably lead to studies of symbolic and metaphysical concepts that express the logic of other realities (Balée 1994; Descola 1994; Murphy 1960; Reichel-Dolmatoff 1976). Most scientists avoid these subjects because they are non-quantifiable and, consequently, non-scientific. Natural scientists tend to be sceptical of the scientific validity of the social sciences, while social scientists are weary of the cognitive limitations of the analytical paradigms and statistical methodologies of the natural sciences.

A bridge between the natural sciences and the social sciences is, however, hypothesis generation and testing (Posey 1986a, 1990c). The investigation of folk sciences not only enriches existent fields of Western science, but can also generate more sophisticated hypotheses through the discovery of new categories of knowledge. This requires the elicitation of indigenous cognitive (emic) categories of classification utilizing a generative methodology that seeks native concepts rather than imposing ethnocentric ones (cf. Posey 1983c, 1986a). The following example will illustrate the purpose of this point.

---

* *Advances in Historical Ecology* (1998), W. Balée (ed.) New York: Columbia University Press. Chapter 5, pp. 104–18.

The felling of enormous trees by Amazonian Indians in order to gather honey too high to reach otherwise is thought to be an anti-ecological practice Ethnobiologists and cultural historians studying these practices from an *emic* point of view, however, inevitably employ a historical analysis as well. In the case of Kayapó Indians, the result of trees felled for this purpose is a *bà-krêti*. For the Kayapó, a *bà-krêti* is a large forest opening that offers a modified ecological zone into which hundreds of useful medicinal and edible plants can be introduced to form a concentrated 'island' of resources near trailsides and campsites (Posey 1985a and 2002). Game animals are also attracted to these enriched areas, since edible foods are scarce in the lower levels of the surrounding high forest; the Indians even plant some species intentionally to attract birds and mammals. In this example the felling of one large tree offers an immediate source of honey and provides a new ecological niche for useful plants that develop into a long-term hunting ground. Indigenous concepts of botanical use and conservation in relation to faunal components are integrated into an overall management system that, without the benefit of an emic analysis and an historical perspective, would escape the scientific eye.

A formidable barrier to research is the scientist's lack of credence in folk specialists. This manifests itself in a reluctance to allow the informant to lead the researcher along unfamiliar lines of logic and into areas of research *that the native chooses*. Scientists resist the loss of control of the questioning paradigm and fear leaving the baseline of the 'reality' that *control* signifies. Concerns about research time also inhibit emic analysis, since restraints on field stays often mean that researchers are reluctant to trade assured results from their project designs for possible 'finds' from informants.

Folk categories may be more elaborate than their Western counterparts – or they may have no corresponding Western categories whatsoever, thereby indicating phenomena unknown to our science. The 'discovery' of such categories may provide the greatest contribution of ethnobiology to scientific development. The description of the fifty-two folk species of stingless bees named, classified, and utilized by the Kayapó led to the 'discovery' of nine species previously unknown to Western science (Posey and Camargo 1985 and 2002). More than fifty types of diarrhoea and dysentery are utilized in Kayapó ethnomedical curing, as compared to less than a dozen utilized by allopathic physicians working in the tropics (Elisabetsky and Posey 1994; Posey and Elisabetsky 1991). The elaboration of taxonomies more complex than scientific ones has also been demonstrated for Amazonian ecological zones (Chapter 8 this volume).

Complex ideas and relationships are often expressed in the highly symbolic codes of myth and ritual and require research over an extended period of time. The Kayapó recognize, for example, two mythological entities that illustrate how beliefs can function as ecological concepts. One is Bepkôrôrôti, the spirit of an ancient shaman unjustly killed by fellow tribesmen while seeking his inherited right to certain parts of his tapir. His spirit now manifests itself in the form of rain, lightning, and dangerous storms, which can kill people or destroy crops. He becomes angry when people do not share food and resources; fear of his vengeance compels the Kayapó to be generous and sharing. To placate Bepkôrôrôti, Indians leave a portion of honey, pollen, and brood comb in raided hives. The result of this practice is that some species of stingless bees will return to re-establish their colonies. Thus belief in Bepkôrôrôti helps to preserve and manage bee colonies whilst insuring continued production.

Another mythological entity is the *mry-kaàk* which takes the form of a twenty- or-more-metre-long electric-eel-like animal that lives in deep pools of water. It is the most feared of all creatures, since it can kill with its powerful electric shock from a distance of five hundred or more metres. It is thought to live on minnows, and therefore whenever the Kayapó see schools of spawning fish or minnows, they stay clear of the areas for fear of the *mry-kaàk*. This practice serves to protect the minnows, which are the basic element of the aquatic foodchain of the river.

There is not a single Kayapó who would tell the investigator that Bepkôrôrôti is a bee-management concept, or that the *mry-kaàk* functions to preserve riverine ecology. I dare say that no Kayapó, not even the wisest and most knowledgeable elder, would even answer 'yes' to questions that ask directly about such ecological management functions as I have described them. This does not mean, however, that they do not exist. Researchers cannot avoid interpreting culture in ways unfamiliar to the people they study, since knowledge – and its interpretation – is codified in different ways in different cultures.

Natural components of extended society

The many 'components' of nature for indigenous peoples become an extension not just of the geographical world, but of human society. This is fundamentally difficult for Western society to understand, since the extension of 'self' is through 'hard technology' not nature (Martins 1993). For indigenous peoples, 'natural models' may even serve as templates for social organization, political thoughts, and modes of subsistence. This also implies radical differences in concepts of time and space. A *Polistes* species wasp nest, for example, serves as the natural model for the Kayapó universe: its parallel broodcombs represent the many layers of the upper and lower worlds, while its circular base prescribes the form of an idealized village (Posey 1981 and 2002).

'Myths' and 'folklore' have been analysed for their structural, metalinguistic and symbolic components, and have even been shown to regulate ecological as well as social cycles. They have perhaps been less studied as sounding boards for cultural and environmental change.

The Kayapó myth known as 'The Journey to become a Shaman' (Posey 1982a and 2002, Chapter 6) is exemplary of how oral tradition works to explain ecological–social relationships and the changes that occur within them.

The story is centred around the capability of the *wayanga* to leave his or her body (*kô*) and be transformed into other physical forms. Energy (*karõn*) can be stored temporarily in rocks, but inevitably gets transformed into armadillos, doves, or bats. The spider's web represents the barrier between the visible and the invisible worlds. Armadillos are persistent animals that know how to burrow under the web; doves are powerful flyers and can break right through the barrier, while bats are such skilful flyers that they manoeuvre through the strands.

The sounds of the doves' and bats' flights represent the different frequencies that their vibrations impart. Frequencies have equivalent sounds and colours. Just to analyse the variations in frequencies of bee sounds would require discussing the fifty-two different folk species of stingless bees, each of which has a distinctive sound and curative properties.

The most powerful shamans can transform themselves into not just one of the animals, but all of them. And once on the other side of the spider's web, after they have passed through the endless dark chasm, they enter into the spectral frequencies of different light (or colours). There is a different spectral frequency for each animal (*mry-karõn*). The general term for undifferentiated energy is *karõn*. Defined energies are given distinctive modifiers (*x-karõn*), where *x* might be *mry* for animals (*mry-karõn*), *tep* for fish, or *kwen* for birds, and so on.

Some shamans learn the secrets of only a few animals and their energies, while others 'know all' (in the words of the myth). They have learned about all of the spectral frequencies and their respective animal energies. Upon return to their bodies, the *wayanga* begin to 'work with' (*nhipex*) the animal energies encountered in their transformation. The basis of the 'work' is to maintain a balance between animal energies and human energies. Eating the meat of, coming in contact with or even dreaming about animals can cause an imbalance in these energies – as can, of course, a well-elaborated list of antisocial actions. *Wayanga* use a great variety of techniques for restoring balance (they can also create imbalances – *kanê* – that lead to sickness), but plants are the most common 'mediators' that manipulate this balance (Posey and Elisabetsky 1991).

Plants themselves have energies (*karõn*), but most do not have distinctive energies or spirits (*x-karõn*) per se. One exception is some of the *mekrakindjà* ('child-want-thing' plants that aid in conception), which have very powerful spirits and cause the user to dream of conceiving a child. Both men and women use these dreaming plants, although men are usually the ones who first 'conceive' – that is, first 'see' (*kra pumunh*) the child in a dream (Elisabetsky and Posey 1989). Other plants with spirits (i.e. defined energies or *x-karõn*) are the *metykdjà* ('the poison plants'), the *mẽudjy* ('witchcraft plants'), and the most deadly and powerful *pitu* (no direct translation): these cause drastic alteration to human beings, such as death, paralyses, blindness, insanity, abortion, etc. Even less-powerful plants have qualities that can either harm or help the balance between human and animal energies (*mẽ-karõn* and *mry-karõn*) – indeed it appears that all plants have curative values.

In any case, the Kayapó respect both plants and animals, since their energies are keys to the health of their own society. Permission is asked of the *mry-karõn* when taking the life of an animal, and songs of appreciation are offered to the spirits of the dead animals. Likewise, annual rituals extol the importance of plants and instil a great sense of respect for their overall role in the socio-ecological balance

(Posey 1981 and 2002, 1982b and 2002). The Kayapó have no question about the dependence of their existence and future health upon plants and animals and the forces of nature.

Normally, spirits of the dead pass easily into the other world (*mẽ-karõn nhon pyka*) and continue their existence in what is roughly the mirror image of what goes on in this world. 'Deceased' (they never really die, for they have already died and just disappear and reappear) *wayanga* live in a special cave in the mountains – hence the reference in the myth of their stone seats. Spirits of dead animals also go to the 'other world'. Devoted pets are sometimes killed and buried with their 'owners' at death, so that the human spirit will not be so lonely (some Kayapó say that dogs are buried with their owners because the dogs can help the human spirit find its way to the 'other world').

Those who attempt a shamanistic transformation and do not succeed, however, have a more tragic end: their spirits are lost forever in the spider's web. There is disagreement among the Kayapó as to what this really means, but there is no doubt that it is a terrible fate. It is little wonder that only a small portion of the Kayapó population have ever tried to become a *wayanga*.

Kwyrà-kà, one of my shaman mentors, showed great concern when the first coffin arrived in Gorotire and his nephew was buried in it instead of in the traditional manner. (The Kayapó traditionally bury the body in a crouched position in deep round pits, covered with logs and soil. Until recently, a secondary burial was practised for four days after the principal burial; this allowed time for the spirit to return to the body in case the 'dead' person was only on a shamanistic journey.) He anguished over the possibility that the soul of the child would not be able to escape from the casket to the other world. Likewise, Kwyrà-kà and Beptopoop (another shaman) both expressed their serious concern with the plants that were taken during ethnobotanical surveys to be pressed and dried in herbaria. They worried about what would happen to the plants' energies. If the plants were kept in such closed, sterile places, would their spirits be trapped, thereby provoking imbalance and danger to the Kayapó, as well as to those who 'kept' them? Like the small child closed within the casket, would their energy not become imprisoned, thereby impeding the 'natural' cycles?

Even deeper concerns are expressed about the massive quantities of plants that would have to be collected to provide the oils, essences, colouring, and the life for the commercialization of plant products. The *wayanga* ask: 'Has anyone ever consulted the plants?' Would the dreaming that is necessary for the conception of healthy children be jeopardized? Would the plants stop mediating between the human and animal *karõns*, thereby leading to the loss of ancient cures and provoking new diseases?

The central concepts of ecological management are deeply embedded and codified in myth from which environmental and social change can also be measured. However, it is important to realize that the forces or energies exemplified in myths are not historical in the Western sense; time may be cyclical, spiral and/or multidimensional. No matter how hard ecologists try, the linearity of time and space that pervades our categories of interpretation will never capture the nonlinearity of some indigenous ecological concepts. This is a serious, inherent limitation to historical ecology.

Basic element of the Kayapó management model

The principal elements of Kayapó management have been previously described in some detail (Posey 1985a and 2002, 1993). They include the following:

(i) overlapping and interrelated ecological categories;
(ii) an emphasis on ecotone utilization;
(iii) the modification of 'natural ecosystems' to create ecotones;
(iv) the extensive utilization of 'semidomesticates';
(v) the transfer of biogenetic materials between similar ecozones; and
(vi) the integration of agricultural with forest management cycles.

These principles are permeated by diachronic processes and historical developments that depend upon interaction within and between ecological zones.

Several options are possible for representing indigenous resource management models. The most inclusive and descriptive representation of the Kayapó system places the *kapôt* (savanna or grasslands) at one end of a continuum, with *kapôt* as the focal type, or the ecozone that most typifies the category, and *bà* (forest) at the other (with *bà* as the focal type) (Posey 2002). Those *kapôt* types with more forest elements would be represented towards the forest pole, while *bà* types that are more open and with grassy elements would lie towards the savanna end of the continuum. This would put *apêtê* (forest patches in savanna) at the conceptual centre, or cognitive interface, since these ecozones introduce forest elements into the savanna. However, *puru* (agricultural plots) also lie conceptually at the same place on the continuum, since these bring sun-tolerant vegetation into forest niches. On this basis, I have also suggested that *apêtê* are conceptual inverses of *puru*, but function in similar ways since they both serve as 'resource islands' where useful plants can be concentrated in known, managed areas.

Ecological types like *bà-kati* (high forest) or *bà-kamrek* (transitional forest) are not, however, uniform. All forests have edges (*kà*), or openings caused by fallen trees (*bà-krêti*). These provisional zonal variations within the conceptual type provide transitions between different types. Thus a plant that likes the margins of a high forest might also grow well at the margin of a field, or an *apêtê* (a forest patch in the savanna created by the Kayapó). A plant that likes light gaps provided by forest openings might also like forest edges or old fields. Plants from open forest types or forest edges could also be predicted to do well along the edge of trails (*pry*) or thicker zones of *apêtê*. Using the same logic, the Kayapó would transfer biogenetic materials between matching microzones so that ecological types are interrelated by their similarities rather than isolated by their differences.

Ecotone recognition and management are, therefore, the uniting elements of the overall system.

In contrast, another interesting dimension to the model emerges when looking diachronically across the system. Agricultural clearings are essentially planted with rapidly growing domesticates, but almost immediately thereafter are managed for secondary forest species. This management depends upon a variety of strategies, which include introducing some varieties (planting and transplanting), removing some elements, allowing others to grow, encouraging some with fertilizer and ash, and preparing or working the soils to favour certain species (Hecht and Posey 1989 and 2002). The introductions are to provide long-term supplies of medicinals and other useful products, as well as food for humans and animals. The old fields (*puru tum*), sometimes erroneously considered inactive 'fallows', are as useful to the Kayapó as are agricultural plots or mature forest. A high percentage of plants in this transition have single or multiple uses (I have estimated 85 per cent, although it is only an estimate based upon surveys of sample plots; elsewhere I have argued that fundamentally the Kayapó believe that *each* and *every* plant has a use or potential use).

When the secondary forest grows too high to provide undergrowth as food for animals (and hunting becomes difficult), then the forest is cut again for use as an agricultural plot. It is, therefore, more useful to think of the Kayapó system as focused on the management of transitional forests (*chronological ecotones*). The Kayapó system depends more on NDRs (non-domesticated resources – varieties that have been managed, but not brought into domestication) than on cultivars, although agricultural produce has become increasingly important for the sedentary, postcontact Kayapó.

I have recently hypothesized in Anna Roosevelt's *Amazonian Indians* (1994) that the dependence on 'resource islands' is related to hostility and warfare. The more unstable the political system, the greater the dispersal of Kayapó groups and the greater the dependence upon concentrations along forest trails, in forest openings and *apêtê* – an overall pattern that I have called 'nomadic agriculture'. When peace and stability return, agriculture begins to dominate, and the reliance on NDRs decreases.

There have been several cycles of warfare–peace–hostility–stability that have caused the shrinkage or expansion of the nomadic or settlement agriculture. Until very recently, the Kayapó were in open warfare against each other and their neighbours; thus, nomadic agriculture was still evident until the early 1980s. Since then, however, settlement agriculture has come to dominate, and most trails, *apêtê*, and distant campsites have been abandoned. Nonetheless, the management of old fields (secondary forest vegetation) continues, and useful varieties of NDRs brought from distant villages or other ecozones still play prominent roles in the management cycle (Anderson and Posey 1989).

The flexibility and complexity of the Kayapó system cannot, therefore, be fully appreciated without a profile that shows the fundamental modifications in their historical past. Likewise, the impact of indigenous warfare, travel, and trade would continue to be undervalued without a diachronic analysis of plant distribution and changing subsistence patterns.

Attacks upon the model

The dynamic of the Kayapó ecological management system is based upon the transfer of useful plants across distances, sometimes great distance, into managed concentrations. In a recent attack on my *apêtê* work, Eugene Parker (1992, 1993) compares the genera and species of managed 'forest islands' with 'natural' *campo-cerrado* vegetation. Based on these crude comparisons, he concludes that *apêtê* are not vegetatively distinct from nonmanaged areas: the Kayapó do not plant NDRS, nor are they conscious manipulators of nature. Parker's methodology is hopelessly flawed with no identified control site, no botanical voucher collection available in any herbarium, and confusion over *cf.* and *sp.* attached to genera as meaning positive field identification to species. His interviews were with monolingual Kayapó informants, but his limited Portuguese and lack of Kayapó language skills meant that no emic data were obtained.

Just as cognitive categories of illness do not necessarily overlap, neither do botanical classification systems. Species determinations (and even more so, generic classifications) are inadequate to describe folk systems that frequently focus on varieties or subvarieties of species. This is not hard for a gardener who searches for new varieties of tulips to understand. The desired variety may be abundant in the garden next door, but does not yet grace his garden: the frequency of the bulb is not the problem, it is the distribution of it. Ethnopharmacologists also know well how annual cycles and ecosystem differences can significantly modify qualities of even the same variety. And woe to any field-worker who does not recognize the difference between bitter and sweet varieties of *Manihot esculenta*. In other words, distinctions made only at the scientific generic (and sometimes even species) levels may be misleading, if not deadly. This fine-tuning of data analysis makes historical ecology problematic when results from different observers utilizing different methods and levels of analysis are compared.

Parker's attack also fundamentally questions whether indigenous peoples have a conservation mentality and are conscious of the effect of their actions on the environment. This is an old debate in anthropology: how conscious is 'common sense'? It is an interesting question when it involves detailed investigation into the actual behaviour. Indians cast seeds, throw them into termite holes, scatter them in ashes, dig little holes to drop them into while they are defecating, step on them as they walk, and otherwise modify the environment in a myriad of ways (Posey 2002). They may not be conscious of these everyday 'common sense' acts, but they may become aware of them when they are properly queried about them.

Over many years of research, my informants and I worked out a common understanding of what was meant by the Portuguese verb 'to plant' (*plantar*), which does not coincide with any single Kayapó word, phrase, or concept. Someone else asking questions about planting would not necessarily get the same answers because the agreed time frame of reference is different. The term 'plantable' refers to a plant that is subject to planting, that is, that the Kayapó in some way propagate or encourage to grow.

Questions about planting and plantable are inherently ambiguous. It is impossible to know, for example, which individual in a patch of daffodils in Central Park was the planted progenitor. We can deduce with certainty that they *were* planted – or their ancestors were planted; in other words, the daffodils are there because of one or more human acts. Likewise the Kayapó may not be able consistently to identify a botanical specimen as planted, but they know that certain species are plantable and that human beings have moulded certain identifiable historic landscapes.

The *apêtê* that Parker attacks are arguably as much human artefacts as Central Park, even if planting (by anyone's definition) does not occur and native species dominate. They are full of trails, paths, human-cut niches, openings, fire pits, charcoal, machete cuts on the trees and shrubs, left-over woven sitting mats, remains of old pots and tools, and discarded food remains: these reflect conscious acts that have a long historical tradition and undeniably create anthropogenic landscapes.

The critical question then is not whether indigenous peoples are conscious of their actions, but rather whether scientists consider such acts as conservation – bearing in mind that there is no general agreement within or between scientific specialities as to what conservation is, how it is measured, or whether it is attainable. Archaeologists have similar difficulties in agreeing upon what constitute 'sites'.

To my knowledge, cultural or anthropogenic landscapes in Amazonia were first detected by Protásio Frickel (1978), who recognized the relationship between historical Indian village sites and enriched forest stands. Nigel Smith (1980), although not the first to recognize the human impact on soils, called attention to the extensiveness and importance of *terra preta do indio* (literally 'black soils of Indians', or anthropologically enriched soils; see Whitehead 1998: ch. 2). Subsequently, I described the Kayapó management principles and processes that affect the Amazonian forest (Posey 1982b and 2002), but it was some time later that I realized that indigenous management practices also had significant impacts on scrub savanna and other landscapes (Posey 1983b, 1984d).

Once scientists are alerted to the nature of ecological 'footprints of the forest' (see Balée 1994), then anthropogenic landscapes become more easily recognized. Dr James Ratter of the Royal Botanic Garden, Edinburgh, and Professor Peter Furley, Department of Geography, University of Edinburgh, for example, have reported two '*apêtê*-like' mounds of vegetation in the Brasilia National Park as having 'no obvious explanation other than being manmade' and they believe that 'many more of these islands may exist' (Furley and Ratter, n.d.). Until relatively recently, the *campo-cerrado* around Brasilia was certainly inhabited by Jê peoples, including the Kayapó.

William Denevan (1966b), Clark Erickson (1995), and William Balée (1995) report thousands of 'forest islands' in the Llanos de Mojos of eastern Bolivia.

Several thousands of these man-made structures, often including earthworks, have been mapped to date. No floristic inventories have been published, although such surveys are in progress. The distances between these islands in eastern Bolivia and those of the Kayapó give only circumstantial support to *apêtê*, but they show that anthropogenic forest islands are a part of Amazonian aboriginal landscapes.

Political dimension of human ecology

In Parker's response (1993) to my 'Reply to Parker' (Posey 1992),[1] the reader is provided with his attempt to 'deconstruct almost every sentence' (p. 721), a careful reading of my corpus (p. 716), and an additional 3,500 or so words that pose as additional data. Alarmingly, his deconstructions have been considered by the former editors of the *American Anthropologist* as having the same scientific validity as field research. This has serious implications for historical ecology and related approaches, since diachronic studies depend upon the highest standards and integrity of historical research and scientific investigation.

Furthermore, the implications of Parker's allegations are extremely dangerous for indigenous peoples, who struggle to maintain their lands and territories against those who see them as detached social entities not linked to their surroundings. The result of such logic is that native peoples have been, and are being, forcefully moved from their homelands without concern for their biocultural environments.

Evidence that indigenous peoples not only interact with, but in fact affect, mould and can even increase the biological diversity on their lands and territories is, therefore, not a collection of detached, irrelevant data to be merely argued over from opposing ivory towers (see Sponsel 1995). The undermining of such finds would be enthusiastically received by some governments, political and economic decision-makers, banks and development agencies that would like nothing more than to prove that culture is divorced from human rights, or development from local communities. Developers could then continue to move and remove indigenous peoples from their lands with impunity and with the implicit blessing of science – and historical ecology.

This is not to suggest that scientific data should be manipulated to fit one's political bent, but it is a warning to those who think that their academic pursuits do not have an impact beyond their fellow specialists. The historical link between a people, their society, and the cultural landscapes with which they interact are essential, for example, in determining intellectual property rights over biogenetic resources commercialized from their doorsteps. Even the term *wild*, carelessly bantered about by scientists, has profound implications for indigenous and traditional peoples in relation to the ownership of, access to, and control over resources. 'Wild' species and landscapes are presumed to be 'natural': local communities can claim no intellectual property rights over biological materials removed from 'nature', even if they have used, conserved, and modified them over millenia.

Environmental impact assessments (EIAs) are increasingly important in guiding development where evidence of anthropogenic impact bears heavily upon whether or not projects proceed and local peoples are forcibly resettled. The Convention on Biological Diversity (CBD) virtually calls for the nationalization of traditional knowledge, innovations, and practices – meaning that the findings of historical ecologists will provide primal evidence for local communities attempting to defend their claim of eminent domain. Finally, as 'free trade' (via GATT, TRIPs – Trade Related Aspects of Intellectual Property – and the new World Trade Organization) further entrenches itself as the basis for the new world order, historical ecologists may find themselves in key roles defending legacies of biological and cultural diversity against the powerful forces that would reduce the earth to private commodities of raw materials.

Conclusion

Historical ecology has an important role in alerting scientists in many disciplines and subdisciplines to the nature and importance of human influence in the conservation, management, and even stimulation of biological and ecological diversity. Anthropogenic qualities of landscapes are becoming increasingly evident, thereby dismissing the assumption that human societies can only be destructive to nature and that traditional resources are 'wild'. Such finds also highlight the necessity of including diachronic profiles in all biological and ecological studies.

The Kayapó of Brazil, for example, practise long-term 'nomadic agriculture' that includes the management of forest openings, trailsides, and rock outcroppings. They are responsible for the highly anthropogenic *apêtê* ('forest islands') of *campo-cerrado*, and essentially create *chronological ecotones* throughout their sophisticated management of disturbed ecological zones and secondary forests emerging from agricultural plots. The system is sufficiently flexible to accommodate changing subsistence requirements during periods of peace or hostility. Yet, to overlook the indigenous cognitive (emic) categories and historical processes central to the system is to miss the genius of Kayapó landscapes.

The debate over indigenous peoples' consciousness of conservation draws attention to the difficulties of conducting interdisciplinary and multidisciplinary research, since the consciousness of conservation, like other 'common sense' aspects of culture, is difficult to elicit and is frequently encoded in myth and ceremony. Direct questioning alone cannot achieve the 'intuitive' nature of research that is based upon another diachronic process affecting historical ecology: that of the long-term relationship between investigators and their cultural consultants.

As important as historical ecology may become in furthering our understanding of environmental processes, it is fundamentally limited by an inextricable tie with Western notions of the linearity of time and space. The metaphysical, cosmic, and invisible forces that permeate indigenous belief will always keep Western scholarship at arm's length from defining the underlying forces of society and nature.

Nonetheless, historical ecology has much to contribute to the human/nature debate through its interdisciplinary and diachronic approaches. Furthermore, the increased global emphasis on locally controlled ecological conservation, countered by a strong resistance from centralized economic and political forces on community empowerment, will thrust historical ecologists, and others who document anthropogenic and cultural landscapes, into significant political debates on the sustained use and management of the components of biological diversity – now and for many years to come.

Chapter 11

Indigenous knowledge, biodiversity, and international rights

Learning about forests from the Kayapó Indians of the Brazilian Amazon*

Introduction

Worldwide deforestation rates, especially in tropical regions, have never been higher. Estimates vary, but the UN Food and Agriculture Organization calculates tropical forest loss at about 110.5 million hectares per annum (UNEP 1995). The UK Forests Network (UKFN 1995) lists the underlying causes of forest destruction as:

- current consumption levels, human greed, inappropriate incentives, and corruption;
- international debt resulting from the above;
- pressure for economic development;
- land tenure and the search for farmland;
- women's position in society; and
- population, settlement, and colonization policies.

Exacerbating these causes are inadequate and inappropriate forest management strategies that ignore local values and the importance of traditional and local knowledge (Pimbert and Pretty 1995). The limited economic parameters imposed by external timber markets undermine non-economic criteria and local values for such things as non-timber forest products (NTFPs) (Shiva et al. 1991). This in turn encourages destruction of biodiversity, which is part of a 'web' of interconnections that undermines local well-being and social stability (Ortiz 1995).

Many of the areas of highest biological diversity are forests inhabited by indigenous and traditional peoples, giving evidence to what the Declaration of Belém calls the 'inextricable link' between biological and cultural diversity (Appendix 2). In fact, of the nine countries which together account for 60 per cent of human languages, six of these 'centres of cultural diversity' are also 'megadiversity' countries with exceptional numbers of unique plant and animal species (Durning 1992). The bulk of these languages are spoken by indigenous peoples.

---

* A. J. Grayson (ed.) *The Commonwealth Forestry Review* (1997), 76:1, 53–60. Oxford Forestry Institute, Oxford. This paper draws upon a discussion report prepared in 1995 by the Working Group on Traditional Resource Rights for the Secretariat of the Convention on Biological Diversity.

It is estimated that there are currently at least 200 million people worldwide who are indigenous (ICHI 1987).[1] Durning (1992) suggests there are between 200 and 600 million people who are indigenous, according to how 'indigenous peoples' are defined. Indigenous peoples inhabit areas of North and South America, Northern Europe, Asia, Africa, and Oceania. They occupy a wide geographical range from the polar regions to the deserts, savannas, and forests of the tropical zone. The fact that 4,000–5,000 of the 6,000 languages in the world are indigenous strongly suggests that indigenous peoples constitute most of the world's cultural diversity. They range from groups as disparate as the Quechua descendants of the Inca civilization in Bolivia, Ecuador, and Peru, who collectively number more than 10 million people, to the Gurumalum band of Papua New Guinea with fewer than ten surviving members. In New Guinea alone, over 600 languages are spoken among a population of only 6 million, and in India there are more than 1,600 languages (Durning 1992).

Cultural diversity is also threatened on an unprecedented scale (Chapter 10 this volume; Dasmann 1991). It has been estimated that half the world's languages – the storehouses of peoples' intellectual heritage and the framework for their unique understanding of life – will disappear within a century (Krauss 1992). According to UNESCO (1993), nearly 2,500 languages are in immediate danger of extinction, and their loss will include much of the traditional knowledge they encode.

Recognizing the inextricable link

The Convention on Biological Diversity (CBD), opened for signature during the 1992 UN Conference on Environment and Development (UNCED), the Earth Summit, and was ratified by over 160 countries. It has become the major global initiative to stop the loss of biological and cultural diversity. Indigenous peoples and local communities are recognized as playing important roles in *in situ* conservation for having sustainably managed the natural resources of fragile, biologically rich ecosystems for millennia. This is specifically noted in the Preamble of the CBD (Appendix 3). The section that is most obviously and directly related to indigenous peoples is Article 8j (Appendix 3).

Indigenous peoples themselves frequently emphasize that conserving biological diversity in areas such as forests requires respect and recognition of their rights, as in the 1992 Indigenous Peoples' Earth Charter (Posey 1996):

> Recognizing indigenous peoples' harmonious relationship with Nature, indigenous sustainable development strategies and cultural values must be respected as distinct and vital sources of knowledge.
>
> (Clause 67)

Similarly, the Final Statement from the 1995 Consultation on Indigenous Peoples' Knowledge and Intellectual Property Rights in Suva, Fiji (PCRC 1995), and the 1992 Charter of the Indigenous-Tribal Peoples of the Tropical Forests (IAI-TPTF

1992) assert that indigenous guardianship of ecosystems is the best method of conserving biological diversity and indigenous knowledge. In the specific context of forests, the Indigenous-Tribal Peoples' Charter states:

> All policies towards the forests must be based on a respect for cultural diversity, for a promotion of indigenous models of living, and an understanding that our peoples have developed ways of life closely attuned to our environment.
> (Article 5)

Thus, the interdependence of cultural and biological diversity is clearly recognized by both the international community and indigenous peoples, as is respect for the rights of indigenous peoples as a *sine qua non* for sustainable use and conservation of forests and their biodiversity. This also requires respect for local values and equitable use of traditional knowledge as a basis for sustainable management.

Local knowledge and sustainable management

The concept of sustainability is embodied in indigenous and traditional livelihood systems. Historical evidence demonstrates the sustained productivity of indigenous forest management systems, in some cases for thousands of years (e.g. Anderson 1990; Gadgil and Thapar 1990; Posey and Balée 1989; Posey Chapter 10 this volume). Indigenous peoples and traditional communities often possess an 'environmental ethic' developed from living in particular ecosystems (Bierhorst 1994; Callicott 1989). This ethic cannot be regarded as universal, but indigenous systems do tend to emphasize the following specific values and features:

- co-operation;
- family bonding and cross-generational communication, including links with ancestors;
- concern for the well-being of future generations;
- local-scale, self-sufficiency, and reliance on locally available natural resources;
- rights to lands, territories, and resources which tend to be collective and inalienable rather than individual and alienable; and
- restraint in resource exploitation and respect for nature, especially for sacred sites.

The CBD language of 'traditional knowledge, innovations and practices' of 'local communities embodying traditional lifestyles' is usually referred to by scientists as Traditional Ecological Knowledge (TEK). It was defined by Gadgil et al. (1993) as 'a cumulative body of knowledge and beliefs handed down through generations by cultural transmission about the relationship of living beings (including humans) with one another and with their environment'. (For other definitions see Posey and

Dutfield 1997.) TEK is far more than a simple compilation of facts. It is the basis for local-level decision-making in areas of contemporary life, including natural resource management, nutrition, food preparation, health, education, and community and social organization (Warren *et al.* 1995). TEK is holistic, inherently dynamic, constantly evolving through experimentation and innovation, fresh insight, and external stimuli.[2] According to the Four Directions Council (FDC 1996):

> What is 'traditional' about traditional knowledge is not its antiquity, but the way it is acquired and used. In other words, the social process of learning and sharing knowledge, which is unique to each indigenous culture, lies at the very heart of its 'traditionality'. Much of this knowledge is actually quite new, but it has a social meaning, and legal character, entirely unlike the knowledge indigenous peoples acquire from settlers and industrialised societies. This is why we believe that protecting indigenous knowledge necessarily involves the recognition of each peoples' own laws and their own processes of discovery and teaching.

The goal of linking indigenous systems and sustainability should be to harness the totality, rather than the components, of TEK systems in sustainability strategies, so that the holistic quality of indigenous management can benefit the wider society. Policy makers need to be aware, however, that indigenous peoples frequently integrate forest and agricultural management systems so that categories of 'forester', 'hunter and gatherer', and 'farmer' cannot be considered as discrete categories, but represent continua of traditional livelihood activities.

The continuum between agriculture and forestry is filled by the vast number of plant and animal species that are *neither* agricultural domesticates *nor* timber species, but nonetheless provide most of the needs of local communities. Many of these species have been genetically selected, planted, and transplanted to enhance and modify local ecosystems. These are sometimes known as 'semi-domesticates' or 'human modified species' (Posey 1993), although *Non-Domesticated Resources* (NDRs) is my preferred term. NDRs have systematically been undervalued and overlooked by scientists, yet provide a vast treasury of useful species for food, medicines, shelter, building materials, dyes, colourings, repellents, fertilizers, and pesticides (FOE 1992; Kvist *et al.* 1995; Plotkin and Famolare 1992).

Many so-called 'natural' landscapes are in fact *cultural or anthropogenic landscapes*, either of cultural significance or modified by human activity.[3] Failure to understand the human impact on 'wild' landscapes has blinded outsiders to NDRs and the traditional management practices that maximize their use and conservation (Gomez-Pompa and Kaus 1992). Indigenous peoples and a growing number of scientists find unacceptable the assumption that just because landscapes and species appear to outsiders to be 'natural' they are 'wild' and, therefore, unowned.

According to a Resolution from the 1995 Ecopolitics IX Conference in Darwin, Australia (NLC 1996):

> The term 'wilderness' as it is popularly used, and related concepts such as 'wild resources', 'wild foods', etc., [are unacceptable]. These terms have connotations of *terra nullius* [empty or unowned land and resources][4] and, as such, all concerned people and organizations should look for alternative terminology which does not exclude indigenous history and meaning.

Scientific studies that document the anthropogenic and cultural aspects of landscapes, therefore, can overturn the 'empty land' concept and begin to recognize the role of indigenous and local peoples in *in situ* conservation. Theoretically, this will in turn strengthen claims by communities to ownership of and rights over land, knowledge, and genetic resources.

Cultural landscapes and Kayapó resource management

Traditionally, Amazonian Indians have been thought of as merely exploiters of their environments – not as conservers, manipulators, and managers of natural resources (e.g. Meggers 1996). Researchers are finding, however, that presumed 'natural' ecological systems may, in fact, be products of human manipulation (Alcorn 1981, 1989; Anderson and Posey 1985; Balée 1989a, 1998; Balée and Gély 1989; Clement 1989; Denevan and Padoch 1988; Frickel 1959; Roosevelt 1994; Sponsel 1995; Sponsel *et al*. 1996; and others). Likewise, old agricultural fallows reflect genetic selection and human-enhanced species diversity (Anderson 1990; Balée 1989b; Denevan and Padoch 1988; Irvine 1989; Redford and Padoch 1992).

The Kayapó Indians of the Middle Xingu Valley, Brazil, provide a good example of how scientific assumptions of 'natural' landscapes have hidden the complexity and potential of local management practices to modify ecosystems. The modern Kayapó population is still under 5,000, but pre-contact populations were many times larger and presumably had even greater impacts on the vast region they exploited (Posey 1994c and 2002, Chapter 3). They live in an ecologically diverse region that comprises nearly 4 million hectares of *reserva indígena* in the States of Para and Mato Grosso. Ethnohistorical research with the Kayapó Indians shows that contact with European diseases came via trade routes and preceded face-to-face contact with colonizers. Epidemics led to intra-group fighting, fission, and the dispersal of sub-groups who carried with them seeds and cuttings to propagate their foods, medicines, and other NDRs (Posey 1987 and 2002, Chapter 2).

A form of 'nomadic agriculture' developed based upon the exploitation of NDRs intentionally concentrated in human-modified environments near trailsides, abandoned villages and at camp sites (Posey 1985a and 2002, Chapter 18). Agricultural practices also spread, along with techniques for management of old fields to enhance the availability of wildlife and useful plants. During times of warfare, the Kayapó could abandon their agricultural plots and survive on non-domesticated species concentrated at trailsides, former village sites, forest openings, and ancient fields.

Agricultural plots were engineered to develop into productive agroforestry reserves dominated by NDR species, thereby allowing the Kayapó to oscillate between (or blend together) agriculture and gathering. Such patterns appear to have been widespread in the lowland tropics, and defy the traditional dichotomies of wild versus domesticated species, hunter-gatherers versus agriculturalists, and agriculture versus agroforestry. Even today, over 76 per cent of the useful plant species collected to date are *not* 'domesticated', nor can they be considered 'wild' (see Chapter 10 this volume; Roosevelt 1994). (I suspect that as a more complete floral inventory is completed, this percentage will approach 98 per cent.)

Nowhere is this more evident than in the formation of *apêtê* (islands of forest) in the *campo-cerrado* (savanna). The Kayapó initiate and simulate the formation of forest patches through the careful manipulation of micro-environmental factors, knowledge of soil and plant characteristics, and intentional concentration of useful species into limited plots. Although most *apêtê* are small (under 10 hectares), elders reported plant varieties in a one hectare plot as having been introduced by villagers from an area the size of Western Europe (Anderson and Posey 1989). *Apêtê* are managed to maximize useful species in all stages of the forest succession. When their centres become dark and unproductive, openings (*irã*) are created that allow light to again penetrate the forest and reinitiate a new cycle.

The Kayapó resource management system is based on the conservation and use of transitional forests in which agriculture is only a useful (albeit critical) phase in the long-term process. *Apêtê* exhibit parallel transitional sequences in the campo-cerrado and depend almost exclusively on NDRs. The degree to which genetic material is transferred between similar microzones of different ecological types points to how the Kayapó exploit ecotones that host the highest diversity of plants. Management over time can be thought of as management of *chronological ecotones*, since management cycles aim to maintain the maximum amount of diversity and the greatest number of ecotones.

The Kayapó model illustrates how previously assumed 'natural' ecosystems in Amazonia have been consciously modified by indigenous residents through time. The degree to which this has taken place has yet to be quantified, but Kayapó 'forest islands' data show concentrations of plant varieties from a vast geographic area. This case underlines the necessity for historical studies to understand the long-term effects of management of cultural and anthropogenic landscapes. Above all, it exposes the inadequacies of our scientific, educational, and political institutions that separate agriculture from forestry and ignore the importance of NDR.

Implications and applications

Can Kayapó TEK be put to 'wider use and application'?

The CBD recognizes various ways in which traditional knowledge, innovations, and practices can be employed to enhance *in situ* biodiversity conservation.

The most fundamental is recognition of community and cultural rights that allow indigenous peoples like the Kayapó to make their own decisions over the future of their land and resources.[5] A second way is through community-controlled conservation and full participation of indigenous and local peoples in all aspects of planning and implementation of conservation and development projects (see Chapter 10).

These strategies are founded upon respect for and preservation of the holistic nature and diversity of indigenous natural resource management systems. But most interest in TEK is not concerned with *in situ* conservation, but rather with the use and application of knowledge and genetic resources for the development of natural products.

Industry has discovered the economic potential for new products 'mined' from the biodiversity rich areas using TEK to provide 'leads' or shortcuts in product discovery (Chadwick and Marsh 1994; Joyce 1994; Posey, Chapter 15 this volume; Reid *et al.* 1993). This is known as 'bioprospecting'[6] and high expectations of profits have led to frenzied collecting and commercial activity on Kayapó lands and elsewhere in Amazonia.

It is difficult to estimate the commercial promise of biodiversity prospecting. For medicines alone, the 1985 market value of plant-based medicines sold in developed countries was estimated at a total of $43 billion (Principe 1989). This frequently cited estimate is unreliable, but whatever the true amount might be, only a minuscule proportion of profits have been returned to indigenous peoples from whom much of the original knowledge came. I have estimated less than 0.001 per cent (Posey 1990b).

Companies that produce seeds and agrochemicals benefit substantially from the free flow of germplasm from indigenous lands. The market value of the seed germplasm utilizing traditional landraces is estimated by the Rural Advancement Foundation International at $50 billion per year in the US alone (RAFI 1994c). Consequently, indigenous peoples are providing subsidies to a modern agricultural system that barely recognizes their contributions. Similar situations exist with timber and non-timber forest products, as well as other natural product markets, such as personal care, foods, industrial oils, essences, pesticides, and preservatives (Burley 1994).

Biodiversity prospectors assume that organisms and ecosystems are 'wild' and, therefore, part of 'the common heritage of humankind'. Even when critical information, or even processed materials, are provided by indigenous peoples, it is the company that makes the protectable or patentable 'invention' and acquires the financial gains. Indigenous peoples see this situation as being parallel to the Europeans' 'discovery' of the New World and are understandably weary of the process. In the Pacific region, indigenous peoples have called for a total moratorium on bioprospecting, a move that has been echoed in Ecuador and is under consideration in indigenous territories around the world.

Scientists and scientific institutions are affected by this situation as they become involved – actively or passively – with the private sector. Plant, animal, and cultural material collected with public funds for scientific, non-profit purposes are now open for commercial exploitation. Research, even in universities and museums, is increasingly funded by corporations, raising questions of who controls the resulting data. 'Purely scientific' data banks have become the 'mines' for 'biodiversity prospecting'. Publishing of information, traditionally the hallmark of academic success, has become a superhighway for transporting restricted (or even sacred) information into the unprotectable 'public domain'.

Many scientific institutions and professional societies are responding to this dilemma by developing their own codes of conduct and standards of practice. These generally follow the well-established principles in international law and customary practice that include *inter alia*: recognition of indigenous land, territorial and intellectual property rights; support of indigenous self-determination; collective or community rights; full disclosure of intent; prior informed consent; and, veto over research and development projects (see Chapter 16 for a detailed profile of these principles).

Nation states rich in biological and cultural diversity are rapidly enacting 'access and transfer' legislation to implement the terms of the CBD. Most countries are not satisfied with voluntary codes and standards, and in some cases call for criminal sanctions against those who illegally remove genetic resources or TEK from their borders. Andean Pact and Amazon Cooperation Treaty countries, including Brazil, are actively seeking adequate legislation to guarantee protection and benefit-sharing. This is hopefully a sign that indigenous peoples and their knowledge are being seriously considered as a national resource in Latin America. One also hopes that the 'wider use and application' of traditional resources will benefit those who have zealously defended – and even moulded – the ecological and biological diversity of regions like Amazonia.

It remains to be seen if scientists can aptly apply the TEK they acquire from indigenous and local peoples like the Kayapó to develop alternative models for sustainable forest management. Adequate historical studies of anthropogenic landscapes, recognition of micro-ecological zones and ecotones, development of NDR-based systems, and exploitation of the forest–agriculture continuum, require major shifts in the way science and scientific institutions are organized and funded. And, even with the popularity of the CBD, enactment of adequate national legislation, and development of professional Codes and Standards of Conduct, there are no guarantees that rates of loss of biological and cultural diversity will slow. The CBD may not have solved many of the problems it identified, but it helps to clarify the basic challenges before us.

Part III

Intellectual property rights and ethical concerns

Chapter 12

Intellectual property rights
What is the position of ethnobiology?*

During the First International Congress of Ethnobiology held in Belém, Para (Brazil), 19–22 July 1988, scientists and native peoples from thirty-five countries met to discuss the importance of traditional knowledge and its application to the development of socially equitable and ecologically sustainable options for the Planet. Although the examples of indigenous knowledge systems, ecological variations in different regions of the world, and suggestions for applications of native concepts varied greatly, common themes appeared and reappeared throughout the Congress. The richness and relevance of traditional knowledge was evident in all cases, as was the global threat of extinction to native peoples and their cultures.

Industry and business discovered many years ago that indigenous knowledge sometimes means money. In the earliest forms of colonialism extractive products were often the basis for colonial wealth. More recently, pharmaceutical industries have become the major exploiters of traditional medicinal knowledge for major products and profits. There are no provisions anywhere for the protection of knowledge rights of native peoples. Despite repeated pleas from indigenous leaders that their traditional culture and knowledge systems are being exploited without just compensation, little action has been taken by legal, professional, environmental, nongovernmental, governmental – or even human rights – groups to secure intellectual property rights (IPR) for native peoples.

The World Intellectual Property Organization (WIPO) and UNESCO have both tried to work within the United Nations system to develop model conventions to protect folklore and 'artistic' aspects of indigenous knowledge. Nothing has gone beyond proposals, however, and currently there is no push to deal with IPR in any existing or future UN Conventions.

There is considerable opposition to IPR for native peoples – even from ethnobiologists and anthropologists – who fear that they will have to drastically change their 'lifestyles'. Incomes from published dissertations and other books, slides,

---

* Extract from 'Intellectual property rights: what is the position of ethnobiology?' First published in *Journal of Ethnobiology*, Summer (1990), 10:1, 93–8.

magazine articles, phonograph records, films and videos – all will have to include a percentage of the profits to the native 'subjects'. It will probably become normal that such 'rights' be negotiated with native peoples prior to the undertaking of initial fieldwork. This kind of behaviour has never been considered as part of the 'professional ethic' of scientific research, but certainly will become so in the near future.

The strongest opposition to IPR comes – as no great surprise – from the companies that have been the major predators upon traditional knowledge in the past: the pharmaceutical industry and seed companies (now subsumed by the 'biotechnology' label). Both groups would have to make major changes in the ways they do business – and paying for the basic information and genetic materials necessary to generate their profits would heavily pinch their profit margins.

An indigenous view

Indigenous leaders lament the difficulties for *their* younger generations to see options for economic security without following the ecologically destructive ways of the 'industrialized world'. How can traditional knowledge be defended and valued within a native society when, in fact, such knowledge offers little economic benefit to indigenous groups caught in the economic maze of consumerism and basic survival?

Ironically, with all of the much-heralded biological and ecological richness of Amazonia, the only products that command stable and reasonable prices are cattle, minerals, and timber – all of which require the destruction of tropical ecosystems in order to be attained. This pattern is repeated time and time again throughout the world.

Native peoples must have economic resources – and, if such income is to preserve the land, the people and their cultures, then traditional knowledge itself must be compensated in financial terms. Otherwise, native peoples themselves must revert to ecological destruction, associated with atrophy of their own knowledge systems, in order to acquire the economic power they need to survive.

Fears of too much success

Ecologists are justifiably concerned with the ecological impact of production of 'natural products' that become too successful. The tendency is always toward monocultures of cash crops. Many worry that international demands may spell the end of biodiversity, rather than encourage conservation of natural resources as initially desired.

Michael Soulé and Kathryn Kohm outline this concern (Soulé and Kohm 1989) in their recently published book, *Research Priorities for Conservation Biology*:

> Increased pressure on biological resources arises because of increasing human populations, changing consumption patterns, and new technologies. Although agricultural intensification will continue to be necessary, its impact

on biological resources is not predetermined. Conservation poses important research questions relevant to the design of new production technologies and land use systems: Can biologically diverse and low energy technologies be extended and/or intensified? Can production systems be differentially intensified so as to maintain biological diversity in other parts of a system? How does increased exploitation of specific species affect other species and general system properties?

Provocations of cultural changes can be equally disconcerting. By establishing mechanisms for 'just compensation' of native peoples, are we not also establishing mechanisms for the destruction of their societies through the subversion of materialism and consumerism?

Given current realities, such concerns are reduced to romantic notions. The fact is that indigenous societies and their natural environments are being destroyed by the dramatic expansion of industrialized society *now*. And, besides, pharmaceutical companies and 'natural products' companies have tasted success in their efforts: they will not go away.

Certainly the mechanisms of *what* is 'just compensation' and *how* such benefits would be distributed opens a 'Pandora's Box'. But to *not* open this Box is to accept the ethical and moral responsibility of 'paternalism' (those from 'advanced societies' know what is good for the 'native' because 'we' have already made the mistakes of squandering our cultural and natural wealth) that has undermined indigenous independence since the first wave of colonialism.

Native peoples must have the right to choose their own futures. Without economic independence, such a choice is not possible. The current devastation of native peoples and the ecological systems that they have conserved, managed, and intimately known for millennia, require that new and drastic steps be taken to reorient world priorities. All channels and organizations – governmental, non-governmental, professional, business – must work together to reverse the current momentum in loss of cultural, ecological, and biological diversity of this planet.

Three major accomplishments must occur:

(i) Giving economic value to the *living* forest and natural habitats through the valorization of 'natural products';
(ii) Recognition that native peoples hold the key to understanding the rational use and management of these living natural areas; and
(iii) Developing legal and practical mechanisms for the 'just compensation' of native peoples for their knowledge through the guarantees of intellectual property rights for traditional knowledge.

I want to make it very clear that I do not advocate the *imposition* of consumer capitalism and ties to market economies upon native peoples. Each group must have the option to enter into market economies, or not, and to what extent and under which circumstances they want to do so, or not do so. I only wish to point out that pressures to exploit traditional knowledge are drastically increasing, and that native peoples ought to at least have the option of just compensation for their knowledge.

To secure IPR and just compensation for traditional knowledge is critical to the survival of ethnobiology and anthropology, since indigenous peoples are increasingly leery of researchers and protective of their knowledge. At the same time, if 'green consumerism' is to function to divert the all-out destruction of remaining planetary natural resources and native peoples, then preservation of the *living* forests and *living* peoples is essential. Ecologists tell us that that is the only way we can save the planet. This can be done only with secure protection of indigenous lands and economic independence for native peoples.

These complex issues will be discussed in several symposia of the Second International Congress of Ethnobiology in Kunming, China, 21–25 October 1990 (see Chapter 7). This Congress will be the next step towards the development of a position of ethnobiologists towards IPR and the 'just compensation' of native peoples for their knowledge. I hope that both the Society of Ethnobiology and the International Society of Ethnobiology will take the intellectual lead – as well as appropriate actions – towards the development of a new ethic that serves as a model for other disciplines.

I suggest the following action be taken:

- Support an international call, through its members in all countries that participate in United Nations activities, for UN action on the question of IPR;
- Seek national legislation to secure indigenous IPR rights in all countries where native populations exist;
- Encourage funding agencies and development banks to support research into traditional knowledge, its practical applications, and ways that native peoples can be 'justly compensated' for their knowledge;
- Establish a special Working Committee to investigate the issues of IPR in relation to native rights and report to the Society with guidelines for international and national legislation;
- Include on the agenda of an Ethics Committee the issues of IPR in relation to activities of researchers with indigenous populations.

Journal of Ethnobiology (Editor's note): It is important to point out that Posey's article on Intellectual Property Rights (IPR) is a position/opinion paper. It was completed on May 10, 1990 and arrived in my office approximately two weeks later. Although the present issue was about ready to go to press, I thought it important that this paper be published in Volume 10, No. 1 because date of issue of Volume 10, No. 2 will be after the meeting of the Second International Congress of Ethnobiology, at which time IPR 'will be discussed in several symposia'. IPR is a complex, multi-faceted issue. It is important that all aspects be intelligently and compassionately considered and assessed before this or any other society or organization makes any firm decisions or rulings about it. In this connection, then,

I encourage members of the Society of Ethnobiology and readers of the *Journal* to contact Dr Darrell Addison Posey as soon as possible, and preferably no later than October 1, 1990, so that he will be aware of the many viewpoints on the many different aspects of IPR.

I wish to make it known that I did not send this paper out for peer review because of lack of time. I felt it was important that the readers of this journal be made aware of the complexities of IPR and be invited to make their opinions and facts at their disposal known so they can be taken into account during the discussions of IPR in China, 21–25 October, 1990. I recognize that many readers of the *Journal* will agree in whole or in part with this chapter. At the same time other readers will object vehemently to it, again, either in whole or in part. Had there been time for the chapter to have been peer-reviewed, it is likely that reviewers would have suggested revisions, given additional or what they might consider better sources of information; it's possible that one of the reviewers might have recommended that the chapter not be published. I decided to publish this paper, which Posey himself recognizes is just a summary, so that any additional references, facts, figures, and viewpoints can be made available to the participants in the symposia at the Second International Congress of Ethnobiology. Please send/telephone/fax any such information to Dr Posey. I also suggest that you send a copy to the *Journal's* News and Comments Editor.

Chapter 13

Indigenous knowledge and green consumerism
Co-operation or conflict?*

A series of meetings in London, in May 1990, signalled a new wave of economic activity to establish a greener road towards saving the planet. Opened by HRH Prince Charles, the international gathering – called 'The Rainforest Harvest' – was sponsored by the Royal Geographical Society, the British Overseas Development Administration, and the Body Shop. The sponsorship sounds like a strange mixture of science, government, and private enterprise, and the participants represented an even stranger mixture of Amazonian Indian leaders, ethnobiologists, human rights activists, environmentalists, economists, Members of Parliament, New Age thinkers, international lawyers, business entrepreneurs, and royalty.

The meetings attempted to show that the *living* rainforest and its *living* inhabitants hold countless secrets about new, natural, and sustainably produced products that are practically bursting out of the trees to reach concerned and enlightened consumers in the developed world. Just imagine, a new generation of soaps, oils, insect repellents, food colourings, clothes softeners, perfumes, foods, and medicines which are produced in ways that preserve the biological and ecological diversity of the planet's endangered rainforests, while at the same time actually benefiting the people who teach us about them and conserve the plants from which they are produced.

In this way, consumers of the world can unite to 'vote' through their individual consumption for the way they want the future of their planet. An international 'consumer democracy' seems a possible pragmatic response to the new world order that depends more upon international economic links than geopolitical alliances.

Miraculous? Perhaps, but miracles are needed to save the rainforest and the peoples of the rainforest – and many think even bigger miracles are needed to halt the destruction of the planet. In recent years an area of tropical rainforest the size of Belgium has been annually destroyed in the Brazilian Amazon alone. No one knows how many cultures have become extinct in the wake of this habitat destruction – and

---

* This extract is taken from Chapter 11 in *Science for the Earth: Can Science make the World a Better Place?* T. Wakeford and M. Walters (eds) (1995), 238–54. © John Wiley & Sons Ltd. Reproduced with permission.

even the most sophisticated scientific studies cannot measure knowledge loss due to cultural degradation.

For many years there have been warnings of the impending destruction of the Amazon and the implications of those losses for all of humanity. As Michael Irwin has pointed out for the Amazonian region:

> Scientists are competing with extinction in their race to inventory what the world contains. Amerindians are the only societies with the necessary knowledge, expertise, and tradition to prosper in the Amazon jungle. Amerindians not only profoundly appreciate what exists, but also understand ecological interrelations of the various components of the Amazonian ecosystem better than do modern ecologists. Indians perceive specific relationships which biologists are only now discovering to be accurate.

Traditional knowledge of medicinal plants, natural insecticides and repellents, fertility-regulating drugs, edible plants, animal behaviour, climatic and ecological seasonality, soils, forest and savanna management, skin and body treatments attest to but a few of the categories of knowledge that can contribute to new strategies for ecologically and socially sound sustained development. However, as work by Richard and Michael McNeil has pointed out (McNeil and McNeil 1989): 'knowledge has sometimes been extracted from rainforest people...in transactions which may be characterized as unjust and illegal. From both moral and legal standpoints we may have obligations to compensate people of these tribal societies for the immensely valuable intellectual property which we obtained from them'.

Yet native peoples and their knowledge systems are threatened with imminent destruction. Eighty-five Brazilian Indian groups became extinct in the first half of this century. In the Amazonian region a conservative estimate would be that, on average, one Amerindian group has disappeared for each year of this century. Unfortunately, we have no calculations showing the worldwide extent of cultural extinction.

In many cases, indigenous societies are becoming extinct at an even faster rate than the regions they have traditionally inhabited. Culture change is so rapid for many groups that young people no longer learn the methods by which their ancestors maintained fragile regions. This is a global tragedy, for with the disappearance of each indigenous group the world loses an accumulated wealth of millennia of human experience and adaptation. One should not be too hasty in the pronouncement that native peoples are all becoming extinct. Demographically, native groups, with guarantees of land rights as well as political and economic independence, have some of the fastest growing populations in the world.

Indigenous communities and the need for economic options

Indigenous leaders frequently voice concerns about the lack of economic options that allow them to avoid the ecologically destructive ways of the industrialized world. How can traditional knowledge be defended and valued within a native society when, in fact, such knowledge offers little economic benefit to indigenous groups caught in the maze of consumerism and basic survival?

Indigenous knowledge and its worth

Industry and business discovered many years ago that indigenous knowledge means money. In the earliest forms of colonialism extractive products (called 'drogas de sertão' in Brazil) were the basis for colonial wealth. More recently, pharmaceutical industries have become the major exploiters of traditional medicinal knowledge for major products and profits. Rarely do native peoples benefit from the marketing of traditional knowledge or natural products that were 'discovered' from native peoples.

Perhaps what is needed is a re-ordering of priorities and values: a new code of ethno-ethics. The code would not depend upon any international laws or conventions, it would not be legislated in congresses or parliaments, nor would it be dependent upon enforcement of copyrights or patents.

It would depend upon scientists who explained to the natives they study what they are doing and why it is important for the people themselves. Researchers should voluntarily sign contracts with native groups guaranteeing a percentage of any profits from medicines, films, new plant varieties, books, or whatever. (See Appendix 2 'The Declaration of Belém'). Businesses should guarantee excellent prices for natural materials, help local peoples add value to those materials and profit from their activities, and help them market the products and return a percentage of the profits to the community. Film and television crews should pay generous prices for filming native peoples and return some of the profits.

But as I realize that, even if this new eco-ethno-ethic were to come to pass, the exceptions would require the rules, and then it is important that our ideals be rooted firmly in international laws that jurisdically protect the Intellectual Property Rights (IPR) of native peoples.

Consumer education, aided by surveillance by NGOs, can go a long way to make a new code of ethics work. Informed consumers have made major differences in production patterns in the past, and can do so in the future. Maybe it is time for an international 'consumer democracy' that empowers each consumer to act in a responsible way that directly affects the planet's human and natural resources.

Planetary resources are already stretched due to current levels of consumption: imagine what will happen with all the new demands. In the euphoria of what it has labelled 'victory', Western capitalism will now be put to the ecological and social test. For 'consumer democracy' to work, alternative products must be developed and the consumers educated to the social and ecological benefits of what may be more costly products.

Nonetheless, many will oppose IPR for indigenous peoples because they know that they too will have to drastically change their working lifestyles. Incomes from published dissertations and other books, slides, magazine articles, phonograph records, films and videos – all will have to include a percentage of the profits to the native subjects. It will probably become normal that such rights be negotiated with native peoples before undertaking initial fieldwork. This kind of behaviour has never been considered as part of the professional ethic of scientific research and business, but certainly must become so in the near future.

Linking biodiversity, intellectual property rights and markets

The links between biological and cultural diversity are inherent in the Biodiversity Convention which was signed by 126 Heads of State during The Earth Summit in June 1992. Specifically with regard to indigenous peoples and their rights, the Preamble establishes the 'desirability of sharing equitably benefits arising from the use of traditional knowledge, innovations and practices relevant to the conservation of biological diversity and the sustainable use of its components' (See Appendix 3). Article 8(j) calls for the promotion of a wider sharing of traditional knowledge, as well as an 'equitable sharing of the benefits arising from the utilization of such knowledge, innovations and practices'. And, in Article 18(4), a call to 'encourage and develop methods of co-operation for the development and use of technologies including indigenous and traditional technologies' can be found.

Although the language of these sections has been harshly criticized by indigenous peoples, the wording nonetheless represents a considerable advancement in international language. If nothing else, the Convention frees up – and gives a clear mandate to – the relevant UN agencies and programmes to do something about indigenous knowledge and its protection.

Chapter 26 of 'Agenda 21' deals specifically with indigenous peoples' traditional knowledge and sustainable development. This list of 'priorities for action' is more than adequate to direct major global resources into the use, application (and protection) of indigenous peoples, their cultures, physical and intellectual resources (see Posey 1996; Posey and Dutfield 1996). The importance of doing such is summarized in Principle 22 of the Rio Declaration:

> Indigenous people and their communities, and other local communities, have a vital role in environmental management and development because of their knowledge and traditional practices. States should recognize and duly support their identity, culture and interests and enable their effective participation in the achievement of sustainable development.

Some kinks in the model

Anthony Anderson (1990) has drawn attention to the relatively low productivity of some traditional models of economic exploitation, including, most specifically, the 'extractive reserves'. He shows how reliance on only Brazil nuts and rubber is not only economically impoverishing, but decreases biodiversity as well. 'Before we can work to improve extractive reserves', he argues, 'we need a critical vision of their limitations. While it is necessary to clear the air of some of the romantic myths associated with extraction, I would disagree with the contention that extractivists are marginal elements in the process of frontier expansion in Amazonia and that we should, therefore, concentrate our efforts in improving land-uses among the numerous colonists'. 'In a practical sense', says Anderson, 'the forces struggling against deforestation in Amazonia are vanishingly small, and it is imperative that allies and battleground be chosen carefully'.

John Browder is yet another persistent voice in pointing out the over-rated productivity of traditional Amazonian models of exploitation. He expounds the somewhat politically incorrect position that Chico Mendés and 'his rubber tappers', for example, were a political movement and not an environmental one. Quite to the contrary, says he, rubber tappers will deplete their resource base as any other group will when given the chance. He maintains that too many funds have gone to 'help one small segment of the rural poor hold onto their cultural heritage and economic way of life', while what is needed are 'solutions for millions of other poor inhabitants of tropical forests'. Thus too many resources have gone towards supporting the limited 'extractive reserve' model, while abandoning the landless peasants, small farmers and even big ranchers to find financially profitable uses for tropical forests.

Likewise, Kent Redford has warned that many 'traditional societies' heavily exploit the fauna of their reserves and provoke reduction, even local extinction of heavily hunted species. This process of 'defaunation' can also lead to 'ecological extinction', defined as 'the reduction of a species' abundance, so that, although it is still present in the community, it no longer interacts significantly with other species'. Indigenous peoples, says he, are not the 'ecological noble savages' we have made them out to be. The degree of ecosystem destruction on the global level may mean that, in some cases, the only way to conserve biodiversity is to abolish all types of human behaviour – from road-building and timber extraction to indigenous hunting and extractivism.

Provocation of cultural changes can be equally concerning. By establishing mechanisms for just compensation of native peoples, are we not also establishing mechanisms for the destruction of their societies through the subversion of materialism and consumerism?

Stephen Cory, Director General of Survival International, one of the major indigenous rights groups, is one of the most radical opponents to 'the harvest'. He points out that, historically, indigenous peoples and local communities have never fared well with the vastly more powerful outside economic system. He has even gone so far as to suggest that in the famous rape case of Kayapó chief Paiakan, it was the Kayapó's relationship with The Body Shop that was ultimately to blame for the chief's alleged disastrous behaviour.

The 'harvest ideology', charges Cory, 'reveals itself to be essentially an integrationist argument dressed in snazzy, green clothes; a retrograde philosophy which, if allowed to gain momentum, could set the campaign for tribal peoples back 25 years or more by playing right into the hands of those who want to *oppose* the movement for land rights'. He continues, 'If allowed to take hold, this new integrationist ethic masquerading as environmentalism will be deeply corrosive to the struggle which so many indigenous peoples' organizations are waging to teach the outside world that their land is not for sale and that they will not put a cash value on it any more than they would sell their own mother'.

In a recent attack on Cultural Survival and The Body Shop, Cory describes all trading with indigenous peoples as 'slow poison' and those involved in such activities as 'not rainforest traders, but rainforest raiders, squeezing what they can out of the public's goodwill and the latest forest fashion'.

Indigenous societies and their natural environments are being destroyed by the dramatic expansion of industrialized society *now*. Good or bad, pharmaceutical companies and 'natural products' companies have tasted success in their efforts: they will not go away. It is also fairly obvious that, like it or not, an ecosystem that has no value will be levelled to make way for whatever system has value – even if only on a limited scale and for only short-term profits in its place.

'Besides', says Jason Clay of Cultural Survival, 'Even the most isolated peoples in the rainforests, with few exceptions, have needs that only the market place can meet. We might leave such groups alone, but others won't. We could even think about building a fence around them, or around the whole Amazon, but these options aren't workable. And if the destruction of their land continues at its present pace, all will be over for them soon'.

'For this reason', Clay continues, 'we must act quickly. This is where the links between human-rights violations and poverty on the one hand and environmental degradation on the other enter in. It turns out that the most successful strategies for conserving rainforests maintain their natural biodiversity *and* meet the economic needs of the forest peoples...Cultural Survival hasn't abandoned its work on land rights, political organizing, and sustainable development; we have added a dimension to it. Simply put, we seek markets for sustainably harvested rainforest products that can help support those who live in the rain forest'.

The 'turf war' between the Body Shop, Cultural Survival and Survival International has received extensive press coverage. More than any other issue in recent memory, 'the harvest' has put researchers, biologists, human and indigenous rights groups, and average citizens in a state of perplexity. It is not a question of the 'good, the bad and the ugly' versus the 'right, the saintly, and the true heroes'. The real tragedy may be that the concern for the rainforest and its peoples gets harshly and unceremoniously divided between patron groups.

In my opinion, the current conflict will result in the ultimate move by indigenous peoples to divest themselves of all intermediaries, taking the opportunity to exert their independence and global consciousness that has been emerging for 30 years – and exploding in the last decade. Thus, in the long run, the whole ordeal will have a positive outcome.

The future

The current devastation of native peoples and the ecological systems that they have conserved, managed, and intimately known for millennia, requires that new and drastic steps be taken to reorient world priorities. All channels and organizations – governmental, nongovernmental, professional, business – must work together to reverse the current momentum in the loss of cultural, ecological, and biological diversity of this planet.

Three major changes that would at least be a move in the right direction are:

1   Recognition that native peoples hold the key to understanding the rational use and management of these living natural areas, and probably others;
2   Giving economic value to the *living* forest and natural habitats by giving increased value to natural products based on traditional knowledge and produced by local communities;
3   Developing legal and practical mechanisms for the just compensation of native peoples for their knowledge through the guarantees of IPR for traditional knowledge.

Chapter 14

Traditional Resource Rights (TRR)

De facto self-determination for indigenous peoples

Introduction

Intellectual Property Rights (IPR) is a rubric under which a great variety of concerns have accumulated. IPR developed as a Western concept that was essentially established to protect individual, technological, and industrial inventions. Until recently, it has been considered an unlikely tool to protect the collective, transhistorical and obliquely defined (legally speaking) qualities of indigenous cultures. As interest has grown, however, IPR has become increasingly difficult to define, but now generally means the intellectual, cultural and scientific knowledge, and resources of indigenous peoples. Many think that IPR is not an appropriate mechanism to strengthen and empower traditional and indigenous peoples. Yet, it is a subject that challenges dialogue across disciplines and cultures and, for that reason alone, merits considerable attention.

For indigenous peoples, IPR is an alien construct that roughly refers to 'culture'. The idea of dividing intellectual, cultural, and scientific property into three separate areas is in itself incomprehensible, since indigenous peoples see these as part of a whole. Furthermore, 'property' may have physical manifestations as well as spiritual manifestations when associated with sacred sites. Many aspects of indigenous culture are sacred or have sacred characteristics. Thus, the basic question is *not* how to use IPR instruments to protect traditional resources, but rather *if* such instruments are relevant and useful.

The classic instruments for IPR protection are patent, copyright, trade secret, know-how, appellation of origin, and licensing agreements. Contracts are probably the most accessible and easily instituted legal instruments and are internationally recognized. As executive director of the Global Coalition for Biological and Cultural Diversity, I have developed a 'Covenant on Intellectual, Cultural and Scientific Resource Rights' to guide contracting parties with essential principles for negotiating (see Appendix 5).

---

* van der Vlist, L. (ed.) (1994). *Voices of the Earth: Indigenous Peoples, New Partners and the Right to Self-determination.* Amsterdam: International Books/NCIP, 217–52.

Issues of protection, recognition and compensation for indigenous peoples' knowledge and resources are not just legal matters: they are profoundly ethical questions based on concepts of universal fairness and justice. In fact, avoiding legal instruments may be the best policy in the long run, since the legal system is stacked against indigenous peoples (access to legal instruments, legal fees, fairness in courts, etc.).

IPR cannot be allowed to become a question of how to fit traditional knowledge into Western legal and conceptual frameworks. Indigenous legal systems and concepts of property rights should guide the debate. The role of scientists, scholars and lawyers should be to provide information and ideas. To this end, I established and continue to co-ordinate an International Working Group on Traditional Intellectual, Cultural and Scientific Resource Rights.

It is indigenous peoples themselves, however, who will redefine IPR. This will undoubtedly occur through experimentation by indigenous communities and will be solved in different ways by many people like the Hawaiians, the Kuna, the Aborigines, the Maori, the Zuni, and the Hopi, who have been working on these issues for a long time. To them, and to me, IPR has no meaning whatsoever unless it is considered as one of the fundamental cornerstones of self-determination.

Control over cultural, scientific, and intellectual property is *de facto* self-determination, although only after rights to land and territory are secured by law and practice (i.e. boundaries are recognized, protected, and guaranteed by law). But, as many indigenous peoples have discovered, even guaranteed demarcation of land and territory does not necessarily mean guaranteed access to resources on that land or territory, nor even the right to exercise one's own culture, or be compensated for the biogenetic resources and local ecosystems that they have kept, conserved, managed, and moulded for thousands of years.

Commoditization, culture change, and indigenous concerns

I entered the IPR issue from a rather practical side, having worked many years with the indigenous peoples of the Amazon basin. Many of them have become very much involved in destroying their own resources: cutting their own forests and polluting their own waters through mining. They have allowed this to occur in part because they felt that they needed an outside income due to the unavailability of resources from the government for medicines or transportation to hospitals. Frequently they just want to buy things like tape recorders, radios, baby carriages, cooking pots, guns, sunglasses, or wristwatches.

Amazonian indigenous groups are frequently told by well-meaning outsiders (environmentalists, human rights groups and 'concerned' representatives from the industrialized world) that they should go back and live in the forest and be like their ancestors. The advice is frequently spurned because it is impractical – and usually impossible – to reverse the processes of history and culture change. But 'unapproved' changes that alter the outsiders' romantic view often mean the indigenous group is no longer exotic enough or 'pure' enough – they are not 'real indians' – to merit outside support. Not uncommonly, the indigenous heroes become the indian villains because they are cutting the forest or are becoming consumers. In effect, indigenous peoples are denied the right to change and adapt.

In the Amazon, like most of the tropics, there are few economic options other than timber extraction, mining, and ranching. Yet, the tropical forest is constantly touted as being one of the richest in biodiversity, with a huge potential for discoveries of new medicines, foods, dyes, fertilizers, essences, oils, and molecules of prime biotechnological use.

Consider at the same time three bits of reality. One is that many indigenous communities need and are looking for economic alternatives. The second is that an increasingly large number of companies are doing 'biodiversity prospecting', that is, looking for biogenetic resources (plants, animals, bacteria, etc.), including human genes, that can be used to develop the biotechnology industry. A third is that the Earth Summit (United Nations Conference on Environment and Development (UNCED)) held in Rio de Janeiro in June 1992, was to a large extent about how biological diversity conservation could be economically exploited through biotechnological development. The Earth Summit effectively called for an all-out assault on traditional knowledge and resources.

The 'biodiversity prospectors' and biotechnology developers are not noted for their ethics and concerns for indigenous peoples. They are noted for capitalizing on opportunity. So there are some urgent reasons why indigenous peoples are worried about the commoditization of their cultural, intellectual, and scientific property – not to mention their plants, animals, seeds and, if the biotechnologists get their way, even indian blood and cells.

I should make it clear that indigenous peoples are not just concerned about who pays and who profits from commercialization of their resources. Frequently they are more concerned about the misuse or misinterpretation of their knowledge, culture, and cultural expressions. For example, when I recently asked my Kayapó father, who is a shaman elder, about his concerns with the commercialization of Brazil nut oil by the village, I thought he would complain about the warriors getting too much money and the old people not getting enough, or something of this sort.

But his response surprised me: he was worried about the plants. He was concerned about what happens to the plant energies when the oil is purified and sent to distant places. When there are only a few plants used, he explained, then it does not matter. But now there are so many plants being used that it upsets the energy balance which is the basis for the health of the entire community. He wanted to know why the company had never consulted the plants before commercializing them. The shaman's concern reminds us that IPR is not just a Western legal concept – IPR and commercialization are very anthropocentric concepts. The assumption is that what is good for humans must be good for the planet, a view that is not universally held (including, no doubt, a considerable number from the plant and animal kingdoms).

Creating TRR

To protect indigenous knowledge, the existing legal concepts that circumscribe intellectual property rights can be accepted as they now exist, or the term can be purposefully moulded, expanded, and re-designed. The former is said by most IPR lawyers to be impossible, given the industrial property connotations, individual property bias, and inequality of access to legal structures faced by local communities. The latter, development of a Traditional Resource Rights legal system, seems to be the better option – albeit a very challenging and difficult one.

The term TRR has been introduced to reflect the necessity of reconceptualizing the limited and limiting concept of IPR, while emphasizing that a wide range of relevant international agreements exist to form the basis for a *sui generis* system of protection for traditional and indigenous peoples and their resources (see Appendix 6). There may be, in other words, much more to build upon in the international community than we have realized.

A number of overlapping areas of international law and practice can be identified to provide the synthesis for an ideological basis for a newly designed TRR.

IPR and the ILO

The International Labour Organization (ILO) was the first UN organization to deal with indigenous issues. A Committee of Experts on Native Labour was established in 1926 to develop international standards for the protection of Native workers. The ILO developed a special convention (107) known as the 'Convention Concerning the Protection and Integration of Indigenous and Other Tribal and Semi-Tribal Populations in Independent Countries' (5 June 1957). The Convention was revised in June 1989 as Convention 169, 'Convention Concerning Indigenous and Tribal Peoples in Independent Countries', and much of the 'integrationist language' of the original was removed.

Its seventh preambular paragraph refers to 'the distinctive contributions of indigenous and tribal peoples to the...ecological harmony of humankind'. Article 7 guarantees the right of indigenous peoples to decide their own development priorities and to control their own economic, social, and cultural development.

Article 13(1) states that governments 'shall respect the special importance for the cultures and spiritual values of the peoples concerned of their relationship with the lands or territories, or both as applicable, which they occupy or otherwise use, and in particular the collective aspects of this relationship'. The recognition of collective aspects is a critical aspect of the Convention and is important in intellectual property rights issues, since collectivity is fundamental to transmission, use, and protection of traditional knowledge.

ILO 169 has not been sufficiently utilized with implementation of IPR in mind. The Convention is not even in the Secretary General's Concise Report on IPR and indigenous peoples. Nonetheless, it uses widely agreed upon terminology that should be exploited in defining the new TRR concept.

Intellectual property and human rights

The 1948 Universal Declaration of Human Rights (UDHR) and subsequent International Covenant on Economic, Social and Cultural Rights (ICESCR UN) guarantee: fundamental freedoms of personal integrity and action; political rights; social and economic rights; and cultural rights. The principal problem with the 'human rights approach' to cultural protection is that action (or inaction) is directed toward nation-states and does not easily 'provide a basis for claims against multinational companies or individuals who profit from traditional knowledge'. (For a detailed discussion and relevant citations, see Shelton 1993.) Nonetheless, Article 1 (ICESCR) establishes the right of self-determination, including the right to dispose of natural wealth and resources. This also implies the right to protect and conserve resources, including intellectual property.

Article 7 (UDHR) allows for equal protection under the law, thereby implying that IPR protection should be available to indigenous peoples as well. Article 17 provides for the right to own collective property and not to be arbitrarily deprived of that property. Article 23 (UDHR) guarantees the right to just and favourable remuneration for work, which can be interpreted as work related to traditional knowledge.

Finally, Article 27 (UDHR) provides for the right to culture and recognition of interest in scientific production, including the right to the protection of the moral and material interests resulting from any scientific, literary, or artistic production.

This language is echoed in the Draft UN Declaration on the Rights of Indigenous Peoples (DDRIP), stating in para. 28 that indigenous peoples have the right to the protection and, where appropriate, the rehabilitation of the total environment and productive capacity of their lands and territories, and the right to adequate assistance including international cooperation to this end. It is clear that IPR should be seen as a basic human right and that human rights organizations should take up the cause as a major part of their activities.

ECOSOC and the Working Group on Indigenous Populations

In 1972, the United Nations Economic and Social Council (ECOSOC) authorized the Commission on Human Rights to form a special sub-commission to conduct a broad study of the problem of discrimination against indigenous peoples (Kahn and Talal 1987). After lengthy delay, a voluminous report found that present international instruments are not 'wholly adequate for the recognition and promotion of the specific rights of indigenous populations as such within the overall societies of the countries in which they now live' (UN Document No. E/CN.4/Sub.2/1986/7/Add.4. para. 625).

ECOSOC created in 1982 a Working Group on Indigenous Populations. Since that time, the Working Group has worked to prepare a Declaration on the Rights of Indigenous Peoples and has become the most open international forum for indigenous representatives and advocates of indigenous rights.

Resolution 1990/27 of the sub-commission recommended that any UNCED convention 'provide explicitly for the role of indigenous peoples as resource users and managers, and for the protection of indigenous peoples' right to control of their own traditional knowledge of ecosystems'. Resolution 1991/31 called for a study on the applicability of collective rights regarding property, including intellectual property.

In 1991, the Sub-Commission on Prevention of Discrimination and Protection of Minorities requested the Secretary General to prepare a concise report on the extent to which indigenous peoples can utilize existing international standards and mechanisms for the protection of their intellectual property, drawing attention to any gaps or obstacles and to possible measures for addressing them. The World Intellectual Property Organization (WIPO) was also specifically requested to help in 'formulating recommendations for the effective protection of the intellectual property of indigenous peoples' (UN Doc. E/C.4/Sub.2/1992/30). A detailed report, whose Special Rapporteur is Ms Erica-Irene Daes, Permanent Secretary of the Sub-Commission, is expected to be published soon.

In May 1992 in Santiago, Chile, the United Nations held a Technical Conference on Indigenous Peoples and the Environment. The Conference established some basic principles that include: 'recognition, protection and respect for indigenous knowledge and practices that are essential contributions to the sustainable management of the environment'. It was also recommended that the United Nations system take effective measures to protect the property rights, including intellectual property, of indigenous peoples to their cultural property, genetic resources, biotechnology and biodiversity (UN Doc. E/CN.4/Sub.2/1992/31).

In these declarations and recommendations, as in the Draft Declaration, there has been a clear call from the Human Rights Commission for protection of and just compensation for the intellectual property rights of indigenous and tribal peoples. Since this forum can activate other UN agencies, it may produce some of the most important results on the international level.

IPR, folklore, and plant variety protection

The United Nations Educational, Scientific and Cultural Organization (UNESCO) should be a logical forum for IPR discussion, but, although UNESCO has heard 'petitions' of complaints by native peoples related to the fields of education, science, culture and information, indigenous questions are still only marginal to its agenda.

The World Intellectual Property Organization (WIPO) in Geneva has 123 Member States that have already reached broad agreements on 'industrial property' and 'copyright'.[1] Folklore, however, represents traditions that transcend the lifespan of individuals and, therefore, are collective property and cannot be protected.

In 1984 WIPO, together with UNESCO, developed 'Model Provisions for National Laws on the Protection of Expressions of Folklore Against Illicit

Exploitation and Other Prejudicial Actions' (WIPO 1985).[2] Both individual and collective folklore traditions are recognized. The words 'expressions' and 'productions' are used instead of 'work' to emphasize that the provisions are *sui generis* and that copyright laws have not proven effective in the protection of folk traditions. Under the Model Provisions, folklore need not be 'reduced to material form' (i.e. written down) to be protected.[3]

Although the Model Provisions have never been adopted, there is renewed interest in the basic issues, especially in the recognition of collective and individual 'expressions' and 'productions' that remove folk expressions from the necessity of having the 'personality' of a creator/artist as required by copyright law. Establishment of the principle that unwritten or oral expressions can be protected and that fees for such expressions should be paid, with criminal penalties for those who disrespect the necessity of authorization, are critical elements. The most important contribution was the application of 'neighbouring rights' to protect native performers, allowing folkloric expressions to be considered the same as the 'performance of a work' and, therefore, protected under international copyright agreements as set out in the 1961 Rome Convention for the Protection of Performers.

For indigenous peoples, it is critical that plant (and animal) genetic resources also be seen as a unique part of their cultural heritage. This approximation is not unusual, inasmuch as plant genetic resource protection falls under WIPO's jurisdiction within the United Nations. The Union for the Protection of New Varieties of Plants (UPOV) is an independent, intergovernmental organization, but it is linked to WIPO, in that its secretariat is located in the same building as WIPO, and its Secretary General is also the Director General of WIPO. UPOV established a Convention in 1961 (amended in 1972 and 1978) for the protection of breeders of new plant varieties. Under the international Convention, natural or legal persons resident in member states can acquire protection for plant varieties they have developed that are 'clearly distinguishable', 'sufficiently homogeneous' and 'stable in essential characteristics' (WIPO 1989: 41).

The Convention calls for compensation of the breeder for use of the protected variety. No cases have appeared before UPOV in which native peoples are considered the breeders of distinctive varieties, although ethnobiologists, geneticists, and botanists can now clearly show that the origins of hundreds of domesticated varieties lie with indigenous selection for and improvement of genetic traits. Even 'wild' varieties may show extensive selection for millennia with resultant genetic improvements, although these varieties were never brought into a 'domesticated' status (Posey and Overal 1990).

The critical factor here is to link folklore and plant genetic resources with intellectual property. It is this complicated legal linkage that allows for the expansion of the concept of IPR to include traditional knowledge not only about species use, but also regarding species management. Thus, ecosystems that are 'moulded' or modified by human presence are a product of indigenous intellectual property as well, and, consequently, are products themselves – or offer products – that can be protected. Furthermore, 'wild' and 'semi-domesticated' (or 'semi-wild'), as well as domesticated plant and animal species, are products of human activity and should also be able to be protected.

FAO farmers' rights

The UN Food and Agriculture Organization (FAO) has tackled in a series of conferences the question of farmers' and breeders' rights. A major goal was to find ways that developing countries and 'Third World farmers' could get a share in the huge seed market. Basic food crops such as rice, maize, and wheat were originally acquired from native peoples, and genetic material from 'wild stock' is still essential to breed into existing varieties the resistance necessary to sustain economic production (Juma 1989; Kloppenburg 1988b; Kloppenburg and Kleinman 1987; Mooney 1983). Third World countries are in enviable positions, since they 'possess the greatest genetic wealth of edible plants at a time when plant genes are in greatest demand in the flourishing biotechnology industry' (Balick 1990; Hamburger *et al.* 1991; Hurtado 1989: 96; Reid *et al.* 1993; Scoones *et al.* 1992). Yet developing countries continue to be reluctant and too timid to press their demands for IPR protection of their genetic resources (Farrington 1989).

In 1987 FAO established a fund for plant genetic resources. The idea was to establish a fund to finance projects for sustainable use of plant genetic resources in the Third World with contributions linked to the volume of total seed sales. Unfortunately, contributions were voluntary and the fund wholly inadequate. Major seed producers, like the United States, have opposed mandatory contributions to the fund. The United States has, in fact, even refused to participate in FAO discussions on the matter. Instead, it has pushed for patent rights for all laboratory improved varieties. Opponents to the US position warn that, if the United States gets its way, 'the only forms of human innovation that will not be patentable will be those of informal innovators in the Third World' (Hurtado 1989: 96).

IPR and the environment: life after UNCED[4]

(a) *The Rio Declaration* clearly establishes the relevance of indigenous peoples and the central importance of their protection in order to attain sustainable development. Given the squeamishness of nation-states regarding indigenous peoples' rights in the past, the tone of the Rio Declaration is indeed progressive and welcome. Principle 22 states:

> Indigenous people and their communities, and other local communities, have a vital role in environmental management and development because of their knowledge and traditional practices. States should recognize and duly support their identity, culture and interests and enable their effective participation in the achievement of sustainable development.

(b) *The Convention on Biological Diversity (CBD)*: Article I of the Convention states:

> The objectives of this convention... are the conservation of biological diversity, the sustainable use of its components and the fair and equitable sharing of the benefits arising out of the utilization of genetic resources, including by appropriate access to genetic resources and appropriate transfer of relevant technologies, taking into account all rights over those resources and to technologies, and by appropriate funding.

The underlying logic behind these objectives is that biodiversity can only be conserved if it is sustainably utilized, particularly by the biotechnology industries, and the economic benefits of such utilization flow back to conservation activities, particularly in developing countries. States retain sovereign rights to their biological and cultural resources, and are responsible for ensuring that the benefits flowing from the utilization of biological resources reach their citizens.

Indigenous peoples, who have largely been marginalized by such processes in the past (if not totally eliminated), are understandably sceptical that this time things will be better. However, for the first time, at least indigenous and local communities embodying traditional lifestyles are expressly mentioned in the Convention, and their central contributions to biodiversity conservation are recognized (Appendix 3).

Yet, again, indigenous groups doubt that existing international and national laws will adequately recognize and protect their knowledge, innovations and practices. They are even more sceptical that 'trickle-down benefits' will occur, since historically they have rarely benefited from the goodwill of nation-states.

(c) *Agenda 21*: Chapter 26 of Agenda 21 deals specifically with indigenous peoples, traditional knowledge, and sustainable development. This list of 'priorities for action' is more than adequate to direct major global resources into the use, application – and protection – of indigenous peoples and their cultures and physical and intellectual resources.

The language of the Rio Declaration, CBD, and Agenda 21 is vague and will be moulded by future political and economic actions. Given that indigenous and traditional peoples are recognized as having special rights and benefits, and that economic livelihood is linked to development and conservation of natural resources, it is definitely worthwhile that energies and efforts be directed toward pushing the relevant sections in the direction of indigenous rights, including the recognition and protection of, as well as compensation for, intellectual property. GATT, FAO, and WIPO will all have to accommodate to this reality in future negotiations due to the large number of signatories to the Biodiversity Convention.

Religious freedom and IPR

In a seminar on IPR at the United Nations Human Rights Convention held in Vienna in June 1993, Ray Apoaka of the North American Indian Congress suggested that

IPR is essentially a question of religious freedom for indigenous peoples. 'Much of what they want to commercialize is sacred to us. We see intellectual property as part of our culture – it cannot be separated into categories as [Western] lawyers would want.' Pauline Tangipoa, a Maori leader, agrees: 'Indigenous peoples do not limit their religions to buildings, but rather see the sacred in all life.'

The Human Genome Project is an example of the dangers indigenous peoples see in the unbridled research and commercialization of genetic resources. In a brochure distributed by the World Council of Indigenous Peoples, a frantic alarm is raised over the genetic 'research' that is taking place on indigenous peoples in the name of global health (WCIP 1993). They are concerned that such research will not only not be used to benefit them, but even be utilized to destroy or weaken them. Minimally, they are concerned that someone else is going to commercially benefit (and in a big way) from their genetic material – and they have not even been consulted on the matter. Certainly no sharing of profits is mentioned, even in the fine print.

The Human Genome Project clearly infringes not only upon the human rights of indigenous groups, but upon their religious freedom. For many of the groups 'chosen' to provide samples of their hair, skin, blood, and other body materials for laboratory examination, the taking of such material is against their religious beliefs.

Indigenous perspectives and non-Western models of IPR

As previously stated, the concept of intellectual property rights is foreign to indigenous peoples. Until very recently, the subject was not on the agenda of indigenous groups. Within the past two years, however, that has changed. For example, in Article 44 of the Charter of the Indigenous-Tribal Peoples of the Tropical Forests (IAI-TPTF 1992) IPR concerns are explicitly stated:

> Since we highly value our traditional knowledge and believe that our biotechnologies can make an important contribution to humanity, including 'developed' countries, we demand guaranteed rights to our intellectual property, and control over the development and manipulation of this knowledge.

In the current Draft of the Declaration on the Rights of Indigenous Peoples, such concerns are also clearly stated in paragraph 19 (see E/CN.4 /Sub.2/1992/28):

> Indigenous peoples have the right to special measures for protection, as intellectual property, of their traditional cultural manifestations, such as literature, designs, visual and performing arts, medicines and knowledge of the useful properties of fauna and flora.

During informal hearings held during the III Prep Com for the United Nations Conference on Environment and Development (UNCED),[5] indigenous representatives discussed their concerns and scepticism regarding the use of IPR regimes to protect their cultural heritage. Several problems were specifically pointed out: (i) the categories between cultural, intellectual, and physical property are not as distinct and mutually exclusive for indigenous peoples as in the Western legal system. 'Sacred sites', for example, are frequently types of ecological reserves that are the result of human knowledge in management and conservation, as well as cultural centres that have both physical and spiritual significance; (ii) knowledge is generally communally held, and, although some specialized knowledge may be held by certain ritual or society specialists (such as shamans), this does not give that specialist the right to privatize communal heritage; (iii) even if legal IPR regimes were to be implemented, most indigenous communities would not have the financial means to implement, enforce, or litigate. It was clear that under some circumstances commercialization of knowledge and plant genetic resources might be desirable, but the prime desire for indigenous peoples was an IPR regime that gave them the right to say no to privatization and commercialization.

One of the areas of IPR research that is most lacking is that of non-Western IPR regimes. Up until now the debate has centred around United Nations and Western concepts of intellectual and genetic property. There are, of course, ancient systems of property utilized by Muslim, Hindu, Chinese and many other civilizations. But what about the property regimes of indigenous peoples themselves? Cunningham (1993) mentions a few African examples, and numerous other examples are to be found in many places. A synthesis and analysis of non-Western systems would be very helpful in finding creative solutions to TRR protection.

Cultural property

In recent years, indigenous peoples have been increasingly successful in reclaiming the tangible aspects of their cultures, or 'cultural property', from museums and institutions (Messenger 1989). Although the term has no clearly defined meaning (O'Keefe 1993), it has come to refer to everything from objects of art to archaeological artefacts, traditional music and dance, and sacred sites. Crewdson (1984) has argued that there is ample justification for establishing a 'distinct legal code' for cultural property. Likewise, Rodata (1988) holds that cultural property already constitutes a 'new category of goods' and needs its own set of new rules.

'Cultural heritage' has appeared as a related 'legal instrument' to link knowledge and information to the cultural artefact. The concept assumes that the property to be protected is not just of historical significance, but is of central interest to living and future generations (O'Keefe *et al.* 1984). Cultural heritage also includes protection for human remains inasmuch as the ancestors are vitally important to modern society. To date, successful use of cultural heritage as a legal tool has been limited to Australia; however, it has recently provoked great interest in international debates.

Although indigenous peoples are interested in following the successes of both cultural heritage and cultural property battles, they have not abandoned the IPR option. During the 1993 United Nations Year for the World's Indigenous Peoples, IPR was on the agenda of nearly every major encounter. One of the most significant was the 'First International Conference on the Cultural and Intellectual Property Rights of Indigenous Peoples' convened by the nine Mataatua Tribes in Whakatane, Aotearoa/New Zealand. The resulting 'Mataatua Declaration on Cultural and Intellectual Property Rights of Indigenous Peoples' reflects the concerns of the 150 delegates from fourteen countries who were present.[6] The Declaration states that cultural and intellectual property are central to the right of self-determination and that, although the knowledge of indigenous peoples is of benefit to all humanity, the first beneficiaries of indigenous knowledge must be the direct indigenous descendants of such knowledge. In the Preamble the Declaration recognizes that 'Indigenous Peoples are capable of managing their traditional knowledge themselves, but are willing to offer it to all humanity provided their fundamental rights to define and control this knowledge are protected by the international community.'

It is in this spirit that fruitful discussion will proceed, and then, only if indigenous peoples themselves take the lead. It would appear from the Mataatua Declaration that indigenous peoples have indeed found that the concepts of intellectual and cultural property are of use to them in the strengthening and protection of their societies.

Conclusion

Traditional Resource Rights has become a very central issue to debates in many major fields of international politics and law, including human rights, labour law, environment and development, trade, religious freedom, and cultural property/cultural heritage. Problems central to the implementation of existing IPR tools (copyright, patent, trade secret, appellation of origin, trademark, etc.) include the collective nature of traditional knowledge and necessity to identify the initiator or inventor of certain knowledge and/or genetic resources. ILO 169 has established an international precedent for the recognition of 'collective' rights', as has the United Nations Commission on Human Rights and the CBD. 'Neighbouring rights', as first described in the WIPO Model Provisions on Folklore but subsequently recognized in a wide range of law relating to expressions of artists, serves as a major advance in the protection of traditional knowledge. Indigenous/traditional knowledge as 'science', however, has only been marginally conceived, but will hopefully be developed as a result of the Declaration of Rights of Indigenous Peoples and other developments called for by the Secretary General of the United Nations. Religious freedom guarantees have, to date, not been adequately utilized to defend TRR, while the provisions of the CBD (together with Agenda 21) are only now being analysed in order to develop effective strategies to empower local communities and indigenous peoples.

It seems that TRR is a major new opportunity for dialogue with indigenous and traditional peoples on their own terms. TRR avoids the stalemate currently seen between indigenous peoples and nation-states over self-determination, while providing a new mechanism for control, compensation, and protection of tangible and non-tangible resources, which is *de facto* self-determination.

Two major steps now need to be taken:

1   TRR debates need to be translated into practical tools for indigenous, traditional peoples, and local communities so they can begin to experiment with on-the-ground methods of dealing with the problem of IPR as they define it; and
2   Non-Western models of intellectual/cultural property need to be analysed to the end of redefining TRR as an entirely new concept. Both of these steps must be taken by indigenous peoples themselves. The role of scientist, scholar, and lawyer should be to provide information and ideas, not to undertake the redefining of TRR. That should occur as the result of practice and experimentation by local communities.

The following specific actions should also be taken:

1   Insist on policy statements and action directives by all relevant agencies and programmes of the United Nations (e.g. WIPO, UPOV, UNCTAD, UNEP, UNDP, Human Rights Center, ILO, GATT, etc.) on how indigenous peoples can acquire protection and compensation for their intellectual and cultural property (including biogenetic resources).
2   Seek national and European Community legislation to secure indigenous TRR rights and guidelines for just compensation.
3   Encourage funding agencies and development banks to support research into traditional knowledge, its practical applications and mechanisms for protection and just compensation.
4   Require that intellectual and cultural property rights protection and compensation be built into each and every project funded by national and international (such as the European Community) aid and assistance programmes, including multinational and multilateral banks (including the World Bank, etc.).
5   Establish a Centre for Traditional Resource Rights to develop educational materials on intellectual and cultural property rights and mechanisms for protection and compensation. This Centre should work to (a) advise indigenous and traditional communities; (b) monitor unethical activities by individuals and institutions who misuse intellectual and cultural property, and (c) establish a network to exchange information about successful and unsuccessful attempts by local communities to secure their rights.
6   Insist that businesses, professional societies, research institutions, and other relevant governmental and non-governmental agencies have Codes of Ethics that insure the intellectual and cultural property protection of indigenous and traditional peoples, as well as guidelines for their members/employees in how to deal practically with such matters.

Whatever TRR may come to mean, to be useful it must assist indigenous peoples by strengthening their expression and practice of self-determination. It must give them, first and foremost, the right to say no to commercialization, exploitation, misuse and abuse of their cultural and biogenetic resources. If they chose to commercialize, donate or provide information, then TRR should protect their interests and provide them with guidelines for compensation and due recourse against those who still do not understand that the future of the planet depends upon the survival of its cultural and biological diversity, and especially of its indigenous peoples.

Chapter 15

Finders keepers won't do any more

Darrell Posey says the time has come for a rethink on bioprospecting*

The indigenous peoples of the world may soon turn away researchers who come to study how they use local plants and animals, or search for rare species on their lands. Their decision to impose a ban on such work follows many years of frustration in their struggle to establish the right to remain in their homelands and gain some compensation for exploitation of their traditional knowledge by others.

The origin of the dispute lies in the growing interest of industrial nations in traditional techniques as a source of new drugs, insecticides, dyes, oils, and foods. But in many countries with indigenous peoples, especially in Africa and Latin America, governments have done little to protect the communities that are stewards of these resources. The governments often allege, sometimes with justification, that they have neither the technical capacity nor the finances to develop these resources. Sometimes, nations only use such excuses to expropriate indigenous lands and resources.

Indigenous peoples now articulate their anger. And against the odds, many have become effective spokespersons decrying the loss of community control over resources, the increased privatization of common resources, and erosion of biological and cultural diversity. Thanks to their campaigning, there has been considerable international recognition of their plight. For example, the Convention on Biological Diversity (CBD) recognizes that effective *in situ* conservation means strengthening and protecting 'indigenous and local communities embodying traditional lifestyles'. This implies that the governments of countries which have done so much to annihilate their 'primitives' and to destroy so-called 'undeveloped' forests and ecosystems, will have to reverse such policies.

The CBD raises questions of access to biogenetic resources and traditional technologies, and the sharing of any benefits that accrue from their commercial use. Traditional technologies are now taken to include know-how (and some say 'do-how') of indigenous medicines, forest management, agriculture, watershed control, animal behaviour, soil fertility maintenance, ecological relationships, and even knowledge of celestial movements.

* Forum, *New Scientist*, 13 July 1996. No. 2038: 48.

Unfortunately, laws on intellectual property rights (IPRs), such as patents, copyright, and trade secrets, are inadequate to protect what the CBD calls the 'knowledge, innovations and practices' of indigenous peoples – because of the lack of identifiable 'inventors', and because they can't afford the services of patent lawyers.

It seems unlikely that existing Western legal structures can ever be adapted to protect indigenous and local communities. Such traditional knowledge usually belongs to all, may not be ownable by any living person, or may even be the domain of ancestral spirits that speak for past and future generations. Under present law, once an indigenous community 'shares' its knowledge or gives a valuable seed or medicine to a scientist, it effectively loses control of that resource forever.

After more than a decade of meetings in the United Nations, the indigenous peoples have now developed a Draft Declaration on the Rights of Indigenous Peoples. Their first demand is that the 's' be kept on 'peoples'. This little letter implies that groups have rights to self-determination, that is, they want the right to deny access to anyone not respecting their languages, cultures, and values.

Nation-states are vehemently opposed to such self-determination and insist on the words 'indigenous populations' – implying that they have no collective or sovereign rights whatsoever. So although the Draft Declaration is now with the UN Commission on Human Rights and on its way to the General Assembly, it has little chance of passage. It is this sad state of affairs that has driven the indigenous peoples to deploy their most powerful weapon so far – the threatened moratorium on all research, collecting, and bioprospecting on their lands and territories until adequate recognition and protection are provided.

Perhaps this is not before time. Shouldn't scientific societies and research institutions be more proactive on behalf of indigenous rights? If they are not, they are likely to find field work far more difficult, more complicated, or impossible.

In fact, these organizations are well-placed to address some of the problems facing the indigenous peoples. For instance, increased recognition of indigenous peoples and their knowledge requires the development of alternative concepts of property, ownership, and value. A recent workshop at the Green College Centre for Environmental Policy and Understanding, University of Oxford, proposed that IPRs be replaced by a system, driven by human rights, that serves to catalyse the needed dialogue between science, industry, and indigenous and local communities (see Chapter 16).

To implement this proposal, work is under way at the Programme for Traditional Resource Rights – an affiliate of the Oxford Centre for the Environment, Ethics and Society – to develop a system of Traditional Resource Rights. The programme, conducted in conjunction with the International Society for Ethnobiology and indigenous lawyers, is developing a model constitution and code of conduct. Governments are also being asked to 'harmonize' their environment, development, and trade laws with internationally agreed human rights principles.

Museums, research institutions and universities are in an excellent position to assist. Sizeable scientific collections and databases, strong interdisciplinary expertise, and cross-cultural experience provide them with the resources necessary to spearhead the dialogue. Given that one of the time-honoured principles of these institutions – free exchange of information – is in jeopardy, this opportunity should be seized.

Chapter 16

Indigenous peoples and Traditional Resource Rights

A basis for equitable relationships?*

Executive summary

Indigenous peoples have increasingly become the focus of international interest in debates on human rights, biodiversity conservation, environment, and development. The United Nations has emerged as a primary forum for the discussion of their problems through its Economic and Social Council's (ECOSOC) Working Group on Indigenous Populations, the Year and Decade of Indigenous People, the proposed Permanent Forum for Indigenous People, and the Commission on Sustainable Development. It is through the Earth Summit agreements – the Earth Charter, the Convention on Biological Diversity (CBD), Agenda 21, and the Commission on Sustainable Development – that traditional and indigenous peoples' issues have received the greatest global attention.

Access to, protection of, and benefit sharing from wider use and application of traditional technologies and genetic resources are essential elements of the CBD. So far it has been thought that the extension of Intellectual Property Rights (IPRs) would be the mechanism by which these issues could be resolved. Many also have seen IPRs as a means to facilitate exploitation of genetic resources for biotechnology. Better use of traditional knowledge could significantly reduce the research and development costs of new products. This is used as an additional argument to justify and attract funds for *in situ* conservation of biodiversity.

These views are not shared by traditional and indigenous peoples, nor by many environmental and human rights groups. For them IPRs represent a serious threat to local economies, cultures, and biodiversity. Many indigenous groups have become well-informed, articulate and effective in representing concerns around the world about the loss of local autonomy; loss of biological and cultural diversity; and the increasing tendency for common property resources (resources held in common for the good of all) to be seen and treated as commodities. Such thinking coincides with wider recognition of the limitations of 'top-down' development; better

---

* Proceedings of a Workshop held at the Green College Centre for Environmental Policy and Understanding, 28 June 1995, Green College, Oxford, UK.

appreciation of traditional systems which use resources sustainably and maintain the diversity and health of ecosystems; and deeper understanding of the potential value of traditional knowledge and genetic resources.

Another source of criticism of IPRs is that they can threaten the free exchange of information and resources that has benefited humanity through research, scholarship, and development of medicines, agriculture, forests, and bioresources generally. Yet the present free-for-all is also unsatisfactory, and grossly inequitable for indigenous peoples. Few companies which exploit their bioresources accept pre-contract and post-profit responsibilities to local communities. In many cases even the most ethically minded companies find it hard to identify legally constituted entities, *bona fide* community representatives, and the form and distribution of benefits.

Another problem arises from the use of public funds to collect plant, animal, and cultural materials for scientific purposes. Research, even in universities and museums, is increasingly funded by commercial interests, leaving unresolved the disconcerting question of who controls the resulting data. Purely scientific data banks have become the mines for 'biodiversity prospecting', that is, searching for species whose genes can provide the raw materials for biotechnology. Publishing of information, traditionally the hallmark of academic success, has become a means for conveying restricted (or even sacred) information into the unprotectable public domain.

Governments are eager to exert control over traditional resources, but often do not have the means to exercise the responsibility that this demands. Even the valuation of indigenous technologies makes assumptions about a 'need for development' which has been historically used to marginalize and exploit indigenous communities and their resources. The likelihood that benefits will ever trickle down to local communities is remote.

International law hardly exists in this area. It seems unlikely that existing legal structures built on or around IPRs could be adapted to enhance the conservation of biological diversity or to empower indigenous, traditional, and local communities. A more promising approach would be to combine systems from a wide range of international agreements to identify 'bundles of rights', which could be brought together to establish Traditional Resource Rights (TRRs) within a new system of national and international law. This will require a process of dialogue between indigenous, local communities and governmental and non-governmental institutions on an agenda which includes local economic interests, accountability, human rights, and environmental concerns for long-term sustainability.

It should also recognize that old notions of sovereignty are being eroded as authority disperses upwards to international institutions to cope with global problems, downwards to local organizations, and sideways in direct communication between individuals anywhere in the world. The result should lead to new attitudes towards indigenous peoples and their knowledge, new codes of ethics and standards of conduct, socially and ecologically responsible business practices, and new concepts of property, ownership, and value.

Museums, research institutes, and universities are in an excellent position to push forward the debate on IPRs, TRRs, and the creation of new and more equitable systems. They should seize the opportunity with urgency and vigour (see Table 16.1).

Table 16.1 Findings and Recommendations from the Workshop held at Green College, Oxford, 28 June 1995.

Finding	Recommendations
Finding 1 Indigenous rights are based on concepts of self-determination as defined in relevant declarations. These should guide science, research, and development policy as well as efforts to protect traditional resources and intellectual property rights (IPRs). They include: • territorial and resource rights; • respect for cultural differences and Indigenous Peoples' own institutions and efforts; • prior informed consent; • veto power over research and development projects.	That governmental and non-governmental institutions: • follow principles already established in indigenous rights documents; • support, disseminate, and integrate these principles into policy guidelines and operations.
Finding 2 Traditional and Indigenous Peoples: • well express concerns around the world about loss of local autonomy and control, erosion of common resources, and destruction of biological and cultural diversity; • have inadequate opportunities for dialogue with institutional representatives; • are under-represented at all levels of governmental and non-governmental decision-making.	That scientists, government and non-government representatives; UN agencies; government departments; scientific and professional institutions: • recognize and value indigenous knowledge as a basis for new models of development and environmental conservation; • establish means to facilitate dialogue and form alliances with indigenous leaders; • strengthen and support local institutions; • involve Indigenous Peoples in planning and executing projects and policies affecting them and the environments in which they live, and let their knowledge guide all levels of decision-making; • ensure transparency in all negotiations of research, results, data management, and benefit-sharing; • establish centres and programmes to guide and facilitate this process.
Finding 3 Modifications of existing practice are necessary to meet the concerns of Indigenous Peoples.	• Ensure *in situ* programmes strengthen local livelihoods; • make community-controlled research[a] standard practice; • give local communities prior informed consent and right of veto regarding projects taking place on their lands or territories or that affect them;

Table 16.1 continued

Table 16.1 Continued.

Finding	Recommendations
	• that determination of the *common good* should reflect indigenous and traditional values.
Finding 4 Research and scientific research organizations do not have adequate operational guidelines to reflect the principles of the Convention on Biological Diversity and indigenous rights.	Form a consortium of institutions to: • establish codes and standards for conduct and policies to reflect indigenous rights and the Convention on Biological Diversity; • identify gaps between policies and practices, and correct these deficiencies; • ensure that scientists, government officials, and non-government representatives are properly informed of indigenous rights and views.
Finding 5 Existing IPR instruments are inadequate and new mechanisms must be developed.	• To pursue the 'bundles of rights' approach, to develop Traditional Resource Rights and to look into other legal systems; • to investigate other ways of protecting intellectual, cultural, and scientific resources, including customary practice; • to observe a moratorium on 'biodiversity prospecting' unless and until adequate and effective mechanisms for protection and compensation have been established.
Finding 6 Institutions may not be able to ensure rights are respected in the countries where Indigenous Peoples reside, but guidelines for institutions can define partners and funding priorities that will affect recognition of indigenous rights.	That as criteria for collaboration: • indigenous rights, including intellectual property rights are recognized; • indigenous rights are guaranteed in countries of activity; • mechanisms are provided to ensure community decision-making, Traditional Resource Rights protection, and benefit-sharing.
Finding 7 Concerns about biosafety are intricately related with concerns about IPRs and TRRs, as release of genetically modified organisms can affect the well-being and livelihoods of local communities.	• To include local communities in the monitoring and evaluation of genetically modified organisms; • for institutions to exercise the 'precautionary principle' in releasing modified organisms into the environment; • to look into the concept of 'Life Patent-free Zones' for indigenous lands.

Note

a Research in which communities control research priorities based on their own criteria. These include self-demarcation, inventories of traditional resources, environmental/social impact assessments, and resource management plans.

Indigenous peoples in international fora

Indigenous peoples and the right to self-determination

Although defining 'indigenous' has proven problematic for international organizations (Clay 1991), indigenous peoples themselves offer several definitions. For example, the World Council of Indigenous Peoples provides the following definition:

> Indigenous peoples are such population groups who from ancient times have inhabited the lands where we live, who are aware of having a character of our own, with social traditions and means of expression that are linked to the country inherited from our ancestors, with a language of our own, and having certain essential and unique characteristics which confer upon us the strong conviction of belonging to a people, who have an identity in ourselves and should be thus regarded by others.

A definition of indigenous peoples which has gained broad international acceptance is that of the 1989 International Labour Organization Indigenous and Tribal Peoples Convention (ILO 169), which is the only international legal agreement specifically on indigenous peoples. It states that people are considered indigenous if they are:

(a) Tribal peoples in countries whose social, cultural and economic conditions distinguish them from other sections of the national community, and whose status is regulated wholly or partially by their own customs or traditions or by special laws or regulations.
(b) Peoples in countries who are regarded by themselves or others as indigenous on account of their descent from the populations which inhabited the country, or a geographical region to which the country belongs, at the time of conquest or colonization or the establishment of present state boundaries and who, irrespective of their legal status, retain, or wish to retain, some or all of their own social, economic, spiritual, cultural and political characteristics, and institutions.

In addition, the Convention establishes another important principle:

> Self-identification as indigenous or tribal shall be regarded as a fundamental criterion for determining the groups to which the provisions of this convention apply.

The 's' on indigenous peoples is very significant, because it implies collective rights as ethnic nations. These rights are subsumed under the *right to self-determination*, that includes rights to land, territory, and resources. Most nation-states have resisted recognition of self-determination, and subsequently, the term 'peoples' (Clay 1991; Colchester 1994b; Kingsbury 1992a,b, 1994). Official UN documents use 'people', or even the weaker term 'populations' that implies lack of collective rights altogether.

Indigenous peoples interpret the right to self-determination to include rights to tangible and intangible cultural, scientific, and intellectual resources. The 1994 Statement from the International Consultation on Intellectual Property Rights and Biodiversity, organized by the Coordinating Body of Indigenous Peoples of the Amazon Basin (COICA) states:

> All aspects of the issue of intellectual property (determination of access to natural resources, control of the knowledge or cultural heritage of peoples, control of the use of their resources and regulation of the terms of exploitation) are aspects of self-determination. For indigenous peoples, accordingly, the ultimate decision on this issue is dependent on self-determination.

The UN Conference on Environment and Development (The Earth Summit)

The UN Conference on Environment and Development (UNCED) produced a number of international agreements that highlight the importance of indigenous peoples and their role in the conservation and sustainable use of the components of biological diversity (Gray 1990; Mead 1994b).

In Article 18.4 of the CBD, knowledge, innovations, and practices of indigenous and local communities specified in the Preamble and Article 8.j (see Appendix 3) are referred to as 'traditional and indigenous technologies'. This is a curious usage of the term because as such they are presumably subject to relevant agreements on transfer, access, and IPR protection. On the one hand, recognition of traditional knowledge as technology elevates indigenous knowledge to an internationally recognized category; on the other hand, indigenous technologies are subsumed under laws of nation-state sovereignty.

Agenda 21 devotes an entire Chapter (26) to 'Recognizing and Strengthening the Role of Indigenous People and their Communities'. Item 26.4b proposes that governments should:

> adopt or strengthen appropriate policies and/or legal instruments that will protect indigenous intellectual and cultural property and the right to preserve customary administrative systems and practices.

Indigenous peoples are actively involved in discussions at The Commission on Sustainable Development (CSD), which was set up to monitor and co-ordinate the CBD and other environmental conventions and agreements. Currently the CSD is evaluating Agenda 21, including Chapter 26. Issues of access and benefit-sharing, focussing upon IPRs, are becoming high-profile.

The CBD provides for two quite distinct approaches to indigenous peoples: (i) *in situ* conservation utilizing knowledge, innovation, and practices of local communities embodying traditional lifestyles, and (ii) wider use and application of indigenous technologies. The latter amounts to a global call to extricate aspects of knowledge from its systems context without providing appropriate mechanisms for protection and equitable benefit-sharing. It should not be of any surprise, therefore, that indigenous peoples are suspicious of the CBD and its expansion of nation-state sovereignty over their knowledge and biogenetic resources.

Biotechnology and 'biodiversity prospecting'

Biodiversity prospecting is the exploration of biodiversity for commercially valuable genetic and biochemical resources, with particular reference to the pharmaceutical, biotechnological, and agricultural industries (Reid *et al.* 1993). Recent advances in biotechnology have increased the ability of scientists to investigate organisms at the genetic level and to find ways to commercialize products developed from such investigations. Expectation of profits from these new products has stimulated biodiversity prospecting that, according to some, will in turn stimulate conservation through the profit motive (Joyce 1994).

It is difficult to estimate the commercial promise of biodiversity prospecting. Table 16.2 shows the quantity and value of natural products that biodiversity-rich countries have provided over the centuries. Given that to date only a small proportion of biodiversity has been exploited, economic potential is thought to be enormous.

For medicines alone, 1985 market value of plant-based medicines sold in developed countries was estimated at a total of $43 billion (Principe 1989). This frequently cited estimate is unreliable, although, whatever the true amount might be, only a minuscule proportion of profits have been returned to indigenous peoples from whom much of the original knowledge came – I have estimated less than 0.001 per cent (Posey 1990b).

Companies that produce seeds and agrochemicals benefit substantially from the free flow of germplasm from indigenous lands. The market value of the seed germplasm utilizing traditional landraces is estimated by RAFI at $50 billion per year in the United States alone (RAFI 1994c: 19). Consequently, indigenous peoples are providing subsidies to a modern agricultural system that barely recognizes their contributions. Similar situations exist with timber and non-timber forest products (Burley 1987, 1994), as well as other natural product markets, such as personal care, foods, industrial oils, essences, pesticides, and preservatives.

Biodiversity prospectors assume that organisms and ecosystems are 'wild' and, therefore, part of 'the common heritage of humankind'. Even when 'leads', or even processed materials, are provided by indigenous peoples, it is the company that makes the protectable 'discovery'. Indigenous peoples see this situation as being parallel to the Europeans' 'discovery' of the New World and are understandably weary of biodiversity prospecting.

In Costa Rica, for example, InBio, an NGO closely linked with the government, was given rights to commercialize biogenetic resources to Merck

Table 16.2 The past and present contribution of biodiversity-rich countries to humanity.

Pharmacy	Industry	Agriculture and food
• Anti-cancer drugs: *the vinca alkaloids*	• Wild relatives of plantation and other species for 'improvement'/protection	• Wild relatives of crops for 'improvement'/protection
• Tranquilizers and heart drugs: *reserpine*	• Exudates: *dyes, insecticides (neem, pyrethrins, rotenone), latexes, resins, tannins, waxes*	• Beverages, sugar, natural sweeteners: *cocoa, coffee, sugar cane, thaumatin*
• Birth control: *Dioscorea (source of many steroidal drugs)*	• Fibres and canes: *bamboos, jute, kapok, rattan, sisal*	• Beans
• Anaesthetics and surgical aids: *cocaine, gum gutta percha, madecassol, picrotoxin, d-tubocurarine, teterodxin*	• Edible and industrial oils: *castor oil, palm oils*	• Roots and tubers: *cassava, sweet potato, yam*
• Ophthalmology and neurology: *atropine, hyoscine, physostigmine, pilocarpine*	• Essential oils: *anise, camphor, cassia, cinnamon, clove, nutmeg, patchouli, sandalwood, sassafras, vanilla, ylang ylang*	• Fruits
• Respiratory disorders: *benzoin tincture, camphor, catechin, emetine, l-dopa, sarsapogenine, tolu balsam*	• Energy plants/biomass conversion: *biomethanation, fermentation to produce ethanol, pyrolysis*	• Vegetables: *aubergine, avocado, breadfruit, cucumber, okra, sweet pepper, pepper, tomato*
		• Spices: *allspice, black pepper, cardamon, cinnamon, cloves, nutmeg, vanilla*
		• Nuts: *brazil, cashew, kola, sesame, macadamia, peanut*
		• Animals: *chickens, water buffalo, wild pigs*

Source: Dutfield 1993 (based on information in Friends of the Earth 1992).

Pharmaceuticals. The agreement included collections on national lands, including those of eight groups of indigenous peoples, none of whom were ever consulted nor named as beneficiaries.

Indigenous peoples are particularly disturbed about the 'discoveries' made from blood samples (Mead 1994a). Under the guise of 'good science', the Human Genome Organization (HUGO) and one of its subsidiary projects (the Human Genome Diversity Project), co-ordinate the collection of blood samples from isolated communities 'threatened with extinction'. The results will supposedly reveal evolutionary links and identify genetic sequences for gene therapy to improve human health (Gannon *et al.* 1995).

The 'Human Vampire Project', as it is known by indigenous peoples, has brought much discredit to scientific research because, once collected, data and cells are available for commercial exploitation. Collections are also made without the prior informed consent of the sample groups.

At least three patent applications have been made for cell lines developed from blood 'donated' by indigenous peoples, including one from a member of a recently contacted group of 260 hunter-cultivators in New Guinea. The co-patent holders are the US Department of Commerce, the US government scientists involved in the project, and the anthropologist who introduced the research team to the tribe. New Guinea has shown no concern over this situation. Indeed, most nation-states show little concern over exportation of traditional genetic resources or knowledge. This may be because the image of indigenous peoples as primitive and savage has been essential for the historic takeover of their lands and resources. Thus, by recognizing the value of traditional resources, the philosophical underpinnings of colonization/ domination are challenged. Predictably this process is slow and meets opposition at all levels of society and government.

Intellectual property rights and ownership of knowledge

Intellectual property rights as legal instruments

Patents are perhaps the best known legal instruments, and discussions of intellectual, cultural, and scientific property usually degenerate into the legal quagmire of patentability (Appendix 7 provides a profile of major IPR instruments). Patents are of very limited interest to most indigenous peoples because of difficulties in documenting 'inventions' and identifying individual inventors. Since indigenous knowledge is considered in the public domain, then 'uniqueness' is also problematic.

Even if technical requirements for patents were satisfied, costs of filing, maintaining, monitoring, legal implementation and enforcement would be prohibitively expensive for most indigenous groups (Colchester 1994b). The same can be said for Plant Breeders' Rights (PBRs), whose requirements for varietal protection can in principle be met by indigenous farmers, but only after considerable laboratory and research investments have been made.

Know-how and trade secrets have potentially greater applicability, but also entail specialized legal advice and corresponding expenses. Appellation of origin and trademarks are relatively accessible IPR tools and can be effectively applied to products coming from indigenous lands or produced under indigenous auspices or licensing agreements.

Copyright is easily obtained and is helpful in the protection of written texts or works of art. Enforcement and monitoring of copyright can be difficult, time-consuming and costly. Scientists regularly depend upon copyright protection for protection of their own works and are increasingly extending that protection through co-publishing with indigenous collaborators.

Copyright-like mechanisms are being attempted in some countries with Community Inventories of useful plant varieties and species. Inventories may be kept by the community under strict rules of access, or published to put registered materials into the public domain in hopes of impeding patent applications by others. This strategy is a form of 'defensive publication', which argues that information in the public domain should not be protectable by IPRs. This is a dangerous tack since most patents are on processes of extraction, purification, or synthesis, not on the original product or compound itself. Publication itself may actually facilitate commercial exploitation of knowledge and resources, given the inequity of IPR application.

Such a case came from the description of 'tiki uba', an anti-coagulant used by the Amazonian Urueu-Wau-Wau tribe, published in an article in a well-known magazine (McIntyre 1989: 807). Based on the published information, Merck Pharmaceuticals found that the plant extract was useful in heart surgery and subsequently patented their 'discovery' (Jacobs *et al*. 1990: 31) without any consideration for the Urueu-Wau-Wau, who were by then threatened with extinction (Posey *et al*. 1995b).

Indigenous problems with IPR

IPRs are problematic for indigenous peoples for the following reasons:

1 They are intended to benefit society through the granting of exclusive rights to 'natural' and 'juridical' persons or 'creative individuals', not collective entities such as indigenous peoples (Boyle 1992, 1993, 1996). As the Bellagio Declaration puts it:

Contemporary intellectual property law is constructed around the notion of the author as an individual, solitary and original creator, and it is for this figure that its protections are reserved. Those who do not fit this model – custodians of tribal culture and medical knowledge, collectives practising traditional artistic and musical forms, or peasant cultivators of valuable seed varieties, for example, are denied intellectual property protection.

2   They cannot protect information that does not result from a specific historic act of 'discovery'. Indigenous knowledge is transgenerational and communally shared. Knowledge may come from ancestor spirits, vision quests, or orally transmitted lineage groups. It is considered to be in the 'public domain' and, therefore, unprotectable.
3   They cannot accommodate complex non-western systems of ownership, tenure, and access. IPR law assigns authorship of a song to a writer or publishing company that can record or publish as it sees fit. Indigenous singers, however, may attribute songs to the creator spirit and elders may reserve the right to limit its performance to certain occasions and to restricted audiences.
4   They serve to stimulate commercialization and distribution, whereas indigenous concerns may be primarily to prohibit commercialization and to restrict use and distribution. The 1994 COICA Statement expresses this clearly:

For members of indigenous peoples, knowledge and determination of the use of resources are collective and inter-generational. No indigenous population, whether of individuals or communities, nor the government, can sell or transfer ownership of resources which are the property of the people and which each generation has an obligation to safeguard for the next.

5   They recognize only market economic values, failing to consider spiritual, aesthetic, or cultural – or even local economic – values. Information or objects may have their greatest value to indigenous peoples because of their ties with cultural identity and symbolic unity.
6   They are subject to manipulation to economic interests that wield political power. *Sui generis* protection has been obtained for semi-conductor chips and 'literary works' generated by computers, whereas indigenous peoples have insufficient power to protect even their most sacred plants, places, or artefacts.
7   They are expensive, complicated, and time-consuming to obtain, and even more difficult to defend.

Intellectual property rights in the global economy

The Trade-Related Aspects of Intellectual Property Rights (TRIPs) section of the GATT Treaty is intended to harmonize national IPR regimes and create what Northern countries call a 'level playing field'. Assuming all nation-states comply fully with TRIPs, national regimes will be virtually identical to the current US system. Opponents feel that this will allow the United States, Europe, and Japan to dictate trading rules.

GATT, and the new World Trade Organization (WTO) that will implement it, have served to stimulate interest in IPRs. Article 27 'Patentable Subject Matter' provides for one interesting option, that of an 'effective' *sui generis* system for plant variety protection. The call for countries to define their own system of protection is an opportunity to introduce a community-based rather than individual-based system. It is unclear what 'effective' means, although some countries are making efforts to define their own alternative systems (e.g. Brazil, India, the Andean Pact).

Indigenous peoples are vociferous in their opposition to GATT/TRIPs with or without a *sui generis* option. They feel that the globalization of trade weakens even further their political and economic influence, while undermining traditional systems of biodiversity conservation (Gray 1990; Mead 1993).

Biopiracy

Northern governments and multinational corporations have been successful in pressuring the rest of the world to accept the argument that extended and strictly enforced IPR regimes are necessary and mutually beneficial. Sometimes by persuasion – and at other times by threats – Southern governments have acquiesced to this view. Piracy of books, designs, trademarks, recordings, and computer programs, as well as illicit sales of pharmaceuticals, have been major targets for attack.

Recently, the Rural Advancement Foundation International (RAFI) has shown how corporations themselves have pirated biogenetic resources and knowledge. Small farmers and indigenous peoples have begun to attack institutions and companies involved in this 'biopiracy'.

Use and abuse of IPRs show that:

(i) Although industries seek legal monopoly for their applications of traditional knowledge and resources, indigenous peoples cannot obtain the same protection.
(ii) Well-meaning scientists involved in non-commercial research become implicated when their data are published or collections made available for commercial interest.
(iii) Many biodiversity-rich countries lack the capacity to adequately exploit the commercial potential of their most valuable resources.
(iv) Even when governments or national scientists benefit from new product development, local communities rarely see even 'trickle down' benefits.
(v) 'Free access' has a negative effect on the environment as well, since local communities have no control over exploitation.

Indigenous views

In recent years indigenous peoples have become well organized, articulate, and politically astute. Their views are widely cited and have come to represent the concerns of local communities – indigenous and non-indigenous – around the world. Sometimes the term 'broader alliance' is used in reference to a political coalition with traditional farmers, foresters, gatherers, fisherfolk, and herders. Increasingly, however, the alliance is growing to include other citizens worried about biosafety, erosion of local institutions, loss of freedom, and environmental degradation.

Indigenous peoples feel that 'development' has been imposed upon them in ways that violate their rights and damage the environment. According to the (1992) *Indigenous Peoples' Earth Charter*: 'The concept of development has meant the destruction of our lands. We reject the current definition of development as being useful to our peoples' (see Appendix 10 for full text).

They also believe that they have an important role to play in conservation. According to the (1995) *Final Statement of the Regional Consultation on Indigenous Peoples' Knowledge and Intellectual Property Rights*, Suva, Fiji:

> [We] assert that *in situ* conservation by indigenous peoples is the best method to conserve and protect biological diversity and indigenous knowledge, and encourage its implementation by indigenous communities and all relevant bodies (2.2).

However, they demand that recognition of this role be used to support territorial and other rights. The *Charter of the Indigenous-Tribal Peoples of the Tropical Forests* (CITP) states that (IAI-TPTF 1992):

> The best guarantee of the conservation of biodiversity is that those who promote it should uphold our rights to the use, administration, management and control of our territories. We assert that guardianship of the different ecosystems should be entrusted to us, indigenous peoples, given that we have inhabited them for thousands of years and our very survival depends on them.

Indigenous societies honour the principle of free exchange and do not necessarily want to close themselves off from others. The CITP declares that:

> Indigenous peoples are willing to share our knowledge with humanity provided we determine when, where and how it is used. At present the international system does not recognize or respect our past, present and potential contributions.

The CITP condemns:

> Those who use our biological diversity for commercial and other purposes without our full knowledge and consent.

The *Mataatua Declaration on the Cultural and Intellectual Property Rights of Indigenous Peoples* (UN Economic and Social Council 1993) adds further restrictions to use of traditional resources:

> Indigenous flora and fauna is inextricably bound to the territories of indigenous communities and any property right claims must recognize their traditional guardianship. Commercialization of any traditional plants and medicines of indigenous peoples must be managed by the indigenous peoples who have inherited such knowledge. A moratorium on any further commercialization of indigenous medicinal plants and human genetic materials must be declared until indigenous communities have developed appropriate protection measures.

Existing IPRs are not viewed by indigenous peoples as adequate to implement 'appropriate protection measures'. According to the Statement from the *COICA Regional Meeting on Intellectual Property Rights and Biodiversity* in Santa Cruz, Bolivia (1994) (Posey and Dutfield 1996):

> For indigenous peoples, the intellectual property system means legitimization of the misappropriation of our peoples' knowledge and resources for commercial purposes.

Therefore:

> There must be appropriate mechanisms for maintaining and ensuring rights of indigenous peoples to deny indiscriminate access to the resources of our communities or peoples and making it possible to contest patents or other exclusive rights to what is essentially indigenous.

As regards biodiversity prospecting and patenting life, the *Pacific Regional Consultation's Final Statement* calls for 'a moratorium on bioprospecting in the Pacific' and urges indigenous peoples 'not to co-operate in bioprospecting activities until appropriate protection measures are in place'. Delegates also agreed on 'the establishment of a treaty declaring the Pacific Region to be a life-forms patent-free zone' including in the treaty 'protocols governing bioprospecting, human genetic research, *in situ* conservation by indigenous peoples, *ex situ* collections and relevant international instruments.'

Indigenous peoples feel threatened by the world trade system, especially since the Uruguay Round negotiations first included discussions on trade-related IPR. Shiva (Shiva 1994b) observes that GATT/TRIPs:

> Has failed to recognize the more informal, communal system of innovation through which Third World farmers produce, select, improve and breed a plethora of diverse crop varieties.

The *Pacific Regional Meeting* urges:

> Those Pacific governments who have not signed the General Agreement on Tariffs and Trade (GATT) (should) refuse to do so, and encourage those

governments who have already signed to protest against any provisions which facilitate the expropriation of indigenous peoples' knowledge and resources and the patenting of life forms.

According to M. Idris, Chairman of Third World Network (TWN 1995), a grouping of organizations and individuals involved in Third World issues:

> Our governments must oppose the TRIPs agreement of the Uruguay Round... that protects the intellectual pirates by giving them the title 'intellectual property owners'.

Confronting the issues

As institutions involved in conservation, exchange, and use of biogenetic resources and indigenous knowledge come under closer scrutiny, new guidelines for collection, storage, transfer, and access are being developed. This process is made complicated by a lack of clarity in what are legal obligations as opposed to what are desirable ethical and moral standards. In this vacuum, some institutions find themselves unexpectedly in pioneering roles of developing the standards and mechanisms that will guide international law and practice.

The Food and Agricultural Organization (FAO) and the Consultative Group for International Agricultural Research (CGIAR)

Farmers' Rights

Third World countries and farmers' groups feel strongly that free access by industry to their resources is inherently unfair. The FAO, and subsequently the Conferences of the Parties to the CBD, have become fora for discussions on farmers' rights which have been proposed to recognize, protect, and compensate traditional farmers for their contributions to global agriculture. FAO defines farmers' rights as:

> Rights arising from the past, present and future contributions of farmers in conserving, improving, and making available plant genetic resources, particularly those in the centres of origin/diversity.
> (UNEP/CBD/IC/2/13, May 1994)

The 1994 First Conference of the Parties to the CBD was derailed by procedural matters, leaving questions of farmers' rights, biosafety, IPRs, and access to genetic resources to the Second Conference, to be held in Indonesia in 1995. This will be followed in 1996 by the Fourth International Conference on Plant Genetic Resources that will consider FAO's first Report on the State of the World's Plant Genetic Resources and a Global Plan of Action for the Conservation and

Sustainable Utilization of Plant Genetic Resources. The outcome is intended to be a revision of the International Undertaking on Plant Genetic Resources (IUPGR) to make it more coherent and compatible with the CBD. The terms of access to agricultural genetic resources and the concept and implementation of farmers' rights are to be renegotiated (GRAIN 1995b).

During 1995, FAO is promoting preparation of country-driven advisory documents for the ITC. This is being effected by a series of meetings taking place at sub-regional level at which members of NGOs and indigenous organizations have the opportunity to discuss country reports and provide major inputs. IPRs will play a major part in these discussions.

Reform of the Consultative Group for International Agricultural Research (CGIAR)

The CGIAR system grew out of the Green Revolution to oversee genetic research and conservation. The CGIAR system has expanded to embrace all types of agriculture and forestry, although its budget has not kept pace (GRAIN 1995b). The germplasm centres of The International Agricultural Research Centres (IARC) controlled by the CGIAR have recently been put under the administrative trust of FAO, with the International Plant Genetic Resources Institute (IPGRI) serving as the IARC point of articulation (Anon 1994: 4). In principle, this move will ensure the neutrality of management and minimize the influence of industrialized countries who are major contributors.

NGOs have formed a Task Force on International Agricultural Research to pursue its proposals at greater depth for presentation at the Ministerial Preparatory Meeting for the World Food Summit in Quebec in October 1995. They feel additional measures are necessary to insure that research and governance are based on true consultation with all involved sectors, including farming communities and indigenous peoples. Five principles have been offered to guide the 'rebirth' of the CGIAR: (i) political commitment to the well-being of the farm community; (ii) broadening of research from commodity-based research to ensuring food security and livelihood systems; (iii) involvement of a wider range of institutions and individuals to provide input from not only hard science, but social, political, ecological, and economic fields as well; (iv) full participation of the South so that indigenous peoples' rights and farmers' rights are fully considered; (v) adoption of a broader mandate so that financial support can be given to initiatives that do not involve the CGIAR Centres.

NGOs, networks, and indigenous alliances

NGOs like RAFI, GRAIN, and the TWN provide valuable information to the public on biopiracy, corporate behaviour, and political activities. Since The Earth Summit, NGOs have become active in lobbying activities and 'pro-active' development of policy statements and model laws (e.g. Nijar 1994). Groups that have worked mostly in indigenous human rights issues, such as Cultural Survival, Survival International, and the International Working Group on Indigenous Affairs (IWGIA) have shown greater interest in IPR issues as they relate to indigenous peoples. Increased monitoring activities have been somewhat effective in checking unauthorized exploitation of community resources.

Likewise, indigenous peoples have set up their own national and international organizations, such as the World Council of Indigenous Peoples (WCIP), World Rainforest Movement (WRM), Coordinating Body of Indigenous Organizations of the Amazon Basin (COICA), Indigenous Peoples' Biodiversity Network (IPBN), and the Mataatua Conference Secretariat.

Governments and nation-states

Some nation-states are responding through discussions on appropriate legislation intended to establish equitable terms for granting access to biogenetic resources and sharing benefits with indigenous peoples.

The Andean Pact

Model laws are being considered by the Andean Pact (Bolivia, Colombia, Ecuador, Peru, and Venezuela) for the conservation and sustainable use of biological material used as a source of genetic resources. Member States are permitted to set terms for access to their biological resources that may include the following: sharing of benefits between receivers of biological resources, members states and providers, which may be legal entities, private individuals, or indigenous or local communities; restrictions on transfer to third parties; reporting on obligations on future uses; obligations related to intellectual property; exclusivity and confidentiality; recognition of the member states or provider in publication of research results. When the provider is an indigenous or local community, member states may take measures to enable them to enter into access agreements.

The Brazilian Indigenous Societies Act

This proposed law was approved in 1994 by the House of Deputies of the National Legislature. It has never passed into the Senate and is still under consideration for its legality.

The proposed law is intended to protect and assure respect for indigenous peoples' social organization, customs, languages, beliefs and traditions, and rights over their territories and possessions. Articles 18–29 deal with the intellectual property of indigenous peoples. Among the important provisions of benefit to indigenous peoples are the following: the right to maintain the secrecy of traditional knowledge; the right to refuse access to traditional knowledge; the right to apply for IPR protection, which, in the case of collective knowledge will be granted in the name of the community or society; the right of prior informed consent (to be given in writing) for access to, use of and application of traditional knowledge; the right to co-ownership of research data, patents and products derived from the research; and, the right of communities to nullify patents illegally derived from their knowledge.

Indian Parliamentary Debates

The government of India has attempted to amend the 1970 Patent Act in conformity with the requirements of GATT-TRIPs, thereby fulfilling part of India's obligations for WTO membership. However, the Upper House of the Indian Parliament, in response to mass protests by farmers groups and opposition parties has voted for a deferment of the amendment. It remains to be seen whether the government will use undemocratic means to push through the Patents Bill (Shiva 1995). A strong traditional and tribal movement in India is pressing for Community Intellectual Rights (CIRs) similar to that proposed by Nijar (Nijar 1994) and described below.

Model Community Intellectual Rights (CIRs)

CIRs are intended 'to prevent the privatisation and usurpation of community rights and knowledge through existing definitions of innovation' (Nijar 1994). Model legislation asserts the existence of knowledge that is communally owned and shared, with 'innovators' being indigenous peoples who have not heretofore revealed their knowledge or resources to the outside world. Local communities are vested with 'custodianship rights of innovation' in two ways:

(i) Constructive Trustee: local community leaders are nominated or appointed to act for the whole community as trustees for the beneficiaries (the community);
(ii) Higher Trust: builds on the concept that governments claiming sovereign rights are, in fact, holding those rights in trust for the community.

Section 5 of the CIR Act calls for a Registry of Invention (similar to the Community Register described above). Here a community may register its innovations simply by declaring their existence. The idea is similar to copyright law, whereby 'protection generally arises with no need for formal acceptance by a registering authority'. Failure to register does not surrender innovation rights, but by making such a register, patent application by others may become more difficult or impossible.

Institutions and professional societies

Several institutions and professional societies have taken the initiative by drawing up ethical guidelines and declarations (Appendix 8 provides a list of professional and scientific societies that have developed ethical guidelines and declarations).

Although they are not legally binding, they are often the result of consensus among concerned scientists, and it is expected that the guidelines will be complied with. Whereas ethical guidelines (or codes of ethics) outline proper conduct for individual scientists, declarations contain more general principles. At its 1994 Congress, the International Society for Ethnobiology (ISE) agreed to develop a Code of Ethics, to be completed in 1995. Both the Code of Ethics and the ISE's new constitution are being co-written with indigenous peoples.

Mechanisms and solutions

Indigenous efforts

Indigenous peoples are making invaluable contributions to debates on IPRs, but are also taking practical initiatives to confront problems in the field.

Self-demarcation of indigenous peoples' territories

Legal title to lands and territories is primary for indigenous peoples. Documentation of traditional land use, including knowledge and use of plants, animals, soils, water systems, forests, and so on can be fundamental to claiming rights. Delimiting sacred sites, and areas of cultural and historical significance become not only legal acts, but also awareness-raising exercises for local communities. Since cultural landscapes are usually difficult to detect and 'read' by outsiders, mapping of these notifies others that lands are not 'wild' and unclaimed, but occupied and significant.

Self-demarcation is a strategy that several indigenous peoples have decided to pursue, such as the Ye'kuana in Venezuela. Self-mapping as a community procedure for demarcation has become an important process in Participatory Rural Appraisal (PRA), Participatory Action Research (PAR), and similar collaborative research methods of oral history and ethnoscience.

Community databases of indigenous knowledge and local biodiversity

1   Community registers have been developed in India as a means of securing community control over traditional ecological knowledge (TEK). Local people document all the known plant and animal species with full details of their uses. Community members are then in a position to refuse access to the register, and to set conditions under which others would be allowed access. Community registers can be used as evidence of intimate knowledge of the local environment in order to support claims to legal title of land and territory.

    Although community registers would be kept locally, they could be components of regional and national registers containing information freely available to communities. This would keep such information in the public domain.[1]

2   Indigenous knowledge databases. Some indigenous peoples have established databases, which they themselves control, ensuring their ability to control access and use of their knowledge and related information. For example, the Canadian Inuit of Nunavik and the Dene have their own information databases to:

> create a dialogue based on respect and equality, not to create a catalogue and make it 'available' to the 'real scientists'. We must not allow indigenous knowledge to be reduced solely to an interesting research topic for Western science.
> (Simon and Brooke 1996)

Community-Controlled Research (CCR)

Community-Controlled Research (CCR) is research where the objectives and methodologies are decided upon by indigenous peoples themselves. Appendix 9 provides a list of basic principles to guide CCR. The Kuna of Panama and the Inuit have established guidelines with the intention that CCR is the only form of research allowed on their territories.

1   The Proyecto de Estudio para el Manejo de Areas Silvestres de Kuna Yala (PEMASKY) and the Asociacion de Empleados Kunas (AEK) of Panama have produced an information manual for researchers on *scientific monitoring and co-operation*. Kuna objectives are outlined with regard to forest management, conservation of biological and cultural wealth, scientific collaboration, research priorities, and guidelines for researchers. Collaboration with Western scientists is encouraged for basic ecological research, botanical and faunal inventories, and the study and recording of Kuna traditions and culture. Research is designed to provide the Kuna with information useful to them and under their control.
2   The Inuit Tapirisat of Canada produced a background paper, *Negotiating Research Relationships in the North*, containing a useful list of principles based on existing ethical guidelines and the concerns expressed by members of Inuit communities, to be followed by all researchers.

Legal agreements

Contracts

Contracts are legal agreements which consist of negotiated promises or actions. Contracts require quite limited legal assistance and may be useful mechanisms for indigenous peoples to ensure that any transfer of knowledge and resources is fairly compensated. Contracts could provide the following benefits: up-front payments, training, technology transfer, royalties, and other financial and non-monetary forms of benefit sharing (Laird 1993; Posey and Dutfield 1996).

Covenants

Covenants serve to establish principles that can lead to a legally binding agreement, but they contain ethical and moral commitments beyond mere commercial agreements. The Global Coalition for Bio-Cultural Diversity developed a model *Covenant on Intellectual, Cultural and Scientific Property* (see Appendix 5) that has been used to guide equitable relationships between The Body Shop International and various indigenous groups. Essential elements of the Covenant include: provisions for immediate benefits, including a trust fund for legal assistance, consultation, negotiation and possible litigation, should such become necessary; an independent monitor to effect a yearly socio-environmental audit of the agreement; and provisions for compensation and profit sharing.

Material transfer agreements

Material Transfer Agreements (MTAs) regulate the transfer of biological resources for research and possible commercialization in exchange for benefits to the party recognized as the supplier. Suppliers might be a government, a collecting organization (such as a botanical garden), or even a local community if material has a commercial application. Such benefits may be in the form of up-front benefits, a trust fund, and future royalties. In exchange, MTAs usually grant the recipient of the material the right to apply for patents if any of the material has commercial potential. The patent holder can then commercialize a product based on the material (Lesser 1994).

Information transfer agreements

Information Transfer Agreements are adaptations of MTAs negotiated between an indigenous group and an outside organization interested in commercial use of traditional knowledge. Since biogenetic resources are often modified by human action, ITAs recognize the processes, preparations, and conservation practices that afford the germplasm improvements. Co-patenting would be an extension of ITAs (Posey and Dutfield 1996).

Traditional Resource Rights (TRR)

Given that knowledge and traditional resources are central to the maintenance of identity for indigenous peoples, the control over these resources is of central concern in their struggle for self-determination. Following COICA (see Posey and Dutfield 1996: 215–18),

> A system of protection and recognition of our resources and knowledge must be designed which is in conformity with our world view and contains formulas that...will prevent appropriation of our resources and knowledge.

Traditional Resource Rights (TRR) has emerged as a concept that more accurately reflects indigenous and traditional peoples' views and concerns. TRR amasses 'bundles of rights' already widely recognized by international legally and non-legally binding agreements in an effort to build a solid foundation for more equitable systems of protection and benefit sharing.

Basic principles upon which TRR is based include: basic human rights, right to development, rights to environmental integrity, religious freedom, land and territorial rights, right to privacy, prior informed consent and full disclosure, farmers' rights, intellectual property rights, neighbouring rights, cultural property rights, cultural heritage recognition, rights of customary law and practice.

Appendix 6 lists 'bundles of rights' and their location within international agreements. Although general principles can be found in these agreements, they are on a very different political footing. Some are enshrined in legally binding conventions, while others are found in non-legally binding documents or model proposals.

Thus, existing 'bundles of rights' are wide ranging, but still inadequate. TRR is more of a *process* than a product. The concept can grow as additional rights accrue, and are adapted through the development of national and international legislation. It goes beyond other *sui generis* models in that it seeks to protect not only knowledge relating to biological resources; it also asserts the right of peoples to self-determination and the right to safeguard 'culture' in its broadest sense.

TRR is rights driven, not economically motivated. Yet by prioritizing indigenous peoples' rights to say *no* to exploitation, and by acknowledging their basic rights to control access over and receive benefits from traditional resources, commercial and research institutions should find equitable agreements and partnerships more easily attainable.

Millennial dilemmas and uncertain conclusions

Intellectual property rights have become important to global economic and commercial debates in part because of the massive perceived potential for exploitation of biogenetic resources for biotechnology. Similarly, traditional knowledge is expected to drastically cut research and development costs. The resulting bioprospecting feeding frenzy may attenuate when, as many experts predict, the highly exaggerated hype converts to disappointing profits. In the meantime, however, expectations are exalted and IPRs have become a code for unethical and unsustainable exploitation of local communities and their resources.

Scientists and scientific institutions are affected by this situation as they become involved – actively or passively – with the private sector. Plant, animal, and cultural material collected with public funds for scientific, non-profit purposes are now open for commercial exploitation. Research, even in universities and museums, is increasingly funded by corporations, leaving questions of who controls the resulting data. 'Purely scientific' data banks have become the 'mines' for 'biodiversity prospecting'. Publishing of information, traditionally the hallmark of academic success, has become a superhighway for transporting restricted (or even sacred) information into the unprotectable 'public domain'.

Companies that seek ethical and equitable relationships with indigenous peoples find their efforts undermined by exploitative practices of unethical corporations. Identification of legally constituted entities and *bona fide* community representatives may be harrowingly difficult, as can be the form and distribution of benefits. Existing business standards and philosophy exclude any obligations to pre-contract and post-profit responsibilities that have become necessary to insure long-term social and ecological commitments.

Nation-states find themselves proclaiming major expansions of sovereignty over traditional resources, but with no means to implement or exercise the responsibility that increased sovereignty demands. Frequently, neither technical capacity nor capital potential are adequate to develop the knowledge or genetic materials that are claimed. Furthermore, valuing indigenous technologies threatens the ideological base that has historically been used to marginalize and exploit local community resources. It is, therefore, problematic that benefits to nation-states will ever 'trickle-down' to local communities.

International law hardly exists, and where it does – as in the case of IPRs – it favours industrialized nations rather than bio-culturally rich nations. There is little evidence that existing Western legal structures can be adapted to enhance conservation of biological diversity or empowerment of indigenous, traditional, and local communities. Any attempts will need to combine 'bundles of rights' from a wide range of agreements to guide a newly emerging system of international law.

The Convention on Biological Diversity, and related UNCED agreements, call for access to, protection of and benefit sharing from the use and wider application of traditional technologies. However, enforcement mechanisms – nor, indeed, even the general basis of agreement as to what to enforce – are far from appearing on the international scene. The fundamental question of what are legal requirements versus moral and ethical responsibilities portends many difficulties for all 'stakeholders'.

Rather than looking hopelessly on, one hopes that the situation will provide opportunities for new dialogues, increased recognition of indigenous peoples and their knowledge, new codes of ethics and standards of conduct, socially and ecologically responsible business practices, holistic approaches to sustainability, and alternative concepts of property, ownership, and value. Intellectual property rights – replaced by a rights-based TRR concept – can serve to catalyse this dialogue, and, indeed, may be one of the most fruitful debates of the next millennium.

Museums, research institutes, and universities are in excellent positions to lead these debates. Sizeable scientific collections and databases, strong interdisciplinary expertise, and cross-cultural experience provide them with the resources necessary to spearhead the dialogue. Given that one of the honoured principles of these institutions, free exchange of information, is in jeopardy – as is the credibility of science itself in the post-Earth Summit context of socio-eco-political correctness – this leadership opportunity should be seized with urgency and vigour.

Chapter 17

The 'balance sheet' and the 'sacred balance'

Valuing the knowledge of indigenous and traditional peoples*

Indigenous and traditional peoples, who often attribute a sacred quality to nature, have made major contributions to the enhancement and conservation of the world's biodiversity. Although this is increasingly recognized in international discourse, rights of these peoples to continue their traditional practices are threatened by the globalized economy. Likewise, science implicitly denies their contribution to biodiversity conservation and enhancement by referring to their lands as 'wild' or 'wilderness'. It also effectively undermines their rights by claiming that the biodiversity fostered by their traditional practices is a global resource. In order to counter these threats, we need, not only to strengthen the rights of indigenous and traditional peoples, but also to reverse global trends that substitute economic and utilitarian models for the holistic concept of the 'sacred balance'.

Introduction

Many of the areas of highest biological diversity on the planet are inhabited by indigenous and traditional peoples, providing what the Declaration of Belém calls an 'inextricable link' between biological and cultural diversity (Posey and Overal 1990). Of the nine countries which together account for 60 per cent of human languages, six of these 'centres of cultural diversity' are also, in the biological sense, 'megadiversity' countries with exceptional numbers of unique plant and animal species (Durning 1992: 6).

More than 300 million people in the world are indigenous (Gray 1999). There are no reliable figures as to how many 'traditional' societies there are, but, excluding urban populations, they could amount to 85 per cent of the world's population. These diverse groups occupy a wide geographical range from the polar regions to the tropical deserts, savannas, and forests (IUCN, UNEP, and WWF 1991). According to UNESCO (1993), between four and five thousand of the

---

* This paper, based on the Introduction to *Cultural and Spiritual Values of Biodiversity* (Posey 1999), was first published in *Worldviews: Environment, Culture, Religion* (1998), 2, 91–106, Brill Academic Publishers, Leiden.

6,000 languages in the world are spoken by indigenous peoples, implying that indigenous groups still constitute most of the world's cultural diversity (also see Maffi 1999).

The terms 'indigenous' and 'traditional' have been defined in various ways, the details of which are beyond the scope of this article (see Posey 1996 for a full discussion). Indigenous peoples insist that they be recognized as 'peoples', not 'people'. The 's' is very important, because it symbolizes not just the basic human rights to which all individuals are entitled, but also land, territorial, and collective rights, subsumed under the right to self-determination. In contrast, the use of terms like 'people', 'populations', and 'minorities' implicitly denies self-determination.

'Traditional knowledge', which characterizes indigenous and traditional cultures, is, contrary to popular understanding, particularly innovative and adaptable (FDC 1996; see Chapter 11 this volume), and traditional livelihood systems are constantly adapting to changing conditions. They are dynamic, but, whatever the changes, they embrace principles of sustainability (Bierhorst 1994; Callicott 1989; Clarkson *et al.* 1992; Johannes and Ruddle 1993; Posey and Dutfield 1997).

The sacred balance

Although conservation and management practices are highly pragmatic, indigenous and traditional peoples generally view this knowledge as emanating from a spiritual base. All creation is sacred, and the sacred and secular are inseparable. Spirituality is the highest form of consciousness, and spiritual consciousness is the highest form of awareness. In this sense, a dimension of traditional knowledge is not local knowledge, but knowledge of the universal as expressed in the local. In indigenous and local cultures, experts exist who are peculiarly aware of nature's organizing principles, sometimes described as entities, spirits, or natural law. Thus, knowledge of the environment depends on the relationship not only between humans and nature, but also between the visible world and the spirit world. According to Opoku (1978) traditional African religion is distinctive in being:

> A way of life, [with] the purpose of... order[ing] our relationship with our fellow men and with our environment, both spiritual and physical. At the root of it is a quest for harmony between man, the spirit world, nature, and society. Thus, the unseen is as much a part of reality as that which is seen – the spiritual is as much a part of reality as the material. In fact, there is a complementary relationship between the two, with the spiritual being more powerful than the material. The community is of the dead as well as the living. And in nature, behind visible objects lie essences, or powers, which constitute the true nature of those objects.

Indigenous and traditional peoples frequently view themselves as guardians and stewards of nature. Harmony and equilibrium are central concepts in most cosmologies. Agriculture, for example, can provide 'balance for well-being' through relationships among, not only people, but also nature and deities. In this concept, the blessing of a new field is not mere spectacle, but an inseparable part of life where the highest value is harmony with the Earth. Most traditions recognize linkages between health, diet, properties of different foods and medicinal plants, and horticultural/natural resource management practices, all within a highly articulated cosmological/social context (see Hugh-Jones 1993).

Local knowledge embraces information about location, movements, and other factors explaining spatial patterns and timing in the ecosystem, including sequences of events, cycles, and trends. Direct links with the land are fundamental and obligations to maintain them form the core of individual and group identity. Chief Oren Lyons (1999) also emphasizes how these relationships and obligations are not to some external objects that possess life, but rather to kin and relatives. Biodiversity, for his Haudenosaunee people, is family and 'all our relations'.

Suzuki (1999) calls the links between life, land, and society the 'Sacred Balance'. Science with its quantum mechanics methods, he says, can never address the universe as a whole. And it certainly can never adequately describe the holism of indigenous knowledge and belief. In fact, science is far behind in the environmental movement. It sees nature as objects ('components' of biodiversity is the term used in the CBD) for human use and exploitation. Technology has used the banner of scientific 'objectivity' to mask the moral and ethical issues that emerge from such a functionalist, anthropocentric philosophy. Strathern (1996) makes this clear when discussing the ethical dilemmas raised (or avoided) when human embryos are 'decontextualized' as human beings to become 'objects' of scientific research. Meanwhile, economists would have us believe that markets provide 'level playing fields' that do not moralize globalization and, therefore, work more efficiently to advance the causes of environmental conservation.

With such philosophies and policies, there can be little surprise that indigenous, traditional, and local communities are hostile to the rhetoric of 'partnerships' and 'sustainable development' – indeed, to the very tenets of 'biodiversity' and 'conservation'. The dominant scientific and economic forces assume that traditional communities must change to meet 'modern' standards, but indigenous and traditional peoples feel the opposite must occur: science and industry must begin to respect local diversity and the 'Sacred Balance'.

Recognizing indigenous and local communities

Western science may have invented the words 'nature', 'biodiversity', and 'sustainability', but it certainly did not initiate the concepts. Indigenous, traditional and local communities have sustainably utilized and conserved a vast diversity of plants, animals and ecosystems since the dawn of *Homo sapiens*. Furthermore, human beings have moulded environments, consciously and unconsciously, for millennia, to the extent that it is often impossible to separate nature from culture.

Sultan et al. (1997) described the relationship between the Aboriginal peoples of Australia and their environment that predated the advent of Europeans.

Recently 'discovered' cultural landscapes include those of Aboriginal peoples, who, 100,000 years before the term 'sustainable development' was coined, were trading seeds, dividing tubers and propagating domesticated and non-domesticated plant species. Sacred sites acted as conservation areas for water sources and species by restricting access and behaviour. Traditional technologies, including fire use, were part of extremely sophisticated systems that shaped and maintained the balance of flora and fauna. Decline of fire management and loss of sacred sites when Aboriginal people were centralized into settlements, led to rapid decline of mammals throughout the arid regions.

The lands of the Kayapó Indians of Brazil provide another example of a 'cultural landscape' (Posey 2002 chs 1 and 18, and 1997b). Kayapó practices of planting and transplanting within and between many ecological zones indicate the degree to which indigenous presence has modified Amazonia. Extensive plantations of fruit and nut trees, as well as 'forest islands' (*apêtê*) created in savanna, force scientists to re-evaluate what have often hastily and erroneously been considered 'natural' landscapes. The techniques of constructing *apêtê* show the degree to which the Kayapó can create and manipulate micro-environments within and between ecozones to actually increase biodiversity. Successful *apêtê* depend on a detailed knowledge of the properties of soil, micro-climates and plants, and of the short- and long-term relationships among components of a human-modified ecological community, relationships that change as the *apêtê* mature. Management becomes more complex, since many plants are grown specifically to attract useful animals, and the *apêtê* become both agro-forestry units and game reserves.

The Kagore Shona people of Zimbabwe have sacred sites, burial grounds, and other sites of special significance deeply embedded in the landscape (Matowanyika 1997). Outsiders often cannot recognize them during land use planning exercises. In societies with no written language or edifices, hills, mountains, and valleys become the libraries and cathedrals that reflect cultural achievement. Many of the forests presumed to be 'wild' are actually managed landscapes, and are more often peoples' back yards than the 'wildernesses' assumed by outsiders.

The failure to recognize anthropogenic (human-modified) landscapes has blinded outsiders to the management practices of indigenous peoples and local communities (Denevan 1992; Gomez-Pompa and Kaus 1992), and has led to cultural landscapes being misrepresented as 'pristine'. This is more than semantics. 'Wild' and 'wilderness' imply that these landscapes and resources are produced by 'nature' and, therefore, have no owners; they are the 'common heritage of all humankind'. This has resulted in local communities having no tenurial or ownership rights, and, thus, in their lands and resources being 'free' to others for the taking. This is why indigenous peoples have come to oppose the use of 'wilderness' and 'wild' to refer to the regions in which they now live or once lived.

Cultural landscapes and their links to conservation of biodiversity are now recognized under the 1972 UNESCO Convention Concerning the Protection of the World Cultural and Natural Heritage (The World Heritage Convention). A new category of World Heritage Site, the 'Cultural Landscape', recognizes 'the complex interrelationships between man and nature in the construction, formation and evolution of landscapes' (UNESCO 1996). The first World Heritage Site of this kind was Tongariro National Park, a sacred region for the Maori people of New Zealand (Rössler 1993), designated because of its importance in Maori beliefs. UNESCO is also now developing new projects to help local communities conserve and protect sacred places (Hay-Edie 1999).

The CBD is one of the major international forces in recognizing the role of indigenous and local communities in *in situ* conservation (Appendix 3) and the obligations of each signatory to the Convention to 'respect, preserve and maintain knowledge, innovations and practices of indigenous and local communities' (Article 8. j).

The Convention also enshrines the importance of customary practice in biodiversity conservation and calls for protection of, and equitable benefit-sharing from the use and application of, 'traditional technologies' (Articles 10(c) and 18.4). Glowka *et al.* (1994) warn that 'traditional' can imply restriction of the Convention only to those embodying traditional lifestyles, keeping in mind that the concept can easily be misinterpreted to mean 'frozen in time'. But Pereira and Gupta (1993) claim, 'it is the traditional methods of research and application, not just particular pieces of knowledge that persist in a tradition of invention and innovation'. Technological changes do not simply lead to modernization and loss of traditional practice, but rather provide additional inputs into vibrant, adaptive and adapting, holistic systems of management and conservation.

'Traditional knowledge, innovations and practices' are often referred to by scientists as Traditional Ecological Knowledge (TEK). TEK is far more than a simple compilation of facts (Gadgil *et al.* 1993; Johnson 1992). It is the basis for local-level decision-making in areas of contemporary life, including natural resource management, nutrition, food preparation, health, education, and community and social organization (Warren *et al.* 1995). TEK is holistic, inherently dynamic, constantly evolving through experimentation and innovation, fresh insight, and external stimuli (Suzuki and Knudtson 1992).

One area where TEK is well understood and exploited is that of agriculture. Many ancient indigenous agricultural systems survived until the colonial period. These systems are complex, based on sophisticated ecological knowledge and understanding, highly efficient and productive, and inherently sustainable. Classic examples are the raised bed systems used for millennia by traditional farmers of tropical America, Asia, and Africa. Known variously in Meso-America as *chinampas*, *waru waru* and *tablones*, these were extremely effective for irrigation, drainage, soil fertility maintenance, frost control, and plant disease management. At Lake Texcoco the pre-conquest Aztecs had 10,000 hectares of land under *chinampas* feeding a population of 100,000 people (Willett 1993). There is evidence that farming in India has continued on the same land for more than two thousand years without a drop in yields, and remained remarkably free of pests. The Indian peasant grew as many as forty-one different crops annually in certain localities, and possessed the ability to vary seeds according to the needs of the soil and the season (Willett 1993).

It becomes obvious that local dependence on traditional varieties of crop plants, non-domesticated resources, and gathered foods serves to stimulate biodiversity conservation, not destroy or homogenize it as most agro-industrial systems do (Thrupp 1997). Indeed 'modern' agriculture has become one of the major threats to indigenous and local communities, as well as to biodiversity, healthy ecosystems and even food security (Mann and Lawrence 1999).

Another important area in which local knowledge plays a major role is in traditional medicines and health systems (Akerele *et al*. 1991; Bodeker 1999). Alternative medical systems are dependent upon and closely tied to healthy environments and biodiversity conservation. It is important to remember that the distinctions between medicine, food, and health are western distinctions. For many indigenous and traditional peoples, foods are medicines and vice versa; in fact, the western division of the two makes little sense to many traditional peoples (Hugh-Jones 1993). And, above all, healthy ecosystems are critical to healthy societies and individuals, because humanity and nature are one, not in opposition to each other.

Equity and rights

Recognition by the Biodiversity Convention of the contributions of indigenous and traditional peoples to maintaining biodiversity may be a major political advance. But there are major dangers. Once TEK or genetic materials leave the societies in which they are embedded, there is little national protection and virtually no international laws to protect community 'knowledge, innovations, and practices'. Many countries do not even recognize the basic right of indigenous peoples to exist, let alone grant them self-determination, land ownership, or control over their traditional resources (Gray 1999).

The concept of 'Farmers' Rights', developed by the Food and Agricultural Organization (FAO) over the last two decades, is one of the few international attempts to recognize the contributions of traditional and indigenous peoples, in this case to global food security. But its legal basis is weak and even meagre guarantees are resisted by some powerful countries. The global fund established to insure forms of compensation for local farmers remains inoperative. FAO is undertaking a revision of its International Undertaking on Plant Genetic Resources (IUPGR) with the view of strengthening or expanding Farmers' Rights, but the political road to such improvements is rocky and uncertain (GRAIN 1995c; Plenderleith 1999; Posey 1996).

The International Labour Organization (ILO) Convention 169 is the only legally binding international instrument specifically intended to protect indigenous and tribal peoples. ILO 169 supports community ownership and local control of lands and resources. It does not, however, cover the numerous traditional and peasant groups that are also critical in conserving the diversity of agricultural, medicinal, and non-domesticated resources. To date the Convention has only ten national signatories and provides little more than a base line for debates on indigenous rights (Barsh 1990).

The same bleak news comes from an analysis of Intellectual Property Rights (IPRs) laws. IPRs were established to protect individual inventions and inventors, not the collective, ancient folklore and TEK of indigenous and local communities. Even if IPRs were secured for communities, differential access to patents, copyright, know-how and trade secret laws and lawyers would generally price them out of any effective registry, monitoring or litigation using such instruments (Posey and Dutfield 1996). Table 17.1 summarizes how IPRs are considered inadequate and inappropriate for protecting the collective resources of indigenous and traditional peoples.

Table 17.1 Inadequacies of intellectual property rights.

Intellectual property rights are inadequate and inappropriate for protection of traditional ecological knowledge and community resources because they:
- recognize individual, not collective rights,
- require a specific act of 'invention',
- simplify ownership regimes,
- stimulate commercialization,
- recognize only market values,
- are subject to economic powers and manipulation,
- are difficult to monitor and enforce,
- are expensive, complicated, time-consuming.

The World Trade Organization's General Agreement on Tariffs and Trade (WTO/GATT) contains no explicit reference to the knowledge and genetic resources of traditional peoples, although it does provide for states to develop *sui generis* (specially generated) systems for plant protection (TRIPs Article 27c, see Dutfield 1997). Considerable intellectual energy is now being poured by governments, non-governmental and peoples' organizations into defining what new, alternative models of protection would include (see Leskien and Flitner 1997). There is scepticism, however, that this *sui generis* option will be adequate to provide any significant alternatives to existing IPRs (Montecinos 1996).

One glimmer of hope comes from the decision in the Biodiversity Convention to implement an 'intersessional process' to evaluate the inadequacies of IPRs and develop guidelines and principles for governments seeking advice on access and transfer legislation to protect traditional communities (UNEP 1997). This provides exciting opportunities for many countries and peoples to engage in an historic debate. Up to now, United Nations agencies have been reluctant to discuss integrated systems of rights that link environment, trade and human rights. However, agreements between the Biodiversity Convention, the FAO, and the

Table 17.2 Some principal rights affirmed by the UN Draft Declaration on the Rights of Indigenous Peoples.

- Right to self-determination, representation, and full participation.
- Recognition of existing treaty arrangements with indigenous peoples.
- Right to determine own citizenry and obligations of citizenship.
- Right to collective, as well as individual, human rights.
- Right to live in freedom, peace, and security without military intervention or involvement.
- Right to religious freedom and protection of sacred sites and objects, including ecosystems, plants, and animals.
- Right to restitution and redress for cultural, intellectual, religious or spiritual property that is taken or used without authorization.
- Right to free and informed consent (prior informed consent).
- Right to control access and exert ownership over plants, animals, and minerals vital to their cultures.
- Right to own, develop, control and use the lands and territories, including the total environment of the lands, air, waters, coastal seas, sea-ice, flora and fauna, and other resources which they have traditionally owned or otherwise occupied or used.
- Right to special measures to control, develop and protect their sciences, technologies and cultural manifestations, including human and other genetic resources, seeds, medicines, knowledge of the properties of fauna and flora, oral traditions, literatures, designs and visual and performing arts.
- Right to just and fair compensation for any such activities that have adverse environmental, economic, social, cultural, or spiritual impact.

WTO, now guarantee broad consultations on *sui generis* systems and community intellectual property rights (CIPRs) among some of the major international bodies. It will take the creative and imaginative input of all these groups, and many more, to solve the complicated challenge of devising new systems of national and international laws that support and enhance cultural and biological diversity.

For indigenous peoples, the Draft Declaration on the Rights of Indigenous Peoples (DDRIP) is the most important statement of basic requirements for adequate rights and protection. DDRIP took nearly two decades to develop by hundreds of indigenous representatives to the UN Working Group on Indigenous Populations of the Geneva Human Rights Centre. It is broad-ranging, thorough, and reflects one of the most transparent and democratic processes yet to be seen in the United Nations. The process itself and many of the principles established will undoubtedly serve as models for traditional societies and local communities seeking greater recognition of rights. Table 17.2 provides some of the principles affirmed by the DDRIP (for the complete text see Appendix 4).

The global balance sheet

Although international efforts to recognize indigenous, traditional, and local communities are welcome and positive, they are pitted against enormous economic and market forces that propel globalization of trade. Critiques of globalization are numerous (e.g. Korten 1995), and point to at least two major shortcomings: (i) value is imputed to information and resources only when they enter external markets, and (ii) expenditures do not reflect actual environmental and social costs. This means that existing values recognized by local communities are ignored, despite knowledge that local biodiversity provides essential elements for survival (food, shelter, medicine, etc.). It also means that the knowledge and managed resources of indigenous and traditional peoples are ascribed no value and assumed to be free for the taking. This has been called 'intellectual *terra nullius*' after the concept (empty land) that allowed colonial powers to expropriate 'discovered' land for their empires. Corporations and states still defend this morally vacuous concept because it facilitates the 'biopiracy' of local folk varieties of crops, traditional medicines, and useful species.

Even scientists have been accomplices to such raids by publishing data they know will be catapulted into the public domain and gleaned by 'bioprospectors' seeking new products. They have also perpetuated the 'intellectual *terra nullius*' concept, both deliberately and through ignorance or negligence, by declaring useful local plants as 'wild' and entire ecosystems as 'wildernesses', despite these having been moulded, managed and protected by human populations for millennia. The result is to declare the biodiversity of a site as 'natural', thereby transferring it to the public domain. Once this has been done, communities are stripped of all rights to their traditional resources.

It is little wonder then, that indigenous groups in the Pacific region have declared a moratorium on all scientific research until protection of traditional knowledge and genetic resources can be guaranteed to local communities by scientists. The 'moratorium movement' began with the 1993 Mataatua Declaration (Clause 2.8): 'A moratorium on any further commercialisation of indigenous medicinal plants and human genetic materials must be declared until indigenous communities have developed appropriate protection mechanisms' (see Posey and Dutfield 1996).

The Mataatua Declaration, in turn, influenced the Final Statement of the 1995 Consultation on Indigenous Peoples' Knowledge and Intellectual Property Rights in Suva, Fiji (Pacific Concerns Resource Centre 1995), in which parties,

- Call for a moratorium on bioprospecting in the Pacific and urge indigenous peoples not to co-operate in bioprospecting activities until appropriate protection mechanisms are in place [adding that, 'Bioprospecting as a term needs to be clearly defined to exclude indigenous peoples' customary harvesting practices'].
- Assert that *in situ* conservation by indigenous peoples is the best method to conserve and protect biological diversity and indigenous knowledge, and encourage its implementation by indigenous communities and all relevant bodies.
- Encourage indigenous peoples to maintain and expand our knowledge of local biological resources.

To allay these deep concerns, many scientific and professional organizations are developing their own codes and standards to guide research, health, educational, and conservation projects with indigenous and local communities (a summary of some of these can be found in Cunningham 1993; Posey Chapter 16 this book; Posey and Dutfield 1996). One of the most extensive of these efforts is that of the International Society for Ethnobiology, which undertook a 10-year consultation with indigenous and traditional peoples, and with its extensive international membership, to establish 'principles for equitable partnerships' (see Appendix 11). These principles, of which there are fourteen, include self-determination, inalienability, prior consent and veto, confidentiality, and so on. The main objective of this process was to establish terms under which collaboration and joint research between ethnobiologists and communities could proceed based upon trust, transparency, and mutual concerns.

Values and principles which promote the rights of indigenous and traditional peoples, and which echo their cultural understandings, have also become established in public environmental discourse. Many people in industrialized countries are recognizing how industrial systems and the power relations on which they depend have operated to separate 'nature' from 'spirit', and are trying to re-integrate the concept of 'sacred balance' into a practical ethic of land, biodiversity, and environment. This movement takes its inspiration from Leopold's (1949) ideas of 'land ethic' and 'environmental citizenship'. Callicott (1989) argues the need for a global ethic formulated around respect for the diversity of cultures and ecosystems. It may be that the 'need' is not just the artefact of human psychology and moral reflection, but also spiritually and psychologically grounded. Roszak (1992) believes that the environmental crisis is rooted in the extreme 'disturbance' of the web of life that is a part of human consciousness. Indeed, a basic precept of ecology itself is that disturbance of one element of an environmental system affects all other elements, as well as the whole (Capra 1999). Indigenous, traditional and local communities are aware of the negative local effects of such disturbance, and express their profound concerns in cultural and spiritual terms precisely because they recognize its deep-rootedness.

The worrisome lesson from all of this is that the global environmental crisis cannot be solved by technological tampering ('quick fixes') or superficial political measures. The Native American leader Black Elk puts it:

> It is the story of all life that is holy and is good to tell, and of us two-leggeds sharing in it with the four-leggeds and the wings of the air and all green things; for these are children of one mother and their father is one spirit.
> (Neihardt 1959, quoted in Suzuki 1998a)

For industrialized society to reverse the devastating cycles it has imposed on the planet, it will have to invent an ecology powerful enough to offset deforestation, soil erosion, species extinction, and pollution, and sustainable practices that can harmonize with growth of trade and increased consumption, and, of course, a 'global environmental ethic' that is not subverted by economically powerful institutions. That may be an impossible task, but there are some viable paths.

One of the best is to relearn the ecological knowledge and sustainable principles that our society has lost. This can come through listening to the peoples of the planet who still know when birds nest, fish migrate, ants swarm, tadpoles develop legs, soils erode, and rare plants seed, and whose worldviews manifest the ecologies and ethics of sustainability. As Bepkororoti Paiakan, a Kayapó Chief (Brazil), puts it: 'We are trying to save the knowledge that the forests and this planet are alive, to give it back to you who have lost the understanding.'

But listening is not enough. We must uphold the basic rights of indigenous and traditional peoples to land, territory, knowledge, and traditional resources. And we must discover how the balance sheet of economic and utilitarian policies can be countered by the 'sacred balance' expressed by such peoples.

Appendices

I Ethnobiology*

Ethnobiology is the comparative study of human beliefs about, and perceptions, categorizations, uses, conservation, and management of, the visible and invisible worlds ('bios') that provide a context for 'life'. The term is roughly synonymous with *ethnoecology*, although some practitioners use ethnobiology as the more general term referring to all 'living things', leaving ethnoecology as the study of how humans understand interactions between elements of ecosystems and landscapes (Toledo 1992). Hardesty (1977: 291) defined ethnoecology as 'the study of systems of knowledge developed by a given culture to classify the objects, activities and events of its universe'. These differences are semantic and reflect variations in the different use of 'ecology' and 'biology' in different languages. Generally, both terms are used interchangeably and in the broadest sense (namely, the human perception of all living things). Subcategories of ethnoecology/ethnobiology are common and mirror the fragmented subdisciplines of Western science (e.g. ethnobotany, ethnozoology, ethnoentomology, ethno-ornithology, ethnopedology, ethnoastronomy, ethnomedicine, and so forth) more than they do the holistic cosmovisions of other traditions (Ellen 1993).

The continuum of research and methodologies that comprises ethnoecology extends from the perception of phenomena (the 'cognition'), to the ordering of cognitive categories (the 'ethnotaxonomy'), the social expression of the system (the 'culture'), the impact of cultural systems on physical surroundings (the 'anthropogenic and cultural landscapes'), the management of those landscapes (the 'conservation and resource management'), the exploitation of knowledge and resources for wider use and application (the 'applied research'), and the moral concerns of how to apply such research equitably while protecting the rights of knowledge holders (the 'ethics and intellectual property rights'). Thus, ethnobiology and ethnoecology inevitably draw from disciplines such as cognitive

---

* Goudie, A. S. and Cuff, D. J. (eds) (2000) *Encyclopedia of Global Change: Environmental Change and Human Society*. Copyright 2000 by Oxford University Press. Used by permission of Oxford University Press Inc.

psychology, linguistics, anthropology (including ethnology and biological and social anthropology), geography, ecology, biology, history of science, philosophy, ethics, and additional areas of study such as forestry and plant sciences, zoology, agriculture, and medicine.

Each phase of the continuum evokes problems of epistemology, terminology, and methodology, since there is no general agreement between disciplines on how to view this spectrum of concerns (Atran 1990). In practical terms, ethnobiology requires cross-disciplinary and interdisciplinary methodologies that are sensitive to profound differences between cultures, especially in relation to 'sacred' categories, places, or domains that may restrict or prohibit access to researchers. Thus, ethnobiologists are constantly torn between maintenance of the rigours of their Western scientific 'discipline' and respect for and understanding of the metaphysical, aesthetic, and spiritual dimensions that define and encompass the societies of the peoples they study.

Conklin (1957) became a pioneer in ethnobiological research when he described the extensive knowledge of natural history of the Hanunoo people of the Philippines, as did Bateson (1979) in his thesis on the 'unity of mind and nature'. Levi-Strauss (1962) provided the neoteric framework for understanding the links between the 'savage mind' and the environment, and drew inspiration from the early (1900) work of Barrows on the Coahuila Indians' knowledge and use of the edible and medicinal plants of the Southern California desert. Berlin *et al.* (1966) set the current standard for comparative studies of ethnobiological classification systems based on their studies of the Tzeltal Maya of Mexico (also see Berlin 1992). Majnep and Bulmer provided another classic standard on the Kalam of New Guinea in *Birds of My Kalam Country* (1977). Debates still rage over whether cognitive, or utilitarian, factors underlie folk classification systems (Hunn 1993). More recently, ethnobiological studies have tended to focus on more practical aspects of ethnobiological knowledge, especially its application to conservation, natural resource management, and environmental change and management (Berkes 1989; Martin 1995; Warren *et al.* 1989).

One goal of ethnobiology is to stimulate dialogue between scientists and local knowledge specialists so that a common scientific language can eventually emerge to discuss and study what is generally known as *Traditional Ecological Knowledge*, or TEK (Slikkerveer 1999). Historically, ethnobiology has concentrated, but not been limited to, studies of indigenous and traditional peoples (such as peasants, hunters, gatherers, fisherfolk, small farmers, and so forth). Today, however, there is increasing interest in knowledge systems of urban dwellers, suburban and periurban communities, and peoples in industrial societies.

Since the 1992 Convention on Biological Diversity (CBD), global interest in the 'wider use and application' of traditional peoples' 'knowledge, innovation and practices' has accelerated. The search for new products and genes for biotechnology (bioprospecting) has highlighted ways in which the knowledge and genetic resources of indigenous and local peoples have been exploited without compensation (known as *biopiracy*), despite requirements of the CBD for equitable benefit sharing with and protection of the 'holders' of TEK. Thus, a debate on the ethics of science and industry in their study and exploitation of 'traditional resources' has ensued (Posey 1996). It is no longer possible to undertake ethnoecological research without dealing with full disclosure of research intentions and outcomes, prior informed consent from affected communities, equitable benefit sharing from any products or derivatives of research, and other ethical issues in research and dissemination (such as publication, films, photos, and so forth). The application of intellectual property rights (IPRs) has become a particularly contentious ethical issue, since industrial 'discoveries' can be protected by law, but collective knowledge of indigenous, traditional, and local communities cannot. The CBD has initiated a process, in conjunction with the Food and Agriculture Organisation (FAO) and the World Intellectual Property Organization (WIPO), to investigate *sui generis* ('unique' or 'specially developed') options for the protection of traditional genetic resources and the TEK associated with them. This process builds upon a long-standing attempt within FAO to develop farmers' rights to guarantee just compensation for traditional farmers who have developed and conserved for millennia the folk varieties and land-races from which high-yielding domesticated crop plants were developed – and upon whose future improvement and adaptation these crops still depend (Posey and Dutfield 1996).

Ethnobiologists and ethnoecologists have become leaders in the struggle to prevent extinction of plant and animal species and the loss of languages and cultures that encode knowledge about biodiversity and management strategies that conserve it. The International Society for Ethnobiology meets biennially and has developed, together with indigenous and traditional peoples, a model Code of Conduct to guide 'equitable partnerships' between experts in TEK and Western scientists. Many countries have their own societies or associations of ethnobiologists (namely, the United States, India, Mexico, Brazil, Thailand, and China). Several journals that deal specifically with ethnobiology and ethnoecology are published, including *Journal of Economic Botany* and *Journal of Ethnobiology* (both published in the United States), *Etnoecologica* (Mexico), and *Indian Journal of Ethnobotany*. There is also a global network of indigenous knowledge resource centres coordinated by the Centre for International Research and Advisory Networks (CIRAN/Nuffic), based in The Hague (Netherlands), which publishes the *Indigenous Knowledge and Development Monitor*. Ethical and benefit-sharing issues are dealt with by the international Working Group on Traditional Resource Rights and the Indigenous Peoples' Biodiversity Network.

2 The Declaration of Belém

The Declaration of Belém was proclaimed in 1988 at the First International Congress of Ethnobiology of the International Society of Ethnobiology (ISE). It outlined the responsibilities of scientists and environmentalists for addressing their efforts to the needs of local communities, and acknowledged the central role of indigenous peoples in all aspects of global environmental planning. Since 1988, several professional societies have followed the ISE example and made similar statements. The Declaration states as follows:

As ethnobiologists, we are alarmed that:
Since

- Tropical forests and other fragile ecosystems are disappearing;
- Many species, both plant and animal, are threatened with extinction; and
- Indigenous cultures around the world are being disrupted and destroyed;

And given

- That economic, agricultural, and health conditions of people are dependent on these resources;
- That native peoples have been stewards of 99 per cent of the world's genetic resources; and
- That there is an inextricable link between cultural and biological diversity;

We, members of the International Society of Ethnobiology, strongly urge action as follows:

1 Henceforth, a substantial proportion of development aid be devoted to efforts aimed at ethnobiological inventory, conservation, and management programmes.
2 Mechanisms be established by which indigenous specialists are recognized as proper authorities and are consulted in all programmes affecting them, their resources, and their environment.
3 All other inalienable human rights be recognized and guaranteed, including cultural and linguistic identity.
4 Procedures be developed to compensate native peoples for the utilization of their knowledge and their biological resources.
5 Educational programmes be implemented to alert the global community to the value of ethnobiological knowledge for human well-being.
6 All medical programmes include the recognition of and respect for traditional healers and the incorporation of traditional health practices that enhance the health status of these populations.
7 Ethnobiologists make available the results of their research to the native peoples with whom they have worked, especially including dissemination in the native language.
8 Exchange of information be promoted among indigenous and peasant peoples regarding conservation, management, and sustained utilization of resources.

3 The Convention on Biological Diversity: extracts from the Preamble, Articles 8.j and 18.4

Preamble

Recognizing the close and traditional dependence of many indigenous and local communities embodying traditional lifestyles on biological resources, and the desirability of sharing equitably benefits arising from the use of traditional knowledge, innovations and practices relevant to the conservation of biological diversity and the sustainable use of its components.

Article 8.j

Each Contracting Party shall, as far as possible and as appropriate:

> Subject to its national legislation, respect, preserve and maintain knowledge, innovations and practices of indigenous and local communities embodying traditional lifestyles relevant for the conservation and sustainable use of biological diversity and promote their wider application with the approval and involvement of the holders of such knowledge, innovations and practices and encourage the equitable sharing of the benefits arising from the utilization of such knowledge, innovations and practices

Article 18.4

The Contracting Parties shall, in accordance with national legislation and policies, encourage and develop methods of cooperation for the development and use of technologies, including traditional and indigenous technologies, in pursuance of the objectives of this Convention. For this purpose, the Contracting Parties shall also promote cooperation in the training of personnel and exchange of experts.

4 United Nations Draft Declaration on the Rights of Indigenous Peoples

(as agreed upon by members of the Working Group on Indigenous Populations at its 11th session, 1993)

Affirming that indigenous peoples are equal in dignity and rights to all other peoples, while recognizing the right of all peoples to be different, to consider themselves different, and to be respected as such,

Affirming also that all peoples contribute to the diversity and richness of civilizations and cultures, which constitute the common heritage of humankind,

Affirming further that all doctrines, policies and practices based on or advocating superiority of peoples or individuals on the basis of national origin, racial, religious, ethnic or cultural differences are racist, scientifically false, legally invalid, morally condemnable and socially unjust,

Reaffirming also that indigenous peoples, in the exercise of their rights, should be free from discrimination of any kind,

Concerned that indigenous peoples have been deprived of their human rights and fundamental freedoms, resulting, *inter alia*, in their colonization and dispossession of their lands, territories and resources, thus preventing them from exercising, in particular, their right to development in accordance with their own needs and interests,

Recognizing the urgent need to respect and promote the inherent rights and characteristics of indigenous peoples, especially their rights to their lands, territories and resources, which derive from their political, economic and social structures, and from their cultures, spiritual traditions, histories and philosophies,

Welcoming the fact that indigenous peoples are organizing themselves for political, economic, social and cultural enhancement and in order to bring an end to all forms of discrimination and oppression wherever they occur,

Convinced that control by indigenous peoples over developments affecting them and their lands, territories and resources will enable them to maintain and strengthen their institutions, cultures and traditions, and to promote their development in accordance with their institutions, cultures and traditions, and to promote their development in accordance with their aspirations and needs,

Recognizing also that respect for indigenous knowledge, cultures and traditional practices contributes to sustainable and equitable development and proper management of the environment,

Emphasizing the need for demilitarization of the lands and territories of indigenous peoples, which will contribute to peace, economic and social progress and development, understanding and friendly relations among the nations and peoples of the world,

Recognizing in particular the right of indigenous families and communities to retain shared responsibility for the upbringing, training, education and well-being of their children,

Recognizing also that indigenous peoples have the right freely to determine their relationships with States in a spirit of coexistence, mutual benefit and full respect,

Considering that treaties, agreements and other arrangements between States and indigenous peoples are properly matters of international concern and responsibility,

Acknowledging that the Charter of the United Nations, the International Covenant on Economic, Social and Cultural Rights and the International Covenant on Civil and Political Rights affirm the fundamental importance of the right of self-determination of all peoples, by virtue of which they freely determine their political status and freely pursue their economic, social and cultural development,

Bearing in mind that nothing in this Declaration may be used to deny any peoples their right of self-determination,

Encouraging States to comply with and effectively implement all international instruments, in particular those related to human rights, as they apply to indigenous peoples, in consultation and cooperation with the peoples concerned,

Emphasizing that the United Nations has an important and continuing role to play in promoting and protecting the rights of indigenous peoples,

Believing that this Declaration is a further important step forward for the recognition, promotion and protection of the rights and freedoms of indigenous peoples and in the development of relevant activities of the United Nations system in this field,

Solemnly proclaims the following United Nations Declaration on the Rights of Indigenous Peoples:

Articles

Part I

1. Indigenous peoples have the right to the full and effective enjoyment of all human rights and fundamental freedoms recognized in the Charter of the United Nations, the Universal Declaration of Human Rights and international human rights law.
2. Indigenous individuals and peoples are free and equal to other individuals and peoples in dignity and rights, and have the right to be free from any kind of adverse discrimination, in particular that based on their indigenous origin or identity.
3. Indigenous peoples have the right of self-determination. By virtue of that right they freely determine their political status and freely pursue their economic, social and cultural development.
4. Indigenous peoples have the right to maintain and strengthen their distinct political, economic, social and cultural characteristics, as well as their legal systems, while retaining their rights to participate fully, if they so choose, in the political, economic, social and cultural life of the State.
5. Every indigenous individual has the right to a nationality.

Part II

6. Indigenous peoples have the collective right to live in freedom, peace and security as distinct peoples and to full guarantees against genocide or any other act of violence, including the removal of indigenous children from their families and communities under any pretext.

    In addition, they have the individual rights to life, physical and mental integrity, liberty and security of person.
7. Indigenous peoples have the collective and individual right not to be subjected to ethnocide and cultural genocide, including prevention of and redress for:

    (a) Any action which has the aim or effect of depriving them of their integrity as distinct peoples, or of their cultural values or ethnic identities;
    (b) Any action which has the aim or effect of dispossessing them of their lands, territories or resources;
    (c) Any form of population transfer which has the aim or effect of violating or undermining any of their rights;

(d) Any form of assimilation or integration by other cultures or ways of life imposed on them by legislative, administrative or other measures;
(e) Any form of propaganda directed against them.

8 Indigenous peoples have the collective and individual right to maintain and develop their distinctive identities and characteristics, including the right to identify themselves as indigenous and to be recognized as such.
9 Indigenous peoples and individuals have the right to belong to an indigenous community or nation, in accordance with the traditions and customs of the community or nation concerned. No disadvantage of any kind may arise from the exercise of such a right.
10 Indigenous peoples shall not be forcibly removed from their lands or territories. No relocation shall take place without the free and informed consent of the indigenous peoples concerned and after agreement on just and fair compensation and, where possible, with the option of return.
11 Indigenous peoples have the right to special protection and security in periods of armed conflict.

States shall observe international standards, in particular the Fourth Geneva Convention of 1949, for the protection of civilian populations in circumstances of emergency and armed conflict, and shall not:

(a) Recruit indigenous individuals against their will into the armed forces and, in particular, for use against other indigenous peoples;
(b) Recruit indigenous children into the armed forces under any circumstances;
(c) Force indigenous individuals to abandon their lands, territories or means of subsistence, or relocate them in special centres for military purposes;
(d) Force indigenous individuals to work for military purposes under any discriminatory purposes.

Part III

12 Indigenous peoples have the right to practice and revitalize their cultural traditions and customs. This includes the right to maintain, protect and develop the past, present and future manifestations of their cultures, such as archaeological and historical sites, artifacts, designs, ceremonies, technologies and visual and performing arts and literature, as well as the right to the restitution of cultural, intellectual, religious and spiritual property taken without their free and informed consent or in violation of their laws, traditions and customs.
13 Indigenous peoples have the right to manifest, practice, develop and teach their spiritual and religious traditions, customs and ceremonies; the right to maintain, protect, and have access in privacy to their religious and cultural sites; the right to the use and control of ceremonial objects; and the right to the repatriation of human remains. States shall take effective measures, in conjunction with the indigenous peoples concerned, to ensure that indigenous sacred places, including burial sites, be preserved, respected and protected.

14 Indigenous peoples have the right to revitalize, use, develop and transmit to future generation their histories, languages, oral traditions, philosophies, writing systems and literatures, and to designate and retain their own names for communities, places and persons. States shall take effective measures, whenever any right of indigenous peoples may be threatened, to ensure this right is protected and also to ensure that they can understand and be understood in political, legal and administrative proceedings, where necessary through the provision of interpretation or by any other appropriate means.

Part IV

15 Indigenous children have the right to all levels and forms of education of the State. All indigenous peoples also have this right and the right to establish and control their educational systems and institutions providing education in their own languages, in a manner appropriate to their cultural methods of teaching and learning.

Indigenous children living outside their communities have the right to be provided access to education in their own culture and language.

States shall take effective measures to provide appropriate resources for these purposes.

16 Indigenous peoples have the right to have the dignity and diversity of their cultures, traditions, histories and aspirations appropriately reflected in all forms of education and public information. States shall take effective measure, in consultation with the indigenous peoples concerned, to eliminate prejudice and discrimination and to promote tolerance, understanding and good relations among indigenous peoples and all segments of society.

17 Indigenous peoples have the right to establish their own media in their own languages. They also have the right to equal access to all forms of non-indigenous media.

States shall take effective measures to ensure that State-owned media duly reflect indigenous cultural diversity.

18 Indigenous peoples have the right to enjoy fully all rights established under international labour law and national labour legislation. Indigenous peoples have the right not to be subjected to any discriminatory conditions of labour, employment or salary.

Part V

19 Indigenous peoples have the right to participate fully, if they so choose, at all levels of decision-making in matters which may affect their rights, lives and destinies through representatives chosen by themselves in accordance with their own procedures, as well as to maintain and develop their own indigenous decision-making institutions.

20 Indigenous peoples have the right to participate fully, if they so choose, through procedures determined by them, in devising legislative or administrative measures that may affect them.

States shall obtain the free and informed consent of the peoples concerned before adopting and implementing such measures.

21 Indigenous peoples have the right to maintain and develop their political, economic and social systems, to be secure in the enjoyment of their own means of subsistence and development, and to engage freely in all their traditional and other economic activities. Indigenous peoples who have been deprived of their means of subsistence and development are entitled to just and fair compensation.

22 Indigenous peoples have the right to special measures for the immediate, effective and continuing improvement of their economic and social conditions, including in the areas of employment, vocational training and retraining, housing, sanitation, health and social security. Particular attention shall be paid to the rights and special needs of indigenous elders, women, youth, children, and disabled persons.

23 Indigenous peoples have the right to determine and develop priorities and strategies for exercising their right to development. In particular, indigenous peoples have the right to determine and develop all health, housing and other economic and social programmes affecting them and, as far as possible, to administer such programmes through their own institutions.

24 Indigenous peoples have the right to their traditional medicines and health practices, including the right to the protection of vital medicinal plants, animals, and minerals. They also have the right to access, without any discrimination, to all medical institutions, health services and medical care.

Part VI

25 Indigenous peoples have the right to maintain and strengthen their distinctive spiritual and material relationships with the lands, territories, waters and coastal seas and other resources which they have traditionally owned or otherwise occupied or used, and to uphold their responsibilities to future generations in this regard.

26 Indigenous peoples have the right to own, develop, control and use the lands and territories, including the total environment of the lands, air, waters, coastal seas, sea-ice, flora and fauna and other resources which they have traditionally owned or otherwise occupied or used. This includes the right to the full recognition of their laws, traditions and customs, land-tenure systems and institutions for the development and management of resources, and the right to effective measures by States to prevent any interference with, alienation of or encroachment upon these rights.

27 Indigenous peoples have the right to the restitution of the lands, territories and resources which they have traditionally owned or otherwise occupied or used;

and which have been confiscated, occupied, used or damaged without their free and informed consent. Where this is not possible, they have the right to just and fair compensation. Unless otherwise freely agreed upon by the peoples concerned, compensation shall take the form of lands, territories and resources equal in quality, size and legal status.
28. Indigenous peoples have the right to the conservation, restoration and protection of the total environment and the productive capacity of their lands, territories and resources, as well as to assistance for this purpose from States and through international cooperation. Military activities shall not take place in the lands and territories of indigenous peoples, unless otherwise freely agreed upon by the peoples concerned. States shall take effective measures to ensure that no storage of hazardous materials shall take place in the lands and territories of indigenous peoples. States shall also take effective measures to ensure, as needed, that programmes for monitoring, maintaining and restoring the health of indigenous peoples, as developed and implemented by the peoples affected by such materials, are duly implemented.
29. Indigenous peoples are entitled to the recognition of the full ownership, control and protection of their cultural and intellectual property. They have the right to special measures to control, develop and protect their sciences, technologies and cultural manifestations, including human and other genetic resources, seeds, medicines, knowledge of the properties of fauna and flora, oral traditions, literatures, designs and visual and performing arts.
30. Indigenous peoples have the right to determine and develop priorities and strategies for the development or use of their lands, territories and other resources, including the right to require that States obtain their free and informed consent prior to the approval of any project affecting their lands, territories and other resources, particularly in connection with the development, utilization or exploitation of mineral, water or other resources. Pursuant to agreement with the indigenous peoples concerned, just and fair compensation shall be provided for any such activities and measures taken to mitigate adverse environmental, economic, social, cultural or spiritual impact.

Part VII

31. Indigenous peoples, as a specific form of exercising their right to self-determination, have the right to autonomy or self-government in matters relating to their internal and local affairs, including culture, religion, education, information, media, health, housing, employment, social welfare, economic activities, land and resources management, environment and entry by non-members, as well as ways and means for financing these autonomous functions.
32. Indigenous peoples have the collective right to determine their own citizenship in accordance with their customs and traditions. Indigenous citizenship does not impair the right of indigenous individuals to obtain citizenship of the States in which they live. Indigenous peoples have the right to determine the

structures and to select the membership of their institutions in accordance with their own procedures.
33 Indigenous peoples have the right to promote, develop and maintain their institutional structures and their distinctive juridical customs, traditions, procedures and practices, in accordance with internationally recognized human rights standards.
34 Indigenous peoples have the collective right to determine the responsibilities of individuals to their communities.
35 Indigenous peoples, in particular those divided by international borders, have the right to maintain and develop contacts, relations and cooperation, including activities for spiritual, cultural, political, economic and social purposes, with other peoples across borders. States shall take effective measures to ensure the exercise and implementation of this right.
36 Indigenous peoples have the right to the recognition, observance and enforcement of treaties, agreements and other constructive arrangements concluded with States or their successors, according to their original spirit and intent, and to have States honour and respect such treaties, agreements and other constructive arrangements. Conflicts and disputes which cannot otherwise be settled should be submitted to competent international bodies agreed to by all parties concerned.

Part VIII

37 States shall take effective and appropriate measures, in consultation with the indigenous peoples concerned, to give full effect to the provisions of this Declaration. The rights recognized herein shall be adopted and included in national legislation in such a manner that indigenous peoples can avail themselves of such rights in practice.
38 Indigenous peoples have the right to have access to adequate financial and technical assistance, from States and through international cooperation, to pursue freely their political, economic, social, cultural and spiritual development and for the enjoyment of the rights and freedoms recognized in this Declaration.
39 Indigenous peoples have the right to have access to and prompt decision through mutually acceptable and fair procedures for the resolution of conflicts and disputes with States, as well as to effective remedies for all infringements of their individual and collective rights. Such a decision shall take into consideration the customs, traditions, rules and legal systems of the indigenous peoples concerned.
40 The organs and specialized agencies of the United Nations system and other intergovernmental organizations shall contribute to the full realization of the provisions of this Declaration through the mobilization, *inter alia*, of financial cooperation and technical assistance. Ways and means of ensuring participation of indigenous peoples on issues affecting them shall be established.

41 The United Nations shall take the necessary steps to ensure the implementation of this Declaration including the creation of a body at the highest level with special competence in this field and with the direct participation of indigenous peoples. All United Nations bodies shall promote respect for and full application of the provisions of this Declaration.

Part IX

42 The rights recognized herein constitute the minimum standards for the survival, dignity and well-being of the indigenous peoples of the world.
43 All the rights and freedoms recognized herein are equally guaranteed to male and female indigenous individuals.
44 Nothing in this Declaration may be construed as diminishing or extinguishing existing or future rights indigenous peoples may have or acquire.
45 Nothing in this Declaration may be interpreted as implying for any State, group or person any right to engage in any activity or to perform any act contrary to the Charter of the United Nations.

5 The Covenant on Intellectual, Cultural, and Scientific Resources

Prologue

Indigenous peoples are unanimous in identifying their primary concern as being self-determination, which subsumes such basic rights as recognition of and respect for their cultures, societies, and languages, as well as ownership over their own lands and territories, and control over the resources that are associated with those lands and territories. Intellectual, cultural and scientific property rights are seen as a starting point to defining a more useful category of traditional values, knowledge, and resources that have often been used and misused without authorization, recognition of origin, or just compensation.

This Covenant should in no way be construed as being a call for commoditization-commercialization of culture, biogenetic resources, or knowledge; nor is it a justification for bringing indigenous peoples unwillingly into commercial relationships with other societies. The Covenant recognizes that trade relationships have been generally harmful to local communities in the past. It is exactly for this reason, together with the fact that an increasing number of indigenous and traditional communities are opting for or are being forced into dangerous trade relationships, that a Covenant is necessary. This is an attempt to provide a basic code of ethics and conduct that will hopefully form the basis for equitable partnerships that lead to economic independence for local communities, while providing for the conservation of natural resources.

Practically, the Covenant is proposed as a model that can be tried in many parts of the world by many partners. There will undoubtedly be failures, but hopefully there will be many successes. The accumulation of these experiences will produce a new category that will replace IPR with a more powerful and decisive concept that, ideally, will catalyse the replacement of markets for temporary gain with trade based upon long term commitments that result in mutual advantages – turning businesses from being vanguards of destruction into equitable partners with local communities in the conservation of biological and cultural diversity.

Implementation of the Covenant will be a long-term process that will require nurturing, patience, and tolerance. The process can only work successfully if both parties come to understand and appreciate the other, and if both see the relationship as a means to improving not just their own lots, but the whole of the Earth.

Spirit of the Covenant

This Covenant is celebrated in order to

Support indigenous and traditional peoples in their fight against genocide and for their land, territory, and control over their own resources, while strengthening the culture and local community through recognition and support of the groups' own goals, values, and objectives, by helping to find ways of responsibly utilizing, while conserving the biological/ecological/cultural richness of the region, through equitable and responsible trade, sourcing, research and development, thereby establishing a long term relationship built through joint decision-making based upon the principles of equality of relationships and protection of traditional values, knowledge and culture; if these basic elements are not respected, then the Covenant is endangered, and along with it, the spirit of trust and partnership between responsible businesses/scientists/institutions and local communities that is essential for the future well-being of the planet.

What is being protected

Although the essence of this Covenant is about the development of responsible research and equitable trade, any Intellectual Property Rights agreement must inevitably deal with protection. The first concern of indigenous peoples is their right not to sell, commoditize or have expropriated from them certain domains of knowledge and certain sacred places, plants, animals and objects. All other elements of the Covenant are preconditioned by this basic right, which is considered a fundamental element of self-determination.

Thus, the first category for protection is

1. Sacred property (images, sounds, knowledge, material, culture or anything that is deemed sacred and, thereby, not commoditizable).

The following categories are recognized as providing the basis for protection and just compensation, if, and only if authorized by the community, society and cultural group.

2   Knowledge of current use, previous use, and/or potential use of plant and animal species, as well as soils and minerals;
3   Knowledge of preparation, processing, or storage of useful species;
4   Knowledge of formulations involving more than one ingredient;
5   Knowledge of individual species (planting methods, care for, selection criteria, etc.);
6   Knowledge of ecosystem conservation (methods of protecting or preserving a resource that may be found to have commercial value, although not specifically used for that purpose or other practical purposes by the local community or the culture);
7   Biogenetic resources that originate (or originated) on indigenous lands and territories;
8   Cultural property (images, sounds, crafts, arts and performances);
9   Classificatory systems of knowledge, such as traditional plant taxonomies.

All of these are protected as part of the larger need to protect land, territory and resources and to stimulate self-determination for indigenous/traditional peoples.

Basic principles to be exercised by all partners

(i)   Equity of partners, including profit-sharing, joint planning and goal-setting, informed consent and full disclosure in all aspects of the project, including results;
(ii) Working to insure that compensation is equitably shared within and among groups, and that compensation is in a form that strengthens the community and ethnic group;
(iii) Non-exclusivity of relationships, meaning that both parties are free to enter into agreements with other parties; priority for exchange will obviously be between partners;
(iv) Confidentiality of information and resources, meaning that information imparted by the indigenous group to the partner cannot be passed on to others without the consent of the giver;
(v)   Continual dialogue and mutual review, supported by independent monitoring and, if necessary, mediation by a third party (as agreed by partners); mandatory review is required if there is a change of status of either party or in the law;

(vi) Diversification of the economic base through diversification of collecting, ingredients and products based upon traditional knowledge, cultural practice and local resources, as well as diversification of markets;
(vii) Cooperation with local (indigenous and non-indigenous) educational, health, research and non-governmental institutions;
(viii) Insuring ecological and cultural sensitivity in all phases of any project, including collecting, screening, sourcing, production and manufacture;
(ix) Encouragement of community autonomy and control over all aspects of the projects as early as possible.

Additional principles to be observed by the company, scientist or institution

(x) Responsibility to be informed about local, regional and national laws, customs and cultures.
(xi) Judicial recognition and registration of this agreement, followed by appropriate legal protection to enable the indigenous group to protect its knowledge and biogenetic resources.

Additional principles to be observed by the indigenous group

(xii) Establishment of a consensus on representation, group participation, ethnic boundaries and 'legal personality(ies) of partner(s)';
(xiii) Commitment to work toward assuming legal, economic and financial independence.

Additional principles for independent monitors

(xiv) Must have no conflict of interests and be able to act as arbitrators or mediators for all parties.
(xv) Must have the professional qualifications and relevant experiences to represent all parties equitably.
(xvi) Must practise full information disclosure and provide a public statement of working procedures and principles.
(xvii) Must serve as the guardian of the Covenant, providing audits when requested by either party, but at least once annually, on actual practice in all areas of the agreement.
(Source: Prepared by the Global Coalition for Bio-Cultural Diversity 1993)

6 Traditional Resource Rights

Category	Supporting agreements	
	Legally binding	Not legally binding
Human rights	ICESCR, ICCPR, CDW, CERD, CG, CRC, NLs	UDHR, DDRIP, VDPA
Right to self-determination	ICESCR, ICCPR	DDRIP, VDPA
Collective rights	ILO169, ICESCR, ICCPR	DDRIP, VDPA
Land and territorial rights	ILO169, NLs	DDRIP
Right to religious freedom	ICCPR, NLs	UDHR
Right to development	ICESCR, ICCPR, ILO169	DDHRE, DDRIP, DHRD, VDPA
Right to privacy	ICCPR, NLs	UDHR
Prior informed consent	CBD, NLs	DDRIP
Environmental integrity	CBD	DDHRE, RD
Intellectual property rights	CBD, GATT, UPOV, WIPO, NLs	
Neighbouring rights	RC, NLs	
Right to enter into legal agreements, such as contracts and covenants	NLs	
Cultural property rights	UNESCO-CCP, UNESCO-WHC, NLs	
Right to protection of folklore	NLs	UNESCO-WIPO, UNESCO-F
Right to protection of cultural heritage	UNESCO-WHC, NLs	UNESCO-PICC
Recognition of cultural landscapes	UNESCO-WHC	
Recognition of customary law and practice	CBD, ILO169, NLs	DDRIP
Farmers' rights		FAO-IUPGR

Notes

CBD, UN *Convention on Biological Diversity* (1992): 140 states parties as of 28 April 1996.

CDW, UN *Convention on the Elimination of all Forms of Discrimination Against Women* (1979): 138 states parties as of 31 December 1994.

CERD, UN *Convention on the Elimination of all Forms of Racial Discrimination* (1966): 142 states parties as of 31 December 1994.

CG, UN *Convention on the Prevention and Punishment of the Crime of Genocide* (1948): 116 state parties as of 31 December 1994.

CRC, UN *Convention on the Rights of the Child* (1994): 168 states parties as of 31 December 1994.

DDHRE, UN *Draft Declaration of Principles on Human Rights and the Environment* (1994).

DDRIP, UN *Draft Declaration on the Rights of Indigenous Peoples* (formally adopted by the UN's Working Group on indigenous Populations in July 1994).

DHRD, UN *Declaration on the Human Right to Development* (1986).

FAO-IUPGR, *International Undertaking on Plant Genetic Resources* (1987 version).

GATT, *Final Document Embodying the Results of the Uruguay Round of Multilateral Trade Negotiations* (1994).

ICCPR, UN *International Covenant on Civil and Political Rights* (1966): 129 states parties as of 31 December 1994.

Appendices 223

ICESCR, UN *International Covenant on Economic, Social and Cultural Rights* (1966): 131 states parties as of 31 December 1994.
ILO169, International Labour Organisation *Convention 169 concerning indigenous and tribal peoples in independent countries* (1989): 7 states parties.
NLs, national laws.
RC, *Rome Convention for the Protection of Performers, Producers of Phonograms and Broadcasting Organisations* (1961): 47 states parties as of 31 December 1994.
RD, Rio Declaration (1992).
UDHR, *Universal Declaration of Human Rights* (1948).
UNESCO-CCP, *Convention on the Means of Prohibiting and Preventing the Illicit Import, Export and Transfer of Ownership of Cultural Property* (1970): 79 states parties as of 1 January 1994.
UNESCO-F, Recommendations on the Safeguarding of Traditional Culture and Folklore (1989).
UNESCO-PICC, Declaration on the Principles of International Cultural Cooperation.
UNESCO-WHC, *Convention Concerning the Protection of the World Cultural and Natural Heritage* (1972): 135 states parties as of 1 January 1994.
UNESCO-WIPO, *Model Provisions for National Laws on Protection of Expressions of Folklore Against Illicit Exploitation and Other Prejudicial Actions* (1985).
UPOV, *International Union for the Protection of New Varieties of Plants Convention* (1961, revised in 1972, 1978, and 1991): 27 states parties as of 31 December 1994.
VDPA, UN *Vienna Declaration and Programme of Action* (1993).
WIPO, World Intellectual Property Organisation (administers international IPR agreements, such as: the *Paris Convention for the Protection of Industrial Property* (1883, revised most recently in 1967): 129 states parties as of 31 December 1994; *Berne Convention for the Protection of Literary and Artistic Works* (1886, revised most recently in 1971): 111 states parties as of 31 December 1994; *Madrid Agreement Concerning the International Registration of Trademarks* (1891, revised most recently in 1967): 43 states parties as of 31 December 1994; *Lisbon Agreement for the Protection of Appellations of Origin and their International Registration* (1958, revised most recently in 1967): 17 states parties as of 31 December 1994; *Patent Cooperation Treaty* (1970): 77 states parties as of 31 December 1994.

7 Summary of Principal Intellectual Property Rights Instruments

Intellectual property rights have a variety of forms. The following four are the most important in the context of this discussion.

Patents

A patent gives an inventor exclusive rights to prevent others from producing, using, selling or importing the invention for a fixed time-period (usually 17–20 years). Legal action can be taken against those who infringe the patent. To be a patentable 'invention' the application must satisfy the patent examiners that it is:

- *useful*: it must have industrial application;
- *novel*: it should be recent and original, but perhaps most importantly it should not already be known (in the public domain). In most countries (except the USA) the patent is awarded to the first person to apply, whether or not this person was the first to invent;
- *non-obvious*: not obvious to a person skilled in the technology, and more inventive than a mere discovery of what already exists in nature (such as a gene with no known function). In the case of an invented *process*, the patent can cover

a 'non-obvious' way of making something already known (i.e. previously invented or discovered). In the case of an invented *product*, the non-obvious requirement does not require it to be made by a novel method.

Patents of the following types may be granted (Lesser 1991):

- *products per se*: covers any use of the product including those as yet undiscovered. For example, a new drug patented as a cure for cancer may later be found to cure heart disease, and the patent will cover this new use;
- *uses*: covers a specific use only. Thus, it would cover the above drug only as a cure for cancer, and not for any uses that are found later;
- *processes*: protects the process when used with *any* product, but it does not protect the invention when it can be manufactured by a different process;
- *products-by-process*: covers only products made by the process described in the application. Therefore, it would cover the drug, but only when made by a specified process.

Copyright

Copyright gives authors legal protection for several types of work, such as:

- literary works;
- dramatic and musical works;
- artistic works and works of applied art;
- motion pictures and sound recordings;
- computer programs and databases.

Copyright law is intended to protect authors by granting them exclusive rights to sell copies of their work in whatever *tangible* form (printed publication, sound recording, film, broadcast, etc.) is being used to convey his or her creative expressions to the public. Legal protection covers the 'expression' of the ideas contained, not the ideas themselves, which are not actually required to be novel at all. Copyright gives owners exclusive rights, usually for the life of the author plus 50 years. Copyright owners have the legal right to stop others from:

- copying or reproducing the work;
- performing the work in public;
- making a sound recording or motion picture of the work;
- broadcasting, translating and adapting the work.

Trade secrets

Know-how is information that may give a person or company a competitive advantage yet fail to fulfil the criteria of patentability. Nevertheless, if the information is known only to a few people it can still have legal recognition and protection as a trade secret. The claim for protection as a trade secret requires that efforts be made to prevent disclosure. Agreements between Indigenous peoples and others to respect the confidential nature of information disclosed, and strictly enforced access restrictions are examples of such efforts. Trade secret law makes the taking without permission of a trade secret an illegal act, but not the discovery by proper means that is, by independent discovery, accidental or actual disclosure, or by reverse engineering.

Plant Breeders' Rights

The UPOV (Union for the Protection of New Varieties of Plants) Convention provides for rights commonly known as Plant Breeders' Rights (PBR). According to the latest 1991 revision of the Convention, breeders are people who breed, discover, or develop crop varieties. These rights prevent other breeders from breeding and selling the same plant varieties. The UPOV Convention only has force in its twenty member countries. To be eligible for protection the plant variety must be:

- *distinct*: distinguishable by one or more characteristics from any other variety whose existence is a matter of common knowledge;
- *stable*: remain true to its description after repeated reproduction or propagation;
- *uniform*: homogeneous with regard to the particular feature of its sexual reproduction or vegetative propagation;
- *novel*: not have been offered for sale or marketed, with the agreement of the breeder or his successor in title, in that country, or for longer than four years in any other country.

8 Scientific and Professional Societies that have developed Guidelines on Intellectual Property Rights

1988: *Declaration of Belém* from the International Society for Ethnobiology
1988: *The Chiang Mai Declaration for Conservation of Medicinal Plants* by WWF/IUCN/WHO
1990: *The Code of Ethics for Foreign Collectors of Biological Samples* developed at the Botany 2000 Herbarium Curation Workshop
1990: *The first Code of Ethics on Obligations to Indigenous Peoples of the World Archaeological Congress*
1991: *Professional Ethics in Economic Botany: A Preliminary Draft of Guidelines of the Society of Economic Botany*
1992: *Conclusions of the Workshop on Drug Development, Biological Diversity and Economic Growth* of the National Institutes of Health/National Cancer Institute
1992: *Williamsburg Declaration* of the American Society of Pharmacognosy

1992: *The Bukittinggi Declaration* at the UNESCO Seminar on the Chemistry of Rainforest Plants
1992: *The Manila Declaration*, developed at the Seventh Asian Symposium on Medicinal Plants, Spices and Other Natural Products (ASOMPS VII)
1993: *Guidelines for Equitable Partnerships in New Natural Products Development* of the People and Plants Initiative of WWF, UNESCO and Kew Gardens

(Source: Derived from Posey and Dutfield 1996)

9 Research Principles for Community-controlled Research with the Tapirisat Inuit of Canada (Selected Principles)

1 Informed consent should be obtained from the community and from any individuals involved in research.
2 In seeking informed consent the researcher should at least explain the purpose of the research; sponsors of research; the person in charge; potential benefits and possible problems associated with the research for people and the environment; research methodology; participation of or contact with residents of the community.
3 Anonymity and confidentiality must be offered and, if accepted, guaranteed except where this is legally precluded.
4 On-going communication of research objectives, methods, findings and interpretation from inception to completion of project should occur.
9 Research must respect the privacy, dignity, cultures, traditions and rights of aboriginal people.
10 Written information should be available in the appropriate language(s).
12 Aboriginal people should have access to research data, not just receive summaries and research reports. The extent of data accessibility that participants/communities can expect should be clearly stated and agreed upon as part of any approval process.

(Source: Derived from Inuit Tapirisit of Canada 1993)

10 Kari-Oca Declaration and Indigenous Peoples Earth Charter (25–30 May 1992)

Preamble

The World Conference of Indigenous Peoples on Territory, Environment and Development (25–30 May 1992).

The Indigenous Peoples of the Americas, Asia, Africa, Australia, Europe, and the Pacific, united in one voice at Kari-Oca Villages express our collective gratitude to the indigenous peoples of Brazil. Inspired by this historical meeting, we celebrate the spiritual unity of the indigenous peoples with the land and ourselves.

We continue building and formulating our united commitment to save our Mother the Earth. We, the indigenous peoples, endorse the following declaration as our collective responsibility to carry our indigenous minds and voices into the future.

Declaration

We the Indigenous Peoples, walk to the future in the footprints of our ancestors.

- From the smallest to the largest living being, from the four directions, from the air, the land and the mountains, the creator has placed us, the indigenous peoples upon our Mother the Earth.
- The footprints of our ancestors are permanently etched upon the land of our peoples.
- We the Indigenous Peoples, maintain our inherent rights to self-determination.
- We have always had the right to decide our own forms of government, to use our own laws to raise and educate our children, to our own cultural identity without interference.
- We continue to maintain our rights as peoples despite centuries of deprivation, assimilation and genocide.
- We maintain our inalienable rights to our lands and territories, to all our resources – above and below – and to our waters. We assert our ongoing responsibility to pass these onto the future generations.
- We cannot be removed from our lands. We the Indigenous Peoples, are connected by the circle of life to our land and environments.
- We the indigenous peoples, walk to the future in the footprints of our ancestors.

(Signed at Kari-Oca, Brazil on the 30th day of May, 1992)

Indigenous Peoples Earth Charter

Human rights and international law

1 We demand the right to life.
2 International law must deal with the collective human rights of indigenous peoples.
3 There are many international instruments which deal with the rights of individuals but there are no declarations to recognize collective human rights. Therefore, we urge governments to support the United Nations Working Group on Indigenous Peoples' (UNWGIP) Universal Declaration of Indigenous Rights, which is presently in draft form.
4 There exist many examples of genocide against indigenous peoples. Therefore, the convention against genocide must be changed to include the genocide of indigenous peoples.
5 The United Nations should be able to send indigenous peoples' representatives, in a peace keeping capacity, into indigenous territories where conflicts

arise. This would be done at the request and consent of the indigenous peoples concerned.

6. The concept of Terra Nullius must be eliminated from international law usage. Many state governments have used internal domestic laws to deny us ownership of our own lands. These illegal acts should be condemned by the World.
7. Where small numbers of indigenous peoples are residing within state boundaries, so-called democratic countries have denied indigenous peoples the right of consent about their future, using the notion of majority rules to decide the future of indigenous peoples. Indigenous peoples' right of consent to projects in their areas must be recognized.
8. We must promote the term 'indigenous peoples' at all fora. The use of the term 'indigenous peoples' must be without qualifications.
9. We urge governments to ratify International Labour Organisation (ILO) Convention 169 to guarantee an international legal instrument for indigenous peoples (Group 2 only).
10. Indigenous peoples' distinct and separate rights within their own territories must be recognised.
11. We assert our rights to free passage through state imposed political boundaries dividing our traditional territories. Adequate mechanisms must be established to secure this right.
12. The colonial systems have tried to dominate and assimilate our peoples. However, our peoples remain distinct despite these pressures.
13. Our indigenous governments and legal systems must be recognized by the United Nations, State governments and International legal instruments.
14. Our right to self-determination must be recognized.
15. We must be free from population transfer.
16. We maintain our right to our traditional way of life.
17. We maintain our right to our spiritual way of life.
18. We maintain the right to be free from pressures from multinational (transnational) corporations upon lives and lands. All multinational (transnational) corporations which are encroaching upon indigenous lands should be reported to the United Nations Transnational Office.
19. We must be free from racism.
20. We maintain the right to decide the direction of our communities.
21. The United Nations should have a special procedure to deal with issues arising from violations of indigenous treaties.
22. Treaties signed between indigenous peoples and non-indigenous peoples must be accepted as treaties under international law.
23. The United Nations must exercise the right to impose sanctions against governments that violate the rights of indigenous peoples.
24. We urge the United Nations to include the issue of indigenous peoples in the agenda of the World Conference of Human Rights to be held in 1993. The work done so far by The United Nations Inter-American Commission on Human

Rights and the Inter-American Institute of Human Rights should be taken into consideration.

25 Indigenous peoples should have the right to their own knowledge, language, and culturally appropriate education, including bicultural and bilingual education. Through recognizing both formal and informal ways, the participation of family and community is guaranteed.

26 Our health rights must include the recognition and respect of traditional knowledge held by indigenous healers. This knowledge, including our traditional medicines and their preventive and spiritual healing power, must be recognized and protected against exploitation.

27 The World Court must extend its powers to include complaints by indigenous peoples.

28 There must be a monitoring system from this conference to oversee the return of delegates to their territories. The delegates should be free to attend and participate in International Indigenous Conferences.

29 Indigenous Women's Rights must be respected. Women must be included in all local, national, regional, and international organizations.

30 The above mentioned historical rights of indigenous peoples must be guaranteed in national legislation.

(*Please note for the purposes of the Declaration and this statement any use of the term 'Indigenous Peoples' also includes Tribal Peoples.)

Land and territories

31 Indigenous peoples were placed upon our Mother, the Earth by the Creator. We belong to the land. We cannot be separated from our lands and territories.

32 Our territories are living totalities in permanent vital relation between human beings and nature. Their possession produce the development of our culture. Our territorial property should be inalienable, unceasable and not denied title. Legal, economic and technical back up are needed to guarantee this.

33 Indigenous peoples' inalienable rights to land and resources confirm that we have always had ownership and stewardship over our traditional territories. We demand that these be respected.

34 We assert our rights to demarcate our traditional territories. The definition of territory includes space (air), land, and sea. We must promote a traditional analysis of traditional land rights in all our territories.

35 Where indigenous territories have been degraded, resources must be made available to restore them. The recuperation of those affected territories is the duty of the respective jurisdiction in all nation states which cannot be delayed. Within this process of recuperation the compensation for the historical ecological debt must be taken into account. Nation states must revise in depth the agrarian, mining and forestry policies.

36 Indigenous peoples reject the assertion of non-indigenous laws onto our lands. States cannot unilaterally extend their jurisdiction over our lands and

territories. The concept of Terra Nullius should be forever erased from the law books of states.
37 We, as indigenous peoples, must never alienate our lands. We must always maintain control over the land for future generations.
38 If a non indigenous government, individual or corporation wants to use our lands, then there must be a formal agreement which sets out the terms and conditions. Indigenous peoples maintain the right to be compensated for the use of their lands and resources.
39 Traditional indigenous territorial boundaries, including the waters, must be respected.
40 There must be some control placed upon environmental groups who are lobbying to protect our territories and the species within those territories. In many instances, environmental groups are more concerned about animals than human beings. We call for indigenous peoples to determine guidelines prior to allowing environmental groups into their territories.
41 Parks must not be created at the expense of indigenous peoples. There is no way to separate indigenous peoples from their lands.
42 Indigenous peoples must not be removed from their lands in order to make it available to settlers or other forms of economic activity on their lands.
43 In many instances, the numbers of indigenous peoples have been decreasing due to encroachment by non-indigenous peoples.
44 Indigenous peoples should encourage their peoples to cultivate their own traditional forms of products rather than to use imported exotic crops which do not benefit local peoples.
45 Toxic wastes must not be deposited in our areas. Indigenous peoples must realize that chemicals, pesticides and hazardous wastes do not benefit the peoples.
46 Traditional areas must be protected against present and future forms of environmental degradation.
47 There must be a cessation of all uses of nuclear material.
48 Mining of products for nuclear production must cease.
49 Indigenous lands must not be used for the testing or dumping of nuclear products.
50 Population transfer policies by state governments in our territories are causing hardship. Traditional lands are lost and traditional livelihoods are being destroyed.
51 Our lands are being used by state governments to obtain funds from the World Bank, the International Monetary Fund, the Asian Pacific Development Bank and other institutions which have led to a loss of our lands and territories.
52 In many countries our lands are being used for military purposes. This is an unacceptable use of the lands.
53 The colonizer governments have changed the names of our traditional and sacred areas. Our children learn these foreign names and start to lose their

identity. In addition, changing the name of a place diminishes respect for the spirits which reside in those areas.
54 Our forests are not being used for their intended purposes. The forests are being used to make money.
55 Traditional activities, such as making pottery, are being destroyed by the importation of industrial goods. This impoverishes the local peoples.

Biodiversity and conservation

56 The Vital Circles are in a continuous interrelation in such a way that the change of one of its elements affects the whole.
57 Climatic changes affect indigenous peoples and all humanity. In addition ecological systems and their rhythms are affected which contributes to the deterioration of our quality of life and increases our dependency.
58 The forests are being destroyed in the name of development and economical gains without considering the destruction of ecological balance. These activities do not benefit human beings, animals, birds, and fish. The logging concessions and incentives to the timber, cattle, and mining industries affecting the ecosystems and the natural resources should be cancelled.
59 We value the efforts of protection of the Biodiversity but we reject being included as part of an inert diversity which pretends to be maintained for scientific and folkloric purposes.
60 The indigenous peoples strategies should be kept in a reference framework for the formulation and application of national policies on environment and biodiversity.

Development strategies

61 Indigenous peoples must consent to all projects in our territories. Prior to consent being obtained the peoples must be fully and entirely involved in any decisions. They must be given all the information about the project and its effects. Failure to do so should be considered a crime against the indigenous peoples. The person or persons who violate this should be tried in a world tribunal within the control of indigenous peoples set for such a purpose. This could be similar to the trials held after the Second World War.
62 We have the right to our own development strategies based on our cultural practices and with a transparent, efficient and viable management and with economical and ecological viability.
63 Our development and life strategies are obstructed by the interests of the government and big companies and by the neoliberal policies. Our strategies have, as a fundamental condition, the existence of International relationships based on justice, equity, and solidarity between the human beings and the nations.

64 Any development strategy should prioritise the elimination of poverty, the climatic guarantee, the sustainable manageability of natural resources, the continuity of democratic societies and the respect of cultural differences.

65 The global environmental facility should assign at best 20 per cent for indigenous peoples' strategies and programs of environmental emergency, improvement of life quality, protection of natural resources and rehabilitation of ecosystems. This proposal in the case of South America and the Caribbean should be concrete in the Indigenous development fund as a pilot experience in order to be extended to the indigenous peoples of other regions and continents.

66 The concept of development has meant the destruction of our lands. We reject the current definition of development as being useful to our peoples. Our cultures are not static and we keep our identity through a permanent recreation of our life conditions; but all of this is obstructed in/the name of so-called developments.

67 Recognizing indigenous peoples' harmonious relationship with Nature, indigenous sustainable development strategies and cultural values must be respected as distinct and vital sources of knowledge.

68 Indigenous peoples have been here since the time before time began. We have come directly from the Creator. We have lived and kept the Earth as it was on the First Day. Peoples who do not belong to the land must go out from the lands because those things (so called 'Development' on the land) are against the laws of creator.

69 (a) In order for indigenous peoples to assume control, management and administration of their resources and territories, development projects must be based on the principles of self-determination and self-management.
(b) Indigenous peoples must be self-reliant.

70 If we are going to grow crops, we must feed the peoples. It is not appropriate that the lands be used to grow crops which do not benefit the local peoples.
(a) Regarding indigenous policies, State Governments must cease attempts of assimilation and integration.
(b) Indigenous peoples must consent to all projects in their territories. Prior to consent being obtained, the peoples must be fully and entirely involved in any decisions. They must be given all the information about the project and its effects. Failure to do so should be considered a crime against indigenous peoples. The person or persons responsible should be tried before a World Tribunal, with a balance of indigenous peoples set up for such a purpose. This could be similar to the Trials held after the Second World War.

71 We must never use the term 'land claims'. It is the non-indigenous peoples which do not have any land. All the land is our land. It is non-indigenous peoples who are making claims to our lands. We are not making claims to our lands.

72 There should be a monitoring body within the United Nations to monitor all the land disputes around the World prior to development.

73 There should be a United Nations' Conference on the topic of 'Indigenous Lands and Development'.

74 Non-indigenous peoples have come to our lands for the purpose of exploiting these lands and resources to benefit themselves, and for the impoverishment of our peoples. Indigenous peoples are victims of development. In many cases indigenous peoples are exterminated in the name of a development program. There are numerous examples of such occurrences.

75 Development that occurs on indigenous lands, without the consent of indigenous peoples, must be stopped.

76 Development which is occurring on indigenous lands is usually decided without local consultation by those who are unfamiliar with local conditions and needs.

77 The eurocentric notion of ownership is destroying our peoples. We must return to our own view of the world, of the land and of development. The issue cannot be separated from indigenous peoples' rights.

78 There are many different types of so-called development: road construction, communication facilities such as electricity, telephones. These allow developers easier access to the areas, but the effects of such industrialisation destroy the lands.

79 There is a world wide move to remove indigenous peoples from their lands and place them in villages. The relocation from the traditional territories is done to facilitate development.

80 It is not appropriate for governments or agencies to move into our territories and to tell our peoples what is needed.

81 In many instances, the state governments have created artificial entities such as 'district council' in the name of the state government in order to deceive the international community. These artificial entities then are consulted about development in the area. The state government, then, claim that indigenous peoples were consulted about the project. These lies must be exposed to the international community.

82 There must be an effective network to disseminate material and information between indigenous peoples. This is necessary in order to keep informed about the problems of other indigenous peoples.

83 Indigenous peoples should form and direct their own environmental network.

Culture, science, and intellectual property

84 We feel the Earth as if we are within our mother. When the Earth is sick and polluted, human health is impossible. To heal ourselves, we must heal the Planet, and to heal the Planet, we must heal ourselves.

85 We must begin to heal from the grassroots level and work towards the international level.

86 The destruction of the culture has always been considered an internal, domestic problem within national states. The United Nations must set up a tribunal to review the cultural destruction of the indigenous peoples.

87 We need to have foreign observers come into our indigenous territories to oversee national state elections to prevent corruption.

88 The human remains and artefacts of indigenous peoples must be returned to their original peoples.
89 Our sacred and ceremonial sites should be protected and considered as the patrimony of indigenous peoples and humanity. The establishment of a set of legal and operational instruments at both national and international levels would guarantee this.
90 The use of existing indigenous languages is our right. These languages must be protected.
91 States that have outlawed indigenous languages and their alphabets should be censored by United Nations.
92 We must not allow tourism to be used to diminish our culture. Tourists come into the communities and view the people as if indigenous peoples were part of a zoo. Indigenous peoples have the right to allow or to disallow tourism within their areas.
93 Indigenous peoples must have the necessary resources and control over their own education systems.
94 Elders must be recognized and respected as teachers of the young people.
95 Indigenous wisdom must be recognized and encouraged.
96 The traditional knowledge of herbs and plants must be protected and passed onto future generations.
97 Traditions cannot be separated from land, territory or science.
98 Traditional knowledge has enabled indigenous peoples to survive.
99 The usurping of traditional medicines and knowledge from indigenous peoples should be considered a crime against peoples.
100 Material culture is being used by the non-indigenous to gain access to our lands and resources, thus destroying our cultures.
101 Most of the media at this conference were only interested in the pictures which will be sold for profit. This another case of exploitation of indigenous peoples. This does not advance the cause of indigenous peoples.
102 As creators and carriers of civilizations which have given and continue to share knowledge, experience and values with humanity, we require that our right to intellectual and cultural properties be guaranteed and that the mechanism for each implementation be in favour of our peoples and studied in depth and implemented. This respect must include the right over genetic resources, genebanks, biotechnology and knowledge of biodiversity programmes.
103 We should list the suspect museums and institutions that have misused our cultural and intellectual properties.
104 The protection, norms and mechanisms of artistic and artisan creation of our peoples must be established and implemented in order to avoid plunder, plagiarism, undue exposure and use.
105 When indigenous peoples leave their communities, they should make every effort to return to the community.
106 In many instances, our songs, dances and ceremonies have been viewed as the only aspects of our lives. In some instances, we have been asked to change a ceremony or a song to suit the occasion. This is racism.

107 At local, national, international levels, governments must commit funds to new and existing resources to education and training for indigenous peoples, to achieve their sustainable development, to contribute and to participate in sustainable and equitable development at all levels. Particular attention should be given to indigenous women, children and youth.
108 All kinds of folkloric discrimination must be stopped and forbidden.
109 The United Nations should promote research into indigenous knowledge and develop a network of indigenous sciences.

11 Principles for 'Equitable Partnerships' established by the International Society for Ethnobiology

1 *Principle of Self-Determination*: This principle recognizes that indigenous peoples have a right to self determination (or local determination for traditional and local communities) and that researchers shall as appropriate acknowledge and respect such rights. Culture and language are intrinsically connected to land and territory, and cultural and linguistic diversity are inextricably linked to biological diversity; therefore, the principle of self-determination includes: (i) The right to control land and territory; (ii) the right to sacred places; (iii) the right to (own / determine the use of / accreditation, protection and compensation for) knowledge; (iv) the right of access to traditional resources; (v) the right to preserve and protect local language, symbols and modes of expression (vi) and the right to self-definition.

2 *Principle of Inalienability*: This principle recognizes the inalienable rights of indigenous peoples and local communities in relation to their traditional lands, territories, forests, fisheries and other natural resources. These rights are both individual and collective, with local peoples determining which ownership regimes are appropriate.

3 *Principle of Minimum Impact*: This principle recognizes the duty of scientists and researchers to ensure that their research and activities have minimum impact on local communities.

4 *Principle of Full Disclosure*: This principle recognizes that it is important for the indigenous and traditional peoples and local communities to have disclosed to them (in a manner that they can comprehend), the manner in which the research is to be undertaken, how information is to be gathered and the ultimate purpose for which such information is to be used and by whom it is to be used.

5 *Principle of Prior Informed Consent and Veto*: This principle recognizes that the prior informed consent of all peoples and their communities must be obtained before any research is undertaken. Indigenous peoples, traditional societies and local communities have the right to veto any programme, project, or study that affects them.

6 *Principle of Confidentiality*: This principle recognizes that indigenous peoples, traditional societies, and local communities, at their sole discretion, have the right to exclude from publication and/or to be kept confidential any

information concerning their culture, traditions, mythologies or spiritual beliefs and that such confidentiality will be observed by researchers and other potential users. Indigenous and traditional peoples also have the right to privacy and anonymity.

7 *Principle of Active Participation*: This principle recognizes the critical importance of communities to be active participants in all phases of the project from inception to completion.

8 *Principle of Respect*: This principle recognizes the necessity for western researchers to respect the integrity of the culture, traditions and relationship of indigenous and traditional peoples with their natural world and to avoid the application of ethnocentric conceptions and standards.

9 *Principle of Active Protection*: This principle recognizes the importance of researchers taking active measures to protect and enhance the relationship of communities with their environment and thereby promote the maintenance of cultural and biological diversity.

10 *Principle of Good Faith*: This principle recognizes that researchers and others having access to knowledge of indigenous peoples, traditional societies and local communities will at all times conduct themselves with the utmost good faith.

11 *Principle of Compensation*: This principle recognizes that communities should be fairly, appropriately, and adequately remunerated or compensated for access and use of their knowledge and information.

12 *Principle of Restitution*: This principle recognizes that where as a result of research being undertaken, there are adverse consequences and disruptions to local communities, those responsible for all undertaking of research will make appropriate restitution and compensation.

13 *Principle of Reciprocity*: This principle recognizes the inherent value to western science and humankind in general from gaining access to knowledge of indigenous peoples, traditional societies, and local communities and the desirability of reciprocating that contribution.

14 *Principle of Equitable Sharing*: This principle recognizes the right of communities to share in the benefits from products or publications developed from access to and use of their knowledge and the duty of scientists and researchers to equitably share these benefits with indigenous peoples.

Notes

1 Introduction to ethnobiology: its implications and applications

1 The First International Congress of Ethnobiology began as a dream in 1984, when I was at the Federal University of Maranhão, in the city of São Luís. With a move to the Museu Paraense Emílio Goeldi, plans were put on hold until support from various quarters could be secured. By 1987, it seemed that the Congress could take place in Belém, symbolically an important place for an international meeting whose theme would be 'Ethnobiology: Implications and Applications'. Soon, I learned the difficulties of organizing an international gathering from an Amazonian base. Difficulties in communications and time-consuming bureaucracy are part of daily reality. But, almost miraculously, many people began to show enthusiasm for the idea and contributed their thoughts, experience, and energies to help with Congress plans.

4 Entomological considerations in south-eastern aboriginal demography

1 For a detailed analysis of various vector and reservoir animals in the Americas, see 'Plague in the Americas', World Health Organization (1965).

6 The application of ethnobiology in the conservation of dwindling natural resources: lost knowledge or options for the survival of the planet

1 In 1982, I initiated a multidisciplinary ethnobiological project called the Kayapó Project that eventually included over twenty scientists and technicians from different scientific fields such as agronomy, botany, entomology, plant genetics, astronomy, geography, anthropology, and linguistics, in efforts to document the traditional biological knowledge of the Kayapó Indians of Para State, Brazil.

My ethnobiological research with the Kayapó began in 1977 with initial grants from the Wenner-Gren Foundation for Anthropological Research. The multidisciplinary Kayapó Project was funded for its first two years (1982–3) by the Brazilian Council for Science and Technology (CNPQ). Since 1984, the Project has received financial aid for various aspects of research from: WWF-US (general ethnobiological investigation), WWF-International (research and education), the National Geographic Society (mapping and ethno-ecological zone definition), NSF (interpretation of satellite images), and the Ford Foundation-Brazil (ethnobiological training).

8 Ethnoecology as applied anthropology in Amazonian development

1 The term *caboclo* is used differently in different parts of Brazil. Here the term refers to those persons who have lived for generations on small farms or in small villages in Amazonia. The true *caboclo* has roots in indigenous cultures and is the intellectual inheritor of indigenous ecological knowledge in many areas. Much of what is said in this chapter concerning the ethnoecological knowledge of Indians also applies to *caboclos*. *Colonos* are considered more recent immigrants to Amazonia, and often know little about the ecology of the region. *Colonos* are often confused with *caboclos* in the literature.
2 For examples of some of the most commonly exploited fish species in the central area of Amazonia, see Goulding (1980) and Smith (1981: 140–3).

10 Diachronic ecotones and anthropogenic landscapes in Amazonia: contesting the consciousness of conservation

1 My reply was prompted by his initial attack on my Kayapó Research Paper (Parker 1992).

11 Indigenous knowledge, biodiversity, and international rights: learning about forests from the Kayapó Indians of the Brazilian Amazon

1 The only international treaty specifically relating to Indigenous Peoples is the 1989 International Labour Organization Convention 169 (the so-called Indigenous and Tribal Peoples Convention). According to this Convention, peoples are considered indigenous if they are: 'regarded by themselves or others as indigenous on account of their descent from the populations which inhabited the country, or a geographical region to which the country belongs, at the time of conquest or colonization or the establishment of present state boundaries and who, irrespective of their legal status, retain, or wish to retain, some or all of their own social, economic, spiritual, cultural and political characteristics and institutions'.
2 Although the word 'traditional' is often used to imply 'antithetic to change', recent discussions indicate a shift towards interpreting 'tradition' as a filter through which innovation occurs (e.g. Hunn 1994; Pereira and Gupta 1993; Vijayalakshmi 1994). Innovation is, therefore, a major part of tradition in indigenous and other traditional societies.
3 Cultural landscapes are necessarily of cultural significance, but do not necessarily have to be anthropogenic (human modified). For indigenous peoples, culture and nature are inseparable, so forests are frequently sacred sites whether they are or are not consciously managed by local residents. Cultural landscapes and their link with the conservation of biological diversity are now recognized under the 1972 UNESCO Convention Concerning the Protection of the World Cultural and Natural Heritage (The World Heritage Convention). Since 1992, there is a new category of World Heritage Site, the 'Cultural Landscape', which recognizes 'the complex interrelationships between man and nature in the construction, formation and evolution of landscapes'.
4 *Terra Nullius* is a legal doctrine used in the past to dispossess indigenous peoples from their lands and territories. In most British colonial countries, this was accomplished by conveniently declaring that lands were uninhabited and, therefore, unowned prior to colonial rule.

5 Indigenous peoples demand recognition of their right to self-determination. According to paragraph 3 of the UN Draft Declaration on the Rights of Indigenous Peoples: 'Indigenous peoples have the right of self-determination. By virtue of that right they freely determine their political status and freely pursue their economic, social and cultural development' (cf. Barsh 1993; Kingsbury 1992b; van der Vlist 1994).
6 The search for commercially valuable genetic and biochemical resources, with particular reference to the pharmaceutical, biotechnological and agricultural industries (Posey and Dutfield 1996).

14 Traditional Resource Rights (TRR): *de facto* self-determination for indigenous peoples

1 'Industrial property' deals chiefly with inventions, trademarks, industrial designs and appellations of origin. 'Copyright' deals chiefly in literary, musical, artistic, photographic and cinematographic works. The application of industrial property agreements has never been applied to indigenous knowledge or handicrafts. Copyright laws have proven ineffective because they depend upon the identification of individuals who produced the work to be copyrighted.
2 The Model Provisions were stimulated by the 'multiple abuses', 'distortions', and 'mutilation' of folklore traditions being provoked by the 'spectacular development of technology' in audiovisual productions, phonograms, broadcasting, cable television, etc. The Model Provisions specifically refer to the problem that 'no share of the returns from ... exploitation is conceded to the communities who have developed and maintained it [folklore]'.
3 The Model Provisions avoid dealing with the concept of ownership, since the 'owner' of folkloric traditions in some countries is legally the State. Emphasis is given to authorization of use by the 'competent authority' or 'community concerned'. Compensation for 'authorized use' would, therefore, be negotiated during the authorization process. The 'competent authorities' are specifically granted the legal right to 'fix and collect a fee' (WIPO 1989: 8). Unauthorized use or wilful distortion of folklore that is 'prejudicial to the cultural interests of the community concerned' would be considered a punishable offence. Fines, seizure and imprisonment are foreseen as enforcement measures.
4 For more detailed examination see Posey 1996 and Posey and Dutfield 1996.
5 Declaration on Intellectual Property Rights and Indigenous Peoples, from a symposium organized by D. Posey for the Global Coalition for Biological and Cultural Diversity, July 1992, Geneva, at the III Preparatory Committee Meeting, United Nations Conference on Environment and Diversity.
6 This Declaration can be obtained from the Conference Secretariat, PO Box 76, Whakatane, Aotearoa, New Zealand (Fax 64-7-307-0762).

16 Indigenous peoples and Traditional Resource Rights: a basis for equitable relationships?

1 For information on community registers contact: Navdanya, A-60, 2nd Floor, Hauz Khas, New Delhi-110016, India.

Bibliography

Ackefors, H. and Rosen, C. (1979) Farming aquatic animals. *Ambio* 8, 132–3.
Adair, J. (1775) *The history of the American Indians*. Reprinted 1930. Watuga Press, Johnson City, TN/Ed. Samuel Cole, London.
Aeschlimann, J. P. (1982) Du role des insectes dans l'alimentation humaine. *Mitt. Entomol. Ges.* 32:4, 99–103.
Akerele, O., Heywood, V., and Synge, H. (eds) (1991) *Conservation of medicinal plants*. Cambridge University Press, Cambridge.
Alcorn, J. B. (1981) Huastec noncrop resource management: implications for prehistoric rain forest management. *Human Ecol.* 9, 395–417.
Alcorn, J. B. (1984) *Huastec Mayan Ethnobotany*. University of Texas Press, Austin.
Alcorn, J. B. (1989) Process as resource: the traditional agricultural ideology of Bora and Huastec resource management and its implications for research. In *Resource management in Amazonia: indigenous and folk strategies* (D. A. Posey and W. L. Balée, eds). New York Botanical Garden, New York, pp. 63–77.
Aldrich, J. M. (1921) *Coloradia pandora* Blake, a moth of which the caterpillar is used as food by the Mono Lake Indians. *Ann. Entomol. Soc. Am.* 14, 36–8.
Allen, W. L. and Tizon, J. H. (1973) Land use patterns among the Campa of the Alto Pachitea, Peru. In *Variations in anthropology: essays in honor of John C. McGregor* (W. W. Lathrap and J. Douglas, eds). Illinois Archaeological Survey, Urbana, pp. 137–53.
Altieri, M. A. (1983a) *Agroecology: the scientific basis of alternative agriculture*. Univ. California Division of Biological Control, University of California, Berkeley, CA.
Altieri, M. A. (1983b) Pest management technologies for peasants: a farming systems approach. *Crop Prot.* 3, 87–94.
Altieri, M. A. (1985) Developing pest management strategies for small farmers based on traditional knowledge. *Dev. Anthro. Network* 3:1, 13–18.
Altieri, M. A. (1987) *Agroecology: the scientific basis of alternative agriculture*. Westview Press, Boulder, CO.
Altieri, M. A. and Letourneau, D. K. (1982) Vegetation management and biological control in agroeco-systems. *Crop Prot.* 1, 405–30.
Alvard, M. S. (1993) Testing the 'ecologically noble savage' hypothesis. *Human Ecol.* 221:4, 355–87.
Alverson, H. (1984) The wisdom of tradition in the development of dry-land farming: Botswana *Hum. Organ.* 43, 1–8.
Alvim, P. d. T. (1972) Potencial Agricola da Amazonia. *Ciência e Cultura* 24, 437–43.

Bibliography 241

Alvim, P. d. T. (1981) Agricultural production potential of the Amazon region. In *Land, people and planning in contemporary Amazonia* (F. Barbira-Scazzocchio, ed.). Cambridge University Press, Cambridge, pp. 27–36.

Anderson, A. B. (1990) *Alternatives to deforestation steps toward sustainable use of the Amazon rain forest*. Columbia University Press, New York.

Anderson, A. B. and Posey, D. A. (1985) Manejo de cerrado pelo indios Kayapó. *Boletim do Museu Paraense Emilio Goeldi, Serie Botanico* 2:1, 77–98.

Anderson, A. B. and Posey, D. A. (1989) Management of a tropical scrub savanna by the Gorotire Kayapo of Brazil. In *Resource management in Amazonia: indigenous and folk strategies* (D. A. Posey and W. Balée, eds), Vol. 7. New York Botanical Garden, New York, pp. 159–73.

Andrewartha, H. G. and Birch, L. C. (1973) The history of insect ecology. In *History of entomology* (R. F. Smith, ed.) Annual Reviews Inc., Palo Alto, pp. 229–66.

Andrews, J. A. J. (1952) The home vegetable garden. In *America's garden book*. Coward-McCann, New York.

Anon (1993) *AgBiotechnology News* 4.

Anon (1994) Consultative Group signs landmark agreement to place CGIAR genebanks under FAO Trusteeship. *Diversity* 10:4, 4.

Araújo, A. M. (1961) *Medicina rústica*. Companhia Editora Nacional, São Paulo.

Armstrong, E. A. (1970) *Insects. Man, Myth, Magic* 52, 1445–51.

Arndt, W. (1923) Bemerkungen uber die rolle der insekten in Arzneischatz der alten kulturvoiker. *Dtsch. Entomol. Z.* 1923, 553–70.

Ashburn, P. M. (1947) *The ranks of death: a medical history of the conquest of America*. (F. D. Ashburn, ed.). Coward-McCann, New York.

Atran, S. (1990) *Cognitive foundations of natural history*. Cambridge University Press, Cambridge.

Axt, J. R., Corn, M. L., Lee, M., and Ackerman, D. M. (1993) *Biotechnology, indigenous peoples, and intellectual property rights*. CRS report for Congress, Washington, DC.

Baldus, H. (1937) *Ensaios de etnologia brasileira*. Companhia Editora Nacional, São Paulo.

Baldus, H. (1970) *Tapirapé, tribo Tupi no Brasil Central*. Companhia Editora Nacional, São Paulo.

Balée, W. L. (1985) Ka'apor Indian forest management. In *84th Annual Meeting, American Anthropological Association*, Washington, DC.

Balée, W. L. (1989a) The culture of Amazonian forests. In *Resource management in Amazonia: indigenous and folk strategies* (D. Posey and W. Balée, eds). New York Botanical Garden, New York, pp. 1–21.

Balée, W. L. (1989b) Cultura na vegetacao da Amazonia. *Boletim do Museu Paraense Emilio Goeldi Colecao Eduardo Galvao*, 95–109.

Balée, W. L. (1994) *Footprints of the forest*. Columbia University Press, New York.

Balée, W. L. (1995) Historical ecology of Amazonia. In *Indigenous peoples and the future of Amazonia* (L. Sponsel, ed.). University of Arizona Press, Tucson, pp. 97–110.

Balée, W., ed. (1998) *Advances in historical ecology*. Columbia University Press, New York.

Balée, W. L. and Gély, A. (1989) Managed forest succession in Amazonia: the Ka'apor case. In *Resource management in Amazonia: indigenous and folk strategies* (D. A. Posey and W. L. Balée, eds). New York Botanical Garden, New York, pp. 129–48.

Balick, M. (1990) Ethnobotany and the identification of therapeutic agents from the rainforest. In *Bioactive compounds from plants* (D. Chadwick and J. Marsh, eds). Wiley, Chichester (Ciba Foundation Symposium 154), pp. 22–39.

Banner, H. (1961) O indio Kayapó em seu acampamento. *Bol. Mus. Parense Emilio Goeldi (ns) Anth.* 13, 1–51.

Barbira-Scazzocchio, F. (1980) From native forest to private property: the development of Amazonia for whom? In *Land, people, and planning in contemporary Amazonia* (F. Barbira-Scazzocchio, ed.). Cambridge University Press, Cambridge, pp. iii–xv.

Barrett, S. A. (1925) *The Cayapa Indians of Ecuador*. Museum of the American Indian, New York.

Barsh, R. L. (1990) An advocate's guide to the Convention on Indigenous and Tribal Peoples. *Oklahama City Univ. Law Rev.* 15, 209–53.

Barsh, R. L. (1993) The challenge of indigenous self-determination. *Univ. Michigan J. Law Reform* 26, 277–312.

Bartram, W. (1909) Observations on the Creek and Cherokee Indians. *Trans. Am. Ethnol. Soc.* 3, 1–81.

Basso, E. B. (1973) *The Kalapalo Indians of Central Brazil*. Holt, Rinehart and Winston, New York.

Bates, H. W. (1862a) Description of a remarkable species of singing cricket. *J. Entomol.* 1, 474–7.

Bates, H. W. (1862b) *The naturalist on the River Amazon*. University of California Press, Berkeley, CA.

Bates, H. W. (1864) A note about the Jaquiranabóia. *Proc. Ent. Soc.*, London.

Bateson, G. (1979) *Mind and nature: a necessary unity*. Dutton, New York.

Beckerman, S. (1979) The abundance of protein in Amazônia: a reply to Gross. *Am. Anthropol.* 81:3, 533–60.

Bell, W. G. (1951) *The great plague in London in 1655*. Bodley Head, London.

Bell, F. W. and Canterbury, E. R. (1976) *Aquaculture for developing countries*. Ballinger Publishing Company, Cambridge, MA.

Bellagio Declaration (1993) *Statement of the Bellagio Conference: cultural agency/cultural authority: politics and poetics of intellectual property in the post-colonial era*. 11 March 1993, Bellagio, Italy.

Bennett, C. F., Jr. (1964) Stingless-bee keeping in western Mexico. *Geogr. Rev.* 54:1, 85–92.

Bennett, C. F., Jr. (1965) Beekeeping with stingless bees in western Panama. *Bee World* 46:1, 23–4.

Bergier, E. (1941) *Insectes comestibles et peuples entomophages*. Impr. Rullière Frères, Avignon.

Bergman, R. (1974) *Shipibo subsistence in the Upper Amazon rainforest*. PhD dissertation, University of Wisconsin, Madison, WI.

Berkes, F., ed. (1989) *Common property resources: ecology and community-based sustainable development*. Belhaven Press, London and New York.

Berlin, B. (1992) *Ethnobiological classification: principles of categorization of plants and animals in traditional societies*. Princeton University Press, Princeton, NJ.

Berlin, B. and Prance, G. T. (1978) Insects galls and human ornamentation: ethnobotanical significance of a new species Licania in Amazonas, Peru. *Biotropica* 10, 81–6.

Berlin, O. B. and Berlin, E. (1979) *Aspectos de la etnobiologica Aguaruna*. University of California, Berkeley, CA.

Berlin, B. *et al.* (1966) Folk taxonomies and biological classification. *Science* 154, 273–5.

Berndt, R. M. and Berndt, C. H. (1964) *The world of the first Australians*. Ure Smith, Sydney.

Biard, A. F. (1862) *Deux années au Brésil.* Hachette Trad. Port, 1945, Paris.

Bierhorst, J. (1994) *The way of the Earth: native America and the environment.* William Morrow and Co., New York.

Blackburn, T. (1976) A query regarding the possible hallucinogenic effects of ant ingestion south-central California. *J. California Anthropol.* 3, 78–81.

Bodeker, G. (1999) Valuing biodiversity for human health and well being: traditional health systems. In *Cultural and spiritual values of biodiversity* (D. A. Posey, ed.). Intermediate Technology Publications/United Nations Environment Programme, Nairobi.

Bodenheimer, F. S. (1951) *Insects as human food: a chapter in the ecology of man.* Junk, The Hague.

Borror, D. J. and de Long, D. M. (1976) *An introduction to the study of insects.* Holt, Rinehart & Winston, New York.

Boster, J. S. (1984) Classification, cultivation and selection of Aguaruna cultivars of *Manihot esculenta* (Euphorbiaceae). In *Ethnobotany in the Neotropics* (G. T. Prance and J. A. Kallunki, eds), Vol. 1. New York Botanical Garden, New York, pp. 34–47.

Bourne, E., ed. (1904) *Narratives of the career of Hernando de Soto.* Trail Marker series, New York.

Boyle, J. (1992) A theory of law and information: copyright, spleens, blackmail and inside trading. *California Law Rev.* 80:6, 1415–540.

Boyle, J. (1993) Alienated information: the international political economy of authorship. Paper presented at conference *Cultural agency/cultural authority: politics and poetics of intellectual property in the post-colonial era,* Bellagio, Italy.

Boyle, J. (1996) *Shamans, software and spleens: law and the construction of the information society.* Harvard University Press, Cambridge, MA.

Brokensha, D., Warren, D. M., and Werner, O., eds (1980) *Indigenous knowledge systems and development.* University Press of America, Lanham.

Browder, J. O., ed. (1989) *Fragile lands of Latin America: strategies for sustainable development.* Westview Press, Boulder, CO; London.

Brown, B. I. and Marten, C. C. (1984) *The ecology of traditional pest management in Southeast Asia.* Working Papers, East-West Center, Hawaii.

Brown, C. H. and Chase, P. K. (1981) Animal classification in Juchitan, Zapotec. *J. Anthropol. Res.* 37, 61–70.

Broyles, B. (1971) Proceedings of the 27th SEAC. In *Southeastern Archaeological Conference* No. 13, USA.

Brush, S. B. (1982) The natural and human environment of the central Andes. *Mt. Res. Dev.* 2, 14–38.

Brush, S. B. (1993) Indigenous knowledge of biological resources and intellectual property rights: the role of anthropology. *Am. Anthropol.* 95:3, 653–86.

Bulmer, R. N. H. (1968) Worms that croak and other mysteries of Karam natural history. *Mankind* 6, 621–39.

Bunker, S. G. (1981) The impact of deforestation on peasant communities in the Medio Amazonas of Brazil. In *Where have all the flowers gone? Deforestation in the Third World* (V. H. Sutlive, N. Altshuler, and M. D. Zamora, eds), Vol. 13. College of William and Mary, Williamsburg, VA, pp. 45–60.

Bunting, A. H. (1972) Pests, population and poverty. *Trop. Sci.* 14, 37–50.

Burley, J. (1987) Applications of biotechnology in forestry and rural development. *Commonwealth Forestry Rev.* 66:4, 357–67.

Burley, J. (1994) *Forests and biodiversity: the researcher's perspective*. Prepared for IVA international symposium on forest products and future society-development and values, Stockholm.

Bushnell, D. I. (1909) The Choctaw of Bayou Lacomb, St Tammany Parish, Louisiana. In *Bureau of American Ethnology, Bulletin*, Vol. 48. Smithsonian Institution, Washington, DC.

Bushnell, D. I. (1910) Myths of the Louisiana Chocktaw. *Am. Anthropol.* 12, 526–35.

Bushvine, J. R. (1976) *Insects, hygiene and history*. Athlone, London.

Cabral, O. (1963) *Histórias de uma região, Mato Grosso, fronteira Brasil-Bolivia*. Editora Himalaya Ltda, Niterói.

Calkins, C. (1974) *Beekeeping in the Yucatan: a study of historical-cultural zoogeography*. PhD dissertation, University of Nebraska, Lincoln.

Callahan, P. S. and Mankin, R. W. (1978) Insects as unidentified flying objects. *Appl. Opt.* 17, 3355–60.

Callicott, J. B. (1989) *In defense of the land ethic: essays in environmental philosophy*. State University of New York Press, Albany, NY.

Calvert, C. C., Martin, R. D., and Morgan, N. (1969) House fly pupae as food for poultry. *J. Econ. Entomol.* 62, 938–9.

Campbell, A. M. (1966) *The black death and men of learning*. AMS Press, New York.

Capra, F. (1999) Reconnecting with the web of life: deep ecology, ethics and ecological literacy. In *Cultural and spiritual values of biodiversity* (D. A. Posey, ed.). Intermediate Technology Publications/UNEP.

Carneiro, R. L. (1960) Slash and burn agriculture: a closer look at its implications for settlement patterns. In *Men and cultures: Selected papers of the fifth International Congress of Anthropology* (A. F. C. Wallace, ed.).

Carneiro, R. L. (1973) Slash-and-burn cultivation among the Kiukuru and its implications for cultural development in the Amazon Basin. In *Peoples and cultures of native South America: an anthropological reader* (D. R. Gross, ed.). Doubleday/Natural History Press, Garden City, NY, pp. 98–123.

Carneiro, R. (1978) The knowledge and use of rain forest trees by the Kuikuru Indians of Central Brazil. In *The nature and status of ethnobotany* (R. Ford, ed.), Vol. 67. Museum of Anthropology, University of Michigan, Ann Arbor, MI, pp. 210–16.

Caron, D. M. (1978) Insects and human nutrition. *Am. Bee J.* 118:6, 388–9.

Carvalho, J. C. M. (1951) Relações entre os indios do Alto Xingu e a fauna regional. In *Publ. Avuls. Mus. Nac.*, Vol. 7, Rio de Janeiro, pp. 1–32.

Catley, A. (1963) Notes on insects as food for native peoples in Papua New Guinea. *Trans. Papua New Guinea Sci. Soc.* 4, 10–12.

Caudell, A. N. (1916) An economic consideration of orthoptera directly affecting man. In *Proceedings of the Entomological Society*, Vol. 18, Washington, DC, pp. 84–92.

Cavalcante, P. (1972) *Frutas comestiveis da Amazonia I*. Publishcações Avulsas do Museu Goeldi, Belém.

Cavalcante, P. (1974) *Frutas comestiveis da Amazonia II*. Publishcações Avulsas do Museu Goeldi, Belém.

Cavalli-Sforza, L. L., Wilson, A. C., Cantor, C. R., Cook-Deegan, R. M., and King, M.-C. (1991) Call for a worldwide survey of human genetic diversity: a vanishing opportunity for the Human Genome Project. *Genomics* 11, 490–1.

Chadwick, D. J. and Marsh, J., eds (1994) *Ethnobotany and the search for new drugs*. John Wiley and Sons, Chichester.

Chagnon, N. (1968) *Yanomamo: the fierce people*. Holt, Rinehart & Winston, New York.
Chagnon, N. (1973) Yanomamo. In *Peoples of the Earth* (E. E. Evans-Pritchard, ed.). Verona, Danbury, pp. 234–47.
Chambers, D. L. (1977) Quality control in mass rearing. *Ann. Rev. Entomol.* 22, 289–308.
Chapin, M. (1991) How the Kuna keep the scientists in line. *Cultural Survival Quarterly* Summer, 17.
Chapman, A. R. (1994) Human rights' implications of indigenous peoples' intellectual property rights. In *Intellectual property rights for indigenous peoples: a sourcebook* (T. Greaves, ed.), pp. 209–22.
Chernela, J. M. (1982) Indigenous forest and fish management in the Uapés basin of Brazil. *Cultural Survival Quarterly* 6:2, 17–18.
Chernela, J. M. (1989) Managing rivers of hunger: the Tukano of Brazil. In *Resource management in Amazonia: indigenous and folk strategies* (D. A. Posey and W. L. Balée, eds). New York Botanical Garden, New York, pp. 238–48.
Chmurny, W. W. (1973) *The ecology of the Middle Mississippian occupation of the American Bottom*. MA dissertation, University of Illinois, Urbana.
Choovivathanavanich, P., Suwanprateep, P., and Kathavichitra, N. (1970) Cockroach sensitivity in allergic Thais. *Lancet* 2, 1362–3.
Clark, L. R., Geier, P. W., Hughs, D. H., and Morris, R. F. (1967) *The ecology of insect populations in theory and practice*. Methuen & Co. Ltd, London.
Clarkson, L., Morrissette, V., and Regallet, G. (1992) *Our responsibility to the seventh generation: indigenous peoples and sustainable development*. International Institute for Sustainable Development, Winnipeg.
Clausen, L. W. (1954) *Insect fact and folklore*. Macmillan, New York.
Clay, J. W. (1988) *Indigenous peoples and tropical forests: models of land use and management from Latin America*. Cultural Survival, Cambridge, MA.
Clay, J. W. (1991) *World Bank policy on tribal people: application to Africa*. Rep. No. 16. Environment Division, Technical Department, Africa Region, The World Bank, Washington DC.
Clay, J. W. (1994) Resource wars: nation and state conflicts of the twentieth century. In *Who pays the price? The sociocultural context of environmental crisis* (B. R. Johnston, ed.). Island Press, Covelo, CA.
Clement, C. R. (1989) A center of crop genetic diversity in Western Amazonia: a new hypothesis of indigenous fruit-crop distribution. *Bioscience* 39:9, 624–30.
Cloudsly-Thompson, J. L. (1976) *Insects and history*. St Martins Press, New York.
Coimbra, C., Jr. (1984) Estudos de ecologia humana entre os Suruí do parque indigena Aripunã, Rondonia. 1. 0 uso de larvas de Coleóp-teros (Bruchidae e Curculionidae) na alimentacão. *Rev. Bras. Zool.* 2:2, 35–47.
Colchester, M. (1994a) *Salvaging nature: indigenous peoples, protected areas and biodiversity conservation*. Rep. No. 55. UNRISD/WRM/WWF, Geneva.
Colchester, M. (1994b) *Some dilemmas in asserting indigenous intellectual property rights*. Background note prepared for brainstorming meeting hosted by GRAIN on Community Rights and Biodiversity, Montezillon.
Colchester, M. and Lohmann, L., eds (1993) *The struggle for land and the fate of the forests*. World Rainforest Movement/The Ecologist/Zed Books, Penang.
Conconi, J. R. E. (1977) Valor nutritovo de ciertos insectos comestibles de Mexico y lista de algunos insectos comestibles del mundo. *Ann. Inst. Biol. Univ. Nacional. Auton. Mex.* 48:1, 165–85.

Conconi, J. R. E. (1982) *Los insectos como fuente de proteinas en el futuro*. Futuro, Limusa, Mexico DF.

Conconi, J. R. E., Moreno, J. M. P., and Gonzales, O. M. (1981) Digestibilidad en vitro de algunos insectos comestibles in Mexico. *Folia Entomol. Mex.* 49, 141–54.

Conconi, J. R. E., Moreno, J. M. P., Mayaudon, C. M., Valdez, F., Perez, M. A. *et al.* (1984) Protein content of some edible insects in Mexico. *J. Ethnobiol.* 4:1, 61–72.

Conklin, H. C. (1957) *Hanunoo agriculture: on an integral system of shifting cultivation in the Philippines*. FAO, Rome.

Conklin, H. C. (1969) An ethnoecological approach to shifting agriculture. In *Environment and cultural behaviour* (A. P. Vayda, ed.). The Natural History Press, Garden City, NY, pp. 221–3.

Conklin, H. C. (1973) *Folk classification: a topically arranged bibliography of contemporary and background references through 1971*. Yale University Press, New Haven, CT.

Cooper, J. I. and Tinsley, T. W. (1978) Some epidemiological consequences of drastic ecosystem changes accompanying exploitation of tropical rain forest. *Terre Vie* 32:2, 221–40.

Cornish, W. R. (1993) The international relations of intellectual property. *Cambridge Law J.* 52:1, 46–63.

Covarrubias, M. (1971) *Indian art of Mexico and Latin America*. A.A. Knopf, New York.

Cowan, F. (1865) *Curious facts in the history of insects*. J.B. Lippincott, Philadelphia.

Crane, E., ed. (1979) *Honey: a comprehensive survey*. International Bee Research Association, Gerrards Cross, England.

Crane, E. (1984) *The archaeology of beekeeping*. Duckworth, London.

Crewdson, R. (1984) Cultural property – a fourth estate. *Law Soc. Gaz.* 18, 126.

Crosby, A. W. J. (1972) *The Colombian exchange: biological and cultural consequences of 1492*. Greenwood Press, Westport.

Crucible Group (1994) *People, plants and patents: the impact of intellectual property on biodiversity, conservation, trade, and rural society*. International Development Research Centre, Ottawa.

CS (1982) Deforestation: the human costs. *Cultural Survival Quarterly* 6:2, 3–7.

Cunningham, A. B. (1993) *Ethics, ethnobiological research, and biodiversity*. WWF-International, Gland, Switzerland.

Curran, C. H. (1939) On eating insects. *Nat. Hist.* 613, 84–9.

Dammerman, K. W. (1929) *The agricultural zoology of the Malay archipelago*. J. H. Buxy, Amsterdam.

Daoust, M. V. (1858) On some eggs of insects employed as human food, and giving rise to the formation of oolites in lacustrine limestone in Mexico. *Ann. Mag. Nat. Hist.* 2, 78–80.

Dasmann, R. F. (1991) The importance of cultural and biological diversity. In *Biodiversity: culture, conservation, and ecodevelopment* (M. L. Oldfield and J. B. Alcorn, eds), Westview Press, Boulder, San Francisco and Oxford, pp. 7–15.

Davis, S. H. (1977) *Victims of the miracle: development and the Indians of Brazil*. Cambridge University Press, Cambridge.

de Foliart, G. R. (1975) Insects as a source of protein. *Bull. Entomol. Soc. Am.* 21:3, 161–3.

de Pratter, C. (1975) *An archaeological survey of P.H. Lewis property, Skidaway Island, Chatham County, Georgia*. University of Georgia Press, Athens.

de Pratter, C. (1976) *The shell mound archaic on the Georgia coast*. MA dissertation, University of Georgia, Athens, GA.

de Spinosa, Fray I. F. (1927) Descriptions of the Tejas of Asinai Indians (translated by M. A. Hatcher). *Southwestern Historical Quarterly* 31, 150–80.

de Voss, A. (1977) Game as Food. *Unasylva* 29:116, 2–12.
Denevan, W. M. (1966a) A cultural ecological view of the former aboriginal settlement in the Amazon region. *Profess. Geogr.* 18, 346–51.
Denevan, W. M. (1966b) *The aboriginal cultural geography of the Llanos de Mojos of Bolivia*. University of California Press, Berkeley.
Denevan, W. M. (1970) The aboriginal population of western Amazonia in relation to habitat and subsistence. *Revista Geografica* 72, 61–86.
Denevan, W. M. (1971) Campa subsistence in the Gran Pajonal, Eastern Peru. *Geogr. Rev.* 61, 496–518.
Denevan, W. M. (1973) Development and the imminent demise of the Amazon rain forest. *Profess. Geogr.* 25:2, 130–5.
Denevan, W. M. (1974) Campa subsistence in the Gran Pajonal, Eastern Peru. In *Native South Americans* (P. J. Lyon, ed.). Little, Brown and Co., Boston, MA, pp. 92–110.
Denevan, W. M. (1976) The aboriginal population of Amazonia. In *The native population of the Americas in 1492* (W. Denevan, ed.). University of Wisconsin Press, Madison, WI, pp. 205–34.
Denevan, W. M. (1981) Swiddens and cattle versus forest: the imminent demise of the Amazon rain forest re-examined. In *Where have all the flowers gone? Deforestation in the Third World* (V. H. Sutlive, N. Altshuler, and M. D. Zamora, eds), Vol. 13. College of William and Mary, Williamsburg, VA, pp. 25–44.
Denevan, W. M. (1984) Ecological heterogeneity and horizontal zonation of agriculture in the Amazon floodplain. In *Frontier expansion in Amazonia* (M. Schmink and C. H. Wood, eds). University of Florida Press, Gainesville, FL, pp. 311–36.
Denevan, W. M. (1992) The pristine myth: the landscape of the Americas in 1492. *Annals, Assoc. Am. Geogr.* 82:3, 369–85.
Denevan, W. M. and Padoch, C., eds (1988) *Swidden-fallow agroforestry in the Peruvian Amazon*. Advances in Economic Botany 5, New York Botanic Garden, New York.
Denevan, W. M., Treacy, J., and Alcorn, J. (1982) *Indigenous agroforestry in the Peruvian Amazon: the example of Bora utilisation of swidden fallows*. Paper presented in the session on 'Change in the Amazon basin' at the 44th International Congress of Americanists, September 1982, Manchester, England.
Denevan, W. M., Treach, J., Alcorn, J., Padoch, C., Denslow, J., and Paitan, J. (1984) Indigenous agroforestry in the Amazon: Bora Indian management of swidden fallows. *Interciencia* 9:6, 346–57.
Dentan, R. K. (1968) Notes on Semai ethnoentomology. *Malayan Nature J.* 21:1, 17–28.
Descola, P. (1994) *In the society of nature: a native ecology in Amazonia*. Cambridge University Press, Cambridge.
Dickinson III, J. C. (1972) Alternatives to monoculture in the humid tropics of Latin America. *Profess. Geogr.* 24, 217–22.
Diniz, E. S. (1962) *Os Kayapó-Gorotire*. Bol. Mus. Paraense Emilio Goeldi, 18.
Dobyns, H. F. (1963) An outline of Andean epidemic history to 1720. *Bull. hist. of Med.* 38:6, 493–515.
Dobyns, H. F. (1966) Estimating aboriginal American population: an appraisal of techniques with a new hemisphere estimate. *Curr. Anthropol.* 7, 395–416.
Dobyns, H. F. (1976) *Native American historical demography: a critical bibliography*. Indiana University Press for the Newberry Library Center for the History of the American Indian, Bloomington, IN.
du Pratz, A. S. le P. (1774) *Histoire de la Louisianne*. London. Reprinted in New Orleans 1947.

Dufour, R. A. (1981) *Insects: a nutritional alternative*. Dep. Med. Pub. Affairs, George Washington University Medical Center, Washington, DC.

Dunn, R. S. (1973) *Sugar and slaves*. University of North Carolina Press, Chapel Hill.

Durning, A. T. (1992) *Guardians of the land: indigenous peoples and the health of the Earth*. Worldwatch, Washington DC.

Dutfield, G. (1993) *Conservation of the tropical forests and the pharmaceutical industry*. Unpublished MPhil dissertation, University of Cambridge, Cambridge.

Dutfield, G. (1997) *Can the TRIPs Agreement protect biological diversity?* African Centre for Technology Studies, Nairobi.

Ealand, C. A. (1915) *Insects and man*. G. Richards Ltd, London.

Earle, A. M. (1901) *Old time gardens*. Macmillan, New York.

Efflaton, B. (1929) The development of entomological science in Egypt. In *Transactions of the First International Congress of Entomology*, Vol. 2, pp. 737–42.

Egger, K. (1981) Ecofarming in the tropics: characteristics and potentialities. *Plant Res. Dev.* 13, 96–106.

Ehrmann, W. W. (1940) The Timucua Indians of sixteenth century Florida. *Florida Historical Quarterly* 18, 168–91.

Elisabetsky, E. and Posey, D. A. (1986) Ethnopharmacology of the Gorotire Kayapó. *Revista Brasileira de Zoologia*, São Paulo.

Elisabetsky, E. and Posey, D. A. (1989) Use of contraceptive and related plants by the Kayapó Indians (Brazil). *J. Ethnopharmacol.* 26, 299–316 (Chapter 14 in Posey 2002).

Elisabetsky, E. and Posey, D. A. (1994) Ethnopharmacological search for anti-viral compounds: treatment of gastrointestinal disorders by Kayapó medical specialists. In *Ethnobotany and the search for new drugs*, CIBA Foundation Symposium 185, London, pp. 77–94 (Chapter 13 in Posey 2002).

Ellen, R. (1993) *The cultural relations of classification*. Cambridge University Press, Cambridge.

Engelhardt, W. (1959) *Was lebt in Tümpel, Bach und Weiher?* Verlag-shdlg., Stuttgart.

Erickson, C. (1995) Archaeological methods for the study of ancient landscapes of the Llanos de Mojos in the Bolivian Amazon. In *Archaeology in the lowland American tropics* (P. W. Stahl, ed.), Cambridge University Press, Cambridge, pp. 66–95.

Essig, E. O. (1931) *A history of entomology*. Macmillan, New York.

Essig, E. O. (1934) The value of insects to the California Indians. *Sci. Mon.* 38, 181–6.

Farrington, J. (1989) *Agricultural biotechnology: prospects for the Third World*. Overseas Development Institute, London.

FDC (1996) *Forests, indigenous peoples and biodiversity: contribution of the Four Directions Council*. Draft paper submitted to the Secretariat of the Convention on Biological Diversity. Four Directions Council.

Fearnside, P. (1979) The development of the Amazon rain forest: priority problems for the formulation of guidelines. *Interciencia* 4:6, 338–42.

Fearnside, P. A. (1982) Deforestation in the Amazon basin: how fast is it occurring? *Interciencia* 7:2, 82–93.

Fernandes, L. (1941) Os caingangues de palmas. *Arq. Mus. Paraense, Curitiba* 1C, 161–209.

Fidalgo, O. and Prance, G. T. (1976) The ethnomycology of the Sanama Indians. *Mycologia* 68:1, 201–10.

Fittkau, E. J. (1973) Crocodiles and the nutrient metabolism of Amazonian waters. In *Amazônia* 5:1, 103–33.

Floericke, K. (1922) *Heuschrecken und Libellen*. Kosmos, Stuttgart.

FOE (1992) *The rainforest harvest: sustainable strategies for saving the tropical forests*. Report of conference held at the Royal Geographical Society. Friends of the Earth, London.

Foweraker, J. (1981) *The struggle for land: a political economy of the pioneer frontier in Brazil, 1930 to the present*. Cambridge University Press, London.

Fowler, C. and Mooney, P. R. (1990) *Shattering: food, politics and the loss of genetic diversity*. University of Arizona Press, Tucson.

Frake, C. O. (1962) Cultural ecology and ethnography. *Am. Anthropol.* 64L1, 53–9.

Frankie, G. W. and Ehler, L. E. (1978) Ecology of insects in urban environments. *Ann. Rev. Entomol.* 23, 367–88.

Frechione, J. (1981) *Economic self-development by Yekuana Amerinds in southern Venezuela*. Doctoral dissertation, University of Pittsburgh, Pennsylvania.

Frickel, P. (1959) Agricultura dos indios Mundurucu. *Boletim Museu Paraense Emilio Goeldi, Antropologia* 8, 1–41.

Frickel, P. (1978) Areas de aboricultura pré-agrícola na Amazônia: notas preliminares. *Revista Antropológica* 21:1, 45–52.

Frost, S. W. (1959) *Insect life and insect natural history*. Dover Publications Inc., New York.

Furley, P. and Ratter, J. (n.d.). *Unpublished report of an ecological survey from central Brazil*. Royal Botanical Garden, Edinburgh.

Gadgil, M. and Thapar, R. (1990) Human ecology in India: some historical perspectives. *Interdisciplinary Sci. Rev.* 15, 209–23.

Gadgil, M., Berkes, F., and Folke, C. (1993) Indigenous knowledge for biodiversity conservation. *Ambio* 22, 151–6.

Ganjian, I., Kubo, I., and Fludzinski, P. (1983) Insect antifeedant elemanolide lactones from *Vernonia amygdalina*. *Phytochemistry* 22:11, 2525–6.

Gannon, P., Guthrie, T., and Laurie, G. (1995) Patents, morality and DNA: should there be intellectual property protection of the Human Genome Project? *Med. Law J.* 1, 321–45.

GATT (1994) *Final act embodying the results of the Uruguay Round of multilateral trade negotiations*. 15 April 1994. Marrakesh.

Geertz, C. (1963) *Agricultural involution*. University of California Press, Berkeley, CA.

Giacone, A. (1949) *Os Tucanos e outras tribos de Rio Uaupês affluente do Negro-Amazonas*. Imprensa Official do Estado, São Paulo.

Gilbert, B. M. and Bass, W. H. (1967) Seasonal dating of burials from the presence of fly pupae. *Am. Antiq.* 32:4, 534–5.

Gilbert, W. H. (1943) The Eastern Cherokee. In *Bureau of American Ethnology Bulletin*, Vol. 133. Smithsonian Institute, Washington DC, pp. 169–413.

Glass, E. H. and Thurston, H. D. (1978) Traditional and modern crop protection in perspective. *Bioscience* 28:2, 109–15.

Gliessman, S. R., Garcia, E. R., and Amador, A. M. (1981) The ecological basis for the application of traditional agricultural technology in the management of tropical agroecosystems. *Agroecosystems* 7, 173–85.

Glock, J. (1891) *Die symbolik der bienen und ihrer produkte in sage, dichtung, kultus, kunst und Bräuchen der Völker*. Heidelberg.

Glowka, L., Burhenne-Guilmin, F. in collaboration with Synge, H., McNeely, J. A., and Gundling, L. (1994) *A guide to the Convention on Biological Diversity*. IUCN, Gland, Switzerland.

Goldman, I. (1963) Tribes of the Uapés-Caquetá region. In *Handbook of South American Indians* (J. Steward, ed.), Vol. 3. Cooper Square Publishers, New York, pp. 763–98.

Gollin, M. A. (1993) An intellectual property rights framework for biodiversity prospecting. In *Biodiversity prospecting: using genetic resources for sustainable development* (W. V. Reid, S. A. Laird, C. A. Meyer, R. Gamez, A. Sittenfeld, D. H. Janzen, M. A. Gollin, and C. Juma, eds). World Resources Institute/Instituto Nacional de Biodiversidad/ Rainforest Alliance/African Centre for Technology Studies, Washington, DC. pp. 159–97.

Golob, P., Mwambula, J., Mhang, V., and Ngulube, F. (1982) The use of locally available materials as protectants of maize grain against insect infestations during storage in Malawi. *J. Stored Prod. Res.* 18, 67–74.

Gomez-Pompa, A. and Kaus, A. (1992) Taming the wilderness myth. *Bioscience* 42, 271–9.

Gomez-Pompa, A., Vázquez-Yanes, C., and Guevara, S. (1972) The tropical rainforest: a non-renewable resource. *Science* 177, 762–5.

Goodland, R. (1980) Environmental ranking of Amazonian development projects in Brazil. *Environmental Conservation* 7:1, 9–26.

Goodland, R. and Bookman, J. (1977) Can Amazonia survive its highways? *Ecologist* 7, 376–80.

Goodland, R. J. and Irwin, H. S. (1975) *Amazon jungle: green hell to red desert?* Elsevier Scientific Publishing Co., Amsterdam.

Goodland, R., Irwin, H. S., and Tillman, G. (1978) Ecological development for Amazônia. *Ciência e Cultura* 30:3, 275–89.

Gorham, J. R. (1975) Filth in foods: implication for health. *J. Milk Food Technol.* 38, 409–18.

Gorham, J. R. (1976a) Insects as food. *Bull. Soc. Vector Ecol.* 3, 11–16.

Gorham, J. R. (1976b) A rational look at insects as food. *FDA Guidelines* 5, 231–9.

Gorham, J. R. (1979) The significance for human health of insects in food. *Ann. Rev. Entomol.* 24, 209–24.

Gottlieb, O. R. (1981) New and underutilized plants in the Americas: solution to problems of inventory through systematics. *Interciencia* 6:1, 22–9.

Goulding, M. (1980) *The fishes and the forest.* University of California Press, Berkeley and Los Angeles.

GRAIN (1995a) The International Technical Conference on Plant Genetic Resources: opportunities for NGOs to get involved. *Biobriefing* No. 5. Genetic Resources Action International, Barcelona.

GRAIN (1995b) The green revolution in the red. *Seedling* 12:1, 16–18. Genetic Resources Action International, Barcelona.

GRAIN (1995c) *Framework for a full articulation of farmers' rights.* Genetic Resources Action International, Barcelona.

Gray, A. (1990) Indigenous peoples and the marketing of the rainforest. *The Ecologist* 20:6, 223–7.

Gray, A. (1991a) *Between the spice of life and the melting pot: biodiversity conservation and its impact on indigenous peoples.* Rep. No. Document 70. IWGIA, Copenhagen.

Gray, A. (1991b) The impact of biodiversity conservation on indigenous peoples. In *Biodiversity: social and ecological perspectives* (V. Shiva, P. Anderson, H. Schuking, A. Gray, L. Lohmann, and D. Cooper, eds). Zed Books Ltd./World Rainforest Movement, London UK/ New Jersey USA / Penang Malaysia.

Gray, A. (1999) Voices of the Earth: introduction. In *Cultural and spiritual values of biodiversity* (D. A. Posey, ed.). Intermediate Technology Publications/UNEP, Nairobi.

Greaves, T., ed. (1994) *Intellectual property rights for indigenous peoples: a sourcebook.* Society for Applied Anthropology, Oklahoma City.

Greenlee, R. (1944) Medicine and curing practices of the modern Florida Seminoles. *Am. Anthropol.* 46, 897–912.

Gregor, T. (1983) *Dark dreams about the white man. Nat. Hist.* 92:1, 8–14.

Griaule, M. (1961) Classification des insectes chez les Dogon. *J. So. Afr.* 31, 7–71.

Grinnel, G. B. (1899) The butterfly and the spider among the Blackfoot. *Am. Anthropol.* 1, 194–6.

Gross, D. (1975) Protein capture and cultural development in the Amazon Basin. *Am. Anthropol.* 77:3, 526–49.

Gudger, E. W. (1925) Stitching wounds with the mandibles of ants and beetles. *J. Am. Med. Assoc.* 84:24, 1861–4.

Hagan, H. (1863) Die insektennamen der Tupi sprach. *Stettiner Entomol. Ztg.* 24, 252–9.

Hall, E. T. (1969) *The hidden dimension.* Doubleday, Garden City, NY.

Hamburger, M., Marston, A., and Hostettemann, K. (1991) Search for new drugs of plant origin. *Adv. Drug Res.* 20, 167–215.

Hames, R. B. (1979) Game depletion and hunting zone rotation among the Yekuana and Yanomamo of Amazônias, Venezuela. In *XLIII International Congress of Americanists*, Vancouver, BC.

Hames, R. B. (1980) Monoculture, polyculture, and polyvariety in tropical forest swidden cultivation. In *79th Annual Meeting of the American Anthropological Association*, Washington, DC.

Hardesty, D. (1977) *Ecological anthropology.* Wiley, New York.

Hare, R. (1954) *Pomp and pestilence.* Gollancz, London.

Harlan, J. R. (1976) The plants and animals that nourish man. *Sci. Am.* 253:3, 89–97.

Harner, M. J. (1972) *The Jivaro: people of the sacred waterfall.* Doubleday-Natural History, Garden City, NJ.

Harpaz, I. (1973) Early entomology in the Middle East. In *History of entomology* (R. F. Smith, ed.). Annual Reviews, Palo Alto, CA.

Harris, D. R. (1971) The ecology of swidden cultivation in the Upper Orinoco rain forest, Venezuela. *Geogr. Rev.* 61, 457–95.

Harris, D. R. (1972) Swidden systems and settlement. In *Man, settlement, and urbanism* (P. J. Ucko, R. Tringham, and G. W. Dimbleby, eds). Gerald Duckworth and Company, Ltd, London, pp. 245–62.

Hay-Edie, T. (1999) Landscape perception and sensory emplacement. In *Cultural and spiritual values of biodiversity* (D. A. Posey, ed.). United Nations Environment Programme/Intermediate Technology Publications, Nairobi.

Hecht, S. B. (1982a) The environmental effect of cattle development in the Amazon basin. Paper presented at the Conference on *Frontier expansion in Amazonia*, Centre for Latin American Studies, University of Florida, Gainesville, 8–11 February 1982.

Hecht, S. B. (1982b) Deforestation in the Amazon Basin: magnitude, dynamics and soil resource effects. In *Where have all the flowers gone? Deforestation in the Third World* (V. H. Sutlive, N. Altshuler, and M. D. Zamora, eds), Vol. 13. College of William and Mary, Williamsburg, VA, pp. 61–101.

Hecht, S. B. and Posey, D. A. (1989) Preliminary results on soil management techniques of the Kayapó indians. In *Resource management in Amazonia: indigenous and folk strategies* (D. A. Posey and W. L. Balée, eds), Vol. 7. New York Botanical Garden, New York, pp. 174–88.

Hedrick, U. P. (1950) *A history of horticulture in America to 1860.* Oxford University Press, New York.

Hendricks, P. K. (1941) Cultivo de abejas indigenas en el Estado de Guerro. *Mex. Antiguo* 5, 365–73.

Hevly, R. H. (1982) Analysis of flotation samples from the Coronado transmission line corridor. In *The specialist volume: biocultural analysis*, Coronado ser. 4, paper 23. Museum of Northern Arizona, Flagstaff.

Hevly, R. H. and Johnson, C. D. (1974) Insect remains from prehistoric pueblo in Arizona. *Pan-Am. Entomol.* 50:3, 307–8.

Hitchcock, S. W. (1962) Insects and Indians of the Americas. *Bull. Entomol. Soc. Am.* 8, 181–7.

Hodge, F. W., ed. (1907) *The narrative of Alvar Nunez Cabeca de Vaca*. Scribner and Sons, New York.

Hoffman, W. E. (1947) Insects as human food. *Proc. Entomol. Soc. Wash.* 49, 223–37.

Hogue, C. L. (1980) Commentaries in cultural entomology – definition of cultural entomology. *Entomol. News* 91:2, 33–6.

Holmberg, A. R. (1950) Nomads of the long bow: the Sirionó of Eastern Bolivia. In *Publications of the Institute of Social Anthropology*, Vol. 10. Smithsonian Institution, Washington, DC.

Holt, V. M. (1885) *Why not eat insects?* E.W. Classey, Middlesex, England.

Horsfall, W. R. (1955) *Mosquitoes: their bionomics and relation to disease*. The Ronald Press, New York.

Hosen, H. W. (1980) Factors associated with the attribution of human traits to nonhumans. *J. Soc. Psychol.* 112:1, 161–2.

Hudson, C. M., ed. (1975) *Four centuries of Southern Indians*. University of Georgia Press, Athens, GA.

Hugh-Jones, S. (1993) 'Food' and 'drugs' in Northwest Amazonia. In *Tropical forests, people and food: biocultural interactions and applications to development* (C. M. Hladik, A. Hladik, O. F. Linares, H. Pagezy, A. Semple, and M. Hadley, eds), Vol. 13. UNESCO and Parthenon Press, Paris.

HUGO (1994) *The Human Genome Diversity Project*. Human Genome Organisation, London.

Hunn, E. S. (1975) A measure of the degree of correspondence of folk to scientific biological classification. *Am. Ethnol.* 2, 307–27.

Hunn, E. (1993) The ethnobiological foundation for TEK. In *Traditional ecological knowledge: wisdom for sustainable development* (N. Williams and G. Baines, eds). Centre for Resource and Environmental Studies, Canberra.

Hunn, E. (1994) What is traditional knowledge? In *Ecologies for the 21st century* (E. Hunn, ed.). Australian National University Press, Canberra, pp. 13–15.

Hurtado, M. (1989) Seeds of discontent. *South*, IUCN September 15, 95–6.

IAFB (1974) *SUPYSAUA: a documentary report of the conditions of Indian peoples in Brazil*. Indigena and American Friends of Brazil, Berkeley, CA.

IAI-TPTF (1992) *Charter of the Indigenous-Tribal Peoples of the Tropical Forests*. International Alliance of the Indigenous-Tribal Peoples of the Tropical Forests, Penang.

ICHI (1987) *Indigenous peoples: a global quest for justice*. Independent Commission on International Humanitarian Issues, Zed Books Ltd, London/New Jersey.

Inuit Tapirisat of Canada (1993) *Negotiating research relationships in the North*. Yellowknife.

Irvine, D. (1989) Succession management and resource distribution in an Amazonian rain forest. In *Resource management in Amazonia: indigenous and folk strategies* (D. A. Posey and W. L. Balée, eds), Vol. 7. New York Botanic Garden, New York. pp. 223–7.

IUCN, UNEP, and WWF (1991) *Caring for the Earth: a strategy for sustainable living.* IUCN, Gland, Switzerland.

Jacob, D. (1974) Chãos de Maiconã. Companhia Editora Americana, Rio de Janeiro.

Jacobs, J. W., Petroski, C., Friedman, P. A., and Simpson, E. (1990) Characterization of the anticoagulant activities from a Brazilian arrow poison. *Thrombosis and haemostasis* 63:1, 31–5.

Janzen, D. H. (1973) Tropical agroecosystems. *Science* 182, 1212–19.

Johannes, R. E. and Ruddle, K. (1993) Human interactions in tropical coastal and marine areas: lessons from traditional resource use. In *Applications of the biosphere reserve concept to coastal marine areas* (A. Price and S. Humphreys, eds). IUCN, Gland, Switzerland.

Johnson, A. (1974) Ethnoecology and planting practices in a swidden agricultural system. *Am. Ethnolog.* 1, 87–101.

Johnson, A. (1989) How the Machiguenga manage resource distribution in an Amazonian rain forest. In *Resource management in Amazonia: indigenous and folk strategies* (D. A. Posey and W. L. Balée, eds.), Vol. 7. New York Botanical Garden, New York. pp. 213–22.

Johnson, C. G. (1969) *Migration and dispersal of insects by flight.* Methuen & Co. Ltd, London.

Johnson, M. (1992) *Lore: capturing traditional environmental knowledge.* Dene Cultural Institute/IDRC, Ottawa.

Joyce, C. (1994) *Earthly goods: medicine-hunting in the rainforest.* Little, Brown and Co., Boston, New York, Toronto, and London.

Juma, C. (1989) *The gene hunters: biotechnology and the scramble for seeds.* Princeton University Press, Princeton, NJ.

Kahn, S. and Talal, H. (1987) *Indigenous peoples: a global quest for justice.* Zed Books, London.

Katter, F. (1883) Die canthariden spec. Meloe als Meilmitel der Tollwurth. *Entomol. Nachr.* 9, 156–83.

Keesing, R. (1980) From the ground up: towards development without dependency. *Human Futures* 80, 1–6.

Kennedy, C. H. (1943) A dragonfly nymph design in Indian pottery. *Ann. Entomol. Soc. Am.* 36, 190–1.

Kerr, W. (1987) Agricultura e selecoes geneticas de plantas. In *SUMA Etnologica Brasileira* (B. Ribeiro, ed.). Vozes/FINEP, Petropolis, Brazil.

Kerr, W. E. (1986) Cipó usado pelos indios Kayapó para matar abelhas africanizadas para extração do mel. *Revista Brasileira de Zoologia*, São Paulo.

Kerr, W. E. and Clement, C. R. (1980) Praticas agricolas com consequencias geneticas que possibilitariam aos indios da Amazonia uma melhor adaptacao as condicoes ecologicas da regiao. *Acta Amazônica* 10, 251–61.

Kerr, W. E. and Posey, D. A. (1984) Algumas notas sobre a agricultura dos indios Kayapó. *Interciência* 9:6, 392–400.

Kerr, W. E. D., Posey, D. A., and Filho, W. W. (1978) Cupá ou cipó babão, alimento de alguns índios amazônicos. *Acta Amazônica* 8:4, 702–5.

Kevan, D. K. (1974) *The land of grasshoppers.* Lyman Entomol. Mus., Ste-Anne-de-Bellevue, Quebec.

Kevan, D. K. (1980) Grigs, graces, graphics and graffiti. *Metaleptea* 2:2, 55–72.

Kevan, K. M. (1979) The place of grasshoppers and crickets in Amerindian cultures. *Proceedings of the Second Triennial meeting, Pan American Acridological Society*, Bozeman, Montana.

Khan, M. M., Rajagopal, D., and Hanumappa, P. (1978) Plant protection practices and problems of chilly growers of Kolar district. *Mysore J. Agric. Sci.* 12, 159–63.

Kilpatrick, J. and Kilpatrick, A. (1970) Notebook of a Cherokee shaman. *Smithson. Cont. Anthropol.* 2:6, 120 pp.

Kingsbury, B. (1992a) Claims by non-state groups in international law. *Cornell International Law J.* 25:3, 481–513.

Kingsbury, B. (1992b) Self-determination and 'indigenous peoples'. In *The American Society of International Law: Proceedings of the 86th Annual Meeting*. American Society of International Law, Washington, DC.

Kingsbury, B. (1994) Whose international law? Sovereignty and non-state groups. In *The American Society of International Law: Proceedings of the 88th Annual Meeting*. ASIL, Washington, DC, pp. 1–13.

Kloos, P. (1971) *The Maroni River Caribs of Surinam*. Royal Van Gorcum and Co. Ltd, Assen, Netherlands.

Kloppenburg, J., Jr (1988a) *First the seed: the political economy of plant biotechnology 1492–2000*. Cambridge University Press, Cambridge.

Kloppenburg, J., Jr (1988b) *Seeds and sovereignty*. Duke University Press, London.

Kloppenburg, J., Jr (1992) Conservationists or corsairs? *Seedling* 9:2/3, 12–17.

Kloppenburg, J., Jr. and Kleinman, D. (1987) Seed wars: common heritage, private property, and political strategy. *Socialist Rev.* 95 (September–October), 7–41.

Klots, A. B. and Klots, E. B. (1959) *Insekten*. Droemersch Verlagsanst, Munich/Zurich.

Knortz, K. (1910) *Die insekten in sage, sitte, und literatur*. Graeser, Annaberg/Sachsen.

Kok, R. (1983) The production of insects for human food. *J. Can. Inst. Food. Sci. Technol.* 16:1, 5–18.

Korten, D. C. (1995) *When corporations rule the world*. Earthscan, London.

Krauss, M. (1992) The world's languages in crisis. *Language* March.

Kreig, M. B. (1964) *Green medicine: the search for plants that heal*. Royal Van Gorcum and Co. Ltd, Chicago.

Kubo, I. and Matsumoto, T. (1984) Abyssinin, a potent insect antifeedant from an African medicinal plant, *Bersame abyssinica*. *Tetrahedron Lett.* 25:41, 4601–4.

Kubo, I., Matsumoto, T., Klocke, J. A., and Kamikawa, T. (1984) Molluscicidal and insecticidal activities of isobutylamides isolated from *Fagara macrophylla*. *Experientia* 40, 340–1.

Kvist, L. P., Andersen, M. K., Hellelsoe, M., and Vanclay, J. K. (1995) Estimating use-values and relative importance of Amazonian flood plain trees and forests to local inhabitants. *Commonwealth Forestry Rev.* 74, 293–300.

Laird, S. A. (1993) Contracts for biodiversity prospecting. In *Biodiversity prospecting: using genetic resources for sustainable development* (W. V. Reid, S. A. Laird, C. A. Meyer, R. Gamez, A. Sittenfeld, D. H. Janzen, M. A. Gollin, and C. Juma, eds), pp. 99–130.

Larson, L. H. J. (1970) *Aboriginal subsistence technology on the Southeastern coastal plain during the Late Prehistoric Period*. PhD dissertation, University of Michigan.

Lathrap, D. W. (1970) *The Upper Amazon*. Praeger/Thames and Hudson, New York/London.

Laudonniére, R. (1586) *Histoire notable de la Florida situee en Indes Occidentales*. Paris.

Laufer, B. (1927) Insect-musicians and cricket champions of China. *Field Mus. Anthropol. Leaflet* 22. Field Museum Natural History, Chicago.

Lawson, J. (1714) *History of Carolina*. Reprints: 1860 Raleigh; 1937 Richmond/Ed., London.
Leeds, A. (1961) Yaruro incipient tropical forest horticulture: possibilities and limits. In *The evolution of horticultural systems in native South America: causes and consequences. A symposium* (J. Wilbert, ed.). Caracas, pp. 13–46.
Lenko, K. and Papavaro, N. (1979) *Insetos no folclore*. Conselho Estadual de Artes e Ciências Humanas, São Paulo.
Leopold, A. (1949) *A Sand County almanac and sketches here and there*. Oxford University Press, New York.
Leskien, D. and Flitner, M. (1997) *Intellectual property rights and plant genetic resources: options for a sui generis system*. International Plant Genetic Resources Institute (IPGRI), Rome.
Lesser, W. (1991) *Equitable patent protection in the developing world: issues and approaches*. Eubios Ethics Institute, Christchurch and Tsukuba.
Lesser, W. (1994) *An approach for securing rights to indigenous knowledge. The bio-diversity/biotechnology programme*. Rep. No. Working Paper No. 15. International Academy of the Environment, Geneva.
Levi-Strauss, C. (1948) *La vie familiale et sociale des Indiens Nambikware*. Societé des Americanistes, Paris.
Levi-Strauss, C. (1996) *The Savage Mind* (First published as *La Pensée Sauvage*. Paris, 1962). University of Chicago Press, Chicago.
Liebrecht, F. (1886) Tocandyrafestes. *Z. Ethnobiol.* 18, 350–2.
Linares, O. (1976) Garden hunting in the American tropics. *Human Ecology* 4:4, 331–49.
Litsinger, J. A., Price, E. C., and Herrera, R. T. (1978a) Filipino farmer use of plant parts to control rice insect pests. *Int. Rice. Res. News* 3:5, 15–16.
Litsinger, J. A., Price, E. C., and Herrera, R. T. (1978b) How the farmers in three provinces control crop pests. *Greenfields* 8:8, 6–16.
Lothrop, S. K. (1964) *Treasures of ancient America*. SKIRA, Geneva.
Lovejoy, T. E. and Schubart, H. O. R. (1980) The ecology of Amazonian development. In *Land, people, and planning in contemporary Amazonia* (F. Barbira-Scazzocchio, ed.). Cambridge University Press, Cambridge, pp. 21–6.
Lowie, R. (1948) The tropical forests: an introduction. In *Handbook of South American Indians. Bulletin* No. 143 (J. H. Steward, ed.), Vol. 3. Bureau of American Ethnology, Washington, DC, pp. 1–56.
Luhrmann, T. M. (1981) *Bee as metaphor: psychodynamic tensions in Maya culture*. Unpublished BA dissertation, Harvard, Cambridge, MA.
Lyon, P., ed. (1974) *Native South Americans: ethnology of the least known continent*. Little, Brown and Co., Boston, MA.
Lyons, O. (1999) Biodiversity: perspectives from indigenous peoples. In *Cultural and spiritual values of biodiversity* (D. A. Posey, ed.). United Nations Environment Programme/Intermediate Technology Publications, Nairobi.
MacCurdy, G. (1913) Shell gorgets from Missouri. *Am. Anthropol.* 15, 402–3.
McDonald, D. R. (1977) Food taboos: a primitive environmental protection agency (South America). *Anthropos* 72, 734–48.
McGowan, J. (1991) Who is the inventor? *Cultural Survival Quarterly* Summer, 20.
MacHargue, J. S. (1917) A study of proteins of certain insects with reference to their value as food for poultry. *J. Agric. Res.* 19, 633–7.
McIntyre, L. (1972) The Amazon. *Nat. Geogr.* 142, 445–95.

McIntyre, L. (1989) Last days of Eden. *Nat. Geogr.* 174:6, 800–17.
McKeown, K. (1944) *Insect wonders of Australia.* Angus and Robertson, Sydney.
McNeil, R. J. and McNeil, M. J. (1989) Ownership of traditional information: moral and legal obligations to compensate for taking. *Northeast Indian Quarterly*, Fall, 30–5.
McNeill, W. H. (1976) *Plagues and people.* Anchor, Garden City, NY.
Maffi, L. (1999) Language diversity: language and the environment. In *Cultural and spiritual values of biodiversity* (D. A. Posey, ed.). United Nations Environment Programme/Intermediate Technology Publications, Nairobi.
Majnep, I. and Bulmer, R. (1977) *Birds of my Kalam country.* Auckland University Press, Auckland.
Malinowski, B. (1929) *The sexual life of savages in north-western Melanesia.* H. Ellis, New York.
Malkin, B. (1956) Seri ethnozoology: a preliminary report. *Davidson J. Anthropol.* 2, 73–83.
Mann, P. and Lawrence, K. (1999) Rebuilding our food system: the ethical and spiritual challenge. In *Cultural and spiritual values of biodiversity* (D. A. Posey, ed.). United Nations Environment Programme/Intermediate Technology Publications, Nairobi.
Marshall, W. (1894) *Neueröffnetes, wundersames Arzenei-Kästlein*, Leipzig.
Martin, G. (1995) *Ethnobotany.* Chapman and Hall, London.
Martins, H. (1993) Hegel, Texas: issues in the philosophy and sociology of technology. In *Knowledge and passion: essays in honour of John Rex* (H. Martins, ed.). Tauris, London, pp. 226–49.
Matheson, R. (1944) *Handbook of the mosquitoes of North America.* Comstock Publishing Co., Ithaca, NY.
Matowanyika, J. Z. Z. (1997) Resource management and the Shona people in rural Zimbabwe. In *Indigenous peoples and sustainability: cases and actions* (D. A. Posey and G. Dutfield, eds). IUCN/International Books, Utrecht.
Matteson, P. C., Altieri, M. A., and Gagne, W. C. (1984) Modification of small farmer practices for better pest management. *Ann. Rev. Entomol.* 29, 383–402.
Mead, A. T. P., ed. (1993) *Delivering good services to the public without compromising the cultural and intellectual property of indigenous peoples: the economics of customary knowledge.* International Association of the Mataatua Declaration, New Zealand.
Mead, A. T. P. (1994a) Biculturalism and cultural sensitivity in human gene therapy and research. In *Draft report and guidelines on the clinical and research use of human genes: report to the Health Research Council Ethics Committee.* Health Research Council of New Zealand.
Mead, A. T. P. (1994b) Indigenous rights to land and biological resources: the Convention on Biological Diversity. Presented to the International Institute for Research (NZ) Ltd and Department of Conservation, *Conference on biodiversity: impacts on government, business and the economy.*
Mead, A. T. P. (1994c) Misappropriation of indigenous knowledge: the next wave of colonisation. *Otago Bioethics Report* 3:1, 4–7.
Meggers, B. (1971) *Amazonia: men and culture in a counterfeit paradise.* Revised Edition 1996. Smithsonian Institution Press, Washington and London/Ed. Aldine Press, Chicago.
Messenger, P. (1989) *The ethics of collecting cultural property: whose cultures? whose property?* University of New Mexico Press, Albuquerque.
Metraux, A. (1948a) The hunting and gathering tribes of the Rio Negro Basin. In *Handbook of South American Indians*, Vol. 3. Smithsonian Institution, Washington, DC, pp. 816–67.

Metraux, A. E. (1948b) Tribes of the Middle and Upper Amazon River. In *Handbook of South American Indians*, Vol. 3. Smithsonian Institution, Washington, DC.

Meyer-Rochow, V. B. (1973) Edible insects in three different ethnic groups of Papua New Guinea. *Am. J. Clin. Nutr.* 26, 673–7.

Meyer-Rochow, V. B. (1975) Can insects help to ease the problem of world food shortage? *Search* 6:7, 261–2.

Meyer-Rochow, V. B. (1976) The use of insects as human food. *Food and Nutr.* 33, 151–2.

Meyer-Rochow, V. B. (1985) The diverse uses of insects in traditional societies. *J. Ethnomed.*

Milanich, J. T. (1971) *The Deptford Phase: an archaeological reconstruction*. PhD dissertation, University of Florida.

Milanich, J. T. (1972) *Excavations at the Richardson site, Alachua County, Florida: an early seventeenth century Potano Indian village*. Florida Department of State, Tallahassee.

Mill, A. E. (1982) Amazon termite myths: legends and folklore of the Indians and Caboclos. *Bull. Royal Entomol. Soc. London* 6:2, 214–17.

Miller, M. F. and Huddelson, R. R. (1921) *Thirty years of field experimentation with crop rotation, manure, and fertilizers*. University of Missouri Agricultural Experiment Station, Columbia, MO.

Miller, J. A. (1981) Space gardening. *Sci. News Lett.* 119, 330–4.

Montague, J. J. (1981) His 'crop' is crocodiles. *International Wildlife* 11:2, 21–8.

Montecinos, C. (1996) *Sui generis*: a dead end alley. *Seedling*, Genetic Resources Action International 13:4, 19–28.

Montgomery, B. F. (1959) Arthropods and ancient man. *Bull. Entomol. Soc. Am.* 5, 68–70.

Mooney, J. (1972) *Myths of the Cherokee and sacred formulas of the Cherokee*. Reprinted from the 7th and 19th Annual Reports of the Bureau of American Ethnology/Ed. Elder Bookseller, Nashville.

Mooney, P. (1983) *The law of the seed*. Zed Books Ltd, London.

Moran, E. F. (1981) *Developing the Amazon*. Indiana University Press, Bloomington, IN.

Morey, R. V. (1978) A joyful harvest of souls: diseases and the destruction of the Llanos Indians. In *Epidemics and native American history in the tropics*. Annual meeting of the American Society for Ethnohistory, Austin, TX.

Morphi, F. J. A. (1932) *History of the province of Texas*.

Murphy, C. (1968) *Patterns of subsistence among Southeastern Indians*. MA dissertation, University of Georgia, Athens, GA.

Murphy, R. F. (1960) *Headhunter's heritage: social and economic change among the Mundurucu indians*. University of California Press, Berkeley, CA.

Myers, N. (1979) *The sinking ark*. Pergamon Press, Oxford.

Myers, N. (1981) Deforestation in the tropics: who wins, who loses? In *Where have all the flowers gone? Deforestation in the Third World* (V. H. Sutlive, N. Altshuler, and M. D. Zamora, eds), Vol. 13. College of William and Mary, Williamsburg, VA, pp. 1–24.

Myers, T. P. (1978) The impact of disease on the Upper Amazon. In *Epidemics and native American history in the tropics*. Annual meeting of the American Society for Ethnohistory, Austin, TX.

NAS (1975) *Underexploited tropical plants with promising economic value*. National Academy of Sciences, Washington, DC.

Nash, C. (1968) *Residence mounds: an intermediate Middle-Mississippian settlement pattern*. Anthropological Research Center Occasional Papers, 2. Memphis State University.

Neihardt, J. G. (1959) *Black Elk speaks*. Washington Square Press, New York.

Nicholson, A. J. (1970) An outline of the dynamics of animal population. In *Insect ecology and population management* (L. Pedigo, ed.). MSS Educational Publishing Co., New York.

Nijar, G. S. (1994) *Towards a legal framework for protecting biological diversity and community intellectual rights – a Third World perspective*. Second Session of the ICCBD, 20 June–1 July 1994, Nairobi. Third World Network Discussion Paper.

Nijar, G. S. and Ling, C. Y. (1993) Intellectual property rights: the threat to farmers and biodiversity. *Third World Resurgence* 39, 35–40.

Nimuendajú, C. (1952) *The Tukuna*. University of California Publications in American Archaeology and Ethnology, Berkeley, CA.

Nimuendajú, C. (1974) Farming among the Eastern Timbira. In *Native South Americans* (P. J. Lyon, ed.). Little, Brown and Co, Boston, MA, pp. 111–19.

NLC (1996) *Ecopolitics IX: Perspectives on Indigenous Peoples' Management of Environment Resources*. Northern Land Council, Darwin.

Nogueira-Neto, P. (1970) A criacão de abelhas indigenas sem ferrão (Meliponinae). *Tecnapis*, São Paulo.

Nordenskjöld, E. (1929) L'apiculture indienne. *J. Soc. Americanistes* 21:1, 169–82.

Nuorteva, P. (1963) Synanthropy of blowflies in Finland. *Ann. Entomol. Fenn.* 29, 1–49.

Oka, I. N. and Pimentel, D. (1974) Corn susceptibility to corn leaf aphids and common corn smut after herbicide treatment. *Environ. Entomol.* 2:6, 911–15.

O'Keefe, P. J. (1992) Intellectual property. Cultural property. Cultural heritage. Do these further indigenous interests? Paper presented at *First International Conference on the cultural and intellectual property rights of indigenous peoples*, Whakatane, New Zealand.

O'Keefe, P. J. (1993) Copyright produced inhibitions on access to the cultural heritage. Paper presented at conference, *Cultural agency/cultural authority: politics and petics of intellectual property in the post-colonial era*, Bellagio, Italy.

O'Keefe, P. J. (1994) *Feasibility of an international code of ethics for dealers in cultural property for the purpose of more effective control of illicit traffic in cultural property: A Report for UNESCO*. UNESCO, Paris.

O'Keefe, P., Prott, L., and Law, L. (1984) *Law and the cultural heritage*. Butterworths, London.

Opoku, K. A. (1978) *West African traditional religion*. FEP International Pvt, Lagos.

Ortiz, R. (1995) Sustainable management of forests and forest biodiversity: the crucial role of the CBD. *Biodiversity Bull.* 1, 6–8.

Outram, I. (1973) Insects in the art and myth of the northwest coast Indians. *Bull. Entomol. Soc. Can.* 5:1, 20–6.

Overal, W. L. and Posey, D. A. (1986) O controle naturale nas rocas Kaiapo. *Rev. Bras. Zool.*, São Paulo.

Packard, F. R. (1931) *History of medicine in the United States*. Reprint 1963, Hafner Publishing Co./Ed. Paul B. Hoeber Inc., New York.

Pandolfo, C. (1978) *A floresta Amazonica Brasileira: enfoque econômico-ecológico*. SUDAM, Belém.

Parent, G., Malaisse, F., and Verstraeten, C. (1978) Les miels dans la forêt claire du shaba méridional. *Bull. Rech. Agron. Gembloux* 13:2, 161–76.

Parker, E. (1981) *Cultural ecology and change: a caboclo varzea community in the Brazilian Amazon*. PhD dissertation, University of Colorado, Boulder, CO.

Parker, E. (1992) Forest islands and Kayapó resource management in Amazonia: a reappraisal of the apêtê. *Am. Anthropol.* 94, 406–28.
Parker, E. (1993) Fact and fiction in Amazonia: the case of the apêtê. *Am. Anthropol.* 95, 715–23.
Parker, E., Posey, D. A., Frechione, J., and da Silva, L. F. (1983) Resource exploitation in Amazônia: Ethnoecological examples from four populations. *Annals, Carnegie Mus.* 52:8, 163–203.
Patiño, V. M. (1963) *Plantas cultivadads y animales domesticos en America equinoccial.* Imprensa Departmental, Cali, Colombia.
PCRC (1995) *Proceedings of the indigenous peoples' knowledge and intellectual property rights consultation.* Pacific Concerns Resource Centre, Suva.
Pereira, N. (1954) *Os indios Maués.* Organização Simoes, Rio de Janeiro.
Pereira, N. (1967) *Noronguetã, um decameron indigena.* Editora Civilizacão Brasileira, Rio de Janeiro.
Pereira, W. and Gupta, A. K. (1993) A dialogue on indigenous knowledge. *Honey Bee* 4, 6–10.
Perrin, R. M. (1980) The role of environmental diversity in crop protection. *Protopathic Ecol.* 2, 77–114.
Pimbert, M. P. and Pretty, J. N. (1995) *Parks, people and professionals: putting 'participation' into protected area management.* Rep. No. 57. UNRISD/IIED/WWF, Geneva.
Pimentel, D. (1971) World food crisis: energy and pests. *Bull. Entomol. Soc. Am.* 22, 20–6.
Pimentel, D., and Goodman, N., (1978) Ecological basis for the management of insect populations. *Oikos* 30, 422–37.
Pimentel, D., Terhune, Dritschilo, W., Gallahan, D., and Kinner, N. (1977) Pesticides, insects in foods, and cosmetic standards. *Bioscience* 27:3, 1789–85.
Pimentel, D., Levin, S. A., and Olson, D. (1978) Coevolution and stability of exploiter-victim. *The American Naturalist* 112:983, 119–25.
Pinel, S. L. and Evans, M. J. (1994) Tribal sovereignty and the control of knowledge. In *Intellectual property rights for indigenous peoples: a sourcebook* (T. Greaves, ed.), Society for Applied Anthropology, Oklahoma City.
Pires, J. (1974) Tipos de vegetação da Amazônia. *Brasil Florest.* 5, 48–58.
Pistorius, R. and van Wijk, G. (1993) Commercializing genetic resources for export. *Biotech. development monitor* 15, 12–15.
Plenderleith, K. (1999) The role of traditional farmers in creating and conserving agrobiodiversity. In *Cultural and spiritual values of biodiversity* (D. A. Posey, ed.). United Nations Environment Programme/Intermediate Technology Publications, Nairobi.
Plotkin, M. and Famolare, L., eds (1992) *Sustainable harvest and marketing of rainforest products.* Conservation International and Island Press, Washington, DC.
Poblete, E. (1969) *Plantas medicinales de Bolivia.* Los Amigos del Libro, Cochambamba.
Porter, P. W. (1965) Environmental potential and economic opportunities: a background for cultural adaptation. *Am. Anthropol.* 67, 409–20.
Posey, D. A. (1978) Ethnoentomological survey of Amerind groups of lowland South America. *Florida Entomologist* 61:4, 225–9.
Posey, D. A. (1979a) *Ethnoentomology of the Gorotire Kayapó of Central Brazil.* PhD dissertation, University of Georgia, Athens, GA.
Posey, D. A. (1979b) Kayapó controla inseto com uso adequado do ambiente. *Revista da Atualidade Indigena* III:14, 47–58.

Posey, D. A. (1980a) Consideraciones etnoentomologicas sobre los grupos amerindios. *América indígena* 40:1, 105–20.
Posey, D. A. (1980b) Algumas observaciones etnoentomológicas sobre grupos Amerindos en la América Latina. *América indígena* 15:1, 105–29.
Posey, D. A. (1981) Wasps, warriors and fearless men: ethnoentomology of the Kayapó Indians of central Brazil. *J. Ethnobiol.* 1:1, 165–74.
Posey, D. A. (1982a) The journey to become a shaman: a narrative of sacred transition of the Kayapó Indians of Brazil. *J. Latin Am. Indian Literature* 7:1, 13–19.
Posey, D. A. (1982b) The keepers of the forest. *Garden* (New York Botanical Garden) 6:1, 18–24.
Posey, D. A. (1982c) Nomadic agriculture of the Amazon. *Garden* (New York Botanical Garden) 6:1, 18–24.
Posey, D. A. (1983a) Indigenous knowledge and development: an ideological bridge to the future. *Ciência e Cultura* 35:7, 877–94.
Posey, D. A. (1983b) Indigenous ecological knowledge and development of the Amazon. In *The dilemma of Amazonian development* (E. Moran, ed.). Westview Press, Boulder, CO, pp. 135–44.
Posey, D. A. (1983c) Enthnomethodology as an emic guide to cultural systems: the case of the insects and the Kayapó Indians of Amazonia. *Rev. Bras. Zool.* 1:3, 135–44.
Posey, D. A. (1983d) The importance of bees to an Indian tribe of Amazonia. *Florida Entomolog.* 65:4, 452–8.
Posey, D. A. (1983e) Keeping of stingless bees by the Kayapó Indians of Brazil. *J. Ethnobiol.* 3:1, 63–73.
Posey, D. A. (1983f) Folk apiculture of the Kayapó Indians of Brazil. *Biotropica* 15:2, 154–8.
Posey, D. A. (1984a) Patterns of superordinate groupings in the entomological classification system of the Kayapó Indians. *J. Ethnobiol.*
Posey, D. A. (1984b) A preliminary report on diversified management of tropical forest by the Kayapó Indians of Brazil. In *Ethnobotany of the neotropics* (G. Prance, ed.), Vol. 1. New York Botanical Gardens, New York, pp. 112–26.
Posey, D. A. (1984c) Diversified management of tropical ecosystems by Brazilian Indians. In *Suma Brasileira de Etnologia*. FINESP, Rio de Janeiro.
Posey, D. A. (1984d) Keepers of the campo. *Garden* (New York Botanical Garden) 8:6, 8–12, 32.
Posey, D. A. (1984e) Hierarchy and utility in a folk biological taxonomic system: patterns in classification of Arthropods by the Kayapó Indians of Brazil. *J. Ethnobiol.* 4, 123–39.
Posey, D. A. (1985a) Indigenous management of tropical forest ecosystems: the case of the Kayapó Indians of the Brazilian Amazon. *Agroforestry Systems* 3:2, 139–58.
Posey, D. A. (1985b) Native and indigenous guidelines for new Amazonian development strategies: understanding biological diversity through ethnoecology. In *Man's impact on forests and rivers* (J. Hemming, ed.), Vol. 1. Manchester University Press, Manchester, England, pp. 156–81.
Posey, D. A. (1986a) Topics and issues in ethnoentomology with some suggestions for the development of hypothesis generation and testing in ethnobiology. *J. Ethnobiol.* 6, 99–120.
Posey, D. A. (1986b) Etnoentomologia dos indios Amazonicos. In *Suma Brasileria de Etnologia*. FINESP, Rio de Janeiro.
Posey, D. A. (1987) Contact before contact: typology of post-Columbian interaction with Northern Kayapó of the Amazon Basin. *Boletim de Museu Paraense Emílio Goeldi*, Serie Antropológica 3:2, 135–54.

Posey, D. A. (1990a) The application of ethnobiology in the conservation of dwindling natural resources: lost knowledge or options for the survival of the planet. In *First International Congress of Ethnobiology* (D. A. Posey, W. L. Overal, C. R. Clement, M. J. Plotkin, E. Elisabetsky, C. N. da Mota, and J. F. P. de Barros, eds). Museu Paraense Emilio Goeldi/CNPq Brazil, Belém, Pará, pp. 47–59.

Posey, D. A. (1990b) Intellectual property rights and just compensation for indigenous knowledge. *Anthropology Today* 6:4, 13–16.

Posey, D. A. (1990c) Introduction to ethnobiology: its implications and applications. In *Proceedings of the First International Congress of Ethnobiology* (Belém, Pará) (D. A. Posey and W. L. Overal, eds). Museu Paraense Emílio Goeldi/CNPq (Brazil), Belém, pp. 1–8.

Posey, D. A. (1990d) Cultivating the forests of the Amazon: science of the Mebêngôkre. *Orion Nature Quarterly* 9.

Posey, D. A. (1992) Reply to Parker. *Am. Anthropol.* 94:2, 441–3.

Posey, D. A. (1993) Importance of semi-domesticated species in post-contact Amazonia: effects of Kayapó Indian dispersal on flora and fauna. In *Food and nutrition in the tropical forest: biocultural interactions* (C. M. Hladik, H. Pagezy, O. Linares, A. Hladik, A. Semple, and M. Hadley, eds), Vol. 15. UNESCO and Parthenon Press, Paris, pp. 63–72.

Posey, D. A. (1994a) International agreements and intellectual property right protection for indigenous peoples. In *Intellectual property rights for indigenous peoples: a sourcebook* (T. Greaves, ed.), Society for Applied Anthropology, Oklahoma City.

Posey, D. A. (1994b) Traditional resource rights (trr): de facto self-determination for indigenous peoples. In *Voices of the Earth: indigenous peoples, new partners and the right to self-determination in practice* (L. van der Vlist, ed.). The Netherlands Centre for Indigenous Peoples, Amsterdam, pp. 217–35.

Posey, D. A. (1994c) Environmental and social implications of pre- and post-contact situations on Brazilian Indians: the Kayapó and a new Amazonian synthesis. In *Amazonian Indians: from prehistory to the present – anthropological perspectives* (A. Roosevelt, ed.). University of Arizona Press, Tucson, pp. 271–86.

Posey, D. A. (1995) *Indigenous peoples and traditional resource rights: a basis for equitable relationships?* Green College Centre for Environmental Policy and Understanding, Oxford.

Posey, D. A. (1996) *Traditional resource rights: international instruments for protection and compensation for indigenous peoples and local communities.* IUCN and International Books, Gland and Utrecht.

Posey, D. A. (1997a) Diachronic ecotones and anthropogenic landscapes: contesting the consciousness of conservation. In *Principles of historical ecology* (W. Balée, ed.). Columbia University Press, New York.

Posey, D. A. (1997b) The Kayapó: the role of intellectual property in resource management in the Brazilian Amazon. In *Indigenous peoples and sustainability: cases and actions* (D. A. Posey and G. Dutfield, eds). IUCN and International Books, Utrecht.

Posey, D. A., ed. (1999) *Cultural and spiritual values of biodiversity.* United Nations Environment Programme/Intermediate Technology Publications, Nairobi.

Posey, D. A. (2002) *Kayapó ethnoecology and culture.* Routledge, London and New York.

Posey, D. A. and Balée, W., eds (1989) *Resource management in Amazonia: indigenous and folk strategies.* Vol. 7. New York Botanical Garden, New York.

Posey, D. A., and Camargo, J. F. (1985) Additional notes on the classification and knowledge of stingless bees (Meliponinae, Apidae, Hymenoptera) by the Kayapó Indians of Gorotire, Pará, Brazil. *Annals Carnegie Mus.* 58:4, 247–74.

Posey, D. A. and Dutfield, G. (1996) *Beyond intellectual property: toward traditional resource rights for indigenous peoples and local communities*. International Development Research Centre, Ottawa.

Posey, D. A. and Dutfield, G., eds (1997) *Indigenous peoples and sustainability: cases and actions*. International Books, Utrecht.

Posey, D. A. and Elisabetsky, E. (1991) Conceitos de animais e seus espíritos em relação a doenças e curas entre os indios Kayapó da Aldeia Gorotire, Pará. *Boletim do Museu Paraense Emílio Goeldi* 7:1, 21–36.

Posey, D. A. and Overal, W., eds (1990) *Ethnobiology: implications and applications. Proceedings of the First International Congress of Ethnobiology*. Volume 1 (Theory & Practice; Ethnozoology). MPEG/CNPq/MCT., Belém, Pará.

Posey, D. A., Frechione, J., Eddins, J., and da Silva, L. F. (1984) Ethnoecology as applied anthropology in Amazonian development. *Human organiz.* 43:2, 95–107.

Posey, D. A., Dutfield, G., and Plenderleith, K. (1995a) Collaborative research and intellectual property rights. *Biodiversity and conservation* 4, 892–902.

Posey, D. A., Argumedo, A., da Costa e Silva, E., Dutfield, G., and Plenderleith, K. (1995b) *Indigenous peoples, traditional technologies and equitable sharing: international instruments for the protection of community intellectual property and traditional resource rights*. IUCN, Gland, Switzerland.

Povolny, D. (1971) Synanthropy. In *Flies and disease* (B. Greenberg, ed.), pp. 856. Princeton University Press, Princeton, NJ.

Prance, G. (1979) Notes on the vegetation of Amazonia III. The terminology of Amazonian forest types subject to inundation. *Brittonia* 31, 26–38.

Prance, G. T., Campbell, D. G., and Nelson, B. W. (1977) The ethnobotany of the Paumari Indians. *Economic Botany* 31:2, 129–39.

Price, J. (1973) *Settlement planning and artifact distribution on the Snodgrass site and their socio-political implications in the Powers Phase of southeast Missouri*. PhD dissertation, University of Michigan.

Price, P. (1975) *Insect ecology*. John Wiley and Sons, New York.

Principe, P. P. (1989) The economic significance of plants and their constituents as drugs. In *Economic and medicinal plants research* (H. Wagner, H. Hikino, and N. R. Farnsworth, eds) Vol. 3, Academic Press, London and San Diego.

RAFI (1993) *'Immortalizing' the (good?) Samaritan: patents, indigenous peoples and human genetic diversity*. Rural Advancement Foundation International Communiqué, April.

RAFI (1994a) *Declaring the benefits*. Occasional paper series 1. October 1994. Rural Advancement Foundation International.

RAFI (1994b) *The patenting of human genetic material*. Rural Advancement Foundation International Communiqué, January/February.

RAFI (1994c) *Conserving indigenous knowledge: integrating two systems of innovation*. An independent study by the Rural Advancement Foundation International, commissioned by the United Nations Development Programme, New York.

Ramirez, J. P., Arroyo, P., and Chavez, A. (1973) Aspectos socio-economicos de los alimentos y la alimentacion en Mexico. *Rev. Comer. Ext. del Bco. de Comer. Ext.* 1, 675–90.

Ramos, A. (1980) Development, integration and the ethnic integrity of Brazilian Indians. In *Land, people, and planning in contemporary Amazônia* (F. Barbira-Scazzocchio, ed.). University of Cambridge Press, Cambridge, pp. 222–9.

Ransome, H. M. (1937) *The sacred bee in ancient times and folklore*. George Allen and Unwin, London.

Raths, A. and Biewald, D. (1974) *Tiere im Experiment*. Aulis Verlag Deubner & Co, Cologne.

Raymond, R. (1994) System-wide program on genetic resources launched by CGIAR, covering centers in IPGRI. *Diversity* 10:3, 25–6.

Read, B. E. (1935) Insect drugs. *Peking Nat. Hist. Bull.* 94, 8–85.

Rebelo, D. (1973) *Transamazônica: integração em marcha*. Ministério dos Trasportes, Centro de Documentação e Publicação, Rio de Janeiro.

Redford, K. H. (1982) Prey attraction as a possible function of bioluminescence in the larvae of *Pyrearinus termitilluminans* (Coleoptera: Elateridae). *Rev. Bras. Zool.* 1:1, 31–4.

Redford, K. H. (1986) Insects as food for humans: some cautionary comments. *J. Ethnobiol.*

Redford, K. H. (1990) The ecologically noble savage. *Orion Nature Quarterly* 9:3, 24–9.

Redford, K. H. and Dorea, J. G. (1984) The nutritional value of invertebrates with emphasis on ants and termites as food for mammals. *J. Zool. London* 203, 395.

Redford, K. H. and Padoch, C., eds (1992) *Conservation of neotropical forests: working from traditional resource use*. Columbia University Press, New York.

Reichel-Dolmatoff, G. (1976) Cosmology as ecological analysis: a view from the rain forest. *Man* 11:3, 307–18.

Reichel-Dolmatoff, G. (1978) Desana animal categories, food restrictions, and the concept of color energies. *J. Latin American Lore* 4:2, 243–291.

Reid, W. V., Laird, S. A., Meyer, C. A., Gamez, R., Sittenfeld, A., Janzen, D. H., Gollin, M. A., and Juma, C., eds (1993) *Biodiversity prospecting: using genetic resources for sustainable development*. World Resources Institute/Instituto Nacional de Biodiversidad/Rainforest Alliance/African Centre for Technology Studies, Washington, DC.

Reim, H. (1962) *Die insektennahrung des Australischen ureinwohner*. Academie Verlag, Berlin.

Reis, A. C. F. (1974) Economic history of the Brazilian Amazon. In *Man in the Amazon* (C. Wagley, ed.). University of Florida Press, Gainesville, pp. 33–44.

Ribeiro, D. (1950) *Religião e mitologia Kadiuéu*. Ministério da Agricultura, Brasilia.

Ribeiro, D. (1970) *Os Índios e a Civilização*. Editora Civilização Brasileira, Rio de Janeiro.

Ribeiro, B. G. and Kenhiri, T. (1989) Rainy seasons and constellations: the Desana economic calendar. In *Resource management in Amazonia: indigenous and folk strategies* (D. A. Posey and W. L. Balée, eds), Vol. 7. New York Botanic Garden, New York, pp. 97–114.

Risch, S. J., Andow, D., and Altieri, M. A. (1983) Agroecosystem diversity and pest control: data, tentative conclusions, and new research directions. *Environ. Entomol.* 12, 625–9.

Ritchie, C. (1979) Insects, the creeping conquerors and human history. *Soc. Sci.* 54:2, 122–32.

Robertson, J. A., ed. (1933) *True relation of the hardships suffered by Governor Fernando de Soto*. Florida Historical Society, Deland.

Rodata, S. (1988) *Explanatory memorandum in Council of Europe. The art trade: report of the Committee on Culture and Education*. Document 5834, Council of Europe, Strasbourg.

Roosevelt, A., ed. (1994) *Amazonian Indians from prehistory to the present: anthropological perspectives*. University of Arizona Press, Tucson.

Roosevelt, A. C. (1980) *Parmana: prehistoric maize and manioc subsistence along the Amazon and Orinoco*. Academic Press, New York.

Ross, E. B. (1978) Food taboos, diet and hunting strategy: the adaptation to animals in Amazonian cultural ecology. *Current Anthropol.* 19:1, 1–16.

Ross, H. H. (1965) *A textbook of entomology*. 3rd edition/Ed. John Wiley & Sons Inc., New York.

Roszak, T. (1992) *The voice of the Earth*. Simon and Schuster, New York.

Rössler, M. (1993) Tongariro: first cultural landscape on the World Heritage List. In *World Heritage Newsletter*, Vol. 4, p. 15.

Ruddell, K. (1973) The human use of insects: examples from the Yukpa. *Biotropica* 5:2, 94–101.

Rutschky, C. W. (1981) Arthropods in the lives and legends of the Pennsylvania Indians. *Mels. Entomol. Ser.* 30, 39–42.

Salazar, E. (1981) La federación Shuar y la frontera de la colonización. In *Amazonian Ecuatoriana: la otra cara del progreso* (N. E. Whitten Jr, ed.). Ediciones Mundo Shuar, pp. 59–82.

Salick, J. (1989) Ecological basis of Amuesha agriculture, Peruvian Upper Amazon. In *Resource management in Amazonia: indigenous and folk strategies* (D. A. Posey and W. L. Balée, eds), Vol. 7. New York Botanic Garden, New York, pp. 189–212.

Santos, P. B. and Coimbra, C. J. (1984) Criacãeo e comercializacão de larvas de *Hermetia illucens* (Diptera: Stratiomydae) em uma comunidade do Distrito Federal. *Ciência e Cultura* 36:1, 2211–15.

Santos, P. B. and Posey, D. A. (1986) Conceitos de saúde, adoecer, vura e morte em relacão as plantas medicinais e o aparecimento de D. Sebastião, Rei Messianico, na ilha de Lencois, Maranhão. *Ciência e Cultura*.

Scarborough, J. (1979a) On the history of early entomology chiefly Greek and Roman, with a preliminary bibliography. *Melsheimer Entomol. Serv.* 26, 17–27.

Scarborough, J. (1979b) Nicander's toxicology: spiders, scorpions, insects, and myriapods. *P. 1. Pharm. Hist.* 21:1, 3–34.

Scarborough, J. (1981) Ancient medicine: some recent books. *Clio Med.* 16:2/3, 141–9.

Schimitschek, E. (1968) Insekten abs nahrung, in Brauchtum, Kukt, und Kultur. In *Kukenthal's Handbook der Zoologie* (J. C. Helmcke, D. Starck, and R. Wekmuth, eds). Walter de Gruyter, Berlin, pp. 1–62.

Schimitschek, E. (1977) Insekten in der bilbenden Kunst im Wandel der Zeiten in psychogenetischer Sicht. *Veroff. Naturhist. Mus. Wein.* 14, 119 ff.

Schmink, M. (1981) *A case study of the closing frontier in Brazil*. Amazon Research and Training Program, Centre for Latin American Studies, University of Florida, Gainesville.

Schmithusen, F. (1978) *Contratos de utilização florestal com referencia especial a Amazônica Brasileira*. IBDF, Brasilia.

Schoolcraft, H. R. (1851–57) *Historical and statistical information respecting the history, condition, and prospects of the Indian tribes of the United States*. Bureau of Indian Affairs, Philadelphia. Vols 1–6.

Schubart, H. O. R. (1977) Ecological criteria for the agricultural development of the dry lands. In *Amazônia Ecuatoriana: La Otra Cara del Progreso* (N. E. Whitten Jr, ed.). Ediciones Mundo Shuar, pp. 59–82.

Schwarz, H. F. (1945) The wax of stingless bees (Meliponidae) and the uses to which it has been put. *J. New York Entomol. Soc.* 53, 137–9.

Schwarz, H. F. (1948) Domestication of stingless bees and rites connected with bee culture. *Bull. Am. Mus. Nat. Hist.* 90, 142–60.

Schwarz, P. M. and Klassen, W. (1981) Estimate of losses caused by insects and mites to agricultural crops. In *CRC handbook of pest management in agriculture* (D. Pimentel, ed.). CRC Press, Boca Raton.

Scoones, I., Melnyk, M., and Pretty, J. (1992) *The hidden harvest: wild foods and agricultural systems – a literature review and annotated bibliography*. International Institute for Environment and Development/WWF, London.

Sharma, D. (1994) *GATT and India: The politics of agriculture*. Konark Publishers, Delhi.

Shelton, D. (1993) *Legal approaches to obtaining compensation for the access to and use of traditional knowledge of indigenous peoples*. WWF-International, Gland, Switzerland.

Shelton, D. (1995) *Fair play, fair pay: strengthening livelihood systems through compensation for access to and use of traditional knowledge and biological resources*. WWF-International, Gland, Switzerland.

Shiva, V. (1994a) Freedom for seed. *Resurgence* March/April, 36–9.

Shiva, V. (1994b) The need for *sui generis* rights. *Seedling* 12:1, 11–15.

Shiva, V. (1995) *Democracy wins on patent laws debate in Indian parliament*. Press release.

Shiva, V., Anderson, P., Schuking, H., Gray, A., Lohmann, L., and Cooper, D., eds (1991) *Biodiversity: social and ecological perspectives*. Zed Books and World Rainforest Movement, London, New Jersey, and Penang.

Silow, C. A. (1976) *Edible and other insects of mid-western Zambia*. Occasional paper 5, Inst. Allm. Jamforand Etnogr., Uppsala.

Silow, C. A. (1983) Notes on Ngangela and Kkoya ethnozoology, ants, and termites. *Etnol. Stud.* 36, 1–177.

Simmons, P. (1976) A specific visual response in dragonflies. *Odonatologica* 5, 285.

Simon, M. M. and Brooke, L. (1996) Inuit science: Nunavik's experience in Canada. In *Indigenous conservation in the modern world: case studies in resource exploitation, traditional practice, and sustainable development*. IUCN, Gland, Switzerland.

Singerest, H. E. (1951) *Civilization and disease*. Cornell University Press, Ithaca, NY.

Sioli, H. (1975) Amazon tributaries and drainage basins. In *Coupling of land and water systems* (A. D. Hasler, ed.). Springer-Verlag, New York, pp. 199–213.

Sioli, H. (1980) Forseeable consequences of actual development schemes and alternative ideas. In *Land, people and planning in contemporary Amazônia* (F. Barbira-Scazzocchio, ed.). Cambridge University Press, Cambridge, pp. 257–68.

Slikkerveer, J. (1999) Traditional ecological knowledge; an introduction. In *Cultural and spiritual values of biodiversity* (D. A. Posey, ed.). United Nations Environment Programme/Intermediate Technology Press, Nairobi.

Smith, C. J. (1907) Proceedings of the English colony of Virginia and general history of Virginia. In *Narratives of early Virginia* (L. Tyler, ed.). Scribner & Sons, New York.

Smith, K. G. V., ed. (1973) *Insects and other arthropods of medical importance*. British Museum Natural History, London.

Smith, N. J. H. (1974) Destructive exploitation of the South American river turtle. In *Yearbook of the Association of Pacific Coast Geographers*, Vol. 36 (c). Oregon State University Press.

Smith, N. J. H. (1977) Human exploitation of terra firma fauna in Amazônia. *Ciência e Cultura* 30:1, 17–23.

Smith, N. J. H. (1980) Anthrosols and human carrying capacity in Amazonia. *Annals, Assoc. Am. Geogr.* 70:4, 553–66.

Smith, N. J. H. (1981) *Man, fishes and the Amazon*. Columbia University Press, New York.

Smith, N. J. H. (1982) *Rainforest corridors: the Transamazon colonisation scheme*. University of California Press, Berkeley, CA.

Smith, N. (1983) Enchanted forest: folk belief in fearsome spirits has helped conserve the resources of the Amazon jungle. *Nat. Hist.* 82:8, 14–20.

Smole, W. J. (1976) *The Yanoama Indians: a cultural geography*. University of Texas Press, Austin, TX.

Soulé, M. and Kohm, K. A. (1989) *Research priorities for conservation biology*. Island Press, Washington, DC.

Southwood, T. R. E. (1977) Entomology and mankind. *Am. Scientist* 65, 30–9.

Spencer, B. and Gillen, F. J. (1899) *The native tribes of central Australia*. Macmillan, London.

Spix, J. B. von and von Martius, C. F. P. (1823–31) *Reise in Brasilien auf Befehl S. M. König Maximilian Joseph I von Bayern, München*. (Translated into Portuguese, no date) Companhia Melhoramentos, São Paulo.

Sponsel, L. E. (1995) *Indigenous peoples and the future of Amazonia: an ecological anthropology of an endangered world*. University of Arizona Press, Tucson.

Sponsel, L. E., Headland, T. N., and Bailey, R. C., eds. (1996) *Tropical deforestation: the human dimension*. Columbia University Press, New York.

Spurgeon, D. (1974) Sea cows eat their way to domestication. *New Scientist* 63, 238–9.

Stearman, A. M. (1994) Revisiting the myth of the ecologically noble savage in Amazonia: implications for indigenous land rights. *Newsletter: Am. Anthropol. Associ.*, 2–6.

Sternberg, H. O. R. (1973) Development and conservation. *Erdkunde* 23, 253–65.

Sternberg, H. (1975) *The Amazon river of Brazil*. Steiner-Verlag, Wiesbaden.

Steward, J. and Metraux, A. (1948) The Peban tribes. In *Handbook of South American Indians*. Smithsonian Institution, Washington, DC.

Steward, J. H., ed. (1948a) *The tropical forest tribes*. Vol. 3. BAE Bulletin 143. US Government Printing Office, Washington, DC.

Steward, J. H. (1948b) The Witotan tribes. In *Handbook of South American Indians*, Vol. 3. Smithsonian Institution, Washington, DC.

Stocks, A. (1980) *Candoshi and Cocamilla swiddens in eastern Peru*. Paper presented at the 79th Annual Meeting of the American Anthropological Association, 7 December, Washington, DC.

Strathern, M. (1996) Potential property. Intellectual rights and property in persons. *Social Anthropol.* 4:1, 17–32.

Sultan, R., Craig, D., and Ross, H. (1997) Aboriginal joint management of Australian national parks: Uluru-kata Tjuta. In *Indigenous peoples and sustainability: cases and actions* (D. A. Posey and G. Dutfield, eds). IUCN and International Books, Utrecht.

Surujbally, R. S. (1977) Game farming is a reality. *Unasylva* 29:116, 13–15.

Suzuki, D. (1999) Finding a new story. In *Cultural and spiritual values of biodiversity* (D. A. Posey, ed.). United Nations Environment Programme/Intermediate Technology Publications, Nairobi.

Suzuki, D. and Knudtson, P. (1992) *Wisdom of the elders: honouring sacred visions of nature*. Bantam Press., London.

Swanton, J. R. (1928) Religious beliefs and medical practices of the Creek Indians. *Ann. Rep. Bur. Am. Ethnol.* 42, 437–672.

Swanton, J. R. (1942) Source material in the history and ethnology of the Caddo Indians. *Bur. Am. Ethnol. Bull.* 132.

Swanton, J. R. (1946) The Indians of the southeastern United States. *Bur. Am. Ethnol. Bull.* 137, Washington, DC.
Taylor, R. L. (1975) *Butterflies in my stomach: or, insects in human nutrition.* Woodbridge Press, Santa Barbara, CA.
Teixeira, F. F. (1937) *Chácaras e Quintais.* Rio de Janeiro.
Teotia, J. S. and Miller, B. F. (1974) Nutritive content of house fly pupae and manure residue. *Br. Poult. Sci.* 15, 177–82.
Thompson, W. R. (1970) On natural control. In *Insect ecology and population management* (L. Pedigo, ed.). MSS Educational Publication Co., New York.
Thresh, J. M. (1982) Cropping practices and virus spread. *Ann. Rev. Phytopathol.* 20, 193–218.
Thrupp, L. A. (1997) *Linking biodiversity and agriculture: challenges and opportunities for sustainable food security.* The World Resources Institute, Washington, DC.
Tihon, L. (1946) A propos des termites au point de vue alimentaire. *Bull. Agric. Congo Belge* 37, 865–90.
Tindale, N. B. (1953) On some Australian Cossidae, including the moth of the Witjuti (Witchey) grub. *Trans. R. Soc. South Aust.* 76, 56–65.
Tocantins, L. (1968) *O rio comanda a vida: uma interpretação da Amazônia.* Gráfica Record Editôra, Rio de Janeiro.
Toledo, V. (1992) What is ethnobiology? Origins, scope, and implications of a rising discipline. *Etnologica* 1:1, 5–21.
TWN (1995) *Patents on life, intellectual property and the environment.* A collection of Third World Network papers and articles. Rep. No. 2. Third World Network, Penang.
Ucko, P. J. and Dimbleby, G. W. (1969) *The domestication and exploitation of plants and animals.* Aldine Publishing Company, Chicago.
UKFN (1995) *Forests memorandum.* UK Forests Network, Norwich.
UN Economic and Social Council (1993) *The Mataatua Declaration on Cultural and Intellectual Property Rights of Indigenous Peoples.* UN Economic and Social Council, Commission on Human Rights, Sub-Commission on Prevention of Discrimination and Protection of Minorities. Working Group on Indigenous Populations.
UN Economic and Social Council Commission on Human Rights (1993) *Discrimination against indigenous peoples: study on the protection of the cultural and intellectual property of indigenous peoples.* Rep. No. E/CN.4/Sub.2/1995/26. UN Economic and Social Council, Commission on Human Rights, Sub-Commission on Prevention of Discrimination and Protection of Minorities. Working Group on Indigenous Populations.
UNEP (1992) *Convention on Biological Diversity.* United Nations Environment Programme, Nairobi.
UNEP (1995) *Forests and biological diversity conservation and sustainable use.* Rep. No. UNEP/CBD/COP/2/Inf.1. United Nations Environment Programme, Geneva.
UNEP (1997) *The biodiversity agenda: decisions from the Third Meeting of the Conference of the Parties to the Convention on Biological Diversity.* Rep. No. UNEP/CBD/97/1. United Nations Environment Programme, Buenos Aires, Argentina.
UNESCO (1993) *Amendment to the draft programme and budget for 1994–1995 (27 C/5), Item 5 of the Provisional Agenda.* Rep. No. 27 C/DR.321. UNESCO, Paris.
UNESCO (1994) *Operational guidelines for the implementation of the World Heritage Convention.* Intergovernmental Committee for the Protection of the World Cultural and Natural Heritage. UNESCO, Paris.
UNESCO (1996) *Revised operational guidelines for the implementation of the World Heritage Convention.* Rep. No. WHC/2/Revised. UNESCO, Paris.

UPOV (1992) *International Convention for the Protection of New Varieties of Plants, of 2 December 1961, as revised at Geneva on 10 November 1972, on 23 October 1978, and on 19 March 1991*. UPOV, Geneva.

van der Vlist, L. ed. (1994) *Voices of the Earth: indigenous peoples, new partners and the right to self-determination in practice*. Netherlands Centre for Indigenous Peoples and International Books, Amsterdam.

Vanderzant, E. S. (1974) Development, significance and application of artificial diets for insects. *Ann. Rev. Entomol.* 19, 139–60.

van Huis, A., Nauta, R. S., and Vulto, M. E. (1982) Traditional pest management in maize in Nicaragua: a survey. *Meded. Landbouwhogesch Wageningen* 82–6, 43.

van Latum, E. B. J. and Gerrits, R. (1991) *Bio-pesticides in developing countries: prospects and research priorities*. ACTS Biopolicy Institute, Maastricht.

Vasey, D. E. (1979) Capybara ranching in Amazônia? *Oryx* 15, 47–9.

Verdoorn, F., ed. (1945) *Plants: plant science in Latin America*. The Ronald Press, New York.

Vickers, W. (1979) Native Amazonian subsistence in diverse habitats: the Siona-Secoya of Ecuador. *Studies in Third World's Societies* 7, 6–36.

Vidal, L. (1977) *Morte e vida de uma sociedade indigena brasileira*. Editora de USP e Hucitec, São Paulo.

Vijayalakshmi, K. (1994) Conserving people's agricultural knowledge. In *Biodiversity conservation: whose resources? whose knowledge?* (V. Shiva, ed.). Indian National Trust for Art and Cultural Heritage, New Delhi, pp. 58–72.

Villas-Boas, O. and Villas-Boas, C. (1972) *Xingú, os índios e seus mitos*. Zahar Ediroa, Rio de Janeiro.

von Spix, J. B., and von Martius, C. F. P. (1823–1831). *Reise in Brasilien auf Befehl S.M. König Maximilian Joseph I von Bayern, München*. Companhia Melhoramentos, São Paulo.

Waddy, J. (1982) Biological classification from a Groote Eylandt aboriginal point of view. *J. Ethnobiol* 2:1, 63–77.

Wagley, C. and Galvão, E. (1948) The Tenetehara. In *Handbook of South American Indians*, Vol. 3, Smithsonian Institution, Washington, DC. pp. 137–48.

Wagner, M. (1895) *Das zeidelwessen und sein ordnung im Mittelalter und in der neuren Zeit*. Munich.

Wallace, A. R. (1852) On the insects used for food by the Indians of the Amazon. *Trans. Entomol. Soc. London* 2, 241–4.

Waring, A. J. J. (1965) The southern cult and Moskogean ceremonial. In *The Waring papers* (S. Williams, ed.). University of Georgia Press and Harvard University Press, Athens/Cambridge.

Waring, A. J. and P. Holder (1965) A prehestoric ceremonial complex in the Southeastern United States. (Reprinted from *Am. Anthropol.* (1945) 47, 1. *The Waring papers* (S. Williams, ed.). University of Georgia Press and Harvard University Press, Athens/Cambridge.

Warren, D. M., Slikkerveer, L. J., and Brokensha, D., eds (1995) *The cultural dimension of development: indigenous knowledge systems*. Intermediate Technology Publications, London.

Warren, D. M., Slikkerveer, L. J., and Titilola, S. O. (1989) *The cultural dimension of development*. Intermediate Technology Publications, London.

WCIP (1993) *Presumed dead... but still useful as a human by-product*. World Council of Indigenous Peoples, Ottawa.

Weaver, N. and Weaver, E. (1981) Beekeeping with the stingless bee *Melipona beecheii* by the Yucatecan Maya. *Bee World* 62:1, 7–19.

Wehner, R. (1972) *Information processing in the visual systems of arthropods.* Springer Verlag, New York.

Wheeler, A. G. J. (1981) The tarnished plant bug: cause of potato rot? *J. Hist. Biol.* 14:2, 317–38.

White, W. N. (1858) *Gardening for the south.* A.O. Moore Agricultural Book Publishers, New York.

Whitehead, N. L. (1998) Ecological history and historical ecology: diachronic modelling versus historical explanation. In *Advances in historical ecology* (W. Balée, ed.). Columbia University Press, New York, pp. 30–41.

WHO (1965) *Plague in the Americas.* World Health Organization, Washington, DC.

Wilbert, J. (1981) Warao cosmology and Yekuana roundhouse symbolism. *J. Lat. Am. Lore* 7:1, 37–72.

Wilken, G. C. (1977) Interpreting forest and small-scale farm systems in Middle America. *Agroecosystems* 3, 291–302.

Willett, A. B. J. (1993) *Indigenous knowledge and its implications for agricultural development and agricultural extension: a case study of the Vedic tradition in Nepal.* PhD dissertation, Iowa State University.

Williams, H. U. (1909) The epidemic of the Indians of New England 1616–1620, with remarks on native American infections. *Johns Hopkins Hospital Bull.* 20, 340–9.

Williams, L. (1960) Little-known wealth of tropical forests. In *Proceedings, Fifth World Forestry Congress,* Vol. 3, Seattle, pp. 2003–7.

WIPO (1985) *Model provisions for national laws on the protection of expressions of folklore against illicit exploitation and other prejudicial actions.* World Intellectual Property Organization/United Nations Educational, Scientific and Cultural Organization, Geneva.

WIPO (1989) *General introductory course on copyright and neighboring rights: protection of expressions of folklore.* World Intellectual Property Organization, Geneva.

World, Bank (1980) World Development Report. World Bank, Washington, DC.

Wright, R. M. (1983) The Great Carajás: Brazil's Mega-Program for the '80s. *The Global Reporter* 1, 3–6.

Wyman, L. C. (1973) *The red antway of the Navajo.* Mus. Navajo Art., Santa Fe NM.

Wyman, L. C. and Bailey, F. L. (1952) Native Navaho methods for the control of insect pests. *Plateau J. Mus. North. Arizona* 24:3, 97–103.

Wyman, L. C. and Bailey, F. L. (1964) *Navaho Indian enthnoentomology.* University of New Mexico Press, Albuquerque.

Yamin, F. and Posey, D. A. (1993) Intellectual property rights, indigenous peoples and biotechnology. *Review of European community and international environmental law: transfer of biotechnology and genetic resources* 2:2, 141–8.

Yde, J. (1965) *Material culture of the Waiwai.* Etnografisk Roekke X, National-museets Skrifter, Copenhagen.

Zinsser, H. (1935) *Rats, lice and history.* Blue Ribbons Books, New York.

Zubillaga, F. (1946) *Monumenta antiquae Floridae.* Monumenta Historica Societatis Jesu, Vol. 69, Rome.

Zurel, R. L. (1976) *Temporal changes in occupation intensity and settlement systems on the Georgia coast.* Paper presented to the 1976 Annual Meeting of the Society for American Archaeology.

Index

Aboriginal peoples 198
Agenda 21 151, 163, 166, 172, 177
agriculture 81–4, 197–200
agroforestry 61, 66, 84, 138
Amazon Cooperation Treaty 140
Amazonia 1–3, 63–7, 70–3, 81–8, 149, 152, 156–7, 198
American Anthropology 130
Amerindian populations 1, 23
Andean Pact 140, 188
Anderson, A. 21, 151–2
anthropology 55, 58, 70–87, 128, 146, 207
ants 13, 17, 20–1, 25, 27, 30, 33, 35, 45–6
apêtê 56, 68, 128–31, 138, 198
appellation of origin 155, 166, 181
aquaculture 78–81
archaeological sites 20, 129

Bailey, F. L. 10, 44
Baldus, H. 18, 26, 31
barriers to research 59, 64
bees 13–14, 19–21, 26, 29, 32, 35, 59–60, 73, 78, 122–4
Bellagio Declaration 181
Bepkôrôrôti 122–3
Biodiversity Convention *see* Convention on Biological Diversity
biodiversity prospecting ('bioprospecting') 139–40, 157, 173, 178, 193, 203
biopiracy 183
biotopes 89
The Body Shop 4, 148, 152–3, 192
Brazil 69, 71–2; Indigenous Societies Act 188–9; *see also* Kayapó Indians
'bundles' of rights 193–4
Bushnell, D. I. 17, 36, 38, 45–6
butterflies 33

Cabeza de Vaca, A. N. 38, 41
caboclos 27, 31, 66, 88–113, 120
Camargo, J. F. 15, 21, 32
caterpillars 26
Chagnon, N. 14, 25–7
Charter of the Indigenous-Tribal Peoples (CITP) 184
Cherokee 17, 35–6, 46–8
China 13, 15
Choctaw 36, 38, 45–6
Clay, J. 2, 153
cockroaches 13, 29
COICA Statement 177, 182, 185
colonialism 3–4
Commission on Sustainable Development (CSD) 177
community-controlled research (CCR) 191, 226
community intellectual rights (CIR) 189, 202
community registers 190–1
consciousness 56–7, 121, 131, 153, 196, 204, 238
conservation 53–5, 129–31, 134, 139, 169, 177–8, 197–9
Consultative Group for International Agricultural Research (CGIAR) 187
contracts 5, 150, 191, 222
Convention on Biological Diversity (CBD) 131, 134–5, 138–40, 151, 163, 166, 169–70, 172, 177–8, 186, 194, 197–201, 210
Coordinating Body of Indigenous Organizations of the Amazon Basin (COICA) 177, 182, 185, 188, 192
copyright 181, 224
cosmology 73
Costa Rica 178–9

Covenant on Intellectual, Cultural and
  Scientific Resources 218–21
covenants 192
cropping systems 16
cultural biases 12
cultural diversity 131–5, 140, 151, 169,
  172, 174, 195–6, 214, 219
cultural entomology 9–10
cultural landscapes 198–9
cultural property 165–6
Cultural Survival 153, 188

da Silva, Luiz Francelino 70, 91–3, 96,
  101, 120
Declaration of Belém 2, 5–6, 133, 195,
  208–9
deforestation 133
Denevan, W. 25, 28, 89–90, 129
development projects 71–2, 80, 139–40,
  174, 232
diachronic processes 126–32
Draft Declaration on the Rights of
  Indigenous Peoples (DDRIP) 159, 202,
  222
Dutfield, Graham 136, 151, 179, 191–2,
  196, 201–4, 208, 226, 239

Earth Summit *see* UN Conference on
  Environment and Development
eco-ethno ethics 4, 150
ecological zones 21, 65, 87–91, 122, 126,
  131, 140, 198
Ecopolitics IX Conference (1996) 137
emic interpretation 9–10, 21–2, 56–8, 60,
  64, 121–2, 131
entomology 9–10, 20, 22
environmental ethic 135
environmental impact assessments 131
'equitable partnerships' 235–6
ethics 4–6, 146, 150, 157, 167, 170, 173,
  194, 205–8, 218, 225; guidelines on
  190, 204–5
ethnoagriculture 66
ethnobiology 5–6, 10, 22, 59–60, 65;
  definition of 64, 206–8
ethnobotany 64, 66, 206, 208
ethnodevelopment 63–9
ethnoecology 64–5, 73, 88–9, 120, 206–8
ethnoentomology 9–11, 33; urban 20
ethnomedicine 206
ethnopedology 65
ethnopharmacology 64, 66, 73

ethnozoology 66
etic interpretation 9–10, 56–8, 64
extinction of native peoples 1–2, 71, 149
extractive products 3, 143, 150

FAO farmers' rights 186, 200
feed conversion ratios 79–80
field patterns 39
fire management 67–8
fishing 80
folk categories 96, 121–2, 128, 207
folk knowledge 10, 22, 35–6, 43, 60, 75,
  88–9, 104
folklore 18, 31, 123, 160–1
Food and Agriculture Organization (FAO)
  162–3, 186–7, 200–2
forest management 133
Four Directions Council 136
Frechione, John 70, 72, 79, 81, 83, 88, 92

game 78–9
gathered products 73–8
gathering 25, 59, 64, 84, 104, 120, 138,
  148, 237
General Agreement on Tariffs and Trade
  (GATT) 201
genetic research 67, 187
Genetic Resources Action International
  (GRAIN) 187, 200
Global Coalition for Bio-Cultural
  Diversity 192
globalization 182–3, 197, 202–3
grasshoppers 26–7, 36, 45–6
Green College Centre for Environmental
  Policy and Understanding 174–5, 261
grubs 13–14, 26–7, 47

Hall, Edward 34, 43–4, 57
hallucinogens 20
historical ecology 130–2
honey 26, 29, 35, 78
horticulture systems 83
Human Genome Organization (HUGO)
  180
human rights 2, 159, 164, 170
hydrology 89–91
hypothesis-testing 20–2, 60

InBio 178–9
India 44–9, 189–90, 200
indigenous knowledge: categories of 65;
  value of 3–4, 150–1

272 Index

indigenous peoples 133–40, 144–5, 149–52, 155–62, 166–70, 173, 195–7, 200, 203; definition of 176; views of 183–8
Indigenous Peoples' Biodiversity Network (IPBN) 188
Indigenous Peoples' Earth Charter 184, 227–35
'inextricable link' 133–4, 195, 209
information transfer agreements 192
insecticides 1, 4, 12, 67, 149, 169, 179
insect repellents 4, 28, 67, 81, 148
insects 11–13, 17–20, 23–33; in India 44–9; in the south-eastern US 34–44
intellectual property rights (IPRs) 2–6, 62, 67–9, 130, 143–7, 149–51, 155–67, 170, 172–3, 180–8, 193–4; in the global economy 182–3; principal instruments for safeguarding of 223–5; problems with 181–2, 201; scientific and professional societies' guidelines on 225–6
interdisciplinary study 20–1, 59, 64, 69, 131–2, 171, 194
International Congress of Ethnobiology: Belém (1988) 1–3, 143; Kunming (1990) 6, 146–7
International Covenant on Economic, Social and Cultural Rights (ICESCR) 159
International Labour Organization (ILO) 158, 166, 176, 200–1
international law 140, 150, 158, 173, 186, 200, 202, 227–8
International Society for Ethnobiology 2, 5–6, 146, 190, 204, 235–6
International Working Group on Indigenous Affairs (IWGIA) 188
interpretation as distinct from reality 57–8
Inuit 191, 226

Journal of Ethnobiology 146–7

Kagore Shona 198
Kari-Oca Declaration 226–35
'karõn' 123–5
Kayapó Indians 3, 13–21, 26–33, 53–61, 68, 73–7, 85–6, 122–31, 137–40, 198, 205
Kerr, W. E. 16, 21
Kevan, K. M. 15, 32
know-how 155, 169, 181, 201, 224
Kuna 3, 156, 191

Lake Coari 88–103, 117, 120
landforms 89–90
languages 133–4, 195–6
Lawson, J. 35, 41
Lelice 19, 27–8, 36, 40–1
Lenko, K. 14, 25–7, 29–30
locusts 27, 35
Lyon, P. 25, 34

maize-squash-bean complex 40
manatees 80
Maori 3, 156, 164, 199
marriage 32
Mataatua Declaration 166, 184–5, 203
Material Transfer Agreement (MTA) 192
Maya culture 14
medicinal plants 1, 4, 58–9, 66, 104, 149, 185, 197, 203, 207, 215, 225–6
Merck Pharmaceuticals 178–81
metaphysical concepts 58
methodological barriers 59
Metraux, A. 14, 25–6, 28
Mooney, J. 17, 35–6, 47
mosquitoes 28, 37
'mry-kaàk' 123
myths 17–18, 30–1, 36–7, 41–2, 45, 49, 123–5

natural landscapes 60, 136–7, 198
natural products 4–5, 62, 67, 69, 139, 144–5, 150, 153–4, 178, 226
New Guinea 180
nomadic agriculture 61, 127, 131, 137
non-domesticated resources (NDRs) 136–8
non-governmental organizations (NGOs) 187

oral literature 18, 30–1
oral traditions 18, 30, 36, 190

Pacific Regional Consultation 185
Paiakan 3, 152, 205
Panama 191
Papavaro, N. 14, 25–7, 29–30
Participatory Rural Appraisal and Participatory Action Research 190
patents 223–4
peoples, self-definition of 176, 235
pest control 15, 21–2, 27

Index

pests 12, 16–17, 28
pitu 58, 85, 124
plague 40–2
plant breeders' rights (PBR) 180, 225
plant genetic materials 4, 67
'planting' 12, 16, 21, 27, 32, 40, 56–7, 83, 103, 127–9, 198, 220
Posey, D. A. 2, 15–21 *passim*, 30, 32, 86
potato famine 15
prickly pears 15

rats 41
religion 163–4, 166, 196
'resource units' 84
resource use 53, 91, 98
Rio Declaration 151, 162
ritual 32, 47, 124–5
rivers, colour of 90, 93, 98
Rural Advancement Foundation International (RAFI) 183

'sacred balance' 197, 204–5
sacred sites 165
Santiago conference on indigenous peoples and the environment (1992) 160
Santos, P. B. 15, 18–19
scientific method 64
self-demarcation 175, 190
self-determination 140, 155–6, 159, 166–70, 174–7, 192–3, 196, 200–4, 211–12, 218–22, 227–8, 232, 235, 239
semi-domestication 14, 61, 66, 87, 162
shamanism 124–5
shifting cultivation 39, 83–5, 87
Shiva, Vandana 133, 185, 189
silk worms 15
social anthropology 121
Society for Ethnobiology 5–6, 146–7
spiders 26, 45
spirituality 196
Steward, J. 25–6, 28
stingless bees 14–15, 18–21, 26, 31–2, 59, 122–4
sui generis systems 158, 161, 182–3, 193, 201–2, 208
Survival International 153, 188
survival of native peoples, conditions for 2–3
sustainable development 134, 151–3, 162–3, 172, 177, 197–8, 232, 235
Suva, Final Statement 134, 184, 203
synanthropy 20

termites 13, 21, 26, 29–32
Third World Network (TWN) 186
tobacco 27–8
Tongariro National Park 199
trademarks 166, 181, 183, 223, 239
Trade Related Aspects of Intellectual Property (TRIPs) 131, 182–6, 189
trade secrets 224–5
traditional ecological knowledge (TEK) 135–6, 139–40, 190, 199–200
traditional knowledge 1–6, 23, 55, 59–69, 131, 134–8, 143–6, 150–1, 154–73, 177, 183, 188–9, 192–3, 196, 203, 210, 221, 229, 234
traditional medicine 200, 203, 215, 229, 234
traditional natural resource management 67
Traditional Resource Rights (TRR) 158, 165–8, 170, 173, 192–4, 222–3
traditional societies 195, 201, 203
turtles 80
typhus 40–2

UK Forests Network 133
Union for the Protection of New Varieties of Plants (UPOV) 161
United Nations 6; Commission on Human Rights 159, 166, 170; Conference on Environment and Development (UNCED) 63, 134, 151, 157, 172, 177, 187; Draft Declaration on the Rights of Indigenous Peoples 159, 202, 210–18; Economic and Social Council (ECOSOC) 159, 172; Educational, Scientific and Cultural Organization (UNESCO) 143, 160, 199; Food and Agriculture Organization (FAO) 162–3, 186–7, 200–1, 208, 222
United States Department of Commerce 180
Universal Declaration of Human Rights (UDHR) 159
Urueu-Wau-Wau 181
Uruguay Round 69, 185–6

Venezuela 78

warfare 127–8, 137–8
wasps 13–14, 21, 25–6, 29–33, 35, 123

water beetle 45–6
water spider 36–7, 46
weeds 16
Wheeler, A.G.J. 10, 15
'wild' 61, 73, 75, 104, 130, 136–9, 161–2, 178, 190, 195, 198, 203
wilderness 137, 195, 198
Working Group on Traditional Resource Rights (WGTRR) 133, 156, 159
World Bank 167

World Council of Indigenous Peoples (WCIP) 176, 188
World Heritage Convention 199
World Intellectual Property Organization (WIPO) 143, 160–3, 166
World Rainforest Movement (WRM) 188
World Trade Organization (WTO) 131, 182, 189, 201–2

Ye'kuana 18–19, 83